CONTENTS

INTRODUCTION

Frequently Asked Questions

1. How Do People Get To Ketosis?

Ketosis is a metabolism process that occurs when a person's body has insufficient glucose. In this, body-stored fats are broken down for energy provision. Some of the reasons why people join the ketosis journey includes; maintaining or regulating their blood sugar levels, reducing risks of heart-related diseases, and shedding weight.

Some of the ways to get to ketosis includes; increasing physical activity, short-period fasting, reducing carbohydrate intake, increasing intake of healthy fats, taking more coconut oils, and getting used to foods with high-protein portions.

Among the mentioned methods, reducing carbohydrate intake is the quickest approach. This requires minimizing your daily carbohydrate intake levels to 50g or less. This is achievable if the person intending to reach ketosis follows a low-carbohydrate meal plan.

Similarly, combining proper diet with exercises such as High-Intensity Interval Training and intermittent (HIIT) assists in faster shedding of excess fats. In this book, more than 500 ketosis recipes have been compiled for an effortless ketosis journey. You can always understand your ketosis status by monitoring your ketone levels through taking urine, blood, or breath test.

2. What Are Advantages Of Ketosis?

The direct obvious good thing about ketosis is improved lipid loss. Due to insufficient glucose, body fats are broken down to energy. To achieve this, consumed calories contents should be lower than your energy requirements. Other medical motives for starting and continuing with ketosis include epilepsy control and cancer therapy.

3. What Are Disadvantages Of Ketosis?

• The process may cause digestion irregularities for beginners. This is because cutting down carbohydrate intake and increasing fat intake might cause gastro-intestinal issues such as diarrhea, nausea, and constipation. However, the problems get resolved after the body adapts to high fat levels.

• Another downfall with ketosis is a restrictive dining instruction since the majority of people cannot follow proper nourishment. Social events, outings, and attempting to find nutrition at eateries, all happen against someone who follows the Ketogenic regimen.

• Also, a permanent low-carb intake may affect your metabolism especially when a person is expected to consume low calories and perform extreme cardio workout. However, this could be managed beating enough healthy fats, avoiding high-intensity exercises, and understanding your body.

Note: Although vegetables and fruits contain vitamins and minerals essential for good fitness, the products also possess anti-oxidants. If you are aiming to burn fats via ketosis, conduct in-depth study of feeding instructions not forgetting fruits and vegetables.

4. How To Drop Weight Through Eating Fat?

Ketogenic meal plans (all-around 50 grams of carbohydrates every day,) remain operational for becoming lean. If you rearrange the enzymatic gear during body utilization, fats transforms to prime fuel which is activated by insufficient carbohydrates.

Some of your refreshments affecting fat loss include; excessive protein, inadequate good fats, and leftover carbohydrates. Ways to disrupt your flat fat-loss phase include;

- Ensure 50% lipid contents in your daily calories.
- Cut down protein contents to around 35% in your daily diet.

5. How Many Carbs Should a Person Eat? How Much Is "Low"?

The fact that everyone is unique means that our body energy requirements are different. The best way to confirm that is checking your emotions. If you find yourself tired and sleepy after eating, chances are that you consumed high levels of carbohydrates which may shoot up your insulin levels.

Surprisingly, if your glucose levels are elevated, you feed more because hunger strikes faster than when glucose level lowers. Large portions of carbohydrates should be avoided not unless they are part of your ketosis diet meal plan. Contrarily, while some individuals cannot take 10g of net carbohydrates per meal, others don't feel significant insulin spikes even after eating 50 grams.

6. How Long It Needs For An Average Healthy Person To Penetrate The Ketosis State?

It takes 72 hours while following a low-carb meal plan strictly. It is wonderful although the feeder may experience massive weight loss. However, consuming healthier and nutritious products such as lean meat, colourful vegetables, and healthful carbs (like sweet potato and brown rice,) keeps you moving.

Since depriving yourself tasty foods is not amusing, it's advisable to balance everything just like the remaining portion of your respective life. Additionally ketosis requires a lot of dieting discipline.

7. Is Ketosis Safe? What Will Function As The Perils Of Ketosis, If Any?

Ketosis is safe but aligned with conditions that vary depending with your health. For instance; diabetes ketoacidosis is a life-threatening disorder that occurs when a diabetic patient doesn't get enough insulin. Without the plasmatic insulin, your system weakens because of hunger since glucose was not transformed to energy.

In situations of hunger, the physique converts lipid and protein into ketones using energy. The difference between this state and nutritious ketosis is how a diabetic individual becomes powerless to generate any insulin causing unsafe feedback.

If you're already diabetic, a Ketogenic nutritional regime might be dangerous. However, you can succeed if monitored closely by a health specialist.

On the other hand, people without diabetes can continue with it without affecting their immune system. The fact remains; nutritional ketosis is a metabolic condition where feeders reduce quantity of carbohydrates in their daily meals to 50% or below. Here, your physique is changed from relying with glycogen to ketones products such as beta-hydroxybutyrate for power.

In short, your body is forced to familiarize its metabolism with different diets containing diverse fuel origins. Since one's body remains overwhelmed, it makes sense. You can maintain the state throughout your life without encountering any related health complications.

8. What Foods Might Be Freely Eaten Inside The Ketogenic Diet?

Consume grass-fed and wild animal resources rich with omega 3. These include;

- Ghee
- Sea food
- Lamb
- Beef
- wild caught
- eggs
- grass-fed venison
- pork and fish
- Goat
- Pastured poultry
- Butter
- Gelatin

Foods to be avoided include;

- Sausages
- Farm fish
- Meat covered with breadcrumbs
- Grass-fed offal including a heart, liver, kidneys and other meat of an animal organ

Examples of;

Wholesome lipids include;

• Saturated fat such as; butter, tallow, lard, chicken, duck and goose fat, clarified butter or ghee, and coconut oil.

• Monounsaturated fat such as; organic olive oil, macadamia, and avocado.

• Polyunsaturated omega-3 extracted from animals including fatty seafood and fish.

Non-starchy vegetables include;

• Green leafy vegetables such as; chives, lettuce, Bok choy, Swiss chard, spinach, chard, endive, and radicchio.

• Some cruciferous veggies like; dark leaf kale, kohlrabi, and radishes.

• Spaghetti squash, asparagus, celery stalk, cucumber, zucchini, and bamboo shoots.

Fruits, seeds and nuts include;

• Coconut, avocado, and macadamia nuts.

Drinks and condiments include:

• Water, black coffee, creamed coffee, coconut milk, and black or herbal tea.

• Cracklings for food coating.

Homemade meals without preservatives and colouring including bone broth, mustard, mayonnaise, pesto, pickles, kimchi, and sauerkraut.

• All herbs and spices, lime or lemon zest, and juice.

• Whey, egg white, and hormone-free grass-fed gelatin.

• Soy lecithin, additives, and non-natural sweeteners.

9. What Foods May Be Occasionally Eaten Within The Ketogenic Diet?

Vegetables, mushrooms, and fruits

• Some cruciferous veggies like; turnips, Brussels sprouts, broccoli, green, red and white cabbage, cauliflower, fennel, rutabaga, and yellow turnip.

• Nightshades like; tomatoes, eggplant, and peppers.

• Some root veggies like; mushrooms, onions, spring onion, parsley root, leek, garlic, winter squash, and pumpkin.

• Sea vegetables like; wax beans, sugar snap peas, bean sprouts, nori, Kombu, okra, French or globe artichokes, and water chestnuts.

• Rhubarb, olives, and berries like; mulberries, raspberries, blueberries, blackberries, strawberries and cranberries.

Dairy and grain-fed animal resources

• Poultry, ghee, beef, and eggs.

• Avoid farmed pig meat as contain omega 6.

• Dairy products like; sour cream, cottage type cheese, plain full-fat yoghurt, cream, and cheese.

• Avoid products packaged and tagged low-fat because they contain quantities of sugar and starch.

Seeds and nuts

• Pumpkin and sesame seeds, pine nuts, walnuts, pecans, almonds, hazelnuts, flaxseed, sunflower, and hemp seeds.

• Brazil nuts except those having very elevated selenium level.

• Avoid GMO and soy fermented products such as; soy sauce, Tempeh, Natto, and paleo-friendly coconut aminos.

• Unprocessed black and green soybeans.

Condiments:

• Healthy carb-free sweeteners such as Stevia, Erythritol, and Swerve.

• Thickeners including powdered arrowroot and xanthan gum.

• Sugar-free products from tomato including puree, pasta, and ketchup.

• Cocoa and powdered carob, hot chocolate mix, and extra dark chocolate.

• Beware of mints, soy lecithin, and sugar-free masticating gums as some have carbohydrates.

Some vegetables, fruits, nuts with average carbohydrates

• Root vegetables like; sweet potato, parsnip, carrot, celery root, and beetroot.
• Fresh cherries, oranges, grapefruit, nectarine, apricot, watermelon, cantaloupe, Gallia, honeydew melons, Pitaya or dragon fruit, peach, apple, kiwi fruit, berries, plums, pears and figs.
• Dried fruit like; berries, dates, raisins or figs, but only within little or no carbohydrate contents.
• Cashew nuts, pistachio and chestnuts.
Alcoholic products such as; red wines, white wines, and unsweetened spirits.

10. Foods To Avoid Completely Inside The Ketogenic Diet

Avoid completely food with high carbohydrate portions like; factory-produced meat and treated foods.
• All granules, even whole meal of amaranth, sorghum, millet, corn, rye, wheat, oats, rice, buckwheat, germinated grains, white potatoes and quinoa. This includes grain-made foods including cookies, bread, pasta, pizza, sweeteners (such as HFCS,) white sugar, cakes, sugary puddings, soft-drinks, and sugar.
• Factory-farmed fish and pork containing high inflammatory omega-6 fats. Besides that, farmed fish might contain PCBs which may trigger cancer and melanomas in human.
• Processed nourishment containing carrageenan for instance; almond milk products, whey proteins, and wheat gluten.
• Artificial sweeteners, for instance: Saccharine, Equal, Splenda, Aspartame sweeteners, and Sucralose.
• Refined fats, trans-fats and oils such as; corn oil, sunflower, grape seed, safflower, soybean, cottonseed, margarine, and canola.
• Low-fat and zero-carbohydrate products like; diet beverages, chewing mints and gums.
• Milked tea and coffee. However, this could be changed by adding a little volume of cream or raw milk. This should be done cautiously done since the products may cause other health issues.
• Alcoholic and sugary drinks like; beer, cocktails, and sweet wine.
• Tropical fruit like; tangerine, mango, grapes, pineapple, banana, and papaya.
• Avoid fruit saps. However, drink shakes and small quantities of smoothies can be taken instead of saps. Juice doesn't add significant health benefits to your body and that's why smoothies are preferred due to their fiber content. Smoothies can be prepared from dried fruits, dates, and raisins
• Avoid wheat gluten found in low-carbohydrate meals.
• When packaging beverages, avoid BPA-lined containers. This is because; BPA traces can cause impaired thyroid functioning and tumours.

11. What May Be a Perfect Demonstration Of a Ketogenic Diet Menu?

Breakfast:
• 4 ounces shredded of spiced beef.
• 1 ounce of sliced onion
• 1 ounce of low-carb vegetables cooked with essential organic olive oil or butter.
• Unsweetened flavored tisane with hefty cream.

Lunch:

• 4 ounces of oven-cooked halibut with sauce of dill butter.

• A cup of cut cauliflower sautéed in extra-virgin organic olive oil or butter.

• A cup of salad greens peppered with blue cheese, and dressed with a tablespoon of full-fat vinaigrette.

• Unsweetened/seasoned/carbonated-plain water or any unsweetened beverage.

Dinner:

• 6 ounces of baked pork chop with mashed garlic

• 2 cups of separation cabbage cooked with buttered caraway

• Salad greens using low-carb and high-fat dressing.

• Unsweetened/flavoured water or any unsweetened liquid refreshment,

• Coffee with plentiful of cream.

12. What would be the supplements to consider and use when on Ketogenic diet?

Below are seven supplements which could support your low-carbohydrate diet journey.

1. Sodium

When you shift to a Ketogenic or low-carbohydrate diet, your physique loses stored carbohydrate, along with water and sodium. When this occurs, your hypertension levels drop causing reduced blood pressure level.

As a result you might feel dizziness or lethargy, especially when exercising regularly. To prevent this, feeding on meat may provide additional sodium. Similarly, taking veggie bouillon cubes or chicken on daily basis may add around 2g of the portion in your body.

In short, ensure that you consume a meal containing around 50% of sodium portions before exercising. This may aid in upholding adequate blood pressure level and plasma capacity to avoid muscle cramps.

2. Branched-chain amino acids or BCAAs

BCAAs contain enzymes that settle in your soft tissues. These makes up in the plasma stream exposing your muscles to high intensities that prevents muscle breakdown when exercising. In this, the supplement retrieves muscular strength that overcomes overstraining when exercising intensely. These supplements limit plasma indicators that cause muscular tissue injury after extended periods of work-outing. They also sustain amino acid portions that induce contention despite suffering from exercising.

Importantly, if you consume a low-carbohydrate diet before working out, BCAAs can boost your lipid oxidation using stored fatty acids as fuel. BCAA dosage consists; 3g of leucine, 1.5g of isoleucine, and a 1.5g of valine.

3. Whole amino acids or Essential Amino Acids

When all eight EAAs have been in attendance during exercising, muscle reparation and revival happens. After getting exhausted from a rough workout, sport or match, high blood intensities of amino acids could encourage the mind and body to stay longer before closing down. This is truly experienced when your carbohydrate content have depleted.

4.   Glutamine

Glutamine is a portion of muscular-glycogen fusion and carbohydrate storage in a body. This was first observed in the American Journal of Physiology research that investigated which glutamine endorsed a re-synthesis of muscle glycogen storage.

A dose of glutamine taken orally (close to 8g,) could increase storage of muscular glycogen. This can be achieved by eating glucose as it improves glucose production during bodybuilding. However, being carbohydrate limited is advantageous to your body health.

Similarly, there is an evidence that glutamine supplementation maintains body immunity while exercising. Its dose involves taking 8g of normal old glutamine directly after training. In this, powdered glutamine is steered with synthetic additives and sweeteners until it clears.

5.   Touraine

From an Amino acid Touraine investigation, it was confirmed that the product is a carb thrifty product that strengthens the insulin upshot enhancing carbohydrate utilization in the body. Another research revealed that when exercising hard caffeine and touraine-containing beverages reduces heart speed and pressure hormones (catecholamine) production.

Based upon this, many people would slam a Red Bull power drink for a long working out period. On the contrary taking 2g of Touraine supplement 45 Minutes would serve you best.

6.   Medium-chain triglyceride (MCT) or coconut oils

Once you exercise while on a low-carbohydrate diet, burning fatty acids produces the fuelling energy. The MCT or medium-chain triglycerides found in coconut and MCT oils could be turned into a fabulous asset for keeping your effort levels elevated.

The supplement dosage involves taking three tablespoons of coconut oil or three dosages of MCT oil before working out. You can technically review this amount at an interval of 3hoursof an extended bike trip.

7.   Magnesium

Even though a low-carbohydrate diet doesn't drain magnesium massively as it does to sodium, people who exercise hardly experiences leg tightness at night and muscle pain while training due to diet switching. This occurs due to low magnesium levels.

Around 70% of folks normally do not attain adequate magnesium level because they do not follow their meal plan. Due to this, they suffer from muscle twitching. Science tells that, over 300 enzymes need magnesium as to enhance them function properly. It is therefore advisable to add magnesium supplementing your low-carb diet meal plan for muscle maintenance.

Its dosage involves preparing a cream using 400Mg of natural magnesium and spraying around 15 sprays of it on every leg before sleeping. In short, magnesium enhances movement of blood sugar to your muscles and disposes lactate which enters your cause muscle pain when exercising.

13. How would you determine whether you are ketosis or not?

The state of ketosis denotes this physique has swapped from being influenced by carb for energy fats. It's a requirement for any person intending to cut down weight.

As you limit carbohydrate consumption and rise using nutritive fat, additional fats are metabolized, forming large quantities of ketones. A significant percentage of your body cells including those in your mind can tap ketones to energy. Unfortunately, this may take several days (low-carb flu) for some people.

Acetone (a variant of ketone,) is not useful in one's body and therefore, excreted as waste through urine and breathing. In this, labeling is a convenient way to measure your ketosis status.

Ketogenic breath

Some people experiences odour change while inhaling due to presence of acetone in their body. If you encounter this when changing nourishments there are chances that you are becoming ketosis.

Urine ketones

The top accurate method to test ketosis is with the use of ketone urine examination bands. These cheap testing bands are the flawless solution designed to instantly determine ketone intensities in your urine.

To accomplish that, pass the examination end from your little paper band directly by your urine stream. Otherwise, amass urine in a spotless parched vessel, and plunge this rock band inside. Allow it to chill for 15-60 minutes.

If your ketosis status is positive, the guitar rock band changes its original shade. Liken the hue as instructed around the package to test if you hit your ketosis intensity. In this, Deep purple signifies progressive ketones level while dimmers hard to interpret. This is because; the majority of males and females find low-to-medium ketosis levels excellent for direct fat lose and muscle strengthening.

You should be cautious while doing this since, ketone levels in your urine is not equal to the actual blood ketone intensities. These results depend on your body water. This is because; water generates a tremendous difference of ketone concentration in your urine.

As time passes, individual living with Ketogenic regimens have low intensities of ketone in their urine due to their fat spend state. Therefore, a blood exam test which is far expensive is recommended for such people.

14. the difference between the Ketogenic diet and Atkins diet.

Ketogenic nutrition is basically a diet that produces energy when following ketosis meal plan. Individuals in this category are allowed to consume a daily limit of 50% carbohydrate. On the other hand, an Atkins loss program is an ordinary plan which involves starting and continuing with ketosis for losing weight reasons. In this, Ketogenic nutrition is plays an introductory phase. After that, you are slowly reintroduced to low carbohydrate intake and advised against intake of junky carbs and sugars.

MEAT RECIPES

Beef Stew

Prep time: quarter-HOUR |Cooking time: 55 minutes | Servings: 9
Ingredients

- 1 pound of beef chuck
- 2 white onions
- 1 tablespoon of paprika
- 1 teaspoon of oregano
- 1 tablespoon of tomato paste
- 1 tablespoon of balsamic vinegar
- 3 cups of water
- 1 tablespoon of thyme
- 1 ounce of leaf
- 1 tablespoon of extra-virgin organic olive oil
- 5 carrots
- 1 cup of wine
- 1 tablespoon of salt
- ½ teaspoon of black pepper (ground)
- 8 ounces of zucchini
- 3 garlic cloves
- 8 ounces of cabbage
- ½ cup of parsley
- 7 ounces of canned tomato
- 1 teaspoon of sour cream

COOKING DIRECTIONS
1. Chop the beef chuck and sprinkle the meat with paprika, oregano, thyme, salt, ground-black pepper and stir well.
2. Set the cooker to "Sauté" mode.
3. Pour any additional virgin extra virgin olive oil into pressure cooker followed by chopped meat.
4. Sauté the poured meat for around ten minutes when, stirring frequently.
5. Peel the onions and chop them roughly. Add the chopped onion into pressure cooker.
6. Peel the carrots and the garlic cloves and add them.
7. Slice the vegetables and add them into pressure cooker.
8. Sauté the mix for 10 more minutes.
9. Add tomato paste, balsamic vinegar, wine followed by canned tomatoes, water, and sour cream.
10. Chop the cabbage and parsley.
11. Add vegetables into the pressure cooker and stir well. Close pressure to succeed cooker lid.
12. Cook the "Sautéd" contents in stew mode for about 35 minutes.
13. When the meal is cooked, transfer it into a bowl and continue to serve.

Nutrition: calories 176, fat 5.1, fiber 3.2, carbs 11.3, protein 17.1

Pulled Beef

Prep time: quarter-hour | Cooking time: 8 hours ten minutes | Servings: 6
Ingredients

- 1 pound of beef chuck
- 1 tablespoon of salt
- A cup of tomato paste
- 1 teaspoon of black pepper(ground)
- 1 tablespoon of sour cream
- 1 tablespoon of mustard
- A teaspoon of paprika
- 1 tablespoon of onion powder
- 1 tablespoon of apple cider vinegar treatment
- 4 cups of beef broth

COOKING DIRECTIONS:
1. Chop the beef chuck into medium-sized pieces, sprinkle it with salt and ground black pepper, and stir well.
2. Set the pressure cooker to "Slow Cook" mode.
3. Pour the chopped beef to the pressure cooker and add the beef broth.
4. Close the lid and cook for 8 hours.
5. Combine the tomato paste, sour cream, mustard, onion powder, paprika, apple cider vinegar treatment, and honey together in a mixing bowl.
6. Whisk the amalgamation until smooth.
7. When the cooking time ends, remove the cooked beef from the pressure cooker and shred it.
8. Return the shredded beef to the pressure cooker and sprinkle it with the honey mixture.
9. Stir it carefully and close the lid.
10. Cook the dish on "Pressure" for ten minutes.
11. When the dish is cooked, allow it to rest briefly before serving.

Nutrition: calories 197, fat 6.7, fiber 1.2, carbs 5.5, protein 27.5

Beef Steak

Prep time: 25 MINUTES | Cooking time: 25 minutes | Servings: 4
Ingredients

- 1 pound of beef steak
- 1 teaspoon of salt
- 1 tablespoon of freshly squeezed lemon juice
- 1 teaspoon of paprika
- 3 tablespoons of fresh rosemary
- 3 tablespoons of balsamic vinegar

- 1 tablespoon of olive oil
- 1 teaspoon of ground black pepper
- 1 cup of red wine
- 1 tablespoon of minced garlic
- 1 onion

COOKING DIRECTIONS

- Mix salt, paprika, fresh rosemary, ground black pepper and minced garlic in a mixing bowl.
- Peel the onion and chop it.
- Place the chopped onion and spice mixture in a blender.
- Add freshly squeezed lemon juice, balsamic vinegar, organic extra virgin olive oil, and burgundy or merlot wine.
- Blend the amalgamation until it smoothens.
- Mix beef steak with all the spice mixture and then leave it in a refrigerator for a quarter-hour to marinate.
- Set the pressure cooker on "Sauté" mode.
- Transfer the marinated steak into pressure cooker and sauté the meat for ten minutes while stirring frequently.
- Close the pressure cooker lid and cook the dish on "Pressure" mode for quarter-hour.
- Release pressure on the cooker and open the lid.
- Serve the beef while hot.

Nutrition: calories 285, fat 11.1, fiber 2.1, carbs 6.2, protein 35.1

Garlic Roasted Beef

Prep time: quarter-HOUR | Cooking time: 40 minutes | Servings: 4
Ingredients

- 2 tablespoons of minced garlic
- 1 teaspoon of garlic powder
- 2 yellow onions
- 7 ounces of mushrooms
- 1 teaspoon of salt
- 1 teaspoon of black pepper (ground)
- 4 cups of chicken stock
- 1 tablespoon of extra-virgin olive oil
- 1 cup of chopped celery stalk
- 1 pound of beef brisket

COOKING DIRECTIONS

1. Mix garlic powder, salt and ground black pepper together in a mixing bowl and stir.
2. Rub the beef brisket with all the spice mixture.
3. Set the pressure cooker to "Sauté" mode.
4. Place the beef brisket in the pressure cooker and sauté the meat for 5 minutes on them, until golden brown.
5. Add celery stalk.
6. Peel the onions, chop vegetables, and slice mushrooms.

7. Remove the beef brisket from the pressure cooker.
8. Put the vegetables into pressure the cooker.
9. Sprinkle the constituents with the organic olive oil and sauté for ten minutes, stirring frequently.
10. Add the chicken stock, garlic and beef brisket.
11. Close the pressure cooker lid and cook the dish on "Keep Warm" mode roughly for 25 minutes.
12. When the cooking time ends, release pressure on the cooker and open the lid.
13. Stir the amalgamation and serve.

Nutrition: calories 542, fat 23.9, fiber 8, carbs 58.59, protein 29

Beef Ragout

Prep time: quarter-HOUR | Cooking time: 35 minutes | Servings: 10
Ingredients

- 2 pounds of beef brisket
- 2 carrots
- 4 white onions
- 1 teaspoon of sugar
- 3 servings of water
- 1 cup of cherry tomatoes
- 1 tablespoon of fresh thyme
- ¼ cup of fresh dill
- ½ cup of fresh parsley
- 1 cup of cream
- 1 cup of tomato juice
- 5 ounces of fennel
- 11 teaspoons of fresh rosemary
- 1 tablespoon of butter

COOKING DIRECTIONS

1. Wash the thyme, dill and parsley and chop them.
2. Chop the beef brisket roughly.
3. Wash cherry tomatoes and cut them into halves.
4. Chop the fennel.
5. Peel the onions and carrots and chop them roughly.
6. Place all of the ingredients into a pressure cooker.
7. Set the pressure cooker on "Sauté" mode.
8. Add water, sugar, cream, tomato juice, fresh rosemary, and butter into the pressure cooker and stir well.
9. Close pressure cooker lid and cook the beef ragout for 35 minutes.
10. When the dish is cooked, remove the food from the pressure cooker to cool briefly and serve.

Nutrition: calories 271, fat 19.5, fiber 2, carbs 8.96, protein 15

Beef with Horseradish

Prep time: ten minutes | Cooking time: 27 minutes | Servings: 6

Ingredients

- 5 ounces horseradish
- 1 cup cream
- 1 pound beef brisket
- 1 tablespoon thyme
- 1 teaspoon coriander
- 1 teaspoon oregano
- 1 tablespoon olive oil
- ½ cup chicken stock
- 1 tablespoon fresh dill
- 1 teaspoon salt
- 3 garlic cloves

COOKING DIRECTIONS

1. Chop the beef rump and sprinkle it with salt.
2. Peel the onions and slice them.
3. Mix the sliced onions with the extra virgin olive oil and stir well.
4. Mix the burgundy or merlot wine, bay leaves, black-eyed peas, ground ginger thyme, red pepper cayenne, freshly squeezed lemon juice, cilantro, oregano, and minced garlic together in a mixing bowl.
5. Set pressure cooker to "Sauté" mode.
6. Add the sliced onion mixture to pressure cooker and sauté for 10 minutes, stirring frequently.
7. Add the chopped beef rump and allow it marinate for a handful of minutes.
8. Stir well and close the strain cooker lid. Cook the dish on "Sauté" mode for 40 minutes.
9. When the cooking time ends, open pressure cooker lid and stir again.
10. Transfer the dish to serving bowls.

Nutrition: calories 273, fat 21.8, fiber 1, carbs 6.26, protein 13

Beef Stifado

Prep time: quarter-HOUR | Cooking time: 50 MINUTES | Servings: 9

Ingredients

- 2 pounds of beef rump
- 2 tablespoons of tomato paste
- 1 teaspoon of salt
- 1 cup of onion
- 3 tablespoons of essential olive oil
- ½ cup of red wine
- 2 ounces bay leaf
- 1 teaspoon of black-eyed peas
- 1 tablespoon of ground ginger
- 1 teaspoon of thyme
- 1 tablespoon of red pepper cayenne
- 4 tablespoons of fresh lemon juice
- 1 teaspoon of cilantro
- 1 teaspoon of oregano
- 1 teaspoon of minced garlic

COOKING DIRECTIONS

1. Chop the beef rump and sprinkle it with salt.
2. Peel the onions and slice them.
3. Combine the sliced onions with the extra-virgin olive oil and stir well.
4. Combine the burgundy or merlot wine, bay leaves, black-eyed peas, ground ginger thyme, red pepper cayenne, freshly squeezed lemon juice, cilantro, oregano, and minced garlic together in a mixing bowl.
5. Set pressure cooker to "Sauté" mode.
6. Add the sliced onion mixture to pressure cooker and sauté for 10 minutes, stirring frequently.
7. Add the chopped beef rump and permit it to marinate for handful of minutes.
8. Stir well and close the strain cooker lid.
9. Cook the dish on "Sauté" mode for 40 minutes.
10. When the cooking time ends, open pressure cooker lid and stir again. Transfer the dish to serving bowls.

Nutrition: calories 218, fat 11.3, fiber 2, carbs 8.07, protein 23

Beef Stroganoff

Prep time: 10 mins | Cooking time: 8 minutes | Servings: 6

Ingredients

- 2 white onions
- 1 teaspoon of salt
- 1 teaspoon of red pepper cayenne
- 1 pound of beef brisket
- 1 teaspoon of oregano
- 7 ounces of Shirataki noodles
- A cup of sour cream
- 6 ounces of mushrooms
- 1 teaspoon of butter
- 3 cups of chicken stock

COOKING DIRECTIONS

1. Peel the onions and dice them.
2. Chop the beef brisket into small pieces.
3. Slice the mushrooms.
4. Mix the ingredients together and mix well.
5. Sprinkle the mixture with oregano, salt and red pepper cayenne.
6. Set the pressure cooker to "Sauté" mode.
7. Add butter into the pressure cooker contents.
8. Add the meat mixture and sauté the dish after the butter has melted.
9. Add chicken stock and Shirataki noodles.
10. Close pressure the cooker lid and cook the dish on "Pressure" mode for 5 minutes.
11. Release the cooker's pressure and open it to add the sour cream.
12. Stir well and transfer it to serving bowls.

Nutrition: calories 258, fat 3.9, fiber 1.3, carbs 7.3, protein 25.9

Shredded Beef

Prep time: 10 minutes | Cooking time: 27 MINUTES | Servings: 9

Ingredients

- ½ cup of lime juice
- 1 teaspoon of curry
- 1 teaspoon of lemon grass paste
- 1 cup of chicken stock
- 1 cup of water
- A tablespoon of extra-virgin organic olive oil
- A teaspoon of chili powder
- 1 ½ pounds of beef chunk
- ½ tablespoon of red pepper cayenne
- ½ cup of fresh parsley

COOKING DIRECTIONS

1. Wash the parsley and chop it.
2. Mix the curry, lemongrass paste, chili powder and red pepper cayenne in a mixing bowl and stir well.
3. Rub the beef using the spice mixture and let it rest for ten minutes.
4. Chop the beef into pieces and pour it in the pressure cooker.
5. Set the load cooker to "Pressure" mode.
6. Add essential extra-virgin olive oil, chicken stock, and water.
7. Close the pressure cooker lid and cook the dish for quarter-hour.
8. When the cooking time ends, release the pressure from the cooker and open the lid to remove the beef from it.
9. Shred it using a fork.
10. Return the shredded beef into the pressure cooker and add chopped parsley and lime juice.
11. Stir well and close pressure cooker lid.
12. Cook for around two minutes.
13. Remove the dish from the pressure cooker and serve.

Nutrition: calories 81, fat 31.7, fiber 1, carbs 9.7, protein 4

Beef Brisket with Red Wine

Prep time: quarter-HOUR | Cooking time: 40 minutes | Servings: 6

Ingredients

- 1 cup of sweet red wine
- 1 lemon
- 1 teaspoon of ground black pepper
- ½ teaspoon of cinnamon
- 1 teaspoon of ground ginger
- 1 teaspoon of cilantro
- 1 tablespoon of butter
- 1 pound of beef brisket
- 1 cup of water
- 1 teaspoon of turmeric

COOKING DIRECTIONS

1. Place the beef brisket in a mixing bowl.
2. Mix the wine with ground black pepper, cinnamon, ground ginger, cilantro, and turmeric in another bowl and stir well.
3. Set pressure to achieve success cooker to "Sauté" mode.
4. Pour the wine mixture inside the brisket bowl and let it to rest for quarter-hour.
5. Transfer the brisket into the pressure cooker and add water.
6. Slice lemon and add it to the meat mixture.
7. Close the pressure cooker lid and cook for 40 minutes.
8. When the cooking time ends, open pressure cooker and separate the meat from the wine mixture.
9. Slice the cooked meat and serve.

Nutrition: calories 182, fat 13.3, fiber 0, carbs 2.2, protein 11

Sweet Beef Ribs

Prep time: 10 MINUTES | Cooking time: 25 minutes | Servings: 8

Ingredients

- 2 pounds of beef ribs
- A teaspoon of extra-virgin organic olive oil
- 4 tablespoons of barbecue sauce
- ½ cup of Erythritol
- 1 teaspoon of onion powder
- 1 teaspoon of garlic powder
- 1 teaspoon of salt
- 2 tablespoons of water

COOKING DIRECTIONS

1. Mix the organic olive oil, barbecue sauce, Erythritol, onion powder, garlic powder, and salt together in a mixing bowl.
2. Stir the mixture until smooth.
3. Rub the beef ribs with all the sauce.
4. Set pressure cooker to "Pressure" mode.
5. Pour water into the pressure cooker.
6. Add ribs and close the pressure cooker lid.
7. Cook for 25 minutes.
8. When the cooking time elapses, release the rest of the pressure and open the pressure cooker lid.
9. Transfer the beef ribs to a plate, cut them into serving pieces and serve.

Nutrition: calories 230, fat 7.7, fiber 0.1, carbs 3.3, protein 34.5

Parmesan Beef Meatloaf

Prep time: quarter-hour | Cooking time: 22 minutes | Servings: 6

Ingredients

- 8 ounces of Parmesan cheese

- 3 eggs
- 1 pound of ground beef
- 1 tablespoon of tomato paste
- 1 teaspoon of ground black pepper
- 1 tablespoon of salt
- 4 tablespoons of butter
- 1 tablespoon of coconut flour
- 1 teaspoon of cilantro
- A large onion
- A teaspoon of minced garlic
- 2 tablespoons of organic olive oil

COOKING DIRECTIONS

1. Peel the onion and chop it roughly.
2. Transfer the onion into a blender and puree until smooth.
3. Mix the onion with the ground black pepper, salt, tomato paste, minced garlic, coconut flour, and cilantro. Stir well.
4. Mix the spice mixture with the ground beef.
5. Beat the eggs in a separate bowl.
6. Mix the eggs and ground beef mixture together in a mixing bowl until fully combined.
7. Form a loaf shape over the meat mixture and wrap it in an aluminum foil.
8. Set pressure cooker to "Steam" mode.
9. Put the meatloaf within the trivet and hang the trivet into the pressure cooker.
10. Cook for 20 minutes.
11. Grate the Parmesan cheese.
12. When the cooking time ends, remove the meatloaf from the pressure cooker and discard it from aluminum foil.
13. Sprinkle the meatloaf with the essential olive oil and grated cheese.
14. Transfer the dish to a pressure cooker and cook it on "Pressure" mode for just two minutes.
15. Remove the dish from pressure cooker, cut into pieces and serve.

Nutrition: calories 420, fat 27.6, fiber 1.2, carbs 5.4, protein 38.6

Spicy Chili Beef Stew

Cooking time: 37 minutes | Servings: 9

Ingredients

- 1 pound of stewing beef
- 1 jalapeño pepper
- A chili pepper
- 1 teaspoon of tomato paste
- ½ cup of cream
- 1 teaspoon of salt
- 1 tablespoon of essential organic olive oil
- ½ cup of dill
- 9 ounces of zucchini
- 3 yellow onions
- 1 teaspoon of paprika
- 1 teaspoon of dried oregano

- 1 teaspoon of turmeric
- 8 ounces of asparagus
- A cup of green beans
- 1 bell pepper
- 3 cups of beef stock
- A teaspoon of cilantro

COOKING DIRECTIONS

1. Chop the beef roughly.
2. Chop zucchini roughly.
3. Mix the chopped components in a mixing bowl.
4. Sprinkle the mixture with salt, olive oil, paprika, oregano, turmeric, and cilantro.
5. Stir well and transfer contents into the pressure cooker.
6. Set the pressure cooker to "Sauté" mode.
7. Cook the mixture for two minutes while stirring frequently.
8. Chop the dill and peel the onions.
9. Dice the onions roughly.
10. Sprinkle pressure cooker with the mixture of onion and dill.
11. Add cream, tomato paste, asparagus, and green beans.
12. Chop the jalapeño pepper, chili pepper, and bell pepper.
13. Add chopped vegetables into the pressure cooker and mix well using a spoon.
14. Close pressure cooker lid and cook the dish on "Sauté" mode for 35 minutes.
15. When the dish is cooked, remove it from pressure cooker and serve.

Nutrition: calories 165, fat 6, fiber 2.9, carbs 10.2, protein 18.7

Sliced Beef with Saffron

Prep time: 10 MINUTES | Cooking time: 47 minutes | Servings: 7

Ingredients

- 14 ounces of beef brisket
- 1 tablespoon of soy sauce
- A teaspoon of oregano
- A teaspoon of salt
- 3 ounces of fresh saffron
- ½ teaspoon of thyme
- 1 tablespoon of ground coriander
- 1 cup of chicken stock
- 1 tablespoon of butter
- 1 teaspoon of rosemary

COOKING DIRECTIONS

1. Mix oregano, salt, thyme, ground coriander and rosemary in a mixing bowl. Stir well.
2. Rub the beef brisket using the spice mixture and sprinkle the meat with soy sauce.
3. Chop the saffron, mix it with butter and mix well.

4. Set pressure cooker to "Pressure" mode.
5. Add the saffron mixture into the pressure cooker and melt for 2 minutes.
6. Add the brisket and chicken stock.
7. Close pressure cooker lid and cook the dish on "Sauté" mode for 45 minutes.
8. When the cooking time ends, remove the meat from pressure cooker and slice it before serving

Nutrition: calories 184, fat 11.6, fiber 1, carbs 9.93, protein 11

Chili

Prep time: 10 MINUTES | Cooking time: 42 minutes | Servings: 10
Ingredients
- 14 ounces of ground beef
- 5 garlic cloves
- A chopped tomato
- A teaspoon of oregano
- 1 tablespoon of essential extra-virgin olive oil
- 1 large onion
- 1 teaspoon of paprika
- 1 tablespoon of ground coriander
- 10 ounces of boiled spinach
- A cup of chicken stock
- 1 teaspoon of salt
- 1 teaspoon of cumin seeds

COOKING DIRECTIONS
1. Peel the garlic cloves and slice them.
2. Set pressure cooker to "Sauté" mode.
3. Pour the additional virgin organic olive oil into the pressure cooker.
4. Add sliced garlic cloves and sauté this mixture for around two minutes.
5. Mix the oregano, paprika, salt, and cumin seeds together in the mixing bowl and stir.
6. Combine the spice mixture with all the ground beef.
7. Peel the onion and dice it.
8. Add the diced onion into the meat mixture.
9. Transfer the beef mixture into the pressure cooker and sauté it for 10 minutes, stirring frequently.
10. Add tomato and chicken stock.
11. Add spinach and mix well.
12. Close the pressure cooker lid and cook the dish on "Sauté" mode for thirty minutes.
13. When the cooking time elapses, transfer the chili to serving bowls.

Nutrition: calories 104, fat 4.2, fiber 1.2, carbs 3.6, protein 13.3

Turmeric Meatballs

Prep time: 10 MINUTES | Cooking time: 10 mins | Servings: 7
Ingredients
- 1 tablespoon of turmeric
- 1 teaspoon of ground ginger
- A teaspoon of salt
- ½ teaspoon of oregano
- 1 teaspoon of minced garlic
- 1 zucchini
- 10 ounces of ground pork
- 1 teaspoon of cilantro
- 1 tablespoon of organic olive oil
- 1 egg yolk

COOKING DIRECTIONS
1. Mix the turmeric, ground ginger, salt, oregano, and cilantro in a mixing bowl and stir well.
2. Add ground pork into the contents and stir again.
3. Add the egg yolk and minced garlic.
4. Chop the zucchini and transfer it to the blender.
5. Blend the vegetable mixture until smooth.
6. Add zucchini into the meat mixture and stir well.
7. Make medium-sized meatballs from your meat mixture.
8. Set pressure to succeed cooker to "Pressure" mode.
9. Pour the organic olive oil into the pressure cooker contents.
10. Place the meatballs in the pressure cooker and close the lid.
11. Cook for 10 minutes.
12. When the dish is cooked, release pressure and open the load cooker lid.
13. Remove the meatballs and serve.

Nutrition: calories 107, fat 5.5, fiber 0, carbs 1.4, protein 13

Meatballs Soup

Prep time: 10 MINUTES | Cooking time: 14 minutes | Servings: 8
Ingredients
- 7 ounces of ground pork
- 1 carrot
- 1 teaspoon of oregano
- A tablespoon of minced garlic
- 1 onion
- 6 cups of chicken stock
- 1 teaspoon of ground black pepper
- ½ cup of dill
- 1 teaspoon of paprika
- 1 tablespoon of flour
- An egg

COOKING DIRECTIONS
1. Peel the carrot and onion. Chop them.
2. Combine the vegetables together and transfer them into the pressure cooker.
3. Set the load cooker to "Pressure" mode.

4. Add chicken stock and paprika.
5. Combine the soil pork, oregano, flour, and ground pork in a mixing bowl.
6. Beat the egg and pour them into the pork mixture. Stir the ingredients carefully.
7. Make small meatballs using the ground pork mixture place them in the pressure cooker.
8. Close the cooker lid and cook for around 14 minutes.
9. Wash the dill and chop it. When the dish is cooked, ladle it into serving bowls.
10. Sprinkle the soup with the dill and serve.
Nutrition: calories 145, fat 5.3, fiber 1, carbs 10.4, protein 14

Pork Stew

Prep time: ten mins | Cooking time: 35 minutes | Servings: 6
Ingredients
- 1 pound of pork chops
- 3 yellow onions
- 4 ounces of chopped asparagus
- 4 cups of beef broth
- 1 teaspoon of salt
- 1 teaspoon of paprika
- 1 teaspoon of chili powder
- A cup of chopped bok choy
- ½ teaspoon of Erythritol
- 1 tablespoon of ground celery

COOKING DIRECTIONS
1. Peel the onions and slice them.
2. Chop the pork chops into bite-sized pieces.
3. Combine the pork with salt, paprika, and chili powder and stir well.
4. Set pressure cooker to "Sauté" mode and pour in the constituents.
5. Close pressure cooker lid and Cook for around 35 minutes.
6. When the cooking time elapses, remove the stew from the pressure cooker and serve.
Nutrition: calories 297, fat 19.9, fiber 2, carbs 7.2, protein 21.5

Pork with every one of the Almonds and Sage

Prep time: quarter-hour | Cooking time: 40 minutes | Servings: 11
Ingredients
- 3 pounds of pork loin
- 3 garlic cloves
- 3 carrots
- 3 tablespoons of sage
- 5 tablespoons of chicken stock
- 1 tablespoon of extra-virgin olive oil
- 1 teaspoon of lemon zest
- 1 tablespoon of almond flakes

- A cup of almond milk
- 1 tablespoon of salt

COOKING DIRECTIONS
1. Rub the pork loin with the sage and leave them to chill for around 10 minutes.
2. Peel the garlic cloves and carrots.
3. Cut the carrots into halves.
4. Place the garlic cloves, halved carrots, and lemon zest into the pressure cooker.
5. Add the fundamental organic olive oil, almond milk, salt, and almond flakes.
6. Set pressure cooker to "Sauté" mode.
7. Put the pork into pressure cooker and close its lid.
8. Cook the dish on meat mode for around 40 minutes.
9. When the cooking time elapses, open the cooker and remove the pork.
10. Allow the pork-meal to cool a bit. Slice it and serve while warm.
Nutrition: calories 293, fat 15.4, fiber 1, carbs 4.54, protein 32

Pulled Pork

Prep time: ten MINUTES | Cooking time: 27 minutes | Servings: 8
Ingredients
- 2 pounds of pork shoulder
- ½ cup of tomato paste
- ½ cup of cream
- ¼ cup of chicken stock
- A tablespoon of salt
- 1 teaspoon of ground black pepper
- 1 teaspoon of red pepper cayenne
- 3 tablespoons of essential olive oil
- 1 tablespoon of fresh lemon juice
- 1 teaspoon of garlic powder
- An onion

COOKING DIRECTIONS
1. Peel the onion and transfer it to a blender.
2. Blend the onion until smooth.
3. Set pressure cooker to "Sauté" mode.
4. Pour in the essential olive oil followed by pork shoulder and cook for around 10 minutes.
5. Add tomato paste, cream, chicken stock, ground black pepper, red pepper cayenne, fresh lemon juice, and garlic powder. Stir the contents well and close pressure cooker lid.
6. Cook the dish on "Pressure" mode for quarter-hour.
7. When the cooking time ends, get rid of the pork shoulder from the pressure cooker and shred it using a fork. Return the shredded pork into the cooker and mix well.
8. Re-cook the dish on "Pressure" mode for around 2 minutes.

9. Transfer the cooked dish into a large plate and serve.

Nutrition: calories 403, fat 28.3, fiber 1, carbs 6.29, protein 30

Pork Brisket with Strawberries

Prep time: 10 mins | Cooking time: 23 MINUTES | Servings: 5

Ingredients

- ¼ cup of strawberries
- 1 red onion
- 1 pound of pork brisket
- 1 teaspoon of Erythritol
- ½ cup of soy sauce
- A cup of beef stock
- 1 tablespoon of butter
- 3 tablespoons of raisins
- 1 teaspoon of garlic sauce
- 1 teaspoon of mayonnaise

COOKING DIRECTIONS

1. Cut the pork brisket into strips.
2. Sprinkle the pork strips with Erythritol and soy sauce. Stir well.
3. Set the pressure cooker to "Sauté" mode.
4. Place the pork strips into the pressure cooker.
5. Add butter and sauté the meat mixture for ten minutes while stirring frequently.
6. Add the beef stock, raisins, garlic sauce, and mayonnaise.
7. Chop the strawberries and add them into the cooker. Stir the mixture well using a spatula.
8. Close the pressure cooker lid and cook the dish on "Pressure" mode for 13 minutes.
9. When the cooking time ends, remove the cooked dish from the pressure cooker, take rest, and serve.
10. Add fresh lemon juice, if desired.

Nutrition: calories 158, fat 4, fiber 1, carbs 10.7, protein 22.1

Pork Schnitzel

Prep time: quarter-hour | Cooking time: ten mins | Servings: 4

Ingredients

- 1 pound of boneless pork chops
- 1 cup of pork rind
- 4 eggs
- 1 teaspoon of salt
- 1 teaspoon of black pepper (ground)
- A tablespoon of extra-virgin olive oil
- 1 cup of almond flour
- 1 tablespoon of coconut milk

COOKING DIRECTIONS

1. First, pound the boneless pork chops flat using a meat mallet.

2. Combine the salt and ground black pepper in a mixing bowl and stir well.
3. Sprinkle the pork with the spice mixture.
4. Beat the eggs, add coconut milk, and stir well.
5. Set pressure cooker to "Sauté" mode. Pour the organic olive oil in the pressure cooker and preheat it.
6. Pour the pork chops to the egg mixture.
7. Dip the pork content to almond flour and return them to the egg mixture.
8. Dip the product to the pork rind and transfer the meat to the strain cooker.
9. Sauté the pork chops for 5 minutes on either side.
10. When the schnitzel is cooked, get rid of it from pressure and allow it rest before serving.

Nutrition: calories 745, fat 46.5, fiber 3.2, carbs 5.9, protein 69.1

Glazed Sausage

Prep time: ten MINUTES | Cooking time: 14 minutes | Servings: 6

Ingredients

- 1 tablespoon of Erythritol
- 1 tablespoon of coconut flour
- 1 pound of ground pork
- 1 tablespoon of butter
- 6 ounces of ground chicken
- 1 tablespoon of salt
- 3 tablespoons of liquid stevia
- 1 teaspoon of oregano
- 1 teaspoon of cilantro
- An onion
- 1 teaspoon of water
- 1 tablespoon of ground black pepper

COOKING DIRECTIONS

1. Peel the onion and grate it.
2. Pour the grated onion, ground pork, ground chicken, salt, oregano, cilantro, and ground black pepper in a mixing bowl.
3. Add the coconut flour and mix well.
4. Combine liquid stevia, Erythritol, and water in another bowl.
5. Stir the mixture well to dissolve erythritol.
6. Make medium-sized sausages patties from the meat mixture.
7. Set the pressure cooker to "Sauté" mode.
8. Add the butter into the cooker and allow it melt.
9. Pour the sausage patties into the pressure cooker and sauté the patties for around 4 minutes.
10. Sprinkle the sausage patties with liquid stevia mixture and close the lid.
11. Cook the dish for another ten minutes on "Sauté" mode.

12. When the cooking time ends, remove the cooked sausage patties from pressure cooker and serve.
Nutrition: calories 195, fat 6.9, fiber 1.2, carbs 3.2, protein 28.5

Pork Satay

Prep time: ten mins | Cooking time: 25 minutes | Servings: 5

Ingredients
- 12 ounces of pork loin
- 3 tablespoons of apple cider vinegar treatment
- 1 tablespoon of essential olive oil
- 1 tablespoon of sesame oil
- 1 teaspoon of turmeric
- ½ teaspoon of red pepper cayenne
- 1 teaspoon of cilantro
- A teaspoon of basil
- A teaspoon of Erythritol
- A teaspoon of soy sauce
- 11 tablespoons of fish sauce

COOKING DIRECTIONS
1. Chop the pork loin into medium-sized pieces.
2. Place the pork loin in the mixing bowl.
3. Sprinkle the meat with apple cider vinegar, organic olive oil, sesame oil, turmeric, cayenne, cilantro, basil, Erythritol, soy sauce, and fish sauce. Stir well.
4. Thread the meat on the skewers.
5. Set the strain cooker to "Sauté" mode.
6. Place the skewers in the pressure cooker and Cook the pork satay for around 25 minutes.
7. When cooked, transfer the satays to a wide bowl and allow them to rest before serving.
Nutrition: calories 231, fat 15.1, fiber 0.2, carbs 2.8, protein 20.7

Ginger Pork Chops

Prep time: ten MINUTES | Cooking time: 35 minutes | Servings: 5

Ingredients
- 2 tablespoons of ground ginger
- A pound of pork chop
- 1 cup of soy sauce
- A teaspoon of parsley
- 1 teaspoon of ground black pepper
- 1 cup of water
- 1 tablespoon of freshly-squeezed lemon juice
- A teaspoon of garlic powder

COOKING DIRECTIONS
1. Combine the soy sauce and water in a mixing bowl.
2. Add fresh lemon juice and mix.

3. Sprinkle the mixture with ground ginger, parsley, ground black pepper, and garlic powder.
4. Add freshly squeezed lemon juice and stir well.
5. Cut the pork chop roughly using a sharp object.
6. Put the pork on the soy sauce mixture and allow it to sit for 15 minutes.
7. Set pressure cooker to "Sauté" mode.
8. Place the amalgamation into the cooker and close its lid.
9. Cook the dish for around 35 minutes.
10. When cooked, open pressure cooker lid and serve the ginger pork chops while hot.
Nutrition: calories 351, fat 19.4, fiber 2, carbs 15.7, protein 27

Pork Belly

Prep time: ten minutes | Cooking time: 32 minutes | Servings: 6

Ingredients
- 1 ½ pound of pork belly
- A tablespoon of ground black pepper
- 1 teaspoon of cilantro
- A cup of soy sauce
- 1 tablespoon of mirin
- 1 tablespoon of fresh ginger
- 4 garlic cloves
- 1 carrot
- A teaspoon of sesame seeds
- 2 tablespoons of organic olive oil
- 1 teaspoon of fresh lemon juice

COOKING DIRECTIONS
1. Peel the garlic cloves and carrot.
2. Chop the vegetables.
3. Combine the black pepper, cilantro, and sesame seeds in a mixing bowl.
4. Rub the pork belly with the spice mixture.
5. Sprinkle it with soy sauce, olive oil, and freshly squeezed lemon juice.
6. Chop the ginger and sprinkle it over the pork belly.
7. Make the tiny cuts from pork belly and grow it with garlic cloves and carrot.
8. Set pressure to "Pressure" mode.
9. Place the pork belly in it and pour some extra-virgin organic olive oil.
10. Close pressure cooker lid and cook the dish on pressure mode for 32 minutes.
11. When the pork belly is cooked, allow it to rest briefly. After that, slice it and serve.
Nutrition: calories 682, fat 67.5, fiber 1, carbs 6.12, protein 12

Spicy Pork Ribs

Prep time: ten MINUTES | Cooking time: 22 minutes | Servings: 5

Ingredients

- A pound of pork ribs
- 1 tablespoon of red pepper cayenne
- A teaspoon of ground black pepper
- 1 teaspoon of chili powder
- ¼ cup of liquid stevia
- 1 tablespoon of butter
- A teaspoon paprika

COOKING DIRECTIONS

1. Set pressure cooker to "Pressure" mode.
2. Add the pork ribs into pressure cooker and add butter.
3. Close the pressure cooker lid and cook for 17 minutes.
4. Combine the black pepper, chili powder, cayenne, stevia, and paprika in a bowl. Mix the ingredients well or until smooth.
5. Preheat the oven to 365 F.
6. When the pork ribs are cooked, transfer these to the oven tray.
7. Spread the pork ribs with stevia and mixture well.
8. Put the pork ribs in the preheated oven and cook for 5 minutes.
9. Remove the ribs from the oven and allow them to rest briefly before serving.

Nutrition: calories 235, fat 14, fiber 0.7, carbs 1.4, protein 25

Vietnam-style Pork Ribs

Prep time: twenty possibly even MINUTES | Cooking time: 23minutes | Servings: 7
Ingredients

- A tablespoon of mirin
- 3 tablespoons of freshly-squeezed lemon juice
- ½ cup of soy sauce
- 1 teaspoon of cilantro
- 1 teaspoon of essential olive oil
- ½ cup of almond milk
- 1 tablespoon of sesame seeds
- A teaspoon of cumin
- 1 teaspoon of Erythritol
- 2 pounds of pork ribs
- 1 teaspoon of ground black pepper

COOKING DIRECTIONS

1. Combine a portion of fresh lemon juice with mirin, soy sauce, cilantro, essential olive oil, sesame seeds, cumin, Erythritol, and ground black pepper in a mixing bowl and stir.
2. Pour the lemon juice mixture to the pork ribs.
3. Mix well and allow it rest for around 15 minutes to marinate.
4. Set the pressure cooker to "Sauté" mode.
5. Pour the olive oil into pressure cooker.
6. Add the ribs and sauté the marinated meat for 10 minutes.
7. Add almond milk and close the lid.
8. Cook the dish on "Pressure" mode for 13 minutes.
9. When the ribs are cooked, remove them from the cooker and serve.

Nutrition: calories 423, fat 28.5, fiber 0.8, carbs 4.1, protein 36.2

Pork Rolls with Apple

Prep time: ten minutes | Cooking time: half an hour |Servings: 6
Ingredients

- 2 green apples
- A pound of pork chop
- 1 tablespoon of cinnamon
- 1 teaspoon of ground ginger
- 1 tablespoon of oregano
- 2 tablespoons of butter
- A teaspoon of salt
- 1 teaspoon of cayenne

COOKING DIRECTIONS

1. Peel the apples and chop them into small pieces.
2. Sprinkle the chopped apples with cinnamon and ginger and mix them well.
3. Pound the pork chops with a meat mallet and sprinkle them with oregano, salt, and cayenne.
4. Add the apple mixture to the pork chops and pin them together using toothpicks.
5. Set the load cooker to "Sauté" mode.
6. Melt the butter in the pressure cooker and add the pork rolls.
7. Close the lid and cook for half an hour.
8. When the cooking time ends, remove the pork rolls from the cooker and allow them rest.
9. Remember to remove the toothpicks before serving.

Nutrition: calories 229, fat 12.4, fiber 2, carbs 9.81, protein 20

Cilantro Pork Tacos

Prep time: 10 mins | Cooking time: 27 minutes | Servings: 6
Ingredients

- 1 tablespoon of cilantro
- 10 ounces of ground pork
- 1 tablespoon of tomato paste
- 1 red onion
- A teaspoon of salt
- 1 teaspoon of basil
- A tablespoon of butter
- 1 cup of lettuce
- 7 ounces of lettuce leaves
- 1 teaspoon of paprika

COOKING DIRECTIONS
1.   Combine the ground pork, salt, cilantro, paprika, and basil together in a mixing bowl.
2.   Add butter and tomato paste and stir well.
3.   Set the pressure cooker to "Sauté" mode.
4.   Place the pork mixture into the pressure cooker and close the lid. Cook for 27 minutes.
5.   Chop the cup of lettuce and peel the onion.
6.   Slice the onion.
7.   When the meat is cooked, remove it from the pressure cooker and add lettuce leaves.
8.   Add chopped lettuce and sliced onion. Wrap the tacos and serve.
Nutrition: calories 96, fat 3.7, fiber 0.7, carbs 2.7, protein 12.8

Pork Belly with Peanuts

Prep time: ten minutes | Cooking time: 25 minutes | Servings: 6
Ingredients
- 5 ounces of peanut
- 1 pound of pork belly
- 1 cup of chicken stock
- A tablespoon of salt
- 1 teaspoon of ground black pepper
- 3 garlic cloves
- 1 teaspoon of onion powder
- A teaspoon of paprika
- A tablespoon of cilantro
- 3 tablespoons of fresh rosemary

COOKING DIRECTIONS
1.   Rub the pork belly with salt, ground black pepper, onion powder, paprika, and cilantro.
2.   Set pressure cooker to "Pressure" mode.
3.   Put the pork belly into the cooker followed by rosemary and chicken stock.
4.   Close pressure cooker lid and cook for around 25 minutes.
5.   Crush the peanuts.
6.   When the cooking time ends, open pressure cooker lid and remove the pork belly.
7.   Dry the pork belly using a paper towel.
8.   After that, slice it and sprinkle crushed peanuts before serving.
Nutrition: calories 554, fat 52.4, fiber 2, carbs 9.19, protein 14

Pork Rolls Covered with Chicken Skin

Prep time: quarter-hour | Cooking time: 35 minutes | Servings: 7
Ingredients
- 5 ounces of chicken skin
- 1 teaspoon of ground black pepper
- 1 teaspoon of oregano
- 1 pound of pork loin
- 6 ounces of mushrooms
- 1 teaspoon of salt
- ¼ cup of chicken stock
- 1 tablespoon of sour cream
- 1 teaspoon of essential olive oil
- ¼ cup of fresh dill

COOKING DIRECTIONS
1.   Chop the pork loin into large pieces.
2.   Sprinkle the pork pieces with all the oregano, ground black pepper, and salt.
3.   Slice the mushrooms and chop the dill.
4.   Mix the vegetables in a mixing bowl.
5.   Fill the chicken skin using pork pieces and mushroom mixture.
6.   Pin the chicken skin to close using toothpicks.
7.   Set the strain cooker to "Sauté" mode.
8.   Place the pork rolls into pressure cooker and sprinkle the dish with extra virgin olive oil and sour cream.
9.   Add the chicken stock and close the cooker's lid. Cook for 35 minutes.
10.   When cooked, allow the pork roll meal to rest briefly.
11.   Remember to remove the toothpicks before serving.
Nutrition: calories 274, fat 12.5, fiber 3, carbs 19.47, protein 23

Pork Cutlets with Blueberry Sauce

Prep time: ten MINUTES | Cooking time: twenty minutes | Servings: 5
Ingredients
- 12 ounces of ground pork
- ½ cup of freshly squeezed lemon juice
- 1/3 cup of blueberries
- 1 tablespoon of Erythritol
- A teaspoon cilantro
- ½ teaspoon of thyme
- An egg
- A tablespoon of ground ginger
- 1 tablespoon of essential organic olive oil
- 1 tablespoon of coconut flour
- 1 teaspoon of paprika

COOKING DIRECTIONS
1.   Combine the ground pork with cilantro, thyme, paprika, and egg and stir well until smooth.
2.   Make medium cutlets of the ground meat mixture.
3.   Set pressure cooker to "Sauté" mode.
4.   Pour the essential olive oil into pressure cooker and add the pork cutlets.
5.   Cook the cutlets for around 10 minutes or until each side turns golden brown.
6.   Put the blueberries in the blender and blend until smooth.
7.   Add the Erythritol, ground ginger, coconut flour, and fresh lemon juice.

8. Blend the amalgamation and cook for 1 minute.

9. When the cutlets are cooked, pour the blueberry sauce over it.

10. Close the lid and cook the dish on "Sauté" mode for around ten minutes.

11. Remove the pork cutlets from the cooker and sprinkle them with plum sauce when serving.

Nutrition: calories 161, fat 6.7, fiber 1.6, carbs 4.5, protein 19.7

Spicy Boiled Sausages

Prep time: quarter-hour | Cooking time: 18 minutes | Servings: 9

Ingredients

- 5 ounces of sausage casings
- 1 tablespoon of minced garlic
- 1 tablespoon of red pepper cayenne
- A teaspoon of chili powder
- ½ teaspoon of ground black pepper
- 1 teaspoon of salt
- 6 ounces of ground pork
- 6 ounces of ground beef
- A tablespoon of organic olive oil
- A cup of water
- 1 teaspoon of turmeric

COOKING DIRECTIONS

1. Mix the ground pork with beef in a bowl.
2. Sprinkle the amalgamation with garlic, cayenne, ground black pepper, salt, and turmeric.
3. Mix well with your hands.
4. Fill the sausage cases with the ground meat mixture.
5. Set the strain cooker to "Sauté" mode.
6. Pour water into the cooker and preheat it for 5 minutes.
7. Transfer the sausages to the strain cooker and close the lid.
8. Cook the sausages for around 10 minutes.
9. Preheat the oven to 365 F. When the cooking time ends, remove the boiled sausages from the pressure cooker and spread them with essential organic olive oil.
10. Transfer the sausages in the oven and cook for 8 minutes.
11. When the sausages turn golden brown, remove them from the oven and allow them to cool before serving.

Nutrition: calories 158, fat 11.5, fiber 1, carbs 2.94, protein 12

Meat Trio with Gravy

Prep time: ten MINUTES | Cooking time: 25 minutes | Servings: 8

Ingredients

- 8 ounces of beef
- 7 ounces of pork
- 8 ounces of lamb
- A cup of red wine
- ¼ cup of freshly squeezed lemon juice
- 1 tablespoon of Erythritol
- 1 tablespoon of ground black pepper
- 1 teaspoon of oregano
- A tablespoon of butter
- 1 tablespoon of fresh rosemary
- A cup of chicken stock
- 1 tablespoon of tomato paste
- 1 tablespoon of minced garlic

COOKING DIRECTIONS

1. Chop the pork, beef, and lamb into medium-sized pieces.
2. Combine the meat mixture with wine together and allow it marinate for 10 minutes.
3. Remove the meat mixture from the burgundy or merlot wine and sprinkle it with Erythritol, ground black pepper, oregano, rosemary, and garlic. Stir well.
4. Set pressure cooker to "Sauté" mode.
5. Add tablespoon of butter to the cooker and allow it melt.
6. Pour the meat mixture in the pressure cooker and sauté it for 10 minutes.
7. Add chicken stock and stir.
8. Close the cooker's lid and cook the dish on "Sauté" mode for quarter-hour.
9. When the meat tenders, remove it from the pressure cooker and allow it chill before serving. Serve the dish with gravy.

Nutrition: calories 188, fat 6.4, fiber 0.6, carbs 2.7, protein 23.5

Italian Beef

Prep time: 25 MINUTES | Cooking time: 35 MINUTES | Servings: 4

Ingredients

- 2 sweet peppers
- 1 tablespoon of cayenne
- ¼ cup of garlic
- A pound of beef
- 1 tablespoon of butter
- A cup of chicken stock
- 1 onion
- A cup of Italian greens
- 1 teaspoon of salt
- 1 teaspoon of Erythritol
- ½ cup of tomato paste
- 1 tablespoon of oregano

COOKING DIRECTIONS

1. Peel the garlic and slice it.
2. Remove the seeds from peppers and dice them.
3. Combine the sliced garlic with the chopped bell pepper.

4.   Sprinkle the combination with salt, Erythritol, greens, tomato paste, and oregano and stir well.

5.   Dip the beef in the tomato mixture until it coats well.

6.   Let the beef marinate for 10 minutes. Set pressure cooker to "Pressure" mode.

7.   Place the beef into the pressure cooker followed by chicken stock and butter.

8.   Sprinkle the meat with red pepper cayenne.

9.   Close pressure cooker lid and cook for 35 minutes.

10.   When the cooking time ends, remove the beef from pressure cooker and slice it into serving pieces.

Nutrition: calories 307, fat 10.7, fiber 3.3, carbs 15.7, protein 37.3

Salisbury Steak

Prep time: quarter-hour | Cooking time: ten mins | Servings: 5

Ingredients

- ½ cup of onion soup mix
- A pound of ground beef
- 2 eggs
- A cup of water
- A tablespoon of mustard
- 1 teaspoon of salt
- A teaspoon of ground white pepper
- 1 tablespoon of extra virgin organic olive oil
- 1 teaspoon of tomato paste

COOKING DIRECTIONS

1.   Beat the eggs in the mixing bowl and whisk them.

2.   Add the mustard, salt, and ground white pepper. Stir well until smooth.

3.   Dip the beef in the egg mixture and ensure it mixes well.

4.   Make mid-sized balls from the meat mixture and flatten them.

5.   Set the pressure cooker to "Sauté" mode.

6.   Pour the olive oil into pressure and preheat it in sauté mode.

7.   Add the steaks and sauté the dish for two minutes on both sides.

8.   Combine the tomato paste and onion soup together and stir well.

9.   Pour the soup mixture to the pressure cooker and close the lid.

10.   Cook the dish on "Pressure" mode for 5 minutes.

11.   When the cooking time elapses, remove Salisbury steak from the pressure cooker and serve with gravy.

Nutrition: calories 323, fat 21.9, fiber 0, carbs 2.92, protein 27

Pork Chili

Prep time: a quarter-hour | Cooking time: 45 minutes | Servings: 8

Ingredients

- A cup of black soybeans
- 10 ounces of ground pork
- 1 teaspoon of tomato paste
- 1 cup of chicken stock
- 1 tablespoon of butter
- A teaspoon of cilantro
- 1 teaspoon of oregano
- 1 cup of chopped bok choy
- ¼ cup of green beans
- 3 servings of water
- 2 carrots
- 3 red onions
- A tablespoon of salt

COOKING DIRECTIONS

1.   Combine the ground pork with tomato paste, butter, cilantro, oregano, and salt. Stir well.

2.   Set pressure cooker to "Sauté" mode and add the ground pork mixture.

3.   Sauté the mixture for 2 minutes while stirring frequently.

4.   Add the green beans and water.

5.   Peel the carrots and red onions.

6.   Chop the vegetables and add them in to the pressure cooker.

7.   Sprinkle the stew mixture with bok choy, and stir.

8.   Close pressure cooker lid and cook the dish on "Pressure" mode for 40 minutes.

9.   When the cooking time elapses, open the pressure cooker lid and mix the chili well.

10.   Transfer the pork chili to serving bowls.

Nutrition: calories 194, fat 7.5, fiber 3.7, carbs 13.1, protein 18.7

Marinated Pork Steak

Prep time: 20 mins | Cooking time: 25 minutes | Servings: 6

Ingredients

- ¼ cup of beer
- ¼ cup of extra virgin olive oil
- 1 teaspoon of cayenne pepper
- A teaspoon of cilantro
- A teaspoon of oregano
- 1 tablespoon of salt
- A teaspoon of ground black pepper
- 1 pound of pork tenderloin
- An onion

COOKING DIRECTIONS

1.   Combine the red pepper cayenne, extra virgin organic olive oil, cilantro, oregano, salt, and ground black pepper together in a mixing bowl.

2.   Peel the onion and grind it.

3. Add the onion to the spice contents and mix it until smooth.
4. Add beer and stir well.
5. Dip the pork tenderloin in the beer mixture and allow it to marinate for at least 10 minutes.
6. Set pressure cooker to "Pressure" mode.
7. Transfer the marinated meat to the pressure cooker and cook for 25 minutes.
8. When the cooking time ends, release the cooker's pressure and open its lid.
9. Remove the cooked meat from the cooker and serve.

Nutrition: calories 219, fat 13.3, fiber 1, carbs 3.35, protein 21

Lemon Beef Steak

Prep time: quarter-hour | Cooking time: 20 MINUTES | Servings: 4

Ingredients

- ¼ cup of lemon juice
- 1 pound of beef steak
- 3 tablespoons of lemon zest
- 1 tablespoon of organic essential olive oil
- 3 tablespoons of sesame oil
- 1 teaspoon of apple cider vinegar
- 1 tablespoon of white pepper
- ½ teaspoon of paprika
- 1 tablespoon of fresh cilantro

COOKING DIRECTIONS

1. Squeeze the juice through the lemon and mix it with lemon zest.
2. Add sesame oil, apple cider vinegar, white pepper, paprika, and cilantro and stir well.
3. Rub the beef steak with the spice mixture and enable it chill for 5 minutes.
4. Pour the excess virgin olive oil into pressure cooker and preheat it on sauté mode.
5. Set the pressure cooker to "Sauté" mode.
6. Place the beef steak into pressure cooker and sauté it for 2 minutes. Close the cooker's lid and cook the dish for around 15 minutes on "Pressure" mode.
7. When the dish is cooked, release the cooker's pressure and open the lid.
8. Transfer the steak to serving plates.

Nutrition: calories 295, fat 20.7, fiber 1, carbs 3.38, protein 23

Corned Beef

Prep time: ten minutes | Cooking time: 68 MINUTES | Servings: 10

Ingredients

- 3 pounds of beef brisket
- A teaspoon of oregano
- 1 teaspoon of cilantro
- A teaspoon of paprika
- 1 teaspoon of basil
- A teaspoon of red pepper cayenne
- 1 tablespoon of mustard seeds
- A tablespoon of minced garlic
- 2 servings of water

COOKING DIRECTIONS

1. Combine the oregano, cilantro, paprika, basil, cayenne, mustard seeds, and garlic together in the mixing bowl and stir well.
2. Set pressure to "Pressure" mode.
3. Pour water into the pressure cooker and add the beef brisket.
4. Sprinkle the meat with the spice mixture.
5. Close the cooker's lid and cook for around 68 minutes.
6. When the cooking time ends, release the cooker's pressure and open its lid.
7. Place the corned beef to a cutting board and allow it to rest. Cut it into slices and serve.

Nutrition: calories 187, fat 8, fiber 0, carbs 0.71, protein 28

Semi-sweet Pork Stew

Prep time: 15 MINUTES | Cooking time: 40 minutes | Servings: 8

Ingredients

- 5 tablespoons of liquid stevia
- 14 ounces of pork tenderloin
- 3 carrots
- A teaspoon cayenne
- 8 ounces of cauliflower
- 2 white onions
- A teaspoon of ground black pepper
- 1 tablespoon of organic olive oil
- 1 teaspoon of cilantro
- 1 cup of green beans
- ½ lime
- 3 cups of chicken stock

COOKING DIRECTIONS

1. Chop the pork tenderloin roughly and sprinkle it with cayenne, ground black pepper, and cilantro. Stir the ingredients well.
2. Peel the onions and carrots.
3. Chop the onions, carrots, and lime.
4. Pour the chopped meat followed by vegetables into pressure cooker.
5. Chop the cauliflower into medium-size pieces and add them into pressure cooker.
6. Add green beans and chicken stock. Stir well.
7. Set pressure to "Pressure" mode.
8. Close pressure cooker lid and cook for 40 minutes.
9. When the cooking time ends, open the cooker and transfer the stew to serving bowls.
10. Remember to sprinkle it with stevia when serving.

Nutrition: calories 124, fat 3.8, fiber 2.6, carbs 8.3, protein 14.6

Pork Chimichangas

Prep time: fifteen minutes | Cooking time: 30 minutes | Servings: 6

Ingredients

- 6 ounces of almond flour tortillas
- 1 tablespoon of extra virgin essential olive oil
- 1 pound of pork
- 1 teaspoon of garlic powder
- ½ teaspoon of chili powder
- 4 tablespoons of tomato paste
- 5 tablespoons of butter
- ½ teaspoon of ground cumin
- 1 teaspoon of salt
- 1 teaspoon of ground black pepper
- 1 teaspoon of cilantro

COOKING DIRECTIONS

1. Grind the pork and combine it with garlic powder and chili powder.
2. Sprinkle the spiced pork with salt, ground black pepper, and cilantro and stir well.
3. Add tomato paste and stir it.
4. Set the pressure cooker to "Sauté" mode and add butter to melt.
5. Add the pork mixture and sauté for 10 minutes. Stir it frequently using a spoon.
6. Close the pressure cooker lid and cook the dish on "Pressure" mode for quarter-hour.
7. When the cooking time ends, remove the pork chimichangas dish from the pressure cooker.
8. Spread the tortillas with the ground meat mixture and wrap them.
9. Pour some virgin essential olive oil into pressure cooker.
10. Add the wrapped tortillas and cook them for 3 minutes.
11. Remove the dish from the pressure cooker and serve.

Nutrition: calories 294, fat 17.7, fiber 1, carbs 18.89, protein 16

Stuffed Meatloaf

Prep time: quarter-hour | Cooking time: a half-hour | Servings: 12

Ingredients

- 2 pounds of ground beef
- Dry bread crumbs
- 5 boiled eggs
- 1 red bell pepper
- 1 white onion
- 4 tablespoons of chives
- 1 tablespoon of starch
- A teaspoon of ground black pepper

- 1 teaspoon of salt
- 2 eggs
- 1 teaspoon of butter
- A teaspoon of essential organic olive oil
- 1 tablespoon of coconut flour
- 1 teaspoon of ground rosemary

COOKING DIRECTIONS

1. Peel the eggs.
2. Peel the onion and remove seeds from the red bell pepper.
3. Chop the onion and the red bell pepper.
4. Add chives and mix well. Combine the ground beef with ground black pepper, starch, salt, butter, coconut flour, and ground rosemary in a bowl. Stir well.
5. Crumble the eggs and mix it with the ground beef combination.
6. Sub-divide the meat into two portions.
7. Pour the organic olive oil in one portion and put it in the pressure cooker.
8. Spread the meat with the onion mixture and set the eggs in the middle.
9. Cover the eggs with the remaining ground meat and pour it over the bread crumbs.
10. Close the pressure cooker lid and cook the dish on "Pressure" mode for a half-hour.
11. When the stuffed meatloaf is cooked, release the pressure from the cooker and open the lid.
12. Remove the meatloaf from the pressure cooker carefully and let it rest. Cut into slices when serving.

Nutrition: calories 165, fat 5.7, fiber 0.9, carbs 3.4, protein 23.9

Stuffed Lettuce

Prep time: 10 MINUTES | Cooking time: ten mins | Servings: 8

Ingredients

- 10 ounces of lettuce leaves
- ½ cup of tomato paste
- 7 ounces of Parmesan
- A pound of ground beef
- 4 ounces of ground pork
- 2 servings of water
- A teaspoon of salt
- A teaspoon of ground black pepper
- A teaspoon of turmeric
- 1 tablespoon of butter
- 1 teaspoon of oregano
- 1/2 cup of cream

COOKING DIRECTIONS

1. Grate the Parmesan put it in a mixing bowl.
2. Add the tomato paste, ground pork, ground beef, salt, ground black pepper, turmeric, butter, and oregano. Stir well.
3. Set the load cooker to "Pressure" mode.

4. Put the beef mixture in the pressure cooker.
5. Combine water and cream in a mixing bowl and stir.
6. Pour the cream mixture into pressure cooker.
7. Close the lid and cook for quarter-hour.
8. When the cooking time elapses, release the cooker's pressure and open its lid.
9. Stuff the lettuce leaves with the ground meat mixture and serve.

Nutrition: calories 245, fat 11.5, fiber 1.1, carbs 5.8, protein 29.9

Mexican Meatballs

Prep time: ten minutes | Cooking time: 8 MINUTES | Servings: 6

Ingredients
- 1 tablespoon of Erythritol
- 1 tablespoon of water
- 1 pound of ground pork
- ½ cup of tomato juice
- 1 teaspoon of oregano
- A tablespoon of essential organic olive oil
- 1 chili pepper
- A cup of chicken stock
- 1 tablespoon of coconut flour
- 1 teaspoon of flax meal
- 1 tablespoon of fresh thyme
- 1 teaspoon of ground coriander
- 1 tablespoon of onion powder

COOKING DIRECTIONS
1. Combine the oregano, coconut flour, flax meal, thyme, ground coriander, onion powder, and ground pork in a mixing bowl.
2. Chop the chili pepper and add it into the pork mixture. Mix well.
3. Preheat the pressure cooker on "Sauté" mode.
4. Pour the essential organic olive oil into pressure cooker.
5. Make medium-sized meatballs from the ground pork mixture and put them in the pressure cooker.
6. Sauté the meatballs for two minutes or until both sides turns golden brown.
7. Remove the meatballs from the load cooker.
8. Pour Erythritol and water into the pressure cooker and stir well.
9. Add meatballs and cook for two minutes.
10. Remove the Mexican meatballs from pressure cooker and serve.

Nutrition: calories 151, fat 5.6, fiber 1.4, carbs 3.9, protein 20.7

Pork Enchiladas

Prep time: fifteen MINUTES | Cooking time: fifteen minutes | Servings: 8

Ingredients
- 7 ounces of almond flour tortillas
- 1 pound of pork tenderloin
- 1 teaspoon of ground black pepper
- 1 cup of cream
- A ½ chili pepper (red)
- 3 tablespoons of ancho chili sauce
- 1 large onion
- 1 teaspoon of garlic powder
- 7 ounces of Cheddar cheese
- 1 teaspoon of paprika

COOKING DIRECTIONS
1. Sprinkle the pork tenderloin with ground black pepper and paprika.
2. Set the load cooker to "Pressure" mode.
3. Place the pork into the cooker and add cream. Close the lid.
4. Cook for 14 minutes.
5. Preheat the oven to 365 F and put the tortillas. Cook them for 4 minutes.
6. Remove them from the oven reserve.
7. Grate the Cheddar cheese and peel the onion.
8. Dice the onion.
9. When the meat is cooked, remove it from the pressure cooker and allow it to rest briefly.
10. Shred the meat using a fork.
11. Combine the shredded meat with chili sauce and mix well.
12. Spread the tortillas with the shredded meat and cover them with the diced onion.
13. Sprinkle the tortillas with the grated cheese and garlic powder.
14. Wrap the tortillas and serve.

Nutrition: calories 263, fat 12.6, fiber 1, carbs 21.81, protein 16

Soy Sauce Pork Strips

Prep time: 20 minutes | Cooking time: quarter-hour | Servings: 6

Ingredients
- A cup of soy sauce
- A tablespoon of Erythritol
- 1 tablespoon of sesame seeds
- 1 teaspoon of cumin seeds
- 1 tablespoon of onion powder
- 1 teaspoon of miso paste
- 10 ounces of pork fillet
- 1 tablespoon of olive oil
- ½ cup of water

COOKING DIRECTIONS
1. Combine the soy sauce, Erythritol, sesame seeds, cumin seeds, onion powder, essential olive oil and water in a mixing bowl.
2. Stir well to dissolve the erythritol sugar.

3.	Cut the pork fillet into strips and place them in the soy sauce mixture.
4.	Mix well and permit the pork to marinate for ten minutes.
5.	Preheat pressure on "Sauté" mode for 2 minutes.
6.	Add the marinated pork strips to a pressure cooker and close its lid.
7.	Cook the dish on "Pressure" mode for 13 minutes.
8.	When the cooking time ends, release the cooker's pressure and open the lid.
9.	Transfer the pork strips to serving plates.
Nutrition: calories 167, fat 9.2, fiber 0.7, carbs 6.7, protein 16.3

Glazed Beef Meatballs with Sesame Seeds
Prep time: fifteen minutes | Cooking time: 10 minutes | Servings: 6
Ingredients
- 1 teaspoon of water
- 2 tablespoons of Erythritol
- 1 tablespoon of butter
- 1 teaspoon of ground black pepper
- 2 tablespoons of sesame seeds
- 12 ounces of ground beef
- An egg
- 1 teaspoon of salt

COOKING DIRECTIONS
1.	Beat the egg in a mixing bowl.
2.	Add the black pepper, sesame seeds, salt, and semolina. Mix well.
3.	Add the ground beef and mix.
4.	Make small meatballs from the ground beef mixture.
5.	Set the pressure cooker to "Sauté" mode.
6.	Add the butter into it and allow it to melt.
7.	Carefully, put the pork meatballs in the pressure cooker and sauté them for 5 minutes on each side.
8.	Pour water to the cooker and Sprinkle the meatballs with Erythritol. Close the pressure cooker lid.
9.	Cook the dish on "Pressure" mode for 5 minutes.
10.	When the cooking time ends, release the remaining pressure and open the lid.
11.	Transfer the cooked meatballs to a serving plate.
Nutrition: calories 151, fat 7.7, fiber 0.4, carbs 1, protein 18.7

Lasagna
Prep time: fifteen minutes | Cooking time: 25 MINUTES | Servings: 8
Ingredients
- 7 ounces of sliced eggplants
- 10 ounces of Parmesan cheese
- 6 ounces of Mozzarella cheese
- 1 teaspoon of salt
- 1 teaspoon of paprika
- A cup of cream
- ½ cup of chicken stock
- 1 onion
- 1 teaspoon of minced garlic
- 10 ounces of ground beef
- A cup of tomato paste
- 1 tablespoon of chives

COOKING DIRECTIONS
1.	Grate the Parmesan and Mozzarella cheeses.
2.	Combine salt, paprika, and chives in a mixing bowl.
3.	Add the garlic and tomato paste and stir well.
4.	Add ground beef and mix well.
5.	Spread the lasagna noodles on the ground beef mixture.
6.	Peel the onion and dice it.
7.	Place the eggplants followed by diced onion and grated cheese in the pressure.
8.	Pour the cream over the pressure cooker contents and close the lid.
9.	Cook the dish on "Sauté" mode for 25 minutes.
10.	When the lasagna is cooked, remove it from the cooker and allow it to rest before serving.
Nutrition: calories 300, fat 15.5, fiber 2.6, carbs 12.2, protein 30.3

Beef Bulgogi
Prep time: 10 mins | Cooking time: 35 minutes | Servings: 10
Ingredients
- 3 pounds of beef
- 1 onion
- A tablespoon chives
- 2 carrots
- ½ tablespoon of sesame seeds
- 1 teaspoon of extra virgin essential olive oil
- ½ cup of soy sauce
- 4 tablespoons of rice wine
- ¼ cup of chicken stock
- A teaspoon of fresh ginger
- 1 teaspoon of Erythritol
- A teaspoon minced garlic

COOKING DIRECTIONS
1.	Peel the onion and dice it.
2.	Peel the carrots and grate them.
3.	Set pressure cooker to "Sauté" mode.
4.	Put the grated carrot and diced onion into the pressure cooker.
5.	Add olive oil, soy sauce, chives, rice wine, chicken stock, fresh ginger, Erythritol, and minced garlic. Stir well.
6.	Add the beef and mix well. Close the pressure cooker lid and cook for around 35 minutes.
7.	When the cooking time ends, remove your beef bulgogi from the cooker and stir again.

8. Place the bulgogi in the serving dish, sprinkle with sesame seeds and serve.
Nutrition: calories 248, fat 11.5, fiber 2, carbs 7.68, protein 30

Rack of Lamb

Prep time: fifteen MINUTES | Cooking time: 25 minutes | Servings: 6

Ingredients

- 13 ounces of lamb rack
- A cup of burgundy or merlot wine
- 1 tablespoon of Erythritol
- A teaspoon of ground black pepper
- 1 teaspoon of cilantro
- 1 cup of chicken stock
- 1 onion
- 3 tablespoons of butter
- 1 tablespoon of extra virgin organic olive oil
- 1 teaspoon of curry
- 1 teaspoon of fresh rosemary

COOKING DIRECTIONS

1. Combine Erythritol, ground black pepper, cilantro, chicken stock, curry, and rosemary in a mixing bowl and stir.
2. Peel the onion and chop it.
3. Add the chopped onion in the mixture and stir again.
4. Place the lamb rack chicken stock mixture and allow it to marinate for around ten minutes.
5. Set pressure cooker to "Pressure" mode.
6. Add the butter into pressure cooker and melt it.
7. Add the marinated lamb rack and sprinkle it with curry.
8. Close the lid and cook for around 25 minutes.
9. When the cooking time elapses, remove your rack of lamb meal from the cooker. Allow it to cool before serving.
Nutrition: calories 208, fat 13.9, fiber 1, carbs 5.49, protein 14

Lamb Espetadas

Prep time: quarter-hour | Cooking time: 25 minutes | Servings: 5

Ingredients

- 2 onions
- 1 pound of lamb
- 1 tablespoon of paprika
- 1 tablespoon of extra virgin essential olive oil
- 1 teaspoon of oregano
- 1 tablespoon of cilantro
- ½ teaspoon of bay leaf
- 1 tablespoon of sea salt
- ¼ chili
- ¼ cup of burgundy or merlot wine
- 1 teaspoon of apple cider vinegar
- 1 teaspoon of black-eyed peas

COOKING DIRECTIONS

1. Chop the lamb roughly.
2. Combine the chopped lamb with oregano, cilantro, sea salt, chili, red, apple cider vinegar treatment, and black-eyed peas in a mixing bowl and stir well.
3. Let the mixture sit for 5 minutes.
4. Peel the onions and blend well using a blender.
5. Take the chopped meat and hang with wooden skewers.
6. Spread the meat with the blended onion.
7. Preheat pressure cooker on "Sauté" mode for 3 minutes.
8. Place the lamb skewers in the pressure cooker and sprinkle the meat with olive oil.
9. Close the lid and cook for 25 minutes.
10. When your lamp espetadas is cooked, remove it from the pressure cooker and allow it to cool before serving.
Nutrition: calories 281, fat 18.2, fiber 1, carbs 5.24, protein 23

Lamb Cutlets

Prep time: ten MINUTES | Cooking time: 12 minutes | Servings: 5

Ingredients

- 14 ounces ground lamb
- 2 white onions
- 1 teaspoon ground black pepper
- 1 egg
- 1 tablespoon salt
- 1 teaspoon cilantro
- ½ teaspoon ground rosemary
- 1 cup fresh basil
- 1 teaspoon organic essential olive oil
- 1 teaspoon minced garlic
- ¼ teaspoon sage
- 1 teaspoon paprika

COOKING DIRECTIONS

1. Combine the ground lamb, ground black pepper, egg, salt, cilantro, ground rosemary, minced garlic, and paprika in a mixing bowl and stir well.
2. Peel the onions and dice them.
3. Add the diced onion on the ground lamb mixture and stir well.
4. Chop the basil and pour sage over it.
5. Set pressure cooker to "Sauté" mode.
6. Pour the virgin organic olive oil in to the pressure cooker and add basil mixture.
7. Sauté the amalgamation for 2 minutes while stirring frequently.
8. Remove the basil mixture from the cooker.
9. Make medium-sized cutlets from the lamb mixture and hang them in the pressure cooker.
10. Cook the cutlets for 10 minutes or until golden brown on both sides.
11. Remove the lamb cutlets from the cooker and allow it to cool before serving.

Nutrition: calories 237, fat 12.9, fiber 2, carbs 11.65, protein 19

Lamb with Thyme

Prep time: ten mins | Cooking time: 45 MINUTES | Servings: 8
Ingredients

- 1 cup of fresh thyme
- 1 tablespoon of essential olive oil
- 2 pounds of lamb
- 1 teaspoon of oregano
- 1 tablespoon of ground black pepper
- 1 teaspoon of paprika
- ¼ cup of rice wine
- 1 teaspoon of Erythritol
- 4 tablespoons of butter
- ¼ cup of chicken stock
- 1 tablespoon of turmeric

COOKING DIRECTIONS

1. Chop the fresh thyme and mix it with oregano, ground black pepper, paprika, rice wine, Erythritol, chicken stock, and turmeric.
2. Sprinkle the lamb with the spice mixture and stir it carefully.
3. Transfer the lamb mixture to a pressure cooker and add olive oil.
4. Close the pressure cooker lid and cook the dish on meat mode for around 45 minutes.
5. When the lamb meal is cooked remove it from the pressure cooker.
6. Allow it to rest and slice it. Enjoy!

Nutrition: calories 313, fat 16.5, fiber 2.8, carbs 8.7, protein 32.7

Asian Lamb

Prep time: ten MINUTES | Cooking time: 45 minutes | Servings: 5
Ingredients

- A cup of soy sauce
- A tablespoon of tahini
- 3 tablespoons of olive oil
- 8 ounces of lamb
- 1 onion
- 1/2 cup garlic herb
- 1 teaspoon of Erythritol
- 1 teaspoon of starch
- 1 teaspoon of salt
- 1 tablespoon of black olives
- 1 tablespoon of coriander
- 1 teaspoon of sage

COOKING DIRECTIONS

1. Combine soy sauce and tahini in a mixing bowl.
2. Set the pressure cooker to "Sauté" mode and pour the extra virgin olive oil into the pressure cooker.
3. Add the garlic and sauté the mixture for 2 minutes.

4. Add the brown Erythritol, starch, salt, black olives, coriander, and sage.
5. Stir the amalgamation and sauté it for thirty seconds.
6. Pour the soy sauce mixture into the pressure cooker contents.
7. Peel the onion and dice it.
8. Add the diced onion and lamb in the cooker and close the lid.
9. Cook the dish on "Sauté" mode for around 40 minutes.
10. When the Asian lamb is cooked, remove it from the cooker and allow it to cool. Serve it while warm.

Nutrition: calories 229, fat 13.6, fiber 1.5, carbs 10.4, protein 17.3

Spinach-stuffed Rack of Lamb

Prep time: quarter-HOUR | Cooking time: thirty MINUTES | Servings: 5
Ingredients

- 3 cups of fresh spinach
- 1 tablespoon of minced garlic
- 1 pound of lamb rack
- 1 tablespoon of curry paste
- ½ cup of chicken stock
- A tablespoon of organic olive oil
- 1 teaspoon of butter
- 1 teaspoon of salt
- 1 teaspoon of fresh ginger
- 3 tablespoons of cream

COOKING DIRECTIONS:

1. Wash the spinach, dry, and chop it.
2. Transfer the spinach to a blender and puree.
3. Put the blended spinach in a mixing bowl and add garlic, curry paste, and fresh ginger. Stir well.
4. Rub the lamb rack with salt, extra virgin organic olive oil, and butter.
5. Make tiny cuts from the lamb rack and stuff it with the spinach mixture.
6. Set pressure cooker to "Pressure" mode.
7. Place the stuffed lamb rack into pressure cooker and add chicken stock.
8. Close the lid and cook for 30 minutes.
9. When the cooking time ends, remove the spinach lamb from the pressure cooker, allow it cool, slice, and serve while warm.

Nutrition: calories 213, fat 13.6, fiber 1, carbs 3.17, protein 20

Lamb and Avocado Salad

Prep time: 10 minutes | Cooking time: 35 minutes | Servings: 7
Ingredients

- 1 pitted avocado
- A cucumber
- 8 ounces of lamb fillet
- 3 servings of water
- 1 teaspoon of salt
- 1 teaspoon of cayenne

- 3 tablespoons of organic extra virgin olive oil
- 1 garlic herb
- 1 teaspoon of basil
- 1 tablespoon of sesame oil
- 1 cup of lettuce

COOKING DIRECTIONS

1. Set the pressure cooker to "Sauté" mode.
2. Place the lamb fillet into pressure cooker and add water.
3. Sprinkle the mixture with salt.
4. Peel the garlic herb and add it to the lamb mixture.
5. Close the lid and cook for 35 minutes.
6. Meanwhile, slice the cucumbers and chop the peeled avocado.
7. Combine the ingredients in the mixing bowl.
8. Chop the lettuce and add it to the mixing bowl.
9. Sprinkle the mix with the red pepper cayenne, extra virgin olive oil, basil, and sesame oil. Toss well.
10. When the meat is cooked, remove it from the cooker and allow it to relax.
11. Chop meat roughly and place it in a mixing bowl.
12. Mix the lamp chops with salad in serving bowl. Serve the dish warm.

Nutrition: calories 203, fat 17.5, fiber 2, carbs 3.47, protein 9

Garlic Lamb Stew

Prep time: quarter-HOUR | Cooking time: 35 minutes | Servings: 8

Ingredients

- 1 cup of garlic
- 1 tablespoon of garlic powder
- 1 teaspoon of cilantro
- 3 carrots
- 1 cup of chopped asparagus
- 4 cups of chickens stock
- ½ cup of half and half
- 2 onions
- A pound lamb
- A cup of parsley
- 1 tablespoon of salt
- 1 tablespoon of essential extra virgin olive oil

COOKING DIRECTIONS

1. Peel the garlic and slice it.
2. Combine the sliced garlic with garlic powder and stir well.
3. Add the cilantro and organic olive oil and stir.
4. Peel the carrots and onions. Chop the vegetables roughly.
5. Set pressure cooker to "Sauté" mode.
6. Place the chopped vegetable and garlic mixture to the pressure cooker.
7. Chop parsley and add it to the cooker.
8. Chop the lamb and add it into pressure cooker.
9. Add asparagus, water, half and half, and salt and stir well.
10. Close the pressure cooker lid and cook for 35 minutes.
11. When the stew is cooked, release the cooker's pressure and open its lid.
12. Ladle the garlic lamb stew into serving bowls.

Nutrition: calories 195, fat 7.9, fiber 2.2, carbs 13, protein 18.7

Soft Lamb Shoulder

Prep time: ten MINUTES | Cooking time: 25 minutes | Servings: 6

Ingredients

- A cup of sour cream
- 1 tablespoon of ground black pepper
- 1 tablespoon of garlic powder
- 1 tablespoon of onion powder
- 1 teaspoon of basil
- 9 ounces of lamb shoulder
- 1 teaspoon of chives
- 3 tablespoons of butter

COOKING DIRECTIONS

1. Combine the sour cream, ground black pepper, garlic powder, onion powder, basil, chives, and butter together in a mixing bowl. Stir the contents well until they smoothen.
2. Put the lamb shoulder in the sour cream mixture and mix well.
3. Let the meat marinate for 3 hours.
4. Preheat pressure on "Pressure" mode and add the lamb mixture.
5. Close the pressure cooker lamb and cook for 25 minutes.
6. When the cooking time ends, release the cooker's pressure and open its lid.
7. Place the soft lamb shoulder on the serving plate and cut into portions.

Nutrition: calories 224, fat 17, fiber 1 carbs 5.58, protein 12

BREAKFAST RECIPES

Aromatic Keto Coffee

Prep time: ten mins | Cooking time: 5 minutes |Servings: 4

Ingredients:

- 4 teaspoon of butter
- 2 servings of water
- 4 teaspoons of instant coffee
- 1 tablespoon of Erythritol
- 1/3 cup of heavy cream
- 1 teaspoon of ground cinnamon
- ½ teaspoon of vanilla flavoring

COOKING DIRECTIONS

1. Pour water, heavy cream, ground cinnamon, and vanilla flavoring into the cooker.
2. Add instant coffee and stir well until they become homogenous.
3. Close and seal the lid.
4. Cook the coffee mixture on high-pressure mode for 4 minutes.
5. Allow the pressure to release naturally for ten minutes.
6. Open the cooker's lid and add butter.
7. Stir well and pour coffee into the serving cups.

Nutrition: calories 71, fat 7.5, fiber 0.3, carbs 0.8, protein 0.3

Zucchini Egg Cups

Prep time: 5 minutes | Cooking time: 7 minutes | Servings: 4

INGREDIENTS:

- 1 zucchini
- 2 tablespoon of almond flour
- ½ teaspoon of salt
- 1 teaspoon of butter
- 4 eggs

COOKING DIRECTIONS:

1. Grate zucchini and mix it with almond flour and salt.
2. Spread the muffin molds with butter and place grated zucchini in the nests.
3. Beat eggs over the "zucchini nests" and place them in the cooker.
4. Lower the fryer lid and cook the zucchini cups for around 7 minutes.
5. When the eggs are solid, the meal is cooked.

Nutrition: calories 99, fat 7.2, fiber 0.9, carbs 2.7, protein 6.9

Egg Clouds

Prep time: ten mins |Cooking time: 6 minutes |Servings: 4

Ingredients:

- 4 egg whites
- ½ teaspoon of freshly squeezed lemon juice
- ½ teaspoon of salt
- 1 teaspoon of almond flour

COOKING DIRECTIONS

1. Whisk the egg whites with freshly squeezed lemon juice.
2. Add salt and almond flour to the mixture. Stir it.
3. Place the egg white clouds in the cooker using a spoon.
4. Lower the mid-air fryer lid.
5. Cook the egg clouds for 6 minutes or until they turn light brown.

Nutrition: calories 21, fat 0.4, fiber 0.1, carbs 0.4, protein 3.7

Avocado Bacon Bombs

Prep time: ten minutes |Cooking time: ten mins |Servings: 4

Ingredients:

- 1 peeled and cored avocado
- 4 oz of sliced bacon
- 1 tablespoon of almond flour
- 1 tablespoon of flax meal
- ½ teaspoon of salt

COOKING DIRECTIONS

1. Blend avocado, almond flour, flax meal, and salt.
2. When the amalgamation is smooth, transfer it into a mixing bowl.
3. Make medium-sized balls and wrap in the bacon.
4. Secure the balls with toothpicks and put them into the cooker set on air crisp mode.
5. Close the lid and cook the meal for 10 minutes.

Nutrition: calories 303, fat 25.8, fiber 4.6, carbs 6.7, protein 13.3

Baked Avocado

Prep time: quarter-hour |Cooking time: 10 minutes |Servings: 2

Ingredients:

- 1 halved avocado
- 2 eggs
- ½ teaspoon of ground black pepper
- 1 teaspoon of butter

COOKING DIRECTIONS:

1. Beat the eggs in the avocado pieces and sprinkle it with ground black pepper.
2. Add butter.
3. Add 1 cup of water into the cooker.
4. Put the avocado halves into the Pressure cooker and close the lid.

5. Cook the breakfast for ten minutes on high-pressure mode.
6. Allow pressure release naturally for ten around ten minutes and serve.
Nutrition: calories 286, fat 25.2, fiber 6.9, carbs 9.3, protein 7.5

Mason Jar Omelet

Prep time: ten mins |Cooking time: 7 minutes |Servings: 4
Ingredients:

- 4 whisked eggs
- ¼ cup of cream
- ½ teaspoon of salt
- 2 oz of chopped bacon
- 1 teaspoon of melted butter
- 1 cup of water for smoking

COOKING DIRECTIONS:
1. Mix whisked eggs, cream, salt, and chopped bacon.
2. Add melted butter and stir the amalgamation.
3. Transfer egg mixture into the mason jars.
4. Pour water in the Pressure cooker and fix the trivet.
5. Place mason jars on the trivet.
6. Close the lid and cook an omelet for 7 minutes on High-pressure mode.
7. Release the pressure immediately.
8. Chill the Mason jar omelet a bit before serving.
Nutrition: calories 234, fat 18, fiber 0, carbs 1.2, protein 16.2

Cauliflower Pancake

Prep time: ten mins |Cooking time: 10 minutes |Servings: 2
Ingredients:

- 7 oz of cauliflower
- 2 whisked eggs
- 2 tablespoons of almond flour
- 1 tablespoon of flax meal
- 1 teaspoon of butter
- 1 teaspoon of chili flakes
- 1 teaspoon of dried dill

COOKING DIRECTIONS:
1. Grind the cauliflower and add in whisked eggs, almond flour, flax meal, dried dill, and chili flakes.
2. Stir the combination well.
3. Preheat Ninja cooker on sauté mode and add butter. Melt it.
4. Place cauliflower mixture into the cooker using a spoon (to acquire pancake shape.)
5. Cook each side for around 4 minutes or until it browns.

Nutrition: calories 161, fat 11.2, fiber 4.3, carbs 8.4, protein 9.9

Scrambled Eggs

Prep time: 5 minutes |Cooking time: 9 minutes |Servings: 5
Ingredients:

- 7 eggs
- ½ cup of almond milk
- 1 tablespoon of butter
- 1 teaspoon of basil
- ¼ cup of fresh parsley
- 1 teaspoon of salt
- 1 teaspoon of paprika
- 4 ounces of sliced bacon
- 1 tablespoon of cilantro

COOKING DIRECTIONS:
1. Beat the eggs in a mixing bowl and whisk well.
2. Add the almond milk, basil, salt, paprika, and cilantro. Stir the amalgamation well.
3. Chop the bacon and parsley.
4. Set pressure cooker mode to "Sauté" mode and add the chopped bacon.
5. Cook it for 3 minutes and add the whisked egg mixture. Cook for 5 more minutes.
6. Stir the eggs carefully with a wooden spoon or spatula.
7. Sprinkle the eggs with the chopped parsley. Cook it for 4 minutes.
8. When the eggs are cooked, remove them from the pressure cooker and serve while warm.
Nutrition: calories 289, fat 23.7, fiber 0.8, carbs 2.6, protein 16.9

Soft-boiled Eggs

Prep time: quarter-hour |Cooking time: quarter-hour |Servings: 6
Ingredients:

- 2 glasses of water
- One pitted avocado
- 4 eggs
- A teaspoon of paprika
- ½ teaspoon of ground black pepper
- 1 sweet bell pepper
- A teaspoon of salt
- 3 tablespoons of heavy cream
- 3 ounces of lettuce leaves

COOKING DIRECTIONS:
1. Pour water into the pressure cooker. Dip the eggs inside and close its lid.
2. Set the pressure cooker mode to "Pressure," and cook for fifteen minutes.
3. Remove the eggs from pressure cooker and place them on ice bath.

4.   Chop the avocado and remove the seeds from the bell pepper.
5.   Dice the sweet pepper chop the eggs after peeling them.
6.   Combine the chopped ingredients in a mixing bowl.
7.   Sprinkle them with paprika, ground black pepper, and salt. Stir.
8.   Transfer the mixture to the lettuce leaves, sprinkle them with cream, and serve.
Nutrition: calories 168, fat 12.9, fiber 3, carbs 6.75, protein 7

Migas

Prep time: ten mins |Cooking time: 10 MINUTES |Servings: 6
Ingredients:
- 10 eggs
- 1 jalapeno pepper
- 8 ounces of tomatoes
- 1 tablespoon of chicken stock
- 7 ounces of cheddar cheese
- 2 white onions
- 2 cups of tortilla chips
- 1 sweet bell pepper
- ½ cup of beef stock
- 1 teaspoon of salt

COOKING DIRECTIONS:
1.   Whisk the eggs in the mixing bowl.
2.   Chop the jalapeno peppers and tomatoes.
3.   Grate the cheddar cheese.
4.   Peel the onions and chop them.
5.   Crush the tortilla chips.
6.   Chop the sweet peppers.
7.   Combine the jalapeno pepper, tomatoes, onion, and chopped bell pepper and stir.
8.   Set pressure cooker to "Sauté" mode and transfer the vegetable mixture.
9.   Cook it for 5 minutes.
10.   Add the whisked eggs mixture followed by stocks, salt, and grated cheese.
11.   Mix them well and cook for 4 minutes.
12.   Add the crushed tortilla chips and cook for one more minute. Stir it and serve.
13.   Note: Adding salt is essential when using low-sodium chicken and beef stock. If otherwise, you can omit it.
Nutrition: calories 295, fat 19.3, fiber 1, carbs 9.27, protein 21

Bacon Eggs

Prep time: 7 minutes |Cooking time: 7 minutes |Servings: 4
Ingredients:
- 7 ounces of sliced bacon
- 4 boiled eggs
- 1 teaspoon of cilantro
- ½ cup of spinach
- 2 teaspoons of butter
- ½ teaspoon of ground white pepper
- 3 tablespoons of heavy cream

COOKING DIRECTIONS:
1.   Lay the bacon flat and sprinkle each of its side with ground white pepper and cilantro.
2.   Peel the eggs and wrap them with the spinach leaves.
3.   Wrap the eggs with sliced bacon.
4.   Set the strain cooker mode to "Sauté" mode and add the wrapped eggs.
5.   Add butter and cook for around ten minutes.
6.   When the cooking time ends, remove the eggs from the strain cooker and spread them with cream.
7.   Serve the bacon egg dish immediately.
Nutrition: calories 325, fat 28.4, fiber 2, carbs 5.24, protein 15

Creamy Soufflé

Prep time: 10 minutes |Cooking time: twenty possibly even minutes |Servings: 6
Ingredients:
- 3 eggs
- A cup of cream
- 6 ounces of cheese
- 4 tablespoons of butter
- ½ cup of dried apricots
- 1 tablespoon of sour cream
- 2 tablespoons of sugar
- 1 teaspoon of vanilla flavoring

COOKING DIRECTIONS:
1.   Whisk the eggs in a bowl and add cream.
2.   Put cheese in a separate bowl and mix them using a hand mixer.
3.   Add the whisked eggs and butter to sour cream, sugar, and vanilla flavoring.
4.   Blend the mixture well until smooth.
5.   Add apricots, and stir the combination well.
6.   Transfer the soufflé in a pressure cooker and close its lid.
7.   Set the pressure cooker mode to Sauté mode and cook for around 20 minutes.
8.   When the cooking time ends, allow the creamy soufflé to cool and serve.
Nutrition: calories 266, fat 21.1, fiber 1, carbs 11.72, protein 8

Delightful Cheese Casserole

Prep time: ten mins |Cooking time: thirty minutes |Servings: 8
Ingredients:
- 6 ounces cheddar cheese
- 1 zucchini
- ½ cup ground chicken
- 4 ounces Parmesan cheese

- 3 tablespoons butter
- 1 teaspoon paprika
- 1 teaspoon salt
- 1 teaspoon basil
- 1 teaspoon cilantro
- ½ cup fresh dill
- ½ cup of tomato juice
- ½ cup cream
- 2 red sweet peppers

COOKING DIRECTIONS:
1. Grate cheddar cheese.
2. Chop the zucchini and mix it with ground chicken.
3. Sprinkle the amalgamation with paprika, salt, basil, cilantro, tomato juice, and cream. Stir this mixture well. Put the contents into the pressure cooker.
4. Chop dill and add it into the cooker followed by butter.
5. Chop the Parmesan cheese and add it to the cooker's content.
6. Chop the peppers and add them too. Sprinkle the ingredients with the grated cheddar cheese and close the lid.
7. Set the load cooker to "Sauté" mode and cook for half an hour.
8. When the cooking time ends, allow the casserole delicacy to rest briefly and serve.
Nutrition: calories 199, fat 14.7, fiber 1, carbs 6.55, protein 11

Spinach Egg Omelet

Prep time: 6 minutes |Cooking time: 6 minutes |Servings: 5
Ingredients:
- 2 cups of spinach
- 8 eggs
- ½ cup of almond milk
- 1 teaspoon of salt
- 1 tablespoon of olive oil
- 1 teaspoon of ground black pepper
- 4 ounces of Parmesan cheese

COOKING DIRECTIONS:
1. Beat the eggs into a mixing bowl and whisk them.
2. Chop the spinach and add it on the egg mixture.
3. Add the almond milk, salt, extra virgin olive oil, and ground black pepper. Stir the amalgamation well. Transfer the egg mixture to the pressure cooker and close the lid.
4. Set the pressure cooker mode to "Steam" mode and cook for 6 minutes.
5. Grate the cheese. When the cooking time elapses, remove the spinach egg omelet from the pressure cooker and place it on a serving plate.

6. Sprinkle the dish with the grated cheese and serve.
Nutrition: calories 257, fat 20.4, fiber 0.9, carbs 3.4, protein 17.1

Spicy Bacon Bites

Prep time: 6 minutes |Cooking time: 20 minutes |Servings: 8
Ingredients:
- 10 ounces of Romano cheese
- 6 ounces of sliced bacon
- 1 teaspoon of oregano
- 5 ounces of puff pastry
- 1 teaspoon of butter
- 2 egg yolks
- 1 teaspoon of sesame seeds

COOKING DIRECTIONS:
1. Chop Romano cheese into small cubes.
2. Roll the puff pastry using a rolling pin.
3. Whisk the egg yolks.
4. Sprinkle them with oregano and sesame seeds.
5. Cut the puff pastry into squares and spread equal amount of butter on each square.
6. Wrap the cheese cubes with the sliced bacon.
7. Place the wrapped cheese cubes on the puff pastry squares.
8. Make the "bites" using the dough and brush them with the egg yolk mixture.
9. Put the bites into the pressure cooker set to steam mode and close its lid.
10. Cook the bites for around twenty minutes.
11. When the cooking time elapses, remove the spicy bacon bites on the serving dish.
Nutrition: calories 321, fat 24.4, fiber 1, carbs 10.9, protein 16

Soft Eggs

Prep time: 4 minutes |Cooking time: 4 minutes |Servings: 3
Ingredients:
- 3 eggs
- 6 ounces of ham
- 1 teaspoon of salt
- ½ teaspoon of ground white pepper
- 1 teaspoon of paprika
- ¼ teaspoon of ground ginger
- 2 tablespoons of chives

COOKING DIRECTIONS:
1. Take three small ramekins and coat them with vegetable oil spray.
2. Beat the eggs add pour them on the ramekins.
3. Treat the eggs with salt, ground black pepper, and paprika.

4. Place the ramekins to the pressure cooker and hang them up having set it to "Steam" mode.
5. Close the lid and cook for 4 minutes.
6. Meanwhile, chop ham and chives and mix them. Add ground ginger and stir them into the ham mixture.
7. Put the amalgamation around the serving plates.
8. When the cooking time elapses, remove the eggs from the cooker and put them alongside the ham mixture. Enjoy!
Nutrition: calories 205, fat 11.1, fiber 1, carbs 6.47, protein 19

Zucchini Quiche

Prep time: quarter-hour |Cooking time: 40 minutes |Servings: 6
Ingredients:
- 3 green zucchini
- 7 ounces puff pastry
- 2 onions
- 1 cup dill
- 2 eggs
- 3 tablespoons butter
- ½ cup cream
- 6 ounces cheddar cheese
- 1 teaspoon salt
- 1 teaspoon paprika

COOKING DIRECTIONS:
1. Wash zucchini and grate the vegetables.
2. Peel the onions and chop them.
3. Grate the cheddar cheese.
4. Whisk the eggs in a mixing bowl.
5. Roll the puff pastry.
6. Spread the butter on the pressure cooker and transfer the dough there.
7. Add grated zucchini and chopped onions, and sprinkle the vegetable mixture with salt and paprika.
8. Chop the dill and add it to the quiche.
9. Sprinkle the dish with grated cheese and egg mixture, and pour the cream ahead.
10. Close the pressure cooker's lid and set it on "Steam" mode.
11. Cook the quiche for around 40 minutes.
12. When the scheduled time finishes, confirm whether your Zucchini quiche is cooked.
13. Remove it from the pressure cooker and allow it to chill before serving.
Nutrition: calories 398, fat 28.4, fiber 2, carbs 25.82, protein 12

Creamy Pumpkin Slow Cook

Prep time: ten mins |Cooking time: 15 minutes |Servings: 5
Ingredients:
- 1 cup of almond milk

- A cup of water
- 1 pound of pumpkin
- 1 teaspoon of cinnamon
- ½ teaspoon of cardamom
- ½ teaspoon of turmeric
- 1 cup of coconut flakes
- 2 teaspoons of Erythritol

COOKING DIRECTIONS:
1. Peel the pumpkin and chop it roughly.
2. Put the chopped pumpkin in the pressure cooker followed by almond milk and water.
3. Sprinkle the amalgamation with cinnamon, cardamom, turmeric, and Erythritol.
4. Add coconut flakes and stir the amalgamation well.
5. Close the strain cooker lid and set it to "Sauté" mode.
6. Cook for quarter-hour.
7. When the cooking time ends, blend the amalgamation until they smoothen using a hand blender.
8. Ladle the pumpkin "Slow Cook" on the serving bowls.
Nutrition: calories 163, fat 13.5, fiber 4.5, carbs 13.1, protein 2.3

Milky Tomato Omelet

Prep time: 8 minutes |Cooking time: 9 minutes |Servings: 6
Ingredients:
- 5 eggs
- ½ cup of coconut milk
- 4 tablespoons of tomato paste
- 1 teaspoon of salt
- 1 tablespoon of turmeric
- ½ cup of cilantro
- 1 tablespoon of butter
- 4 ounces of Parmesan cheese

COOKING DIRECTIONS:
1. Whisk the eggs with coconut milk and tomato paste in a mixing bowl.
2. Add salt and turmeric and stir the mix.
3. Grate the Parmesan cheese and add it to the egg mixture.
4. Mince cilantro and add it on the egg mixture.
5. Spread butter in the pressure cooker and pour the egg mixture.
6. Close the pressure cooker lid having set it to "Steam" mood. Cook for 9 minutes.
7. Open the cooker and allow the omelet to rest.
8. Serve it on flat plates and enjoy.
Nutrition: calories 189, fat 14.6, fiber 1.2, carbs 4.9, protein 11.7

Poached Tomato Eggs

Prep time: 5 minutes |Cooking time: 5 minutes |Servings: 4

Ingredients:

- 4 eggs
- 3 medium tomatoes
- 1 red onion
- 1 teaspoon of salt
- 1 tablespoon of organic olive oil
- ½ teaspoon of white pepper
- ½ teaspoon of paprika
- 1 tablespoon of fresh dill

COOKING DIRECTIONS:

1. Spread the extra virgin olive oil on the ramekins.
2. Beat the eggs in a mixing bowl and add equal portions to each ramekin.
3. Mix paprika, white pepper, fresh dill, and salt in a bowl and stir them to mix.
4. Dice the red onion and tomatoes and combine.
5. Add the seasonings and stir the mixture.
6. Sprinkle the eggs with the tomato mixture.
7. Put the eggs in a pressure cooker and close the lid.
8. Set the cooker to steam mode and cook the ingredients for 5 minutes.
9. Remove it from the cooker and serve immediately.

Nutrition: calories 194, fat 13.5, fiber 2, carbs 8.45, protein 10

Chicken Breakfast Burrito

Prep time: ten mins |Cooking time: 45 minutes |Servings: 6

Ingredients:

- 6 large almond flour tortillas (keto tortillas)
- 1 pound of chicken
- ½ cup of chicken stock
- 1 tablespoon of tomato paste
- 1 teaspoon of sour cream
- 1 teaspoon of ground black pepper
- ½ teaspoon of paprika
- 1 teaspoon of cilantro
- ½ teaspoon of turmeric
- 1 white onion
- 2 sweet peppers
- ½ cup of cauliflower rice
- 1 cup of water

COOKING DIRECTIONS:

1. Chop the chicken roughly and put it into a strain cooker.
2. Add chicken stock, tomato paste, sour cream, and water.
3. Sprinkle the amalgamation with ground black pepper, paprika, cilantro, and turmeric.
4. Peel the onion and remove the pepper seeds.
5. Dice onion and peppers and put them aside.
6. Sprinkle the strain cooker mixture with cauliflower rice and close the lid.
7. Set pressure to "Steam" mode and cook for around 30 minutes.
8. Add the chopped onion and peppers and cook for around 15 minutes.
9. When the cooking time ends, shred the chicken place the mixture on flour tortillas.
10. Wrap the tortillas and serve the dish immediately.

Nutrition: calories 295, fat 10.8, fiber 5.2, carbs 14.3, protein 35.1

Stuffed Buns with Egg

Prep time: 8 minutes |Cooking time: 10 mins |Servings: 6

Ingredients:

- 3 large keto bread rolls
- 4 eggs
- 7 ounces of cheddar cheese
- 1 teaspoon of salt
- ½ teaspoon of red chili flakes
- ½ teaspoon of sour cream
- 1 tablespoon of butter

COOKING DIRECTIONS:

1. Cut the keto bread rolls into halves.
2. Make a hole at the center of each half.
3. Mix salt, pepper flakes, and sour cream in a bowl and stir gently.
4. Whisk the eggs in a mixing bowl and Add butter.
5. Pour equal amount of egg mixture over the bread halves.
6. Transfer the bread contents into the pressure cooker.
7. Treat the ingredients with the spice mixture.
8. Grate the cheddar cheese and sprinkle the bread with grated cheese.
9. Close the lid and set the cooker to "Steam" mode.
10. Cook for 10 minutes. Let the dish rest before serving it.

Nutrition: calories 259, fat 19.2, fiber 3.6, carbs 2.6, protein 17.5

Ham Frittata

Prep time: 10 minutes |Cooking time: ten minutes |Servings: 6

Ingredients:

- 7 eggs
- ½ cup of coconut milk
- 1 teaspoon of salt
- ½ teaspoon of paprika
- ½ cup of parsley

- 8 ounces of ham
- 1 teaspoon of white pepper
- 1 tablespoon of lemon zest
- 1 teaspoon of essential olive oil
- A tomato

COOKING DIRECTIONS:

1. Beat the eggs in a mixing bowl.
2. Add coconut milk, salt, paprika, white pepper, and lemon zest.
3. Blend the mixture well using a hand mixer.
4. Chop the tomato and add it to your egg mixture.
5. Chop the ham, and top the egg mixture with it.
6. Stir it carefully until smooth.
7. Chop the parsley.
8. Smear the pressure cooker with olive oil.
9. Pour the egg mixture in the pressure cooker.
10. Sprinkle it with chopped parsley and close the lid.
11. Cook the frittata for 10 minutes on "Steam" mode.
12. When the cooking time elapses, remove ham frittata and allow it to cool.

Nutrition: calories 193, fat 14, fiber 1.4, carbs 4.2, protein 13.5

Veggie Frittata

Prep time: 10 mins |Cooking time: a quarter-hour |Servings: 6

Ingredients:

- 10 eggs
- 1 cup of coconut milk
- 1 teaspoon salt
- ½ teaspoon ground black pepper
- 1 sweet bell pepper
- ½ jalapeno pepper
- 3 tomatoes
- 1 zucchini
- 1 tablespoon butter
- 5 ounces asparagus
- ½ cup cilantro

COOKING DIRECTIONS:

1. Beat the eggs in a mixing bowl and whisk.
2. Add the coconut milk followed by butter and mix.
3. Season the contents with salt and ground black pepper. Mix well.
4. Chop zucchini, tomatoes, asparagus, and cilantro.
5. Remove the seeds from the bell pepper and chop it.
6. Slice the jalapeno pepper.
7. Transfer the egg mixture into a pressure cooker.
8. Top it with vegetables and cilantro.

9. Close the lid having set the cooker to "Steam" mode.
10. Cook for quarter-hour.
11. Remove veggie frittata from the pressure cooker and serve immediately.

Nutrition: calories 145, fat 11.4, fiber 1.7, carbs 5.4, protein 7.1

Suffed Peppers with Eggs

Prep time: ten mins |Cooking time: a quarter-hour |Servings: 3

Ingredients:

- 4 boiled eggs
- 9 ounces of feta cheese
- 1 tablespoon of butter
- 2 sweet peppers
- 1 teaspoon of salt
- A cup of chicken stock
- ½ cup of cilantro
- 1 teaspoon of heavy cream
- 2 tablespoons of sour cream
- 1 tablespoon of tomato paste

COOKING DIRECTIONS:

1. Remove seeds from the sweet peppers.
2. Peel the eggs and stuff the sweet peppers with it.
3. Chop the feta cheese and cilantro and mix them.
4. Sprinkle the cheese mixture with salt, cream, sour cream, and tomato paste.
5. Blend the mixture until smooth.
6. Add the cream mixture to the sweet peppers.
7. Smear the pressure cooker with butter and put the stuffed peppers contents there.
8. Add chicken stock and close the lid.
9. Set the pressure cooker to "Steam" mode and cook for quarter-hour.
10. When the cooking time ends, let the dish rest briefly before serving.

Nutrition: calories 513, fat 37.2, fiber 1, carbs 17.23, protein 28

Marinated Eggs

Prep time: ten mins |Cooking time: 5 minutes |Servings: 5

Ingredients:

- 1 teaspoon of red chili flakes
- ½ cup of water
- 5 boiled eggs
- 1 teaspoon of salt
- 1/2 cup of soy sauce
- 1 teaspoon of cilantro
- ½ teaspoon of ground black pepper
- 1 tablespoon of freshly squeezed lemon juice

- 1 tablespoon of sugar
- 2 tablespoons of mirin

COOKING DIRECTIONS:

1. Peel the cooked eggs and pour them to the strain cooker.
2. Add water, chili flakes, salt, soy sauce, cilantro, ground black pepper, fresh lemon juice, and mirin in a bowl. Stir the amalgamation well until smooth, and then pour the mixture in the pressure cooker.
3. Stir it gently, close the lid, and set it to "Sauté" mode.
4. Cook for 5 minutes. Transfer the content to the casserole dish and allow it to cool.
5. Cool marinated eggs can be served immediately or stored in the refrigerator for later serving.

Nutrition: calories 189, fat 12.8, fiber 1, carbs 7.7, protein 10

Creamy Cauliflower Rice

Prep time: ten mins |Cooking time: a half-hour |Servings: 3
Ingredients:

- A cup of cauliflower rice
- 1 cup of heavy cream
- A cup of coconut milk
- ¼ cup of water
- 1 teaspoon of salt
- 4 tablespoons of Erythritol
- 1 teaspoon of cinnamon

COOKING DIRECTIONS:

1. Pour cream, coconut milk, and water in a pressure cooker.
2. Stir the combination gently and then add salt, Erythritol, and cinnamon.
3. Blend them gently to mix well.
4. Add cauliflower rice.
5. Close pressure cooker lid having set it to "Slow Cook" mode.
6. Cook for a half-hour.
7. When the cooking time ends, open the lid and stir the cauliflower gently.
8. Transfer the cooked dish to bowls and serve while hot.

Nutrition: calories 343, fat 34.5, fiber 2.2, carbs 8.4, protein 4

Cauliflower Rice with Bacon

Prep time: 10 mins |Cooking time: 40 minutes |Servings: 7
Ingredients:

- 7 ounces of sliced bacon
- 2 cups of cauliflower rice
- 1 tablespoon of essential organic olive oil
- 1 onion
- 4 cups of chicken stock

- 1 teaspoon of butter
- A teaspoon of basil
- 1 teaspoon of oregano
- A teaspoon of thyme

COOKING DIRECTIONS:

1. Chop the bacon and put it in the pressure cooker.
2. Close the cooker's lid and set it to "Sauté" mode. Cook the bacon for 4 minutes.
3. Open the lid and add the cauliflower rice.
4. Sprinkle the amalgamation with extra virgin extra-virgin olive oil and stir.
5. Add chicken stock, butter, basil, oregano, and thyme.
6. Peel the onion and chop it.
7. Sprinkle the cauliflower rice with the chopped onion and mix well. Close the lid.
8. Set the cooker mode to "Slow Cook" and cook for 40 minutes.
9. When the dish is cooked, remove the cauliflower rice from the cooker and stir.
10. Transfer the dish to serving plates and serve.

Nutrition: calories 273, fat 19.6, fiber 8, carbs 25.03, protein 11

Chia Slow Cook

Prep time: 5 minutes |Cooking time: 5 minutes |Servings: 4
Ingredients:

- A cup of Greek yogurt
- 1 cup of water
- 1 cup of Chia seeds
- 1 tablespoon of liquid stevia
- ½ teaspoon of cinnamon
- 1 teaspoon of lemon zest
- 2 apples
- ¼ teaspoon of salt
- A teaspoon of clove

COOKING DIRECTIONS:

1. Add water to the yoghurt and mix well.
2. Transfer the liquid mixture to the pressure cooker and add Chia seeds.
3. Stir the ingredients and add liquid stevia, cinnamon, lemon zest, salt, and cloves.
4. Peel the apples and chop them into small chunks.
5. Add the chopped apple in the pressure cooker and stir well.
6. Close the cooker's lid having set it to "Steam" mode. Cook for 7 minutes.
7. When the dish is cooked, remove it from the pressure cooker and mix. Serve the Chia Slow Cook while hot.

Nutrition: calories 259, fat 13.3, fiber 12.8, carbs 29.5, protein 8.5

Tomato Cups

Prep time: 5 minutes |Cooking time: 3 minutes |Servings: 4

Ingredients:

- 4 big tomatoes
- 4 eggs
- 7 ounces of ham
- 1 tablespoon of chives
- 1 teaspoon of mayonnaise
- ½ teaspoon of butter
- 4 ounces of Parmesan cheese
- ½ teaspoon of salt

COOKING DIRECTIONS:

1. Wash the tomatoes and peel it to obtain cups. Put its flesh, jelly, and seeds in a mixing bowl.
2. Chop the ham and chives and add them to the mixing bowl.
3. Add mayonnaise, butter, and salt to the ham mixture and blend well.
4. Grate the Parmesan cheese and beat the eggs into the tomato cups.
5. Fill the cups with the ham mixture.
6. Sprinkle each cup with grated cheese.
7. Wrap the tomato cups with an aluminum foil and put them in the success cooker.
8. Close the lid and set it to "Sauté" mode. Cook for ten minutes.
9. When the cooking time ends, remove the tomato cups from the cooker and place it on a flatter.
10. Discard the foil and serve immediately.

Nutrition: calories 335, fat 19.8, fiber 1, carbs 12.17, protein 27

Light Chicken Casserole

Prep time: quarter-hour |Cooking time: 30 minutes |Servings: 6

Ingredients:

- 1 pound chicken fillets
- 4 egg yolks
- An onion
- 1 cup cream
- 10 ounces cheddar cheese
- 1 tablespoon butter
- ½ teaspoon ground black pepper
- 1 teaspoon salt
- 1 tablespoon freshly squeezed lemon juice

COOKING DIRECTIONS:

1. Cut the chicken into strips and season them with salt, freshly squeezed lemon juice, and ground black pepper. Mix well.
2. Grate the cheddar cheese.
3. Peel and dice the onion.
4. Combine the chopped onion with butter and blend well.
5. Transfer the chopped onion mixture in the pressure cooker and make a layer from the chicken

mixture. Whisk the egg yolks, and pour the amalgamation in the success cooker.
6. Add cream and grated cheese.
7. Close the lid, and set the cooker mode to "Pressure." Cook for a half-hour.
8. When the casserole is cooked, let it cool briefly.
9. Ladle the dish on plates and serve.

Nutrition: calories 424, fat 27.7, fiber 2, carbs 26.58, protein 18

Hot Pepper Eggs

Prep time: 8 minutes |Cooking time: 7 minutes |Servings: 3

Ingredients:

- 4 eggs
- 1 teaspoon of red pepper cayenne
- ½ teaspoon of red chili flakes
- ½ teaspoon of cilantro
- ½ teaspoon of white pepper
- 1 pitted avocado
- ½ cup of sour cream
- 2 tablespoons of butter
- 3 tablespoons of chives

COOKING DIRECTIONS:

1. Combine cayenne, chili flakes, cilantro, and white pepper in a wide bowl. Mix the amalgamation.
2. Chop the chives and slice the avocado.
3. Mix the sour cream with butter and blend until they smoothen.
4. Pour the sour cream mixture in the pressure cooker.
5. Add spice mixture.
6. Beat the eggs over the pressure cooker contents.
7. Add chives and avocado and close the lid.
8. Set the load cooker mode to "Steam," and cook for 7 minutes.
9. When the peppered eggs are cooked, remove them from the cooker and serve.

Nutrition: calories 410, fat 2, fiber 34.6, carbs 11.82, protein 15

Breakfast Strata

Prep time: 10 minutes |Cooking time: a quarter-hour |Servings: 6

Ingredients:

- 6 slices of keto bread
- 1 tablespoon of mustard
- 1 teaspoon of salt
- ½ cup of parsley
- ¼ cup of dill
- 1 cup of cream
- 4 eggs
- A cup of spinach
- 2 tablespoons of butter

COOKING DIRECTIONS:
1. Cut the keto bread into cubes.
2. Put half of the bread portion in a pressure cooker.
3. Whisk the eggs in a mixing bowl add salt, mustard, and cream.
4. Chop the spinach and parsley.
5. Add the chopped greens to the egg mixture.
6. Add butter and whisk.
7. Pour half of the egg mixture pressure cooker and cover the contents with the remaining bread.
8. Add the remaining egg mixture.
9. Close the lid and set the pressure cooker mode to "Steam."
10. Cook for a quarter-hour.
11. When the dish is cooked, let it cool briefly and cut it into pieces.
12. Serve the strata while warm.

Nutrition: calories 171, fat 10.3, fiber 3.2, carbs 11.9, protein 9.9

Egg Sandwiches

Prep time: ten mins |Cooking time: ten mins |Servings: 4
Ingredients:
- 8 slices of keto bread
- 6 ounces of ham
- 6 ounces of cheddar cheese
- 1 tablespoon of mustard
- 4 eggs
- 1 tablespoon of mayonnaise
- 1 teaspoon of basil
- 1 teaspoon of cilantro
- ½ teaspoon of ground black pepper
- 1 teaspoon of paprika

COOKING DIRECTIONS:
1. Slice the ham and cheddar cheese.
2. Combine mayonnaise, basil, cilantro, ground black pepper, and paprika in a mixing bowl.
3. Add mustard and stir the mixture well.
4. Spread every slice of bread with the mayonnaise mixture.
5. Add ham and cheddar cheese to the four bread pieces. Cover it remaining bread pieces.
6. Whisk the eggs and add the sandwiches in the egg mixture.
7. Put the sandwiches to the pressure cooker and close the lid.
8. Set the pressure cooker mode to "Sauté" and cook for 10 minutes.
9. When the cooking time ends, put the egg sandwiches on a flatter and serve immediately.

Nutrition: calories 399, fat 23.3, fiber 4.9, carbs 17.5, protein 31.3

Sweet Egg Toasts

Prep time: 10 mins |Cooking time: 8 minutes |Servings: 7
Ingredients:
- 4 eggs
- 1 cup of coconut milk
- 3 tablespoons of Erythritol
- 1 teaspoon of vanilla flavoring
- 1 tablespoon of butter
- 7 slices of carb bread

COOKING DIRECTIONS:
1. Beat the eggs in a mixing bowl and add coconut milk.
2. Whisk the contents well and add Erythritol.
3. Sprinkle the egg mixture with the vanilla extract and stir.
4. Dip the bread slices into the egg mixture.
5. Smear the pressure cooker with butter, add the egged bread slices, and close the lid.
6. Set the cooker mode to "Sauté" and cook for 4 minutes on either sides.
7. When the toasts are cooked, remove them from the cooker and allow them to rest briefly.

Nutrition: calories 175, fat 12.3, fiber 2.8, carbs 9.2, protein 8

Tortilla Ham Wraps

Prep time: ten minutes |Cooking time: 10 minutes |Servings: 5
Ingredients:
- 5 almond flour tortillas
- 10 ounces of ham
- 2 tomatoes
- 1 cucumber
- 1 red onion
- 1 tablespoon of mayonnaise
- 2 tablespoons of extra virgin olive oil
- 2 tablespoons of ketchup
- 1 teaspoon of basil
- 1 teaspoon of paprika
- ½ teaspoon of cayenne
- 4 ounces of lettuce

COOKING DIRECTIONS:
1. Wash the tomatoes and slice them.
2. Chop cucumbers and hum.
3. Peel the red onion and chop it.
4. Combine the mayonnaise, organic olive oil, ketchup, basil, paprika, and cayenne and stir.
5. Spread tortillas with the mayonnaise mixture and add chopped ham.
6. Sprinkle the dish with the chopped onion, sliced tomatoes, and chopped cucumbers.
7. Add lettuce and wrap the tortillas.
8. Put the tortilla wraps in the pressure cooker and close its lid.
9. Set the pressure cooker mode to "Steam" and cook for ten minutes.

10.   Remove your tortilla ham wraps from the load cooker and allow them to rest before serving.
Nutrition: calories 249, fat 15, fiber 4.1, carbs 14.7, protein 15.6

Breakfast Panini

Prep time: 5 minutes |Cooking time: 2 minutes |Servings: 4
Ingredients:
- 1 banana
- 8 slices of low-carbohydrate bread
- 2 tablespoons of butter
- 1 teaspoon of vanilla flavoring
- 1 teaspoon of cinnamon

COOKING DIRECTIONS:
1.   Peel the banana and slice it.
2.   Spread each bread slice with butter.
3.   Sprinkle the buttered-bread with vanilla and add banana making sandwiches.
4.   Put the sandwiches in the pressure cooker and close the lid.
5.   Set its mode to "Sauté," and cook for 1 minute.
6.   Remove the sandwiches from the strain cooker and allow them to rest briefly before serving.
Nutrition: calories 127, fat 6.4, fiber 3.1, carbs 14.3, protein 4.4

Egg Balls

Prep time: quarter-hour |Cooking time: a half-hour |Servings: 5
Ingredients:
- 5 boiled eggs
- A cup of ground chicken
- 1 teaspoon of salt
- 1 teaspoon of ground black pepper
- ½ cup of pork rinds
- A teaspoon of butter
- ½ teaspoon of tomato paste
- 2 tablespoons of almond flour
- A teaspoon of oregano

COOKING DIRECTIONS:
1.   Peel the eggs.
2.   Combine the ground chicken with salt, ground black pepper, tomato paste, and oregano in a mixing bowl. Blend chicken mixture well.
3.   Make the balls from the ground chicken mixture and flatten them.
4.   Put peeled eggs in the balls and roll the meat mixture around them.
5.   Dip the contents in a mixture of almond flour and pork rinds.
6.   Add the butter in the pressure cooker and put the egg balls.
7.   Close the lid and set the cooker mode to "Sauté." Cook for a half-hour.

8.   Open the cooker after releasing built-in pressure.
9.   When the egg balls are cooked, remove them from the pressure cooker and serve immediately.
Nutrition: calories 237, fat 15.8, fiber 1.5, carbs 3.3, protein 21.

Cheesy Chorizo Topping

Prep time: ten mins |Cooking time: 8 minutes |Servings: 6
Ingredients:
- 8 ounces of chorizo
- ½ cup of tomato juice
- 1 teaspoon of cilantro
- 1 tablespoon of coconut flour
- 1 teaspoon of organic essential olive oil
- 1 teaspoon of butter
- 1 sweet pepper
- 3 eggs
- ½ cup of coconut milk
- 1 teaspoon of coriander
- ¼ teaspoon of thyme
- ½ cup of fresh basil

COOKING DIRECTIONS:
1.   Combine the tomato juice, cilantro, coconut flour, extra virgin organic olive oil, coriander, and thyme.
2.   Stir the combination well.
3.   Remove the sweet pepper's seeds and chop it.
4.   Wash the fresh basil and chop it.
5.   Add coconut milk in the tomato juice mixture and beat the eggs.
6.   Blend the amalgamation with a hand mixer until they smoothen.
7.   Add the chopped peppers and butter.
8.   Chop the chorizo and add it to the mixture.
9.   Put the combination to the load cooker and close the lid.
10.   Set the pressure cooker mode to "Steam" and cook for 6 minutes.
11.   Open the lid and blend well using a wooden spoon.
12.   Close pressure cooker lid and cook for 2 minutes.
13.   When the cooking time elapses, let the cheesy chorizo dish rest briefly before serving.
Nutrition: calories 260, fat 21.4, fiber 1.1, carbs 4.6, protein 12.7

Egg Muffins

Prep time: 10 minutes |Cooking time: 10 mins |Servings: 6
Ingredients:
- 4 eggs
- ¼ cup of almond flour

- 1 teaspoon of salt
- ¼ cup of cream
- A teaspoon of baking soda
- 1 tablespoon of freshly squeezed lemon juice
- 1 white onion
- 5 ounces of cooked-sliced bacon

COOKING DIRECTIONS:

1. Beat the eggs and whisk in a bowl.
2. Add almond flour and cream and mix until they smoothen.
3. Peel the onion and dice it.
4. Chop the cooked bacon.
5. Add the diced onion and chopped bacon to the egg mixture. Stir it carefully.
6. Add salt, freshly squeezed lemon juice and baking soda and mix again.
7. Take muffin cups and fill each with the egg dough halfway.
8. Put the muffin cups in the pressure cooker basket and close the lid.
9. Set pressure mode to "Pressure," and cook the muffins for ten minutes.
10. When the muffins are cooked and let them rest before serving.

Nutrition: calories 211, fat 15.7, fiber 0.9, carbs 3.6, protein 13.7

Chocolate Slow Cook

Prep time: ten mins |Cooking time: 13 minutes |Servings: 3

Ingredients:

- 1 cup of flax meal
- 3 tablespoons of hot chocolate mix
- 1 tablespoon of Erythritol
- 1 teaspoon of vanilla flavoring
- 1 cup of water
- ½ cup of coconut milk
- A tablespoon of dark chocolate
- 1 tablespoon of butter
- 1 teaspoon of sesame seeds
- 3 tablespoons of almonds
- 1 teaspoon of raisins
- 1 teaspoon of extra virgin olive oil

COOKING DIRECTIONS:

1. Crush the almonds.
2. Combine the hot chocolate mix with Erythritol, vanilla flavoring, and chocolate in a bowl and stir the amalgamation.
3. Spread the strain cooker with olive oil.
4. Put the flax meal in the pressure cooker and add the hot chocolate mix mixture.
5. Add the crushed almonds, raisins, coconut milk, and water.
6. Blend the mix using a wooden spoon.

7. Close the cooker's lid and set it to "Pressure "mode. Cook for 13 minutes.
8. When the cooking time ends, mix the chocolate with a wooden stick until they smoothen.
9. Transfer the cooked chocolate Slow Cook to wide bowls and serve.

Nutrition: calories 347, fat 30.3, fiber 13.9, carbs 19.7, protein 11.4

Spinach Muffins

Prep time: ten mins |Cooking time: 8 minutes |Servings: 5

Ingredients:

- 2 cups of chopped spinach
- 5 whisked eggs
- 1 tablespoon of flax meal
- ½ teaspoon of salt
- A teaspoon of turmeric
- ½ teaspoon of butter
- A cup of water for smoking.

COOKING DIRECTIONS:

1. In the mixing bowl add chopped spinach, whisked eggs, flax meal, salt, turmeric, and butter.
2. Transfer the mixture to the muffin molds.
3. Pour water in the cooker and fix a trivet.
4. Place muffin molds on the trivet and close the lid.
5. Cook the muffins for 8 minutes on high-pressure mode.
6. Release the cooker's pressure instantly.
7. Chill the spinach muffins until warm and serve with muffin molds.

Nutrition: calories 77, fat 5.3, fiber 0.8, carbs 1.5, protein 6.2

Creamy Porridge

Prep time: 5 minutes |Cooking time: ten mins |Servings: 6

Ingredients:

- 1 cup of chia seeds
- A cup of sesame seeds
- 2 servings of coconut milk
- A teaspoon of salt
- 3 tablespoons of Erythritol
- ½ teaspoon of vanilla flavor
- 3 tablespoons of butter
- 1 teaspoon of clove
- ½ teaspoon of turmeric

COOKING DIRECTIONS:

1. Combine coconut milk with salt, Erythritol, vanilla flavor, clove, and turmeric in a pressure cooker.
2. Blend the amalgamation.
3. Close the lid set its mode to "Pressure."
4. Cook the liquid for ten minutes.
5. Open the lid and add Chia seeds followed by sesame seeds.

6. Stir the combination well and close the lid.
7. Cook for two minutes.
8. Remove the creamy porridge from the pressure cooker and allow it to cool briefly before serving.
Nutrition: calories 467, fat 42.6, fiber 11.2, carbs 18.4, protein 9.3

Chicken Quiche

Prep time: 10 minutes |Cooking time: a half-hour |Servings: 6
Ingredients:
- A pound of chicken
- 1 cup of dill
- 2 eggs
- 8 ounces of dough
- 1 teaspoon of salt
- ½ teaspoon of nutmeg
- 9 ounces of cheddar cheese
- ½ cup of cream
- 1 teaspoon of oregano
- 1 teaspoon of organic olive oil

COOKING DIRECTIONS:
1. Chop the chicken and season it with salt, oregano, and nutmeg.
2. Blend the mixture.
3. Chop the dill and add it to the chopped chicken.
4. Grate cheddar cheese.
5. Take the round pie pan and spray its base with extra-virgin essential olive oil.
6. Transfer the yeast dough in the pan and flatten it.
7. Add the chicken mixture.
8. Whisk the eggs and add dough mixture.
9. Sprinkle it with the grated cheese and add cream.
10. Transfer the quiche to the pressure cooker and close the lid.
11. Set the pressure cooker mode to "Sauté" and cook for a half-hour.
12. When the cooking time ends, remove the chicken quiche from the pressure cooker and chill it.
13. Cut it into slices and serve.
Nutrition: calories 320, fat 14.1, fiber 3, carbs 13.65, protein 34

Cinnamon Chia Pudding

Prep time: ten mins |Cooking time: a quarter-hour |Servings: 4
Ingredients:
- A cup of chia seeds
- 4 tablespoons of Erythritol
- 2 glasses of coconut milk
- 2 tablespoons of heavy cream
- A teaspoon of butter
- A teaspoon of cinnamon

- 1 teaspoon of ground cardamom

COOKING DIRECTIONS:
1. Combine Chia seeds, Erythritol, and coconut milk in a pressure cooker.
2. Stir the amalgamation gently and close the lid.
3. Set the pressure cooker mode to "Slow Cook" and cook for ten minutes.
4. When the cooking time ends, leave the chia seeds to rest.
5. Open the pressure cooker lid and add cream, cinnamon, cardamom, and butter.
6. Blend the amalgamation well with a wooden spoon.
7. Transfer the Chia pudding on the serving bowls.
8. You can serve it alongside cherry jam.
Nutrition: calories 486, fat 43.3, fiber 15.3, carbs 22.6, protein 8.8

Seeds Mix

Prep time: 10 mins |Cooking time: 25 minutes |Servings: 6
Ingredients:
- ½ cup of flax seeds
- ½ cup of flax meal
- ½ cup of sunflower seeds
- 1 tablespoon of tahini paste
- 3 cups of chicken stock
- A teaspoon of salt
- 1 diced onion
- 3 tablespoons of butter
- 3 ounces of dates

COOKING DIRECTIONS:
1. Combine flax seeds, flax meal, and sunflower seeds in a mixing bowl.
2. Add salt and diced onion.
3. Chop the dates and add the crooks to the amalgamation.
4. Transfer the mixture into a pressure cooker followed by chicken stock.
5. Blend the mixture and close the lid.
6. Set pressure to "Slow Cook," and cook for 25 minutes.
7. When the cooking time ends, remove the mixture from the pressure cooker and transfer in a mixing bowl. Add butter and stir. Transfer the dish to serving plates.
Nutrition: calories 230, fat 15.7, fiber 7.3, carbs 19.4, protein 5.9

Scotch Eggs

Prep time: quarter-hour |Cooking time: 30 mins |Servings: 4
Ingredients:
- 4 boiled eggs
- 1 cup of ground beef

- A teaspoon of salt
- 1 teaspoon of turmeric
- A teaspoon of cilantro
- ½ teaspoon of ground black pepper
- ½ teaspoon of butter
- A tablespoon of fresh lemon juice
- ½ teaspoon of lime zest
- A tablespoon of almond flour
- ½ cup of pork rinds
- ¼ cup of cream

COOKING DIRECTIONS:
1. Peel the eggs.
2. Combine the ground beef, salt, turmeric, cilantro, ground black pepper, fresh lemon juice, and lime zest in a bowl. Stir them well.
3. Mould medium-sized balls from your meat mixture and flatten them well.
4. Place peeled eggs at the middle of the flattened balls and roll them.
5. Dip the balls in the almond flour.
6. Dip the meatballs from the cream and sprinkle them with the pork rind.
7. Transfer the balls to the pressure cooker and close the lid.
8. Set the cooker mode to "Sauté," and cook for a half-hour.
9. When the cooking time ends, remove scotch eggs from the pressure cooker and serve immediately.

Nutrition: calories 230, fat 13, fiber 0.4, carbs 1.8, protein 25.8

Broccoli Rice

Prep time: ten mins |Cooking time: a quarter-hour |Servings: 4
Ingredients:
- 2 cups of broccoli rice
- 4 servings of water
- 1 tablespoon of salt
- 3 tablespoons of heavy cream

COOKING DIRECTIONS:
1. Combine broccoli rice with salt, and water in a pressure cooker. Add cream.
2. Stir the mix gently and close the cooker's lid.
3. Cook for around 15 minutes with the cooker set to "Slow Cook" mode. When the broccoli rice is cooked, remove it from the pressure cooker and allow it to rest.
4. Transfer broccoli rice to bowls. Serve the dish while warm.

Nutrition: calories 54, fat 4.3, fiber 1.2, carbs 3.3, protein 1.5

Breakfast Pasta Casserole

Prep time: 10 mins |Cooking time: 20 mins |Servings: 6
Ingredients:

- 6 ounces of cooked palmini pasta
- 8 ounces of Romano cheese
- 1 cup of cream
- 3 tablespoons of butter
- 1 teaspoon of salt
- A teaspoon of paprika
- 1 teaspoon of turmeric
- A cup of parsley
- 1 teaspoon of cilantro

COOKING DIRECTIONS:
1. Grate the cheese.
2. Place pasta in the pressure cooker.
3. Sprinkle it with half of the cheese.
4. Chop the parsley and add it to the pressure cooker mixture.
5. Season the mixture with salt, paprika, turmeric, and cilantro.
6. Sprinkle the casserole with the remaining cheese.
7. Add butter and cream and close the lid.
8. Set the load cooker mode to "Pressure" and cook for 20 minutes.
9. When the casserole is cooked, remove it from the pressure cooker and cut into serving pieces.

Nutrition: calories 256, fat 18.5, fiber 1.9, carbs 6.7, protein 17.5

Creamy Pumpkin Puree

Prep time: 10 minutes |Cooking time: twenty or so minutes |Servings: 5
Ingredients:
- ¼ cup of raisins
- A pound of pumpkin
- ½ cup of water
- A teaspoon of butter
- 4 tablespoons of heavy cream
- 1 teaspoon of cinnamon
- ½ teaspoon of vanilla flavoring
- A tablespoon of liquid stevia

COOKING DIRECTIONS:
1. Peel the pumpkin and chop it.
2. Transfer the chopped pumpkin into the pressure cooker.
3. Add water, butter, cinnamon, and vanilla flavoring.
4. Close the lid and cook for 20 minutes with the cooker set to "Pressure" mode.
5. When the cooking time ends, remove the mixture from the cooker, and transfer it to a blender.
6. Blend it until smooth.
7. Add raisins followed by cream and stir the mixture well.
8. Add liquid stevia and stir it again. Chill the puree briefly and serve.

Nutrition: calories 82, fat 3.3, fiber 3.1, carbs 13.7, protein 1.4

Cauliflower Balls

Prep time: ten minutes |Cooking time: twenty minutes |Servings: 4

Ingredients:

- A pound of cauliflower
- 1 white onion
- 3 tablespoons of coconut flour
- 1 teaspoon of extra virgin olive oil
- ¼ cup of tomato juice
- A teaspoon of salt
- 2 tablespoons of flax meal
- 1 teaspoon of chicken stock
- 2 eggs

COOKING DIRECTIONS:

1.   Chop the cauliflower roughly and transfer it to a blender.
2.   Peel the onion and chop it.
3.   Add the chopped onion in a blender.
4.   Add flax meal and eggs to the blender contents and blend until smooth.
5.   Remove the smoothen amalgamation from the blender and add chicken stock, salt, and flour.
6.   Knead the smooth cauliflower dough.
7.   Make small-sized balls from the cauliflower mixture and transfer the crooks to the pressure cooker.
8.   Add tomato juice and close the lid.
9.   Set pressure cooker mode to "Steam" and cook for twenty minutes.
10.   When the cooking time ends, transfer the cauliflower balls to a flatter and give it around 10 minutes to unwind.
11.   Serve while warm.

Nutrition: calories 121, fat 5.3, fiber 6.7, carbs 14.1, protein 6.9

Breakfast Yogurt

Prep time: ten minutes |Cooking time: thirty minutes |Servings: 6

Ingredients:

- 8 cups of almond milk
- 2 tablespoons of plain Greek yogurt

COOKING DIRECTIONS:

1.   Pour the almond milk in the pressure cooker and close the lid.
2.   Set the pressure cooker mode to "Slow Cook" and boil the milk for 30 minutes or until it hits 380 degrees Fahrenheit.
3.   Remove the milk from pressure cooker and cool it to 100 F.
4.   Add the plain Greek yogurt and blend well.
5.   Let the mixture chill in the refrigerator overnight.
6.   Stir the yogurt gently with a wooden spoon and pour it into serving bowls.

Nutrition: calories 82, fat 3.4, fiber 0, carbs 10.8, protein 1.4

Bread Pudding

Prep time: 10 minutes |Cooking time: a half-hour |Servings: 7

Ingredients:

- A cup of cream
- ½ cup of coconut milk
- 10 slices of low-carb bread
- 2 tablespoons of butter
- 1 teaspoon of vanilla extract
- 3 eggs
- A teaspoon of salt
- 4 tablespoons of stevia powder

COOKING DIRECTIONS:

1.   Chop the bread into medium cubes and put it in the success cooker.
2.   Combine coconut milk and cream in a bowl.
3.   Add eggs and whisk the combination using a hand mixer.
4.   Add vanilla flavoring, salt, and stevia. Stir the mixture well.
5.   Pour the amalgamation in the pressure cooker and close the lid.
6.   Leave it for 15 minutes to allow the bread absorb the coconut milk liquid.
7.   Set the pressure cooker mode to "Pressure" and cook for 30 minutes.
8.   When the cooking time ends, open the pressure cooker lid and let the bread pudding rest.
9.   Transfer the dish to serving plates.

Nutrition: calories 255, fat 15.4, fiber 6.1, carbs 13.7, protein 17.4

Creamy Mac Cups

Prep time: ten minutes |Cooking time: 25 minutes |Servings: 6

Ingredients:

- 8 ounces of chopped cauliflower
- A cup of cream
- 1 cup of water
- 3 tablespoons of butter
- A teaspoon of salt
- 1 teaspoon of basil
- 6 ounces of Romano cheese
- A teaspoon of paprika
- 1 teaspoon of turmeric
- 3 ounces of ham

COOKING DIRECTIONS:

1.   Coat six ramekins with butter.
2.   Combine cauliflower, cream, and water in a mixing bowl.
3.   Add salt, basil, paprika, and turmeric.
4.   Chop the ham and Romano cheese.

5.	Add the chopped ingredients to the cauliflower mixture and stir it.
6.	Sub-divide the cauliflower mixture among the six ramekins and place them in the pressure cooker.
7.	Close the lid and set the cooker's mode to "Steam" Cook for 25 minutes.
8.	When the creamy mac cup is ready, allow it to cool before serving.
Nutrition: calories 221, fat 17, fiber 1.3, carbs 5.3, protein 12.6

Flax Meal with Almonds

Prep time: 10 mins |Cooking time: 7 minutes |Servings: 3
Ingredients:
*	1 cup of flax meal
*	3 glasses of coconut milk
*	2 tablespoons of Erythritol
*	A teaspoon of vanilla flavor
*	3 tablespoons of almond flakes
*	½ teaspoon of cinnamon
*	½ teaspoon of nutmeg

COOKING DIRECTIONS:
1.	Put the flax meal in the pressure cooker and add coconut milk.
2.	Sprinkle the mixture with Erythritol, vanilla flavoring, cinnamon, and nutmeg.
3.	Blend the combination well until smooth.
4.	Close the pressure cooker's lid, having set it to "Slow Cook" mode. Cook for 7 minutes.
5.	Open the pressure cooker lid and stir the dish carefully.
6.	Transfer it to serving bowls and sprinkle with the almond flakes.
Nutrition: calories 739, fat 72.4, fiber 16.6, carbs 25, protein 14.2

Zucchini Pasta with Chicken

Prep time: 10 mins |Cooking time: 25 minutes |Servings: 5
Ingredients:
*	1 zucchini
*	A cup of ground chicken
*	½ cup of cream
*	½ cup of chicken stock
*	A teaspoon of salt
*	1 teaspoon of ground black pepper
*	A teaspoon of paprika
*	½ teaspoon of ground coriander
*	A teaspoon of cilantro
*	An onion

COOKING DIRECTIONS:
1.	Wash zucchini and peel the onion.
2.	Grate the vegetables and put them in a mixing bowl.

3.	Add ground chicken, cream chicken stock, salt, ground black pepper, paprika, ground coriander, and cilantro. Blend the amalgamation well, and transfer it to the pressure cooker.
4.	Close the lid having set it to "Sear/Sauté." Cook for 25 minutes.
5.	Open the strain cooker lid and stir. Transfer the dish to a serving bowl and chill well.
Nutrition: calories 87, fat 3.6, fiber 1.2, carbs 4.7, protein 9.2

Zucchini Scramble

Prep time: 10 mins |Cooking time: 6 minutes |Servings: 2
Ingredients:
*	½ grated zucchini
*	2 whisked eggs
*	1 teaspoon of butter
*	¼ cup of cream
*	A teaspoon of ground black pepper

COOKING DIRECTIONS:
1.	Preheat the cooker on Sauté mode and toss the butter.
2.	Melt it and add grated zucchini.
3.	Sprinkle the vegetables with ground black pepper and cream. Stir well. Cook them for 3 minutes.
4.	Add whisked eggs and cook for 1 minute.
5.	Scramble eggs and cook them for two minutes.
6.	Close the cooker and shut it off. Let the scramble rest for ten minutes before opening and serving.
Nutrition: calories 110, fat 8.1, fiber 0.8, carbs 3.6, protein 6.5

Cottage Cheese Soufflé

Prep time: 10 minutes |Cooking time: 45 minutes |Servings: 4
Ingredients:
*	8 ounces of cottage cheese
*	4 eggs
*	½ cup of cream
*	4 tablespoons of butter
*	3 tablespoons of Erythritol
*	1 teaspoon of vanilla flavoring

COOKING DIRECTIONS:
1.	Pour the cream in the pressure cooker and close the lid.
2.	Set the cooker mode to "Slow Cook" and hest the cream the 20 minutes or until it reaches 180 F.
3.	Combine cheese with eggs.
4.	Add Erythritol, vanilla flavoring, and butter.
5.	Blend the amalgamation using a hand blender.
6.	Add the cheese mixture to the preheated cream contents.

7.   Stir it carefully until smooth.

8.   Close the lid and cook the mixture for 25 minutes in yogurt mode.

9.   Remove cottage cheese soufflé from the pressure cooker and rest briefly. Serve it warm.

Nutrition: calories 362, fat 28.3, fiber 0, carbs 12.99, protein 14

Coconut Porridge with Cream

Prep time: ten mins |Cooking time: 20 mins |Servings: 5

Ingredients:

- A cup of chia seeds
- ½ cup of raisins
- ½ cup of coconut cream
- 2 tablespoons of butter
- ½ teaspoon of ground ginger
- A teaspoon of vanilla flavoring
- 1 cup of almond milk
- 2 tablespoons of Erythritol

COOKING DIRECTIONS:

1.   Combine coconut cream with almond milk in a bowl.

2.   Add ground ginger, vanilla extract, and Erythritol and mix them well.

3.   Add butter and stir the mixture again.

4.   Chop the raisins.

5.   Transfer the coconut cream mixture in the pressure cooker.

6.   Add Chia seeds and chopped fruit. Stir it.

7.   Close the cooker's lid and set it to "Slow Cook" mode. Cook for quarter-hour.

8.   When the porridge is cooked, open the pressure cooker lid and stir it gently.

9.   Transfer the coconut porridge into serving bowls and enjoy.

Nutrition: calories 266, fat 19.1, fiber 10.7, carbs 21.2, protein 5.6

Cauliflower Rice Balls

Prep time: 10 minutes |Cooking time: quarter-hour |Servings: 4

Ingredients:

- A cup of cooked cauliflower rice
- 2 eggs
- 1 carrot
- 1 white onion
- 1 teaspoon of salt
- 3 tablespoons of almond meal
- 1 tablespoon of butter
- A cup of ground chicken

COOKING DIRECTIONS:

1.   Peel the carrot and onion.

2.   Grate the vegetables and put them in a mixing bowl.

3.   Add salt, almond meal, and ground chicken. Mix it up.

4.   Make medium-sized balls from the mixture.

5.   Add butter in the pressure cooker. Pour the balls.

6.   Close the pressure cooker lid and set its mode to "Steam." Cook for 15 minutes.

7.   When the cooking time ends, leave the balls to rest. Serve them warm.

Nutrition: calories 128, fat 8.2, fiber 2.2, carbs 6.5, protein 8.1

POULTRY RECIPES

Chicken and Mushrooms Bowl

Prep time: quarter-hour | Cooking time: 35 minutes | Servings: 8

Ingredients

- A cup of cauliflower rice
- 3 cups of chicken stock
- A tablespoon of salt
- 2 tablespoons of butter
- 2 big carrots
- 1 white onion
- 8 ounces of mushrooms
- 1 tablespoon of dry dill
- A tablespoon of cream
- 1 teaspoon of rosemary
- A teaspoon of ground cumin
- 1 teaspoon of paprika
- A teaspoon of oregano
- 1 tablespoon of cilantro
- A teaspoon of chives
- 1 pound of chicken

COOKING DIRECTIONS:

1. Peel carrots and onions and slice them together with mushrooms.
2. Combine cream with rosemary, ground black pepper, paprika, oregano, cilantro, and chives in a mixing bowl and stir.
3. Chop the chicken white meat roughly.
4. Place the chopped chicken in the cream mixture and allow it to sit for a few minutes.
5. Set the pressure cooker to "Pressure" mode.
6. Put butter to the pressure cooker and let it melt.
7. Add the sliced vegetables and cook for 10 minutes while stirring frequently.
8. Add the creamy chicken mixture, chicken stock, and cauliflower rice.
9. Close the lid and cook on "Sauté" mode for 25 minutes.
10. When the dish is cooked, remove it from the strain cooker, stir well, and serve.

Nutrition: calories 121, fat 4.8, fiber 1.6, carbs 5.7, protein 14

Aromatic Whole Chicken

Prep time: quarter-hour | Cooking time: a half-hour | Servings: 9

Ingredients

- 2 pounds of chicken
- A tablespoon of salt
- 1 teaspoon of ground black pepper
- A tablespoon of organic olive oil
- 1 teaspoon of butter
- A teaspoon of fresh rosemary
- 1 lemon
- A tablespoon of sugar
- 1 cup of water
- A teaspoon of coriander
- ½ teaspoon of red pepper cayenne
- ¼ teaspoon of turmeric

COOKING DIRECTIONS:

1. Wash the chicken thoroughly, detaching the neck and gizzards.
2. Combine the salt with ground black pepper, fresh rosemary, sugar, coriander, red pepper cayenne, and turmeric in a mixing bowl and stir.
3. Rub the chicken with the spice mixture.
4. Wash the red apples and chop them, removing the cores.
5. Combine the chopped apples with butter and stuff the chicken with the fruit mixture.
6. Sprinkle the chicken with extra virgin organic olive oil.
7. Set pressure cooker to "Pressure" mode.
8. Pour water to it and put the stuffed chicken. Close the lid and cook for 30 minutes.
9. When the cooking time ends, release the cooker's pressure and open its lid.
10. Remove your aromatic chicken and let it rest.
11. Cut the chicken into pieces and serve.

Nutrition: calories 217, fat 9.5, fiber 0.3, carbs 2.3, protein 29.3

Tomato Chicken Stew

Prep time: fifteen minutes | Cooking time: 35 minutes | Servings: 8

Ingredients

- ½ cup of tomato juice
- A tablespoon of sugar
- 1 teaspoon of salt
- 1 pound of boneless chicken
- 1 tablespoon of oregano
- A teaspoon of cilantro
- 1 teaspoon of fresh ginger
- 2 carrots
- 3 red onion
- 5 ounces of shallot
- 1 tablespoon of ground black pepper
- ½ cup of cream
- 3 cups of chicken stock
- 3 ounces of scallions
- 2 tablespoons of essential olive oil
- 3 ounces of eggplants

COOKING DIRECTIONS:

1. Combine tomato juice with salt, oregano, cilantro, ground black pepper, and cream in a mixing bowl and stir. Peel the eggplants, onions, and carrots.

2. Chop the vegetables into medium-sized pieces.
3. Set the pressure cooker to "Sauté" mode.
4. Place the chopped vegetables into the pressure cooker and sprinkle them with essential extra virgin olive oil. Cook the chopped vegetables for around 5 minutes.
5. Add the tomato juice mixture and stir.
6. Chop the shallot and scallions.
7. Add the chopped ingredients into the pressure cooker.
8. Chop the boneless chicken breast roughly and add it into the pressure cooker followed by chicken stock.
9. Stir well using a spoon and close the pressure cooker lid.
10. Cook the dish on "Sauté" mode for half an hour.
11. When the tomato chicken stew is cooked, remove it from the pressure cooker and transfer it to serving bowls.
Nutrition: calories 205, fat 9, fiber 2.5, carbs 13.7, protein 18.4

Shredded Chicken
Prep time: ten mins | Cooking time: 22 minutes | Servings: 7
Ingredients
- 1 pound of chicken white meat(boneless)
- A tablespoon of Erythritol
- 1 teaspoon of ground black pepper
- 1 teaspoon of extra virgin olive oil
- 2 cups of water
- 1 ounce of bay leaves
- 1 tablespoon of basil
- A tablespoon of butter
- ½ cup of cream
- A teaspoon of salt
- 3 garlic cloves
- 1 teaspoon of turmeric

COOKING DIRECTIONS:
1. Set the pressure to "Pressure" mode.
2. Pour water into it and add the chicken white meat.
3. Add the bay leaf. Close the lid and cook for 12 minutes.
4. When the cooking time ends, release the residual pressure and open cooker's lid.
5. Transfer the chicken in a mixing bowl and shred it.
6. Sprinkle the shredded chicken with Erythritol, ground black pepper, basil, butter, cream, salt, and turmeric and stir well.
7. Peel the garlic cloves and mince them.
8. Spray pressure cooker with organic extra virgin olive oil and transfer the shredded chicken into it.

9. Cook the dish on "Sauté" mode for ten minutes.
10. When the shredded chicken is cooked, transfer it to serving plates. Enjoy!
Nutrition: calories 122, fat 5.3, fiber 1.3, carbs 4.4, protein 14.4

Stuffed Chicken Breast
Prep time: 10 MINUTES | Cooking time: 20 mins | Servings: 7
Ingredients
- ½ cup of basil
- 3 ounces of dry tomatoes
- 1 pound of chicken white meat
- 1 tablespoon of extra virgin olive oil
- 3 ounces of dill
- A teaspoon of paprika
- ½ teaspoon of ground ginger
- 1 teaspoon of salt
- ½ teaspoon of ground coriander
- ½ teaspoon of cayenne pepper
- 2 tablespoons of freshly squeezed lemon juice
- ¼ cup of sour cream

COOKING DIRECTIONS:
1. Wash basil and chop it.
2. Chop the dried tomatoes.
3. Combine the chopped ingredients in a mixing bowl and add paprika followed by ground ginger. Stir well. Pound the chicken breast with a meat mallet to flatten it.
4. Rub the chicken with dill, salt, ground coriander, red pepper cayenne, and fresh lemon juice.
5. Fill the chicken white meat with the chopped basil mixture.
6. Set pressure cooker to "Steam" mode.
7. Pour the extra virgin olive oil into the pressure cooker.
8. Spread the stuffed chicken white meat with the sour cream.
9. Close the chicken breasts with toothpicks and put it in the pressure cooker.
10. Close cooker's lid and cook for twenty or so minutes.
11. When the cooking time ends, open the pressure cooker lid and remove the stuffed chicken breast.
12. Unpin the toothpicks and slice it before serving.
Nutrition: calories 179, fat 9.4, fiber 2 carbs 8.89, protein 16

Spicy Chicken Strips
Prep time: ten mins | Cooking time: 8 minutes | Servings: 7
Ingredients
- 1 cup of almond flour

- A teaspoon of kosher salt
- 1 teaspoon of red pepper cayenne
- ½ teaspoon of cilantro
- ½ teaspoon of oregano
- ½ teaspoon of paprika
- ½ cup of coconut milk
- A pound of chicken fillet
- 3 tablespoons of sesame oil
- A teaspoon of turmeric

COOKING DIRECTIONS:
1. Pour the flour in the mixing bowl.
2. Add kosher salt, red pepper cayenne, cilantro, oregano, paprika, and turmeric and mix well.
3. Pour the coconut milk in a separate bowl.
4. Cut the chicken into strips.
5. Set the pressure cooker to "Sauté" mode.
6. Pour the organic olive oil to the pressure cooker.
7. Dip the chicken strips into the coconut milk.
8. Dip it again in almond flour mixture.
9. Repeat this task two more times.
10. Add the dipped chicken strips to the pressure cooker.
11. Sauté the chicken strips for 3 minutes.
12. Remove spicy chicken strips from the pressure cooker and dry excess oil using a paper towel. Serve.

Nutrition: calories 244, fat 18.1, fiber 1.6, carbs 10.6, protein 11.9

Chicken Pancake Cake

Prep time: twenty approximately minutes | Cooking time: quarter-hour | Servings: 9
Ingredients
- 1 cup of almond flour
- 3 eggs
- 1 teaspoon of salt
- 1 teaspoon of Psyllium husk powder
- ½ cup of half and half
- ½ tablespoon of baking soda
- 1 tablespoon of apple cider vinegar treatment
- 1 medium onion
- ½ teaspoon of ground black pepper
- 7 ounces of ground chicken
- 1 teaspoon of paprika
- 1 tablespoon of tomato paste
- 1 tablespoon of butter
- 1 tablespoon of extra virgin olive oil
- 1 tablespoon of sour cream

COOKING DIRECTIONS:
1. Beat the eggs in a mixing bowl.
2. Add half & half and almond flour. Whisk the mixture until smooth batter forms.
3. Add baking soda, salt, apple cider vinegar, and psyllium husk powder. Stir well.

4. Let the batter rest for 10 minutes in your refrigerator.
5. Peel the onion and dice it.
6. Combine the chicken with ground black pepper, paprika, tomato paste, kosher salt, and sour cream in a mixing bowl.
7. Set the pressure cooker to "Sauté" mode.
8. Add the ground chicken mixture and sauté the meat for ten minutes while stirring frequently.
9. Remove the chicken from the strain cooker.
10. Pour sesame oil to enhance cooking pancakes.
11. Put the batter in the pressure cooker and cook the pancakes for 1 minute.
12. Place one pancake into the pressure cooker and spread it with the ground chicken.
13. Repeat the step until you form a pancake cake.
14. Close the lid and cook the dish on "Pressure" mode for ten minutes.
15. When the pancake cakes are cooked, remove them from the cooker and allow them to rest.
16. Serve in slices.

Nutrition: calories 134, fat 9.4, fiber 1, carbs 3.4, protein 9.6

Dill Chicken Wings

Prep time: ten mins | Cooking time: 20 MINUTES | Servings: 7
Ingredients
- 4 tablespoons of dry dill
- A cup of Greek yogurt
- 1 teaspoon of salt
- 1 teaspoon of ground black pepper
- ½ teaspoon of red chili flakes
- 1 teaspoon of oregano
- 1 tablespoon of essential organic olive oil
- 1 pound of chicken wings
- 1 teaspoon of fresh lemon juice

COOKING DIRECTIONS:
1. Combine the yogurt with salt, ground black pepper, chili flakes, oregano, and fresh lemon juice in a mixing bowl. Blend them until smooth.
2. Add half of the dry dill and Stir well.
3. Add the chicken wings and Coat them with the yogurt mixture.
4. Let the chicken wings rest for some hours.
5. Set the pressure cooker to "Pressure" mode.
6. Pour the additional virgin olive oil into the pressure cooker.
7. Add the chicken wings.
8. Sprinkle the chicken wings with the remaining dill.
9. Close the load cooker and cook for twenty minutes.

10.   When the chicken wings are cooked, take them out from the cooker and allow them to rest before serving.

Nutrition: calories 122, fat 4.5, fiber 1 carbs 2.77, protein 17

Italian Chicken

Prep time: 10 MINUTES | Cooking time: 25 minutes | Servings: 6

Ingredients
- 13-ounce of Italian-style salad dressing
- 1 teaspoon of butter
- 1-pound of skinless chicken

COOKING DIRECTIONS:

1.   Chop the chicken breasts roughly and put it in the mixing bowl.
2.   Sprinkle the chopped meat with the Italian-style salad dressing and mix well using your hands.
3.   Put the chicken breast in your refrigerator for around one hour to marinate.
4.   Set the pressure cooker to "Pressure" mode and add butter.
5.   Add marinated chicken and cook for 25 minutes.
6.   When the cooking time ends, remove the chicken from the cooker and allow it to rest.
7.   Transfer the dish to a serving plate and enjoy.

Nutrition: calories 283, fat 20.6, fiber 0, carbs 7.45, protein 16

Teriyaki Chicken

Prep time: 10 minutes | Cooking time: a half-hour | Servings: 6

Ingredients
- 1 pound of chicken thighs
- ½ cup of soy sauce
- 2 tablespoons of mirin
- 1 teaspoon of starch
- 2 garlic cloves
- 1 teaspoon of salt
- 2 ounces of fresh ginger
- 3 tablespoons of sake
- 1 teaspoon of sugar
- 1 tablespoon of sesame oil
- 1 tablespoon of sesame seeds

COOKING DIRECTIONS:

1.   Peel the garlic cloves and slice them.
2.   Chop the fresh ginger. Combine the soy sauce with mirin, starch, salt, sugar, and sake in a mixing bowl. stir until they are dissolved.
3.   Set the pressure cooker to "Pressure" mode.
4.   Pour the teriyaki sauce into the cooker and close the lid.
5.   Cook the sauce for ten minutes or until it starts boiling.

6.   When the sauce begins boiling, open the cooker's lid and add the chicken thighs.
7.   Close the lid and cook the dish on "Pressure" mode for ten minutes.
8.   Preheat the oven to 365 F.
9.   When the chicken thighs are cooked, release the built-in pressure and open the lid.
10.   Transfer the chicken thighs into the oven tray and sprinkle it with sesame oil.
11.   Also, add sesame seeds and put the tray in the oven.
12.   Cook for 5 minutes and put transfer it to serving bowls. Enjoy!

Nutrition: calories 167, fat 7.8, fiber 1 carbs 7.06, protein 15

Sweet Chicken Breast

Prep time: fifteen MINUTES | Cooking time: 40 minutes | Servings: 8

Ingredients
- 2 pounds of chicken breasts
- 2 tablespoons of ketchup
- ½ cup of Erythritol
- ½ cup of soy sauce
- 1 teaspoon of salt
- 2 ounces of fresh rosemary
- 1 teaspoon of ground white pepper
- ¼ cup of garlic
- 2 tablespoons of extra virgin essential olive oil
- 1 white onion
- 4 tablespoons of water
- 1 tablespoon of flax meal
- ½ teaspoon of red chili flakes
- 1 teaspoon of oregano

COOKING DIRECTIONS:

1.   Place the chicken into pressure cooker.
2.   Set the cooker to "Pressure" mode.
3.   Combine ketchup with Erythritol, soy sauce, salt, rosemary, and ground white pepper in a mixing bowl.
4.   Whisk until smooth.
5.   Peel the garlic and white onion and then slice the vegetables.
6.   Combine the sliced vegetables with chili flakes and oregano and stir.
7.   Pour the Erythritol mixture into the pressure cooker.
8.   Mix well, close the lid, and cook for ten minutes.
9.   Combine the flax meal with water in a mixing bowl and stir.
10.   When the cooking time ends, release the rest of the pressure and open the lid.
11.   Remove the chicken from the cooker and chop it.

12. Pour the starch mixture into the cooker and stir.
13. Add chicken and close the lid.
14. Cook the dish on "Sauté" mode for 30 minutes.
15. When the cooking time ends, remove the chicken breast from the pressure cooker and serve.
Nutrition: calories 295, fat 13.4, fiber 3.9, carbs 9.5, protein 34.6

Salsa Verde Chicken

Prep time: ten minutes | Cooking time: thirty
MINUTES | Servings: 6
Ingredients
* 10 ounces of Salsa Verde
* 1 tablespoon of paprika
* A pound of boneless chicken breasts
* 1 teaspoon of salt
* A teaspoon of ground coriander
* 1 teaspoon of cilantro

COOKING DIRECTIONS:
1. Rub the boneless chicken breasts with paprika, salt, ground black pepper, and cilantro.
2. Set the pressure cooker to "Pressure" mode.
3. Place the boneless chicken into the pressure cooker.
4. Sprinkle the meat with salsa verde and stir well.
5. Close pressure cooker lid and cook for half an hour.
6. When the cooking time ends, release the pressure and transfer the verde chicken into your mixing bowl. Shred the chicken well and serve.
Nutrition: calories 222, fat 11.3, fiber 3 carbs 21.02, protein 9

BBQ Chicken Balls

Prep time: ten MINUTES | Cooking time: 25 minutes | Servings: 8
Ingredients
* ½ cup of BBQ sauce
* 1 teaspoon of salt
* 1 teaspoon of sugar
* 3 tablespoons of chives
* 12 ounces of ground chicken
* 1 egg
* A tablespoon of coconut flour
* 1 tablespoon of extra-virgin organic olive oil
* 1 teaspoon of oregano
* 1 red onion

COOKING DIRECTIONS:
1. Place the ground chicken in a mixing bowl.
2. Sprinkle it with sugar, salt, chives, coconut flour, and oregano.
3. Peel the red onion, dice it, and add it to the chicken mixture.

4. Beat the egg and combine it with chicken. Mix everything well with your hands until smooth.
5. Make small balls from the chicken mixture.
6. Set the cooker to "Sauté" mode.
7. Pour the organic extra virgin olive oil into pressure cooker.
8. Put the chicken balls in the pressure cooker and sauté them for 5 minutes.
9. Stir them constantly until each ball browns on every side.
10. Pour the barbecue sauce into pressure cooker and close the lid.
11. Cook the dish on "Sear/Sauté" mode for 20 approximately minutes.
12. When the cooking time ends, remove the chicken balls from the pressure cooker and serve.
Nutrition: calories 131, fat 5.7, fiber 0.8, carbs 6.3, protein 13.3

Thai Chicken Fillet

Prep time: ten minutes | Cooking time: 35
MINUTES | Servings: 8
Ingredients
* 14 ounces of boneless chicken white meat
* 1 teaspoon of ground black pepper
* 1 teaspoon of paprika
* 1 teaspoon of turmeric
* 3 tablespoons of fish sauce
* ½ teaspoon of curry
* 1 teaspoon of salt
* 3 tablespoons of butter
* ¼ cup of fresh basil
* 1 teaspoon of essential olive oil

COOKING DIRECTIONS:
1. Cut the boneless chicken white meat into medium pieces.
2. Combine the black pepper with paprika, turmeric, curry, and salt in a mixing bowl. Stir.
3. Sprinkle the chicken with the spice mixture and stir again.
4. Chop basil and combine it with butter in a small bowl. Stir the mixture until smooth.
5. Set the load cooker to "Sauté" mode and add the butter mixture. Melt it.
6. Put the chicken filets to the pressure cooker and sauté them for ten minutes.
7. Add the organic essential olive oil and fish sauce.
8. Close the pressure cooker lid and cook the dish on "Sear/Sauté" mode for 25 minutes.
9. When the chicken fillet is cooked, remove it from the pressure cooker. Let the dish rest briefly and serve.
Nutrition: calories 182, fat 12, fiber 1, carbs 12.7, protein 6

Onions Stuffed with Ground Chicken

Prep time: quarter-hour | Cooking time: 40 minutes | Servings: 5
Ingredients

- 5 large white onions
- 1 pound of ground chicken
- 1 cup of cream
- 1 cup of chicken stock
- 1 teaspoon of salt
- 1 teaspoon of oregano
- 1 teaspoon of basil
- 1 egg
- 1 teaspoon of turmeric
- 5 garlic cloves

COOKING DIRECTIONS:
1.   Peel the onions removing its stem and roots such that it sits down flat.
2.   Use a paring knife or apple corer to pull out the inner layers of the onions leaving several outer layers.
3.   Place the ground chicken in a mixing bowl and sprinkle it with salt, oregano, basil, and turmeric.
4.   Mix the chicken products using well your hands.
5.   Beat the egg and pour it into the mix. Stir well.
6.   Peel the garlic cloves, mince them, and add them to the chicken mixture. Mix well again.
7.   Fill the onions with the ground chicken mixture.
8.   Set the pressure cooker to "Sear/Sauté" mode.
9.   Transfer the stuffed onions to the pressure cooker.
10.   Add the chicken stock and cream.
11.   Close the lid and cook for 40 minutes.
12.   When the cooking time ends, open the lid and allow the onions to rest briefly.
13.   Transfer the crooks to a serving platter and sprinkle them with the gravy from the load cooker. Serve while warm.
Nutrition: calories 318, fat 19.3, fiber 2, carbs 15.56, protein 22

Mexican Chicken

Prep time: 13 minutes | Cooking time: fifteen minutes | Servings: 6
Ingredients

- A cup of salsa
- 1 teaspoon of paprika
1 teaspoon of salt
- 2 tablespoons of minced garlic
- 15 ounces of boneless chicken
- 1 teaspoon of oregano

COOKING DIRECTIONS:
1.   Combine the paprika with salt, minced garlic, and oregano in a mixing bowl and stir.

2.   Chop the boneless chicken and sprinkle it with the spice mixture.
3.   Set the pressure cooker to "Pressure" mode.
4.   Transfer the chicken mixture into pressure cooker.
5.   Add salsa and mix well using a wooden spoon.
6.   Close the lid and cook for quarter-hour.
7.   When the cooking time ends, release the built-in pressure and open the pressure cooker lid.
8.   Transfer the cooked chicken to some serving bowl.
Nutrition: calories 206, fat 10.3, fiber 3, carbs 20.49, protein 9

Buffalo Chicken Wings

Prep time: 10 minutes | Cooking time: 15 MINUTES | Servings: 7
Ingredients

- 4 tablespoons of hot sauce
- 1 teaspoon of salt
- 1 teaspoon of stevia extract
- ½ cup of water
- 1 teaspoon of garlic sauce
- 1 tablespoon of fresh cilantro
- 1 pound of chicken wings
- A tablespoon of essential olive oil
- 1 teaspoon of tomato paste

COOKING DIRECTIONS:
1.   Combine salt with cilantro in a shallow bowl and stir.
2.   Combine the chicken wings with the spice mixture to coat them fully.
3.   Set the pressure cooker to "Pressure" mode.
4.   Pour water into the pressure cooker and fit a trivet.
5.   Transfer the chicken wings on the trivet and close the pressure cooker lid.
6.   Cook for 10 minutes.
7.   Combine sauce with stevia extract, garlic sauce, and tomato paste in a bowl and stir well until they smoothen.
8.   When the cooking time ends, open the pressure cooker and take out the chicken wings.
9.   Spray the oven tray with olive oil.
10.   Preheat the oven to 365 F.
11.   Place the chicken wings in the tray and coat them with the sauce mixture.
12.   Transfer the chicken wings to the oven and cook for 5 minutes.
13.   When the wings turn golden brown, remove it from the cooker and serve.
Nutrition: calories 142, fat 6.8, fiber 0.1, carbs 0.3, protein 18.8

Creamy Garlic Shredded Chicken

Prep time: quarter-hour | Cooking time: 25 minutes | Servings: 7
Ingredients

- A cup of cream
- 1 cup of chicken stock
- 1 tablespoon of garlic sauce
- 1 tablespoon of minced garlic
- A teaspoon of nutmeg
- 1 teaspoon of salt
- 12 ounces of chicken breasts
- 1 tablespoon of fresh lemon juice

COOKING DIRECTIONS:

1. Combine nutmeg with salt and stir well.
2. Sprinkle the chicken breasts with nutmeg mixture. Ensure that they are well coated.
3. Set the pressure cooker to "Pressure" mode.
4. Place the chicken into the cooker.
5. Add chicken stock, minced garlic, and cream. Stir well and close the lid. Cook for 25 minutes.
6. When the cooking time ends, release the rest of the pressure and open the cooker's lid.
7. Transfer your shredded chicken in a mixing bowl and shred it using a fork.
8. Add garlic sauce, mix well, and serve.

Nutrition: calories 169, fat 11.8, fiber 0, carbs 3.32, protein 12

Feta Cheese Chicken Bowl

Prep time: quarter-hour | Cooking time: half an hour | Servings: 6
Ingredients

- 7 ounces of Feta cheese
- 10 ounces of boneless chicken breast
- 1 teaspoon of basil
- 1 tablespoon of onion powder
- A teaspoon of organic essential olive oil
- 1 tablespoon of sesame oil
- 4 ounces of green olives
- 2 cucumbers
- 1 cup of water
- A teaspoon of salt

COOKING DIRECTIONS:

1. Set the pressure cooker to "Pressure" mode.
2. Place the boneless chicken white meat into pressure cooker.
3. Add water, basil, and onion powder. Stir well and close the lid. Cook for half an hour.
4. Chop the Feta cheese roughly and spray it with essential organic olive oil.
5. Slice the green olives and chop the cucumbers into medium-sized cubes.
6. Combine the chopped cheese with sliced green olives, and cucumbers in a mixing bowl.
7. Sprinkle the amalgamation with the salt and sesame oil.

8. When the chicken is cooked, open the cooker and take it out.
9. Chill briefly and chop the chicken into pieces.
10. Add the chicken to the cheese mixture. Mix well and serve.

Nutrition: calories 279, fat 19.8, fiber 2 carbs 15.37, protein 11

Steamed Chicken Cutlets

Prep time: 10 MINUTES | Cooking time: 25 minutes | Servings: 8
Ingredients

- 14 ounces of ground chicken
- 1 teaspoon of ground black pepper
- 1 teaspoon of paprika
- A teaspoon of cilantro
- 1 teaspoon of oregano
- ½ teaspoon of minced garlic
- 2 tablespoons of starch
- A teaspoon of red chili flakes
- 1 tablespoon of oatmeal flour
- An egg

COOKING DIRECTIONS:

1. Place the ground chicken in a mixing bowl.
2. Sprinkle it with the ground black pepper, cilantro, and oregano.
3. Add paprika and minced garlic and mix using your hands.
4. Beat an egg in a separate bowl.
5. Add starch and oatmeal flour to the egg and stir well until smooth.
6. Add the egg mixture in the chicken mixture.
7. Add chili flakes and mix well.
8. Make medium-sized cutlets from the ground chicken mixture.
9. Set the pressure cooker to "Steam" mode.
10. Put the cutlets on the trivet and place it in the pressure cooker.
11. Close the lid and cook the dish on steam mode for 25 minutes.
12. When the dish is cooked, remove the steamed cutlets from the pressure cooker. Allow it to rest and serve.

Nutrition: calories 96, fat 5.3, fiber 0, carbs 1.89, protein 10

Parmesan Chicken

Prep time: ten MINUTES | Cooking time: half an HOUR | Servings: 8
Ingredients

- 1 cup of chopped tomatoes
- 3 tablespoons of butter
- 1 pound of boneless chicken
- 1 teaspoon of salt
- 1 teaspoon of paprika
- 7 ounces of Parmesan cheese

- ½ cup of fresh basil
- 1 teaspoon of cilantro
- 1 tablespoon of sour cream

COOKING DIRECTIONS:

1. Grate Parmesan cheese and combine it with cilantro and paprika in a mixing bowl. Stir.
2. Wash the basil and chop it.
3. Set the pressure cooker to "Sear/Sauté" mode.
4. Sprinkle the boneless chicken with salt and put it in the cooker.
5. Add basil, butter, tomato, and sour cream.
6. Sprinkle the chicken with the grated cheese mixture and close the lid.
7. Cook the chicken for thirty minutes.
8. When the cooking time ends, release the rest of the pressure and open the cooker's lid.
9. Transfer the dish to serving plates and enjoy.

Nutrition: calories 234, fat 14.2, fiber 0.4, carbs 2, protein 24.8

Chicken Pilaf

Prep time: quarter-hour | Cooking time: 6 minutes | Servings: 10

Ingredients

- A cup of cauliflower rice
- 7 ounces of boneless chicken breasts
- 1 teaspoon of salt
- 4 ounces of mushroom
- 1 tablespoon of organic olive oil
- 1 white onion
- 1 tablespoon of oregano
- 4 ounces of raisins
- 5 ounces of kale
- 7 ounces of green beans
- 3 cups of chicken stock
- 2 tablespoons of oyster sauce

COOKING DIRECTIONS:

1. Slice the mushrooms and put them in the pressure cooker.
2. Chop the chicken breasts into medium-sized pieces and add them to the cooker.
3. Peel the onion and dice it.
4. Chop the kale and green beans.
5. Add the vegetables in the cooker.
6. Sprinkle the amalgamation with extra virgin essential olive oil, salt, oregano, raisins, and chicken stock.
7. Set the pressure cooker to "Pressure" mode and stir well.
8. Add cauliflower rice and close its lid. Cook for 6 minutes.
9. When the cooking time ends, release the remaining pressure and open the lid.
10. Let your chicken pilaf rest to cool a bit. Stir before serving.

Nutrition: calories 111, fat 3.2, fiber 2.1, carbs 14.4, protein 7.8

Chicken Puttanesca

Prep time: quarter-hour | Cooking time: 25 minutes | Servings: 8

Ingredients

- 1 ½ pounds of chicken thigh
- ½ cup of tomato paste
- 2 tablespoons of capers
- 1 teaspoon of salt
- 1/2 teaspoons of black-eyed peas
- 3 garlic cloves
- 3 tablespoons of organic extra virgin olive oil
- 4 ounces of black olives
- 1 tablespoon of chopped fresh basil
- ½ cup of water

COOKING DIRECTIONS:

1. Set the pressure cooker to "Sauté" mode.
2. Pour the organic olive oil into it and heat it for 1 minute.
3. Put the chicken thighs and sauté for 5 minutes.
4. When the chicken thighs are browned, remove them from the strain cooker.
5. Add tomato paste, capers, olives, black-eyed peas, and basil in the pressure cooker contents.
6. Peel the garlic and slice it.
7. Add the sliced garlic to the pressure cooker mixture.
8. Add salt and water. Stir the amalgamation well and sauté it for 3 minutes.
9. Add the chicken thighs and close the lid. Cook the dish on "Pressure" mode for 17 minutes.
10. When the cooking time ends, open pressure cooker lid and transfer your chicken puttanesca on serving bowl. Enjoy.

Nutrition: calories 170, fat 8.8, fiber 1, carbs 4.48, protein 18

Coconut Chicken Strips

Prep time: 10 mins | Cooking time: 12 minutes | Servings: 8

Ingredients

- ½ cup of coconut
- 4 tablespoons of butter
- 1 teaspoon of salt
- ½ cup of almond flour
- ½ teaspoon of Erythritol
- ¼ teaspoon of red chili flakes
- 1 teaspoon of onion powder
- 15 ounces of boneless chicken

COOKING DIRECTIONS:

1.	Cut the boneless chicken white meat into strips.
2.	Sprinkle them with salt and chili flakes, and stir.
3.	Combine the coconut with almond flour, Erythritol, and onion powder in a mixing bowl and stir well.
4.	Set pressure cooker to "Sauté" mode.
5.	Add butter in the pressure cooker and cook for two minutes.
6.	Dip chicken strips into the coconut mixture and put them to the cooker.
7.	Sauté the dish for 10 minute or until each strip turns golden brown.
0.	Remove your coconut chicken strip from the cooker and drain excess oils using a paper towel.
9.	Let the dish rest briefly before serving.
Nutrition: calories 197, fat 13.7, fiber 1 carbs 2.3, protein 16.6

Fragrant Drumsticks

Prep time: 5 minutes | Cooking time: 18 minutes | Servings: 7
Ingredients
•	A pound of chicken drumsticks
•	1 teaspoon of salt
•	1 teaspoon of paprika
•	1 teaspoon of white pepper
•	A cup of water
•	1 teaspoon of thyme
•	½ teaspoon of oregano
COOKING DIRECTIONS:
1.	Sprinkle the chicken drumsticks with salt, paprika, thyme, oregano, and white pepper and stir well.
2.	Set pressure cooker to "Pressure" mode.
3.	Add the chicken drumsticks into the cooker and add the drumstick mixture.
4.	Close the lid and cook for 18 minutes.
5.	When the cooking time ends, release the remaining pressure and open the lid.
6.	Remove the drumsticks from pressure cooker and transfer them to the serving platter.
Nutrition: calories 112, fat 3.8, fiber 0 carbs 0.5, protein 17.9

Light Chicken Soup

Prep time: quarter-hour | Cooking time: 29 minutes | Servings: 9
Ingredients
•	6 ounces of Shirataki noodles
•	8 cups of water
•	1 carrot
•	1 tablespoon of peanut oil
•	1 yellow onion
•	½ tablespoon of salt
•	3 ounces of celery stalk

•	1 teaspoon of ground black pepper
•	½ lemon
•	A teaspoon of minced garlic
•	10 ounces of chicken breast
COOKING DIRECTIONS:
1.	Peel the carrot and onion and dice them.
2.	Cut the chicken white meat into halves.
3.	Set pressure cooker to "Pressure" mode.
4.	Pour the peanut oil into the cooker and preheat it for 1 minute.
5.	Add the onion and carrot and stir well. Cook it for 5 minutes while stirring constantly.
6.	Add 4 portions of water and chicken.
7.	Close the lid and cook the dish on "Pressure" mode for ten minutes.
8.	When the cooking time ends, take off the chicken from the cooker and shred it.
9.	Return the shredded chicken to pressure cooker and close the lid.
10.	Cook the dish for 7 minutes.
11.	Add 4 servings of water and Shirataki noodles.
12.	Close the lid and cook the dish on "Pressure" mode for 7 minutes.
13.	When the soup is cooked, remove it from the pressure cooker and ladle it into serving bowls.
Nutrition: calories 64, fat 2.3, fiber 2.7, carbs 2.6, protein 7.2

Chicken Cream Soup

Prep time: 15 MINUTES | Cooking time: 22 minutes | Servings: 8
Ingredients
•	4 servings of water
•	2 cups of cream
•	1/2 cup of half and half
•	1 tablespoon of minced garlic
•	5 ounces of chopped mushrooms
•	1 onion
•	1 tablespoon of organic olive oil
•	½ tablespoon of salt
•	1 teaspoon of fresh basil
•	1 teaspoon of fresh dill
•	7 ounces of chicken
COOKING DIRECTIONS:
1.	Peel the onion.
2.	Set the pressure cooker to "Sauté" mode.
3.	Transfer the onion and mushroom to the pressure cooker and add essential extra virgin olive oil.
4.	Sauté the vegetable mixture for 5 minutes while stirring constantly.
5.	Add chicken and cream.
6.	Add the half and half and water.
7.	Sprinkle the amalgamation with the garlic, salt, dill, and basil. Stir well and close the lid.

8. Cook the dish for 25 minutes on "Pressure" mode.
9. Open the cooker lid and remove the chicken white meat and shred it.
10. Blend the soup mixture using an immersion blender until smooth.
11. Add the shredded chicken and close the pressure cooker lid.
12. Cook the chicken soup on "Pressure" mode for two minutes.
13. Ladle the cooked soup into serving bowls.
Nutrition: calories 106, fat 6.9, fiber 0.5, carbs 4.6, protein 6.9

Duck Tacos
Prep time: 10 mins | Cooking time: 22 minutes | Servings: 7
Ingredients
- A pound of duck breast fillet
- 1 teaspoon of salt
- A teaspoon of chili powder
- 1 teaspoon of onion powder
- A teaspoon of oregano
- 1 teaspoon of basil
- A cup of lettuce
- 1 teaspoon of ground black pepper
- 1 tablespoon of tomato sauce
- 1 cup of chicken stock
- 1 tablespoon of organic essential olive oil
- 6 ounces of cheddar cheese
- 7 almond of flour tortilla
- 1 teaspoon of turmeric

COOKING DIRECTIONS:
1. Chop the duck fillet and put it in the blender.
2. Blend the amalgamation well.
3. Set the pressure cooker to "Sauté" mode.
4. Add the blended duck fillet into the cooker.
5. Sprinkle it with extra virgin olive oil and stir well.
6. Saute the blended fillet mixture for around five minutes.
7. Combine salt with chili powder, onion powder, oregano, basil, ground black pepper, and turmeric in a mixing bowl and stir.
8. Add tomato sauce. Sprinkle the blended duck fillet with the spice mixture.
9. Mix well and add chicken stock. Stir gently and close the lid.
10. Cook the mixture on "Pressure" mode for 17 minutes.
11. Wash the lettuce and chop it roughly.
12. Grate the Cheddar cheese.
13. When the duck mixture is cooked, take it off from the cooker and allow it to rest.
14. Place the chopped lettuce in the tortillas and add the duck mixture.

15. Sprinkle the tortillas with the grated cheese and serve.
Nutrition: calories 246, fat 12.9, fiber 1.6, carbs 4.1, protein 28.9

Spicy Shredded Duck
Prep time: 10 mins | Cooking time: 27 minutes | Servings: 8
Ingredients
- ½ cup of red merlot wine
- 1/2 cup of chicken stock
- 1 teaspoon of onion powder
- 14 ounces of duck fillet
- 2 teaspoons of red pepper cayenne
- ¼ teaspoon of minced garlic
- ½ cup of fresh dill
- 1 teaspoon of salt
- 1 teaspoon of ground black pepper
- 1 tablespoon of sour cream
- 1 tablespoon of tomato puree

COOKING DIRECTIONS:
1. Combine the burgundy or merlot wine with the chicken stock in a mixing bowl and stir.
2. Set pressure cooker to "Sauté" mode.
3. Pour the chicken stock mixture into the pressure cooker and preheat it for 1 minute.
4. Combine the onion powder with cayenne, salt, ground black pepper, and garlic in a mixing bowl.
5. Stir the combination and pour it over the duck fillets.
6. Place the duck fillet into the pressure cooker and close the lid.
7. Cook the dish on "Pressure" mode for 25 minutes.
8. When the cooking time ends, remove the dish from pressure cooker and allow it to rest.
9. Shred the duck using a fork.
10. Leave the liquid in the pressure cooker and add the shredded duck there.
11. Add tomato puree and sour cream.
12. Chop the dill and sprinkle the dish with it.
13. Stir gently and close the lid.
14. Cook the dish on "Sauté" mode for two minutes.
15. When the cooking time ends, ladle the shredded duck to serving bowls.
Nutrition: calories 119, fat 7.9, fiber 0, carbs 1.81, protein 9

Cheddar Chicken Fillets
Prep time: ten mins | Cooking time: quarter-hour | Servings: 7
Ingredients
- 1 cup cream of cheese
- 6 ounces of Cheddar cheese
- 1 yellow onion
- 14 ounces of boneless chicken

- 1 teaspoon of extra virgin organic olive oil
- 1 tablespoon of ground black pepper
- 1 teaspoon of red chili flakes
- 4 ounces of pitted apricot
- 3 tablespoons of chicken stock

COOKING DIRECTIONS:
1. Cut the chicken into fillets.
2. Sprinkle the boneless chicken breasts with the ground black pepper, essential organic olive oil, and chili flakes.
3. Set the pressure cooker to "Sauté" mode.
4. Transfer the chicken breasts into the cooker and sauté the dish for 5 minutes.
5. Meanwhile, grate Cheddar cheese and combine it with cream cheese.
6. Add chicken stock and mix well with a spoon.
7. Peel the onion and slice it.
8. Chop apricots and combine them with the sliced onion.
9. When the cooking time ends, open the pressure cooker lid.
10. Sprinkle the chicken with the onion mixture.
11. Add the Cheddar cheese mixture.
12. Close the lid and cook the boneless chicken breasts on "Pressure" mode for 10 minutes.
13. When the cooking time ends, release the cooker's pressure and open it.
14. Ladle the chicken fillets on the serving plates.
Nutrition: calories 282, fat 18.1, fiber 1 carbs 11.88, protein 18

Duck Cutlets

Prep time: ten mins | Cooking time: twenty or so minutes | Servings: 8
Ingredients
- ¼ cup of vermouth
- 1 pound of ground duck
- 1 teaspoon of salt
- 4 ounces of keto bread
- ¼ cup of cream
- 1 teaspoon of paprika
- 1 teaspoon of coconut flour
- A teaspoon of white pepper

COOKING DIRECTIONS:
1. Combine the ground duck with vermouth in a mixing bowl.
2. Chop the bread and combine it with cream. Stir well until they smoothen. You can even use a blender.
3. Add the bread mixture to the ground duck.
4. Sprinkle the meat mixture with salt, paprika, and white pepper.
5. Add coconut flour and mix well with a spoon.

6. Make medium cutlets from the duck mixture and place them in the trivet.
7. Set the pressure cooker to "Steam" mode.
8. Fit the trivet into the cooker and close the lid.
9. Cook the dish on steam mode for 20 minutes.
10. When the cooking time ends, remove the cutlets from the cooker and allow them to rest before serving.
Nutrition: calories 121, fat 5.4, fiber 1.4, carbs 4.9, protein 12.3

Chicken Breast with Pomegranate Sauce

Prep time: ten mins | Cooking time: 29 minutes | Servings: 6
Ingredients
- ½ cup of pomegranate juice
- 2 tablespoons of Erythritol
- 1 teaspoon of cinnamon
- ¼ cup of chicken stock
- 2 pounds of chicken
- 1 teaspoon of starch
- 1 teaspoon of butter
- 1 tablespoon of oregano
- 1 teaspoon of turmeric
- ½ teaspoon of red chili flakes

COOKING DIRECTIONS:
1. Set the pressure cooker to "Pressure" mode.
2. Put the chicken breast into the cooker and sprinkle it with oregano, butter, chicken stock, and chili flakes.
3. Stir to mix and close pressure cooker lid. Cook the meat for 20 minutes.
4. Combine the pomegranate juice with Erythritol, cinnamon, starch, and turmeric and stir well until everything dissolves.
5. When the cooking time ends, open the cooker's lid and remove the chicken.
6. Set the cooker to "Sauté" mode.
7. Pour the pomegranate sauce in the pressure cooker and sauté it for 4 minutes. Return the chicken in the pressure cooker and stir well using a spoon.
8. Close the lid and cook the chicken on "Pressure" mode for 5 minutes.
9. When the cooking time ends, release the cooker's pressure and open its lid.
10. Transfer the chicken breast dish to serving plates and sprinkle it with pomegranate sauce. Enjoy.
Nutrition: calories 198, fat 4.6, fiber 0.6, carbs 4.7, protein 32.2

Creamy Chicken Pasta

Prep time: ten minutes | Cooking time: 27 minutes | Servings: 8
Ingredients

- 5 ounces of cooked zoodles
- 1 pound of boneless chicken white meat
- 1 teaspoon of cilantro
- 1 cup of cream
- ½ cup of chicken stock
- 1 teaspoon of butter
- 1 teaspoon of salt
- ½ cup of cream cheese
- 1 teaspoon of paprika
- 1 teaspoon of garlic powder

COOKING DIRECTIONS:

1. Combine cilantro with salt, paprika, and garlic in a mixing bowl and stir well.
2. Sprinkle the boneless chicken white meat with spice mixture and mix well with your hands.
3. Set pressure cooker to "Pressure" mode.
4. Place the spiced chicken in the cooker.
5. Add cream, chicken stock, and cream cheese.
6. Stir the mixture and close the pressure cooker lid.
7. Cook the dish for 25 minutes.
8. Open the lid and transfer the chicken to a mixing bowl. Shred it using a fork.
9. Transfer the shredded chicken into the cooker and add the cooked zoodles. Stir well and close the lid.
10. Cook the dish on "Pressure" mode for two minutes.
11. Remove the cooked chicken pasta from the cooker and serve it warm.

Nutrition: calories 186, fat 18.911.5, fiber 0.3, carbs 2.2, protein 18

Chicken Bread

Prep time: fifteen minutes | Cooking time: 40 minutes | Servings: 8

Ingredients

- ½ tablespoon of garam Masala powder
- 8 ounces of keto dough
- 1 teaspoon of sesame seeds
- 1 egg yolk
- 1 teaspoon of ground cilantro
- 1 teaspoon of dill
- 10 ounces of ground chicken
- ¼ cup of fresh parsley
- 1 teaspoon of extra virgin olive oil
- 1 tablespoon of ground black pepper
- 1 onion

COOKING DIRECTIONS:

1. Roll the dough using a rolling pin.
2. Combine the chicken with the ground cilantro and ground black pepper. Stir well.
3. Wash the parsley and chop it.
4. Add the chopped parsley in the chicken mixture.
5. Peel the onion and dice it.
6. Add the onion to the chicken mixture.
7. Mix the meat mixture using your hands.
8. Set the pressure cooker to "Pressure" mode.
9. Place the meat mixture at the middle of the rolled dough.
10. Wrap the dough with the bread.
11. Smear the strain cooker with extra-virgin olive oil and put the chicken bread there.
12. Whisk the egg yolk and pour it over the chicken bread.
13. Sprinkle the chicken breast with sesame seeds.
14. Close the pressure cooker lid and cook the dish for 40 minutes.
15. When the cooking time ends, open the pressure cooker lid and confirm whether it's cooked using a toothpick. Place the chicken bread on your serving plate and allow it to cool. Slice it and serve.

Nutrition: calories 189, fat 5.3, fiber 4.2, carbs 8.1, protein 27.3

Peanut Duck

Prep time: ten minutes | Cooking time: 25 minutes | Servings: 6

Ingredients

- 4 tablespoons of creamy peanut butter
- ½ cup of fresh dill
- 1 teaspoon of oregano
- 1 tablespoon of freshly squeezed lemon juice
- A teaspoon of lime zest
- ¼ teaspoon of cinnamon
- 1 teaspoon of turmeric
- 1 teaspoon of paprika
- ½ teaspoon of cumin
- ½ teaspoon of ground black pepper
- 1 cup chicken of stock
- 1 tablespoon of butter
- 1 pound of duck breast
- ¼ cup of burgundy or merlot wine

COOKING DIRECTIONS:

1. Wash the fresh dill and chop it.
2. Combine the chopped dill with lime zest, cinnamon, turmeric, lemon juice paprika, cumin, and ground black pepper and stir well.
3. Set pressure cooker to "Pressure" mode.
4. Rub the duck using the spice mixture and place it in the cooker.
5. Sprinkle the meat with oregano and add chicken stock, red, and butter.
6. Close the pressure cooker lid and cook the dish for 18 minutes.
7. When the cooking time ends, release the cooker's pressure and open its lid.
8. Set the pressure cooker to "Sauté" mode.

9.   Remove the dish from the pressure cooker.
10.   Add peanut butter into pressure cooker and sauté it for 1 minute.
11.   Add the duck and sauté the dish for 5 minutes. Stir the duck constantly.
12.   When the duck is cooked, place it on your serving plate and let it sit before serving.
Nutrition: calories 198, fat 11.5, fiber 1 carbs 4.74, protein 19

Orange Duck Breast

Prep time: ten mins | Cooking time: 37minutes | Servings: 9
Ingredients
- 2 pounds of duck breast
- 2 oranges
- 2 tablespoons of honey
- 1 cup of water
- A teaspoon of cayenne pepper
- 1 teaspoon of salt
- 1 teaspoon of curry powder
- 2 tablespoons of freshly squeezed lemon juice
- 2 tablespoons of butter
- 1 teaspoon of sugar
- 1 teaspoon of turmeric

COOKING DIRECTIONS:
1.   Make zest from the oranges and chop them.
2.   Combine orange zest with chopped oranges in a mixing bowl.
3.   Sprinkle the amalgamation with honey, red pepper cayenne, salt, curry powder, lemon juice, sugar, and turmeric and stir well.
4.   Set pressure cooker to "Sauté" mode.
5.   Put the duck in the orange mixture and stir it.
6.   Smear the pressure cooker base with butter and sauté it for two minutes.
7.   Add water.
8.   Add the duck mixture and close the lid.
9.   Set the pressure cooker mode to "Poultry" and cook the dish for 35 minutes.
10.   When the cooking time ends, open the cooker's lid and remove your duck breast.
11.   Put it on a serving plate and slice it.
12.   Pour the orange sauce over the duck meal when serving.
Nutrition: calories 174, fat 7, fiber 1, carbs 7.18, protein 20

Chicken Satay

Prep time: 10 MINUTES | Cooking time: 16 minutes | Servings: 8
Ingredients
- 10 ounces of boneless chicken thighs
- ½ cup of sweet soy sauce
- ½ cup of dark soy sauce
- 1 teaspoon of lemongrass paste
- 1 tablespoon of almond oil
- 1 teaspoon of salt
- 1 tablespoon of scallions
- ½ tablespoon of sriracha

COOKING DIRECTIONS:
1.   Chop the chicken thighs and sprinkle them with lemongrass paste and salt.
2.   Set the pressure cooker to "Pressure" mode.
3.   Place the chicken thighs in the pressure cooker and add the soy sauces.
4.   Chop the scallions and add them into the cooker.
5.   Sprinkle the amalgamation with sriracha and almond oil. Stir well using a spoon and close the lid.
6.   Cook the dish for 16 minutes.
7.   When the dish is cooked, release pressure and open the lid.
8.   Transfer the chicken satay to your serving plate and sprinkle it with the sauce from the load cooker.
9.   Serve the dish while hot.
Nutrition: calories 85, fat 4.7, fiber 0, carbs 1.98, protein 9

Juicy Duck Legs

Prep time: ten mins | Cooking time: 25minutes | Servings: 6
Ingredients
- 1 pound of duck legs
- ½ cup pomegranate juice
- ½ cup of dill
- 1 teaspoon of salt
- 1 teaspoon of ground black pepper
- 1 teaspoon of ground ginger
- 1 tablespoon of extra-virgin olive oil
- ½ cup of water
- A teaspoon of brown sugar
- 1 tablespoon of lime zest
- 2 teaspoons of soy sauce
- ½ teaspoon of peppercorn

COOKING DIRECTIONS:
1.   Combine the black pepper with salt, ground ginger, lime zest, brown sugar, and peppercorn in a mixing bowl and stir well.
2.   Sprinkle the duck legs with the spice mixture and mix well using your hands.
3.   Add the soy sauce, water, organic olive oil, and pomegranate juice.
4.   Wash the dill and chop it.
5.   Sprinkle the duck legs mixture with the chopped dill.
6.   Set pressure cooker to "Pressure" mode.
7.   Transfer the duck legs mixture into the pressure cooker and close the lid.

8. Cook for 25 minutes.
9. When the dish is cooked, open the pressure cooker lid and pour the content on the serving dish.
10. Sprinkle the juicy duck legs with the pomegranate sauce and serve.
Nutrition: calories 209, fat 11.4, fiber 0, carbs 5.11, protein 21

Miso Chicken Dip

Prep time: quarter-hour | Cooking time: 30 MINUTES | Servings: 8
Ingredients
- 2 tablespoons of miso paste
- 1 teaspoon of liquid stevia
- 1 teaspoon of apple cider vinegar treatment
- ¼ cup of cream
- ½ teaspoon of white pepper
- 3 tablespoons of chicken stock
- 7 ounces of boneless chicken
- 1 teaspoon of black-eyed peas
- 3 water servings

COOKING DIRECTIONS:
1. Chop the chicken roughly and put it into the pressure cooker.
2. Set pressure cooker to "Sear/Sauté" mode.
3. Add water, black-eyed peas, and white pepper. Stir the amalgamation and close the lid.
4. Cook the dish on poultry mode for around 30 minutes.
5. Combine the miso paste and chicken stock in a mixing bowl.
6. Add liquid stevia and apple cider vinegar.
7. Whisk the amalgamation carefully to dissolve miso paste.
8. When the chicken is cooked, remove it from the cooker and let it rest briefly.
9. Transfer the chicken to your blender and add cream.
10. Blend the mixture for 5 minutes or until they smoothen.
11. Add the miso paste mixture and blend the combination for 1 minute.
12. Transfer the miso chicken dip into the serving bowls and enjoy.
Nutrition: calories 62, fat 2.5, fiber 0.3, carbs 1.6, protein 7.8

Egg Yolk Chicken Rissoles

Prep time: ten MINUTES | Cooking time: fifteen minutes | Servings: 8
Ingredients
- 4 egg yolks
- 1 tablespoon of turmeric
- 1 teaspoon of salt
- 1 teaspoon of dried parsley
- A tablespoon of cream
- 12 ounces of ground chicken

- 1 tablespoon of almond oil
- 1 tablespoon of sesame seeds
- 1 teaspoon of minced garlic

COOKING DIRECTIONS:
1. Combine turmeric with salt, dried parsley, and sesame seeds in a mixing bowl.
2. Whisk the egg yolks and combine with ground chicken.
3. Add the spice mixture to the garlic and combine.
4. Make small rissoles from the ground chicken mixture.
5. Set the pressure cooker to "Sauté" mode.
6. Pour the essential olive oil into the pressure cooker and add chicken rissoles.
7. Sauté the chicken rissoles for quarter-hour while stirring frequently.
8. When the dish is cooked, allow it to go rest briefly and serve.
Nutrition: calories 117, fat 8.4, fiber 0, carbs 1.42, protein 9

Chicken Dumplings

Prep time: ten MINUTES | Cooking time: 25 minutes | Servings: 7
Ingredients
- 1 teaspoon of salt
- ¼ teaspoon of Erythritol
- A cup of almond flour
- ¼ cup of whey
- 10 oz of boneless chicken
- 1 tablespoon of extra-virgin olive oil
- 1 cup of water
- 1 onion
- A teaspoon of ground black pepper
- 1 teaspoon of paprika

COOKING DIRECTIONS:
1. Combine salt with Erythritol and almond flour in a mixing bowl and stir.
2. Add whey and mix well.
3. Knead the dough. Mould a long log from the dough and subdivide it into small dumpling pieces.
4. Chop the chicken roughly and sprinkle it with ground black pepper.
5. Place the chopped chicken into pressure cooker.
6. Set the pressure cooker to "Pressure" mode.
7. Sprinkle the chopped chicken with olive oil. Add water.
8. Close the pressure cooker lid and cook for quarter-hour.
9. Peel the onion and slice it.
10. When the cooking time elapses, release the residual pressure and open the cooker lid.
11. Remove the cooked chicken and shred it.
12. Return the chicken in the pressure cooker.
13. Add the dumplings and sliced onion.

14. Sprinkle the dish with paprika.
15. Close the pressure cooker lid and cook on "Pressure" mode for ten minutes.
16. When the cooking time ends, remove your chicken dumplings from the pressure cooker. Allow it to rest and serve.

Nutrition: calories 133, fat 7.1, fiber 1, carbs 4.5, protein 13.1

Chicken Bone Broth with Fresh Herbs

Prep time: 10 minutes | Cooking time: 45 minutes | Servings: 13

Ingredients

- 8 ounces of drumsticks
- 8 ounces of chicken wings
- ½ cup of fresh thyme
- ¼ cup of fresh dill
- ¼ cup of fresh parsley
- A teaspoon of ground black pepper
- 10 cups of water
- 1 teaspoon of salt
- 2 tablespoons of fresh rosemary
- 1 garlic clove
- An onion

COOKING DIRECTIONS:
1. Wash the drumsticks and chicken wings thoroughly.
2. Chop them roughly and put them into the pressure cooker.
3. Set the cooker to "Sauté" mode.
4. Sprinkle the mixture with salt and ground black pepper and mix well using your hands.
5. Wash the thyme, dill, and parsley and chop them.
6. Put the chopped greens into the pressure cooker and add water followed by rosemary.
7. Peel the onion and garlic.
8. Add the vegetables in the chicken mixture.
9. Close the pressure cooker lid and cook the dish for 45 minutes.
10. When the cooking time ends, remove the greens from the pressure cooker.
11. Then, remove the chicken from the cooker.
12. Strain the chicken stock and serve it with cooked chicken. You can also store the remainder in the refrigerator for later servings.

Nutrition: calories 35, fat 0.7, fiber 1 carbs 3.06, protein 4

Cauliflower Rice and Chicken Soup

Prep time: ten MINUTES | Cooking time: 31 minutes | Servings: 8

Ingredients

- A cup of cauliflower rice
- 1 pound of chicken drumsticks
- 1 tablespoon of salt
- 1 teaspoon of curry

- 1 teaspoon of dill
- A teaspoon of ground celery root
- 1 garlic herb
- 3 tablespoons of sour cream
- 1 teaspoon of cilantro
- 6 portions of water
- ½ cup of tomato juice
- 1 teaspoon of oregano
- 1 tablespoon of butter
- 8 ounces of kale

COOKING DIRECTIONS:
1. Combine the salt with curry, dill, ground celery, and cilantro in a mixing bowl and stir.
2. Peel the garlic cloves and slice it.
3. Set the pressure cooker to "Pressure" mode.
4. Add butter into it and allow it melt.
5. Add the sliced garlic and cook the dish for thirty seconds.
6. Add the spice mixture and cook the dish for 10-seconds while stirring constantly.
7. Add the drumsticks, sour cream, water, oregano, tomato juice, and cauliflower rice.
8. Chop the kales and pour them over the soup. Stir well. Close the lid and cook the dish on "Sauté" mode for 30 minutes.
9. When the cooking time ends, open the pressure cooker lid allow the chicken soup rice to cool a little.
10. Ladle it into serving bowls and enjoy.

Nutrition: calories 140, fat 5.7, fiber 1, carbs 4.9, protein 17.1

Chicken Curry

Prep time: 10 minutes | Cooking time: 21 MINUTES | Servings: 7

Ingredients

- 1 teaspoon of garam Masala
- A tablespoon of curry paste
- 1 teaspoon of coriander
- A teaspoon of ground cumin
- 1 onion
- 3 garlic cloves
- A pound of chicken thighs
- 1 teaspoon of ginger
- 1 tablespoon of butter
- 1 cup tomatoes
- A teaspoon of salt
- 3 cups of chicken stock
- 3 tablespoons of chives
- ¼ cup of coconut milk

COOKING DIRECTIONS:
1. Combine the garam Masala with curry paste, and coriander in a mixing bowl.
2. Stir the mixture and add cumin, ginger, and salt. Stir again.
3. Set the pressure cooker to "Pressure" mode.

4.   Add the butter followed by the spice mixture.
5.   Cook the combination for 1 minute while stirring frequently.
6.   Peel the garlic and onion.
7.   Chop the vegetables and add them into the pressure cooker.
8.   Chop the tomatoes and add them into the cooker.
9.   Sprinkle the mix with chives and mix well.
10.   Add the chicken thighs, coconut milk, and chicken stock.
11.   Close the cooker lid and cook the dish on "Pressure" mode for around 20 minutes.
12.   When chicken curry is cooked, remove it from the cooker, shred it, and serve.
Nutrition: calories 160, fat 6.9, fiber 1, carbs 7.57, protein 17

Sour Cream Chicken Liver

Prep time: ten MINUTES | Cooking time: 18 minutes | Servings: 7
Ingredients
- A pound of chicken livers
- 1 onion
- 1 teaspoon of garlic powder
- 1 tablespoon of cilantro
- ¼ cup of dill
- 1 teaspoon of extra-virgin organic olive oil
- 1 cup of cream
- ¼ cup of cream cheese
- 1 teaspoon of salt
- 1 teaspoon of ground white pepper

COOKING DIRECTIONS:
1.   Chop the chicken livers roughly and put them in the pressure cooker.
2.   Set the cooker to "Sauté" mode.
3.   Sprinkle the liver with organic olive oil and sauté it for 3 minutes while stirring frequently.
4.   Combine the sour cream with cream cheese in a mixing bowl.
5.   Sprinkle the mixture with cilantro, garlic powder, salt, and ground black pepper and stir well.
6.   Pour the sour cream mixture into the cooker and stir well.
7.   Close its lid and cook the dish on "Sear/Sauté" mode for 15 minutes.
8.   When the chicken liver is cooked, allow it to rest briefly and serve.
Nutrition: calories 239, fat 18.2, fiber 0, carbs 8.22, protein 11

Tomato Ground Chicken Bowl

Prep time: 10 MINUTES | Cooking time: 30 mins | Servings: 5
Ingredients
- A cup of tomatoes

- ½ cup of cream
- 1 onion
- 1 teaspoon of chili powder
- 3 tablespoons of tomato paste
- 1 bell pepper
- 1 jalapeño pepper
- A tablespoon of essential organic olive oil
- 15 ounces of ground chicken

COOKING DIRECTIONS:
1.   Peel the onion and dice it.
2.   Combine the onion with chili powder, tomato paste, and cream. Stir well.
3.   Chop the jalapeño pepper and bell pepper.
4.   Wash the tomatoes and chop them.
5.   Set pressure cooker to "Sauté" mode.
6.   Place the prepared ingredients to the pressure cooker.
7.   Add ground chicken and mix.
8.   Close the load cooker lid and cook for 30 minutes.
9.   When the cooking time ends, remove the dish from the pressure cooker and stir well.
10.   Transfer it to serving bowls.
Nutrition: calories 220, fat 14.5, fiber 2, carbs 7.24, protein 17

Butter Chicken Cutlets

Prep time: quarter-hour | COOKING time: 25 MINUTES | Servings: 8
Ingredients
- 3 tablespoons of cream
- 5 tablespoons of butter
- 1 teaspoon of starch
- 2 tablespoons of chicken stock
- 9 ounces of ground chicken
- ½ cup of dill
- 1 teaspoon of ground black pepper
- 1 teaspoon of paprika
- 1 teaspoon of tomato paste
- 2 eggs
- 3 tablespoons of semolina

COOKING DIRECTIONS:
1.   Combine the cream with butter and whisk.
2.   Sprinkle the combination with starch, paprika, tomato paste, semolina, and ground black pepper. Stir well.
3.   Set the pressure cooker to "Sear/Sauté" mode.
4.   Chop the dill and add it in the pressure cooker. Add eggs and ground chicken and mix.
5.   Form medium-sized balls from the ground chicken mixture, and then flatten them.
6.   Pour the chicken stock into the cooker and add the flattened chicken balls.
7.   Close the load cooker lid and cook for 25 minutes.

8.   When the chicken cutlets are cooked, allow them to rest a bit before serving.
Nutrition: calories 172, fat 13.4, fiber 0, carbs 4.32, protein 9

Warm Chicken Salad

Prep time: ten minutes | Cooking time: 25 minutes | Servings: 7
Ingredients
- A pound of boneless chicken
- 1 cup of spinach
- 1 tablespoon of mayonnaise
- 1 teaspoon of freshly squeezed lemon juice
- 4 boiled eggs
- A tablespoon of chives
- ½ cup of dill

COOKING DIRECTIONS:
1.   Put the chicken in the trivet and place in the pressure cooker.
2.   Set the pressure cooker to "Steam" mode. Cook the dish for 25 minutes.
3.   Peel the eggs and chop them.
4.   Chop the spinach and dill.
5.   Transfer the chopped greens to a mixing bowl.
6.   Add chives and chopped eggs.
7.   Sprinkle the mixture with freshly squeezed lemon juice and mayonnaise.
8.   When the chicken salad is cooked, remove it from the strain cooker and let it rest briefly.
9.   Grind the cooked chicken and transfer it to the egg mixture.
10.   Mix until smooth and serve.
Nutrition: calories 154, fat 8, fiber 0, carbs 0.92, protein 19

Chicken Meatballs

Prep time: 10 MINUTES | Cooking time: ten MINUTES | Servings: 8
Ingredients
- 1 cup of cooked broccoli rice
- 10 ounces of ground chicken
- 1 carrot
- An egg
- 1 teaspoon of salt
- ½ teaspoon of cayenne
- A teaspoon of extra virgin olive oil
- 1 tablespoon of flax meal
- A teaspoon of sesame oil

COOKING DIRECTIONS:
1.   Peel the carrot and chop it roughly.
2.   Transfer the chopped carrot in the blender and puree it.
3.   Combine the blended carrot with ground chicken in a mixing bowl and stir.

4.   Sprinkle the meat mixture with broccoli rice, egg, cayenne pepper, salt, and flax meal and combine well.
5.   Set the strain cooker to "Sauté" mode.
6.   Pour the organic olive oil and sesame oil to the pressure cooker.
7.   Make meatballs from the meat mixture and put them into the pressure cooker.
8.   Cook the dish on sauté mode for ten minutes.
9.   Stir the meatballs until each side turns light brown.
10.   Remove the chicken meatball from the cooker and drain excess oils using a paper towel. Serve.
Nutrition: calories 96, fat 4.7, fiber 0.8, carbs 1.9, protein 11.5

Chicken Tart

Prep time: ten MINUTES | Cooking time: 35 minutes | Servings: 8
Ingredients
- A cup of almond flour
- 1 egg
- 7 ounces of butter
- 1 teaspoon of salt
- 10 ounces of ground chicken
- 1 teaspoon of essential olive oil
- 1 red onion
- A tablespoon of cream
- 1 teaspoon of ground pepper
- 4 ounces of celery stalk

COOKING DIRECTIONS:
1.   Combine almond flour with butter in a mixing bowl.
2.   Add egg and knead the dough.
3.   Place the dough inside a freezer.
4.   Peel the onion and grate it.
5.   Combine the onion with salt, ground chicken, cream, ground pepper.
6.   Chop the celery stalk and add it to the ground chicken mixture. Stir.
7.   Set the pressure cooker to "Pressure" mode.
8.   Pour the essential extra virgin olive oil into the cooker.
9.   Remove the dough from the freezer and half it.
10.   Put half dough into the pressure cooker.
11.   Add the remaining dough in the chicken mixture.
12.   Grate the remaining dough and add it to the chicken mixture.
13.   Close pressure cooker lid and cook for 35 minutes.
14.   When the chicken tart is cooked, allow it to rest briefly. Serve it while sliced.

Nutrition: calories 348, fat 31, fiber 2.1, carbs 5, protein 14.4

Raspberries Chicken Fillets

Prep time: ten MINUTES | Cooking time: 25 MINUTES | Servings: 8

Ingredients

- 8 ounces of raspberries
- A pound of boneless chicken white meat
- 1 teaspoon of sour cream
- ½ cup of cream
- 6 ounces of Parmesan
- 2 tablespoons of butter
- 1 teaspoon of cilantro
- A tablespoon of white pepper

COOKING DIRECTIONS:

1. Pound the chicken breasts using a meat mallet.
2. Set the pressure cooker to "Sauté" mode.
3. Add butter into the cooker and allow it melt.
4. Grate the Parmesan cheese.
5. Sprinkle the chicken with cilantro and white pepper.
6. Place the boneless chicken breasts in the pressure cooker and sprinkle them with raspberries.
7. Add sour cream and cream.
8. Sprinkle the contents with the grated cheese.
9. Close the pressure cooker lid and cook on "Sear/Sauté" mode for 25 minutes.
10. When the cooking time ends, the chicken fillets from the cooker and allow it to unwind. Serve while warm.

Nutrition: calories 226, fat 12.5, fiber 2.1, carbs 5, protein 23.8

Chicken Pies

Prep time: 15 minutes | Cooking time: 24 minutes | Servings: 8

Ingredients

- 8 ounces of puff pastry
- 4 ounces of ground chicken
- 1 teaspoon of paprika
- 1 teaspoon of ground ginger
- ½ teaspoon of cilantro
- An egg
- 1 tablespoon of butter
- 1 onion
- A teaspoon of essential extra virgin olive oil

COOKING DIRECTIONS:

1. Roll the puff pastry using a rolling pin.
2. Cut the rolled puff pastry into medium-sized squares.
3. Combine the ground chicken with cilantro, ground ginger, paprika, and egg in a mixing bowl and stir well. Peel the onion and dice it.

4. Add the diced onion on the meat mixture and stir well.
5. Place the chicken mixture in the pastry squares and wrap them to form pies.
6. Set the strain cooker to "Sear/Sauté" mode.
7. Smear the cooker's base with essential extra virgin olive oil and pour the chicken pies.
8. Close the pressure cooker lid and cook the dish for 24 minutes.
9. When the chicken pies are cooked, remove them from the pressure cooker. Serve while warm.

Nutrition: calories 217, fat 15.2, fiber 1, carbs 14.52, protein 6

Garlic Chicken Thighs

Prep time: quarter-HOUR | Cooking time: 40 MINUTES | Servings: 6

Ingredients

- A tablespoon of garlic powder
- ½ cup of garlic
- ½ lemon
- 1 teaspoon of onion powder
- 2 tablespoons of mayonnaise
- 1 teaspoon of ground white pepper
- A tablespoon of butter
- 1 teaspoon of cayenne
- A pound of chicken thighs
- 4 ounces of celery root

COOKING DIRECTIONS:

1. Peel the garlic cloves and mince them.
2. Combine the garlic with chicken thighs using your hands.
3. Sprinkle the meat with onion powder, ground white pepper, cayenne, and butter.
4. Peel celery root and grate it.
5. Chop the lemon into thin slices.
6. Add the celery root and lemon into the chicken mixture.
7. Add garlic powder and mayonnaise and stir well. Put it to the pressure cooker.
8. Set the cooker to "Sear/Sauté" mode.
9. Close the lid and cook the dish on poultry mode for 40 minutes.
10. When the cooking time ends, open the pressure cooker lid and transfer the chicken thighs to serving bowls.

Nutrition: calories 142, fat 5.7, fiber 1, carbs 5.7, protein 17

Duck Pot Pie

Prep time: 10 mins | Cooking time: 50 minutes | Servings: 8

Ingredients

- 7 ounces of keto dough
- 1 teaspoon of onion powder
- A pound of duck breast
- ½ teaspoon of anise

- A cup of green beans
- 1 cup of cream
- An egg
- 1 teaspoon of salt

COOKING DIRECTIONS:

1. Place the duck breast on the trivet and fix it on the pressure cooker.
2. Set the cooker to "Steam" mode.
3. Steam the duck for 25 minutes.
4. When the cooking time ends, remove the duck pot pie from the cooker and shred it.
5. Place the shredded duck in the mixing bowl.
6. Add onion powder, anise, cream, salt, and green beans and stir well.
7. Beat the egg.
8. Roll the keto dough and subdivide it into halves.
9. Put one portion in the pressure cooker to make a pie crust.
10. Fit the fillings in the pie crust and cover it with the second part of the dough.
11. Spread the pie using whisked egg and close the lid.
12. Cook the dish on "Pressure" mode for 25 minutes.
13. When the cooking time ends, allow the duck pie to rest briefly. You can slice it when serving.

Nutrition: calories 194, fat 5.6, fiber 3.8, carbs 7.8, protein 28

Duck Patties

Prep time: 10 MINUTES | Cooking time: quarter-hour | Servings: 6

Ingredients

- A tablespoon of mustard
- 1 teaspoon of ground black pepper
- 9 ounces of ground duck
- ½ cup of parsley
- A teaspoon of salt
- 1 tablespoon of extra virgin olive oil
- A teaspoon of oregano
- 1 teaspoon of red pepper
- ½ teaspoon of cayenne pepper
- A tablespoon of flax meal

COOKING DIRECTIONS:

1. Combine mustard with ground black pepper, ground duck, salt, oregano, red pepper, cayenne, and flax meal in a mixing bowl and stir well.
2. Wash parsley and chop it.
3. Sprinkle the duck mixture with chopped parsley and stir well.
4. Mould medium-sized patties from the duck mixture.
5. Set the pressure cooker to "Sauté" mode.
6. Pour extra virgin olive oil into the pressure cooker.

7. Add duck patties and cook the dish on sauté mode for quarter-hour or until they brown. Serve immediately.

Nutrition: calories 106, fat 6.9, fiber 1.3 carbs 3.3, protein 8.6

Asian-style Chicken Strips

Prep time: ten mins | Cooking time: a half-hour | Servings: 7

Ingredients

- ½ cup of soy sauce
- 1 tablespoon of liquid stevia
- 1 tablespoon of sesame seeds
- ½ cup of chicken stock
- 1 tablespoon of oregano
- 1 teaspoon of cumin
- 1 pound of boneless chicken
- 1 teaspoon of butter

COOKING DIRECTIONS:

1. Cut the chicken into the strips and transfer them to a mixing bowl.
2. Combine soy sauce with the liquid stevia in another mixing bowl. Stir to mix.
3. Add sesame seeds, chicken stock, oregano, cumin, and butter.
4. Whisk the amalgamation and blend it with the chicken strips.
5. Let the chicken strips marinate for 10 minutes.
6. Set the pressure cooker to "Pressure" mode.
7. Transfer the chicken strips mixture to the cooker and close the lid. Cook for thirty minutes.
8. When the chicken strip dish is cooked, release extra pressure and open the cooker's lid.
9. Transfer the chicken strips and soy sauce mixture to serving bowls.

Nutrition: calories 149, fat 6.2, fiber 0.6, carbs 2.3, protein 20.3

Indian Chicken

Prep time: 10 minutes | Cooking time: half an hour | Servings: 8

Ingredients

- A tablespoon of curry paste
- A tablespoon of lemongrass paste
- ½ cup of fresh thyme
- 2 pounds of chicken breasts
- 1 cup of almond milk
- ½ cup of cream
- 1 teaspoon of salt
- A teaspoon of cilantro
- 1 tablespoon of organic-extra virgin olive oil

COOKING DIRECTIONS:

1. Wash the thyme and chop it.
2. Combine the almond milk with curry paste and lemongrass paste.

3. Stir the mixture until they dissolve well.
4. Add cilantro, salt, and cream.
5. Add the chopped thyme and chicken breasts.
6. Let the chicken sit for ten minutes.
7. Set the pressure cooker to "Sear/Sauté" mode.
8. Transfer the chicken mixture into the cooker and close the lid.
9. Cook the chicken for half an hour.
10. When the cooking time ends, remove the Indian chicken from the cooker and separate it from the cream mixture. Slice and serve.
Nutrition: calories 261, fat 15.6, fiber 1, carbs 4.77, protein 25

Crunchy Oregano Drumsticks
Prep time: ten mins | Cooking time: 11 minutes | Servings: 8
Ingredients
- 1 cup of pork rind
- A tablespoon of salt
- 1 tablespoon of paprika
- 1 teaspoon of ground black pepper
- 1 teaspoon of cayenne pepper
- 1 teaspoon of oregano
- ½ cup of essential olive oil
- 1 tablespoon of minced garlic
- 1 pound of chicken drumsticks
- ½ cup of cream
- 1 cup of cream cheese

COOKING DIRECTIONS:
1. Combine the pork rind with salt, paprika, ground black pepper, red pepper cayenne, oregano, and minced garlic in a mixing bowl and stir well.
2. Combine cream with the cream cheese in a separate bowl.
3. Whisk it until smooth.
4. Pour the organic olive oil into pressure cooker and preheat on "Sauté" mode for 3 minutes.
5. Dip the drumsticks in the cream cheese mixture.
6. Dip the mixture again in the pork rind mixture.
7. Put the chicken into the pressure cooker and cook for 8 minutes or until it turns golden brown.
8. When the drumsticks are cooked, transfer them to a bowl.
9. Remember to dry it with paper towel to remove excess oil.
Nutrition: calories 421, fat 33.2, fiber 0.6, carbs 2.5, protein 29.4

Chicken Piccata
Prep time: 10 minutes | Cooking time: 17 minutes | Servings: 8
Ingredients

- 2 tablespoons of capers
- 1 ½ pound of boneless chicken
- 1 teaspoon of ground black pepper
- 3 tablespoons of organic extra-virgin olive oil
- 3 tablespoons of butter
- 1 teaspoon of salt
- ½ cup of fresh lemon juice
- 1 cup of chicken stock
- ½ cup of fresh parsley
- 1 teaspoon of oregano
- A tablespoon of coconut flour
- A teaspoon of paprika

COOKING DIRECTIONS:
1. Cut the chicken into medium-sized pieces.
2. Sprinkle the chicken with the ground black pepper, salt, oregano, and paprika and stir well.
3. Set the pressure cooker to "Sauté" mode.
4. Smear the pressure cooker with extra virgin olive oil and butter.
5. Stir the ingredients well and sauté for 1 minute.
6. Add the chicken pieces in the pressure cooker, and cook them for 6 minutes while stirring frequently.
7. Remove the chicken from the cooker.
8. Add capers, freshly squeezed lemon juice, chicken stock, and coconut flour and stir well. Cook the mixture for 1 minute.
9. Add the cooked chicken and close the cooker's lid.
10. Cook for ten minutes on "Pressure" mode.
11. When the cooking time ends, release the pressure from the cooker and open the lid.
12. Serve chicken piccata immediately.
Nutrition: calories 257, fat 16.3, fiber 0.8, carbs 1.6, protein 25.2

Stuffed Tomatoes with Ground Chicken
Prep time: 10 MINUTES | Cooking time: ten mins | Servings: 6
Ingredients
- 5 big tomatoes
- 10 ounces of ground chicken
- 1 teaspoon of ground black pepper
- 1 tablespoon of sour cream
- 6 ounces of Parmesan cheese
- 1 onion
- A tablespoon of minced garlic
- 5 tablespoons of chicken stock
- 1 teaspoon of red pepper cayenne

COOKING DIRECTIONS:
1. Use a paring knife or apple corer to remove the tomato fresh.

2.   Combine the floor chicken, ground black pepper, sour cream, minced garlic, and red pepper cayenne in a mixing bowl.
3.   Peel the onion and grate it.
4.   Add the onion to the ground chicken mixture and stir well.
5.   Fill the tomatoes with ground chicken mixture.
6.   Grate Parmesan cheese and sprinkle the stuffed tomatoes it.

7.   Set the pressure cooker to "Pressure" mode. Pour the chicken stock to the pressure cooker and add the stuffed tomatoes. Close the pressure cooker lid and cook for 20 minutes.
8.   When the cooking time ends, let the stuffed tomato dish rest briefly. Serve.
Nutrition: calories 222, fat 12.4, fiber 1, carbs 10.55, protein 18

LUNCH RECIPES

Chicken Salad in Jar

Prep time: ten mins |Cooking time: quarter-hour |Servings: 4
Ingredients:

- 1-pound of boneless and skinless chicken breast
- 1 teaspoon of ground black pepper
- ½ teaspoon of paprika
- ½ teaspoon of ground coriander
- 1 tablespoon of butter
- 1 cup of chopped spinach
- 1 chopped cucumber
- 1 teaspoon of chili flakes
- 1 teaspoon of freshly squeezed lemon juice
- 1 teaspoon of avocado oil
- 1 cup of lettuce
- 1 cup of water

COOKING DIRECTIONS:

1. Rub the chicken with ground black pepper, paprika, and ground coriander.
2. Then place the treated chicken in the cooker.
3. Add water and close the lid. Cook the chicken on high-pressure mode for quarter-hour.
4. Make a quick pressure release and take out the chicken from the cooker. Let it rest.
5. Meanwhile, combine lettuce with spinach in a bowl.
6. Sprinkle the greens with chili flakes, lemon juice, and avocado oil.
7. Add cucumber and mix.
8. Shred the chicken breast and spread it with butter.
9. Fill the serving jars with the shredded chicken and add the green salad mixture.
10. You can store the remaining chicken meat and salad in the refrigerator.

NUTRITION: CALORIES 174, FAT 6.1, FIBER 1, CARBS 4, PROTEIN 25

Brie Cheese in Phyllo

Prep time: 10 mins |Cooking time: ten mins |Servings: 8
Ingredients:

- 10 oz of round brie cheese
- 10 sheets of phyllo dough
- 1 tablespoon of butter
- 1 teaspoon of Erythritol

COOKING DIRECTIONS:

1. Place Brie cheese on the phyllo pastry and sprinkle it with Erythritol.
2. Add butter and wrap the cheese carefully.
3. Place the brie cheese combination on a trivet.

4. Fit the trivet in the cooker and close the mid-air fryer lid.
5. Cook the meal for ten minutes.
6. Allow it to chill for 3-5 minutes. Serve in pieces.

Nutrition: calories 204, fat 11.1, fiber 0.6, carbs 7, protein 7.4

Cheesy Pulled Beef

Prep time: 20 min |Cooking time: half an hour |Servings: 4
Ingredients:

- 12 oz of boneless beef
- 1 cup of water
- ½ cup of cream
- 1 teaspoon of butter
- 1 teaspoon of salt
- 4 oz of grated Parmesan
- 1 teaspoon of tomato paste
- 1 teaspoon of chili flakes
- 1 teaspoon of turmeric
- 1 teaspoon of dried cilantro

COOKING DIRECTIONS:

1. Pour water and cream in the cooker.
2. Add beef and salt.
3. Close the lid and cook the meal on high-pressure mode for around 30 minutes.
4. Allow the pressure to release naturally for 10 minutes.
5. Open the lid and shred the meat using a fork.
6. Add butter, tomato paste, chili flakes, turmeric, and dried cilantro. Mix them.
7. Sprinkle the pulled beef with grated cheese and stir gently.
8. Let the cheese melt. Transfer the cooked pulled beef to bowls and serve.

Nutrition: calories 280, fat 14.1, fiber 0.2, carbs 2.6, protein 35.3

Portobello Cheese Sandwich

Prep time: 10 minutes |Cooking time: 6 minutes |Servings: 2
Ingredients:

- 2 Portobello of mushroom hats
- 3 oz of sliced cheddar cheese
- 1 tablespoon of chopped cilantro(fresh)
- ½ teaspoon of ground black pepper
- 2 teaspoons of butter
- 2 bacon slices

COOKING DIRECTIONS:

1. Take off the mushroom fresh.
2. Sprinkle the vegetables with chopped cilantro and ground black pepper.

3. Fill the mushroom hats with sliced bacon and cheese.
4. Add butter to the combination.
5. Place the mushrooms in the Ninja cooker and close the fryer lid.
6. Cook the mushroom hats for 6 minutes.
7. When the meal is cooked, transfer it to bowls and serve immediately.

Nutrition: calories 307, fat 24.9, fiber 1.2, carbs 3.9, protein 17.7

Pasta Bolognese

Prep time: ten minutes |Cooking time: 14 minutes |Servings: 6

Ingredients:

- 8 ounces of black bean pasta
- 1 teaspoon of organic essential olive oil
- 2 white onions
- 1 cup of ground beef
- 3 tablespoons of chives
- 1 teaspoon of salt
- 4 cups of chicken stock
- ½ cup of tomato sauce
- 2 tablespoons of soy sauce
- 1 teaspoon of turmeric
- 1 teaspoon of cilantro
- ½ tablespoon of paprika

COOKING DIRECTIONS:

1. Peel the onions and slice it.
2. Place the sliced onions in the pressure cooker.
3. Add ground beef, salt, turmeric, cilantro, and paprika.
4. Stir the mixture and sauté it for 4 minutes. Stir again.
5. Remove the mixture from the cooker and add soy sauce, tomato sauce, and chives.
6. Saute them for 3 minutes and return them to the cooker.
7. Add the black bean paste, chicken stock, and ground beef mixture .Close the lid.
8. Cook the dish on "Pressure" mode for 7 minutes.
9. When the dish is cooked, release the built-in pressure and open the lid.
10. Mix it and serve.

Nutrition: calories 99, fat 2.1, fiber 5.5, carbs 11.7, protein 10

Warm Chicken Salad

Prep time: a quarter-hour |Cooking time: thirty minutes |Servings: 6

Ingredients:

- 5 ounces of romaine lettuce
- 3 medium tomatoes
- 2 cucumber
- 1 tablespoon of organic essential olive oil
- 1 teaspoon of red pepper cayenne
- 1 pound of chicken
- 1 teaspoon of basil
- 1 tablespoon of apple cider vinegar
- 1 teaspoon of ground black pepper
- 3 ounces of black olives
- 1 teaspoon of salt
- ½ lemon

COOKING DIRECTIONS:

1. Sprinkle the chicken meat with basil, salt, apple cider vinegar treatment, and cayenne, and stir it carefully.
2. Transfer the seasoned meat to the pressure cooker and close the lid.
3. Set the pressure cooker mode to "Sear/Sauté," and cook for thirty minutes.
4. Meanwhile, chop the lettuce, cucumbers, and tomatoes. Also, slice the olives.
5. Combine the vegetables in a mixing bowl.
6. Sprinkle the dish with essential olive oil.
7. Squeeze in the fresh lemon juice.
8. When the chicken is cooked, remove it from the cooker and allow it to rest briefly.
9. Slice the chicken into medium pieces.
10. Add the sliced meat in the mixing bowl.
11. Mix the salad with wooden spoons.

Nutrition: calories 141, fat 8.1, fiber 2, carbs 8.82, protein 9

Spaghetti Squash Bolognese

Prep time: 10 minutes |Cooking time: 10 minutes|Servings: 6

Ingredients:

- 15 ounces of spaghetti squash
- 2 servings of water
- 1 cup of ground beef
- 1 teaspoon of salt
- 1 tablespoon of paprika
- 1 teaspoon of sour cream
- 1/2 cup of tomato paste
- 1 teaspoon of thyme

COOKING DIRECTIONS:

1. Combine the ground beef with salt, paprika, sour cream, tomato paste, and thyme in a mixing bowl.
2. Blend the amalgamation well until smooth and pour them into the pressure cooker.
3. Set pressure cooker mode to "Sauté" mode and cook for around 10 minutes while stirring frequently.
4. Open the cooker's lid and transfer the cooked dish in a bowl.
5. Pour water into the pressure cooker.
6. Cut the spaghetti squash into four parts and dip it in the cooker.

7.   Close pressure cooker lid and cook the spaghetti squash on pressure mode for ten minutes.
8.   Release the cooker's pressure and open its lid.
9.   Transfer the cooked spaghetti squash in the bowl containing the ground meat using two forks.
10.   Mix them well and serve while warm.
Nutrition: calories 109, fat 5.5, fiber 2, carbs 7.18, protein 9

Chicken Soup

Prep time: ten mins |Cooking time: 45 minutes |Servings: 8
Ingredients:
- 2 white onions
- 1 teaspoon of salt
- 2 tablespoons of sour cream
- 5 cups of chicken stock
- ½ cup of cream
- 1 teaspoon of paprika
- 2 sweet bell pepper
- 1 pound of boneless thighs
- 4 carrots

COOKING DIRECTIONS:
1.   Peel the onion and chop it.
2.   Peel the carrot and grate it.
3.   Pour the cream followed by chicken stock in a pressure cooker.
4.   Add the boneless thighs and season with salt.
5.   Close the cooker's lid and cook the mixture on "Sear/Sauté" mode for 25 minutes.
6.   Add the sour cream, chopped onion, and carrot.
7.   Detach the seeds from the sweet peppers. Slice them.
8.   Add the sliced peppers in the pressure cooker mixture and close the lid.
9.   Cook for 25 minutes.
10.   When the soup is cooked, remove it from the pressure cooker and sprinkle it with paprika. Serve immediately.
Nutrition: calories 111, fat 3.7, fiber 4, carbs 15.98, protein 6

Garlic Cream Soup

Prep time: ten mins |Cooking time: 3 hours |Servings: 10
Ingredients:
- 1 pound of garlic cloves
- 1 teaspoon of salt
- 1 cup of cream
- ½ cup of almond milk
- 5 servings of water
- 1 teaspoon of basil
- 1 teaspoon of oregano
- ½ teaspoon of fresh lemon juice
- 6 oz of turnip
- 1 teaspoon of ground black pepper
- 1 tablespoon of butter

COOKING DIRECTIONS:
1.   Peel the garlic cloves and slice them.
2.   Combine cream with almond milk and in a mixing bowl.
3.   Add basil, oregano, freshly squeezed lemon juice, and ground black pepper.
4.   Peel the turnips and chop them.
5.   Add the chopped turnips to the cream mixture.
6.   Put the cream mixture in a pressure cooker.
7.   Add the sliced garlic and butter.
8.   Close the pressure cooker lid having set it to "Slow Cook" mode.
9.   Cook the soup for 3 hours or until all the soup ingredient softens.
10.   Remove your soup from the strain cooker and blend it with a blender until smooth.
11.   Ladle the soup to serving bowls and enjoy.
Nutrition: calories 101, fat 2.9, fiber 1.4, carbs 17.2, protein 3.3

Chicken and yogurt Salad

Prep time: fifteen minutes |Cooking time: 35 minutes |Servings: 6
Ingredients:
- 1 cup of walnuts
- A cup of cranberries
- 1 pound of chicken
- 1 cup of plain yogurt
- 1 teaspoon of salt
- 1 teaspoon of cilantro
- ½ cup of fresh dill
- 2 glasses of water

COOKING DIRECTIONS:
1.   Sprinkle the chicken with salt and put it in the pressure cooker.
2.   Add water and close the lid.
3.   Set the strain cooker mode to "Sear/Sauté" mode and cook for around 35 minutes.
4.   Crush walnuts and chop the cranberries.
5.   Pour the ingredient in a large mixing bowl.
6.   Chop the fresh dill and mix it with the plain yogurt.
7.   Add cilantro and stir.
8.   When the chicken is cooked, remove it from the cooker and shred.
9.   Add the shredded chicken to the salad mixture.
10.   Pour the yogurt mixture over the cooked chicken. Serve the chicken salad immediately.
Nutrition: calories 287, fat 15.3 fiber 2.3, carbs 8, protein 30

Spicy Tomato Soup

Prep time: 15 minutes |Cooking time: 35 minutes |Servings: 6
Ingredients:
- 1 pound of tomatoes
- 4 cups of beef stock
- 1 teaspoon of thyme
- 1 teaspoon of coriander
- 1 teaspoon of cilantro
- 1 tablespoon of ground black pepper
- ½ tablespoon of red chili flakes
- 1 teaspoon of turmeric
- 2 tablespoons of sour cream
- 5 ounces of Parmesan cheese
- 1 teaspoon of salt
- 1 jalapeno pepper
- 2 yellow onions
- 4 ounces of celery stalks
- 1 bay leaf
- ½ cup of tomato paste

COOKING DIRECTIONS:
1. Wash tomatoes, peel their skin, and chop.
2. Combine the thyme with coriander, cilantro, ground black pepper, chili flakes, turmeric, and salt in a mixing bowl.
3. Stir the mixture well.
4. Place the beef stock and chopped tomatoes in the pressure cooker.
5. Add the spiced mixture.
6. Remove the seeds from the jalapeno pepper and add it to the tomato mixture.
7. Add bay leaf and close the lid.
8. Cook the dish on "Sauté" mode for quarter-hour.
9. Peel the onions together with the celery stalks.
10. Add the vegetables to the tomato mixture followed by the sour cream.
11. Close the lid and cook for 20 minutes.
12. Grate the Parmesan cheese.
13. When the tomato soup is cooked, ladle it to the serving bowls.
14. Sprinkle it with grated cheese and serve it.

Nutrition: calories 144, fat 6.6, fiber 3.1, carbs 11.9, protein 11.6

Cheese Soup

Prep time: quarter-hour |Cooking time: 40 minutes |Servings: 8
Ingredients:
- 8 ounces of broccoli
- ½ cup of parsley
- 10 ounces of beef brisket
- 1 teaspoon of salt
- 1 tablespoon of sour cream
- 7 portions of water
- 1 carrot
- 1 cup of green beans
- 10 ounces of cheddar cheese
- 1 teaspoon of cilantro
- 1 teaspoon of ground black pepper
- ¼ cup of coriander leaves
- 1 teaspoon of fresh lemon juice

COOKING DIRECTIONS:
1. Place broccoli, beef brisket, green beans, and salt in a pressure cooker.
2. Peel the carrot and chop it.
3. Add chopped carrot and water to the cooker's content.
4. Close the lid and cook the dish on "Pressure" mode for half an hour.
5. Remove the cooker's pressure and open its lid. Remove the beef brisket and set aside. Blend them until they smoothen.
6. Return the pressure pan on the cooker again.
7. Pour in sour cream, cilantro, ground black pepper, and freshly squeezed lemon juice.
8. Chop the parsley and coriander leaves. Add them to the soup.
9. Grate cheddar cheese and pour it in the soup. Cook for 10 minutes.
10. Remember, the cheese should have melted at the end of the cooking time.
11. Mix the soup until you obtain a smooth texture.
12. Remove it from the pressure cooker and add beef brisket.
13. Ladle the cheese soup to bowls and enjoy.

Nutrition: calories 152, fat 8.9, fiber 2, carbs 7.15, protein 11

Kale Rolls

Prep time: ten mins |Cooking time: 25 minutes |Servings: 8
Ingredients:
- 1 cup of cauliflower rice(cooked)
- 1 tablespoon of curry
- 1 teaspoon of salt
- ½ teaspoon of tomato paste
- ¼ cup of cream
- A cup of chicken stock
- 1 teaspoon of oregano
- A pound of kale
- 1 teaspoon of organic extra virgin olive oil
- 1 yellow onion
- 3 tablespoons of chives
- 1 tablespoon of paprika
- ½ tablespoon of ground black pepper
- 1 teaspoon of garlic powder
- 1 egg
- 1 cup of beef stock

COOKING DIRECTIONS:

1. Combine the cooked cauliflower rice with curry in a mixing bowl.
2. Beat an egg in the mixture.
3. Peel the yellow onion and chop it.
4. Chop the chives and add the vegetables in the bowl.
5. Sprinkle the dish with salt, oregano, paprika, ground black pepper, and garlic powder.
6. Blend the ingredients until they smoothen using your hands.
7. Separate the kale leaves.
8. Put the cauliflower rice mixture at the middle of each kale leaf and roll them.
9. Combine the tomato paste with cream, chicken stock, extra virgin organic olive oil, and beef in a bowl and mix.
10. Transfer the kale rolls to the pressure cooker.
11. Add the tomato paste mixture and close the lid.
12. Set its mode to "Sauté," and cook for 25 minutes.
13. When the cooking time ends, open the cooker's lid and allow your kale rolls to rest.
14. Transfer the kale rolls to the serving plates. Sprinkle it with tomato sauce and serve.
Nutrition: calories 66, fat 2, fiber 2.3, carbs 9.9, protein 3.7

Spinach Casserole

Prep time: 15 minutes |Cooking time: 25 minutes |Servings: 6
Ingredients:
- 2 cups of spinach
- 1 cup of cream
- 3 tablespoons of coconut flour
- 1 teaspoon of salt
- 8 ounces of Parmesan cheese
- 2 onions
- 1 teaspoon of oregano
- ½ teaspoon of red chili flakes
- 1 cup of green peas

COOKING DIRECTIONS:
1. Wash the spinach and chop into tiny strands.
2. Transfer the chopped spinach to a mixing bowl.
3. Peel the onions and dice them.
4. Combine salt with coconut flour and chili flakes in a separate bowl.
5. Add oregano and cream. Whisk them to smoothen.
6. Grate the Parmesan cheese and subdivide it into three.
7. Put the peas in a pressure cooker and sprinkle it with a portion of grated cheese to form a thin layer.

8. Add the diced onion and pour cheese again.
9. Add the chopped spinach and the remaining cheese.
10. Pour the cream mixture and close the lid.
11. Set pressure cooker mode to "Steam" and cook for 25 minutes.
12. When the cooking time ends, allow it to cool before serving.
Nutrition: calories 200, fat 11, fiber 3.6, carbs 12, protein 15

Stuffed Meatloaf

Prep time: a quarter-hour |Cooking time: half an hour |Servings: 8
Ingredients:
- 2 cups of ground beef
- 3 eggs (boiled and peeled)
- 1 tablespoon of flax meal
- 1 teaspoon of salt
- 1 teaspoon of chili flakes
- 1 teaspoon of ground coriander
- 1 tablespoon of butter
- 1 cup of water (for smoking)
- Loaf mold

COOKING DIRECTIONS:
1. Put the ground beef in the mixing bowl.
2. Add flax meal and salt.
3. Add chili flakes and ground coriander.
4. Mix up the ground beef mixture thoroughly.
5. Pour water in the Ninja Pressure cooker and insert trivet.
6. Take the loaf mold and spread it with butter generously.
7. Place the ground beef mixture on the loaf mold and flatten.
8. Place the boiled eggs on the beef mixture.
9. Flatten the beef mixture again to cover the eggs completely.
10. Cover the mold a foil and secure all its perimeters.
11. Place it across the trivet and close the lid.
12. Cook the contents on high-pressure mode for half an hour.
13. Then, let the cooker's pressure to release naturally for 10 minutes.
14. Allow the stuffed meatloaf to cool and serve it sliced.
Nutrition: calories 105, fat 7.5, fiber 0.3, carbs 0.4, protein 8.8

Tender Schnitzel

Prep time: 10 mins |Cooking time: 16 minutes |Servings: 6
Ingredients:
- 1 pound of pork chops
- 1 teaspoon of salt
- 1 teaspoon of turmeric

- 2 eggs
- ¼ cup of coconut milk
- 1 teaspoon of cilantro
- ½ cup of coconut flour
- 1 teaspoon of freshly squeezed lemon juice
- 1 teaspoon of ground black pepper

COOKING DIRECTIONS:
1. Hammer the pork chops carefully.
2. Combine salt with turmeric, cilantro, and ground black pepper and stir.
3. Rub the pork chops with the spice mixture.
4. Spray the meat with the lemon juice and leave it for 10 minutes to marinate.
5. Meanwhile, beat the eggs in a mixing bowl. Stir well. And add milk.
6. Dip the marinated pork chops in the egg mixture.
7. Coat them by dipping the chops in the coconut floor.
8. Add a little organic olive oil to the pressure cooker and preheat it on "Sauté" mode.
9. Pour the coated pork chops to cooker and cook the schnitzels for 8 minutes.
10. Release the cooker's pressure and transfer your dish on a flatter. Serve while warm.

Nutrition: calories 258, fat 25.2, fiber 6.4, carbs 10.2, protein 22.2

Stuffed Chicken Caprese

Prep time: quarter-hour |Cooking time: 30 minutes |Servings: 6
Ingredients:
- 13 oz of chicken (skinless and boneless)
- 1 sliced tomato
- ½ cup of fresh basil
- 5 oz of sliced Mozzarella
- ½ teaspoon of salt
- 1 tablespoon of butter
- 1 teaspoon of paprika
- 1 tablespoon of extra-virgin essential olive oil
- 1 teaspoon of chili flakes
- ½ teaspoon of turmeric
- 1 cup of water (for cooking)

COOKING DIRECTIONS:
1. Beat the chicken meat gently using the graceful side of a kitchen hammer.
2. Make a longitudinal cut on the breast to make a pocket.
3. Chop the fresh basil and rub the chicken with salt, paprika, chili flakes, and turmeric.
4. Grow it with sliced Mozzarella, butter, and chopped fresh basil.
5. Brush the white meat with extra-virgin olive oil and wrap it in the foil.

6. Pour water in a Ninja cooker and insert a trivet.
7. Place the chicken on the trivet and close the lid.
8. Cook the meal on high-pressure mode for 30 minutes.
9. After this, use quick pressure release and discard the foil from your chicken.
10. Slice it and serve. Enjoy.

Nutrition: calories 182, fat 11.2, fiber 0.3, carbs 1.3, protein 18.5

Beef Lasagna

Prep time: a quarter-hour |Cooking time: 35 minutes |Servings: 6
Ingredients:
- 1 cup of ground beef
- 1 cup of tomato juice
- 9 ounces of zucchini(sliced)
- 1 tablespoon of butter
- 1 teaspoon of sour cream
- ½ cup of half and half
- 10 ounces of Parmesan cheese
- ½ cup of cream cheese
- 1 white onion
- A teaspoon of ground black pepper
- 1 teaspoon of cilantro
- ½ teaspoon of salt
- ½ cup of beef stock

COOKING DIRECTIONS:
1. Combine the tomato juice with sour cream, half and half, beef stock and salt together in a mixing bowl. Stir the ingredients.
2. Grate the Parmesan cheese. Peel and slice the onion.
3. Combine the beef with ground black pepper and cilantro. Stir the amalgamation.
4. Add butter in the pressure cooker add the ground beef mixture. Cook the mixture on "Sauté" mode for around 10 minutes while stirring frequently.
5. Remove beef from the pressure cooker.
6. Place the sliced zucchini in the cooker followed by the tomato juice mixture.
7. Add a layer of sliced onion, grated cheese, and the ground beef mixture.
8. Close the lid and cook on manual mode for 25 minutes.
9. When your beef lasagna is cooked, allow it to cool and serve.

Note: It's advisable to subdivide the ingredients well after preparation.
Nutrition: calories 330, fat 24.1, fiber 1.1, carbs 8.2, protein 22.9

Pork Taco

Prep time: ten mins |Cooking time: 35 minutes |Servings: 6

Ingredients:

- 1 pound of ground pork
- ½ cup of spinach
- ½ cup of cilantro
- 1 tablespoon of salt
- 1 teaspoon of oregano
- 1 teaspoon of cumin
- ½ teaspoon of ground coriander
- 1 teaspoon of ground black pepper
- 1 teaspoon of cayenne
- 1 tablespoon of onion powder
- 2 cups of chicken stock
- 1 tablespoon of tomato paste
- 1 tablespoon of olive oil

COOKING DIRECTIONS:

1. Wash the spinach and cilantro and chop them. Mix the ingredients on a wide bowl.
2. Add ground pork followed by salt, oregano, and cumin. Blend the resultant mixture.
3. Transfer the amalgamation to the pressure cooker and sprinkle it with the essential organic olive oil.
4. Sauté it for 10 minutes while stirring frequently.
5. Add the ground black pepper, onion powder, and tomato paste.
6. Add chicken stock and blend well.
7. Pour the mixture in the pressure cooker and cook on "Pressure" mode for 25 minutes.
8. When the pork taco is cooked, allow it to relax briefly and serve with tortillas.

Nutrition: calories 286, fat 19.1, fiber 1, carbs 5.53, protein 22

Pressure Cooker Cottage Cheese

Prep time: 5 minutes |Cooking time: 5 minutes |Servings: 5

Ingredients:

- 6 cups of almond milk
- ¼ cup of apple cider vinegar
- 1 teaspoon of salt
- ½ cup of sour cream
- 3 tablespoons of Erythritol
- ½ cup of almonds
- Cheese

COOKING DIRECTIONS:

1. Pour the almond milk in a pressure cooker.
2. Set the cooker to "Slow Cook" mode and cook it with the lid open until it boils.
3. Whisk the almond milk and add salt followed by vinegar.
4. Close the lid and unplug the pressure cooker.
5. Leave the almond milk for 25 minutes.

6. Cover a sieve with cheesecloth and squeeze cheese out (to reduce whey protein.)
7. Transfer the cheese into a blender and blend it.
8. Add Erythritol and sour cream.
9. Blend the mixture for 3 minutes.
10. Transfer the cottage cheese on serving bowls and sprinkle it with almonds. Serve.

Nutrition: calories 120, fat 10, fiber 0.8, carbs 2.1, protein 3

Lunch Wraps

Prep time: 10 minutes |Cooking time: 8 minutes |Servings: 5

Ingredients:

- 5 almond flour tortillas
- 8 ounces of ham
- ½ cup of lettuce
- ¼ cup of tomato paste
- 6 ounces of tomatoes
- 1 red onion
- 1 teaspoon of salt
- 1 teaspoon of ground black pepper
- 1 teaspoon of oregano
- 3 tablespoons of fresh lemon juice

COOKING DIRECTIONS:

1. Chop the ham and lettuce.
2. Slice the tomatoes and onions.
3. Combine salt with ground black pepper and oregano in a bowl and mix.
4. Spread the tortillas with tomato paste.
5. Add lettuce, ham, sliced onions, and tomatoes.
6. Add the spice mixture and fresh lemon juice.
7. Wrap the tortillas and place them in a pressure cooker.
8. Set it to manual mode and cook for around 8 minutes.
9. When the cooking time ends, remove your lunch wrap from the cooker.
10. Unwrap the tortillas and serve while hot.

Nutrition: calories 195, fat 9, fiber 4.7, carbs 13.2, protein 6

Mushroom and Bacon Bowl

Prep time: ten mins |Cooking time: couple of hours |Servings: 3

Ingredients:

- 1 ½ cup of white mushrooms (chopped)
- 5 oz of bacon(chopped)
- 2 tablespoons of butter
- 1 white onion (diced)
- 1 teaspoon of salt
- 1 teaspoon of ground black pepper
- ½ cup of cream
- 1 teaspoon of oregano

- ¾ teaspoon of cayenne pepper

COOKING DIRECTIONS:

1. Place butter and cream in a Ninja cooker.
2. Add diced onion, mushrooms, chopped bacon, and salt.
3. Sprinkle the constituents with ground black pepper, oregano, and cayenne. Mix up well.
4. Close the lid and cook the meal on low-pressure mode for two hours.
5. When the cooking time elapses, open the lid and stir using spoon.
6. Transfer it to the bowls and serve while warm.

Nutrition: calories 376, fat 29.9, fiber 1.7, carbs 7.5, protein 19.6

Pizza

Prep time: fifteen minutes |Cooking time: 35 minutes |Servings: 12
Ingredients:

- 8 ounces of soda keto dough
- 1 egg
- ½ cup of tomatoes
- 6 ounces of pepperoni
- 5 ounces of mozzarella cheese
- 3 tablespoons of tomato paste
- 1 tablespoon of sour cream
- 1 teaspoon of oregano
- 2 tablespoons of basil
- 4 ounces of black olives
- 1 tablespoon of fresh cilantro
- 1 teaspoon of extra virgin olive oil

COOKING DIRECTIONS:

1. Roll the dough using a rolling pin to a circular shape.
2. Spray the pressure cooker with extra-virgin organic olive oil and line it using pizza crust.
3. Combine the tomato paste with sour cream and stir.
4. Spread the pizza crust with the tomato mixture.
5. Slice pepperoni and black olives.
6. Sprinkle the pizza crust with the sliced ingredients.
7. Grate cheddar cheese.
8. Chop cilantro and pour it over the crust.
9. Slice tomatoes and add them to the pizza crust.
10. Add grated cheese, basil, and oregano.
11. Sprinkle the pizza with the grated cheese and close the lid.
12. Cook the dish on manual mode for 35 minutes.
13. When the cooking time ends, open the lid and let the pizza cool.
14. Place it on flatter and serve in slices.

Nutrition: calories 187, fat 11.5, fiber 1, carbs 12.2, protein 8.7

Calzone

Prep time: ten minutes |Cooking time: 35 minutes |Servings: 7
Ingredients:

- 6 ounces of soda dough
- 1 cup of ricotta cheese
- 8 ounces of ham
- 7 ounces of Parmesan cheese
- 1 tablespoon of butter
- 1 teaspoon of paprika
- 1 teaspoon of freshly squeezed lemon juice

COOKING DIRECTIONS:

1. Roll the soda dough using a rolling pin.
2. Grate the Parmesan cheese and chop the ham.
3. Sprinkle one side of the rolled dough with grated cheese and chopped ham.
4. Add ricotta cheese.
5. Add paprika and wrap it to form a calzone.
6. Add the butter in the pressure cooker and melt it.
7. Transfer the calzone to the cooker and pour over it freshly squeezed lemon juice.
8. Close the lid and cook on manual mode for 35 minutes.
9. Turn the calzone to the other side once the initial one is cooked.
10. When your calzone is cooked, remove it from the cooker and serve.

Nutrition: calories 249, fat 14.2, fiber 0.8, carbs 11.4, protein 19.6

Pasta Salad

Prep time: ten minutes |Cooking time: twenty or so minutes |Servings: 6
Ingredients:

- 5 ounces of black bean pasta
- ½ lemon
- 3 cups of chicken stock
- 2 tomatoes
- ½ cup of pork rind
- 3 tablespoons of mayonnaise
- ½ cup of lettuce
- 1 teaspoon of basil
- 1 teaspoon of paprika
- 5 ounces of Romano cheese
- ½ cup of cream
- 5 ounces of sliced bacon(fried)

COOKING DIRECTIONS:

1. Place the pasta and chicken stock in the pressure cooker.
2. Add paprika and basil and stir the amalgamation.

3. Close the pressure cooker and cook on "Pressure" mode for 20 minutes.
4. Tear the lettuce and put it in a mixing bowl.
5. Squeeze fresh juice from the lemon and pour it over the lettuce.
6. Combine mayonnaise with cream together in another bowl and mix.
7. Chop the Romano cheese and fried bacon.
8. Slice the tomatoes and cut each side by a half.
9. When the pasta is cooked, remove it from the pressure cooker and rinse with hot water.
10. Add the pasta to the lettuce mixture followed by sliced tomatoes, Romano cheese, and fried bacon.
11. Sprinkle the mixture with cream sauce and pork rinds. Mix and serve.
Nutrition: calories 392, fat 23.6, fiber 5.9, carbs 13.5, protein 32.4

California Hot Sandwich

Prep time: ten mins |Cooking time: 4 minutes |Servings: 6
Ingredients:
- 5 ounces of keto naan bread
- 1 teaspoon of sesame seeds
- 1 tablespoon of mustard
- 2 tablespoons of fresh lemon juice
- 3 tablespoons of garlic sauce
- 5 ounces of cheddar cheese
- ¼ cup of sunflower sprouts
- 1 teaspoon of onion powder
- 1 avocado(pitted)
- 8 ounces of smoked chicken
- 1 teaspoon of butter

COOKING DIRECTIONS:
1. Combine the mustard with freshly squeezed lemon juice, garlic sauce, and onion powder in a bowl. Stir. Spread the keto naan bread slices with the mustard sauce.
2. Slice cheddar cheese and avocado.
3. Chop the smoked chicken.
4. Place the sliced cheese, avocado, and chopped smoked on the bread slices.
5. Sprinkle it with the sesame seeds.
6. Cover the mixture with naan bread slices to make a sandwich.
7. Add the butter in the pressure cooker.
8. Transfer the sandwiches into the cooker and cook on sauté mode for two minutes per side.
9. Put the California sandwich on a flatter. Serve in slices.
Nutrition: calories 264, fat 17.2, fiber 2.8, carbs 8.7, protein 18.8

Miso Soup

Prep time: 8 minutes |Cooking time: ten mins |Servings: 6
Ingredients:
- 1 tablespoon of miso paste
- 1 teaspoon of turmeric
- ½ tablespoon of ground ginger
- 1 teaspoon of cilantro
- 5 cups of chicken stock
- 5 ounces of celery stalk
- 1 teaspoon of salt
- 1 tablespoon of sesame seeds
- 1 teaspoon of lemon zest
- ½ cup of soy sauce
- 1 white onion

COOKING DIRECTIONS:
1. Combine turmeric with ground ginger, cilantro, salt, lemon zest, and chicken stock in the pressure cooker. Peel the onion.
2. Chop celery stalks and white onion.
3. Add the vegetables in the cooker. Mix them and close the lid.
4. Set pressure cooker mode to "Pressure" and cook for 8 minutes.
5. Add miso paste and soy sauce.
6. Stir the mixture until miso paste dissolves.
7. Cook for two minutes.
8. Ladle your soup into serving bowls and enjoy.
Nutrition: calories 155, fat 7.3, fiber 1, carbs 14.66, protein 7

Chipotle Burrito

Prep time: 10 minutes |Cooking time: 35 minutes |Servings: 5
Ingredients:
- 3 tablespoons of chipotle paste
- 1 pound of chicken
- 2 cups of water
- 1 tablespoon of tomato paste
- 1 teaspoon of cayenne
- 5 keto tortillas
- 1 teaspoon of mayo sauce
- 1 tablespoon of garlic powder
- ½ cup fresh parsley
- 3 ounces of lettuce
- ¼ cup of salsa

COOKING DIRECTIONS:
1. Chop the chicken and put it in the pressure cooker.
2. Add red pepper cayenne, garlic powder, and chili pepper.
3. Pour water and close the lid.
4. Set pressure cooker mode to "Sear/Sauté" and cook the spiced chicken for thirty minutes.
5. Tear the lettuce in a mixing bowl.
6. Add salsa and mayo sauce and mix.

7. Spread the keto tortillas with salsa and chipotle paste.
8. Chop the parsley and subdivide it among tortillas.
9. Add tomato paste and lettuce mixture.
10. When the chicken is cooked shred it and put it on tortillas.
11. Wrap the tortillas to form burritos.
12. Put burritos in the pressure cooker and cook on "Sauté" mode for 5 minutes.
13. When the cooking time ends, remove your chipotle burrito from the cooker and serve it immediately.
Nutrition: calories 244, fat 7.6, fiber 2.5, carbs 10.4, protein 32.6

Tuna Salad

Prep time: a quarter-hour |Cooking time: twenty approximately minutes |Servings: 6
Ingredients:
- 1 pound of fresh tuna(fish)
- 2 red onions
- 2 sweet peppers
- 1 cup of lettuce
- ½ cup of pecans
- 2 tablespoons of lemon juice
- 1 teaspoon of organic olive oil
- 2 tablespoons of butter
- ½ teaspoon of rosemary
- ¼ cup of cream
- 5 ounces of tomatoes
- 1 teaspoon of salt
- ½ cup of water

COOKING DIRECTIONS:
1. Sprinkle the fresh tuna with rosemary and salt. Stir.
2. Smear the pressure cooker base with butter and add tuna.
3. Add water and close the lid.
4. Set cooker's mode to "Pressure" and cook the fish for approximately25 minutes.
5. Peel the onions and slice them.
6. Chop the lettuce, sweet peppers, and tomatoes. Crush the pecans.
7. Pour the freshly squeezed lemon juice, essential organic olive oil, and cream in a bowl and mix.
8. Add the sliced/ crushed vegetables in the lemon mixture bowl.
9. When the tuna is cooked, remove it from pressure cooker and shred.
10. Add the shredded tuna in the vegetable mixture.
11. Mix the tuna salad using two spoons.
12. Transfer the salad to a bowl and sprinkle it with the cream sauce. Serve and enjoy.

Nutrition: calories 190, fat 11.3, fiber 2, carbs 7.29, protein 17

Cabbage Casserole

Prep time: ten mins |Cooking time: 40 minutes |Servings: 6
Ingredients:
- 1 pound of cabbage
- 2 carrots
- 1 onion
- ½ cup of tomato juice
- 5 eggs
- 1 teaspoon of salt
- 1 teaspoon of paprika
- ½ tablespoon of coconut flour
- 1 teaspoon of cilantro
- 1 tablespoon of butter
- ½ cup of pork rinds

COOKING DIRECTIONS:
1. Chop the cabbage and season it with salt.
2. Combine the tomato juice with cilantro.
3. Add the butter in the pressure cooker and melt it.
4. Add the chopped cabbage and sauté it for ten minutes while stirring frequently.
5. Beat the eggs in a mixing bowl and whisk.
6. Add flour and stir until you obtain a smooth mixture.
7. Put the tomato mixture in the pressure cooker and stir.
8. Add egg mixture and pork rinds.
9. Sprinkle the mixture with paprika.
10. Peel onion and carrots and chop them.
11. Add the chopped ingredients in the pressure cooker and stir.
12. Close the lid and cook on manual mode for 35 minutes.
13. When your cabbage casserole is cooked, allow it rest and serve.

Nutrition: calories 178, fat 10, fiber 3.2, carbs 9.8, protein 13.8

Cheese Baguette

Prep time: quarter-hour |Cooking time: 30 minutes |Servings: 6
Ingredients:
- 2 cups of almond flour
- ½ cup of whey
- 1 teaspoon of baking powder
- A tablespoon of Erythritol
- 1 teaspoon of salt
- 5 ounces of Parmesan cheese
- 8 ounces of Mozzarella cheese
- 1 teaspoon of parsley
- 1 teaspoon of cilantro
- A teaspoon of oregano

- 1 tablespoon of rosemary
- 2 eggs
- 1 tablespoon of butter
- 1 cup of fresh spinach

COOKING DIRECTIONS:
1. Combine whey with baking powder and stir.
2. Add Erythritol, salt, and cilantro and stir the mixture.
3. Add the almond flour and knead the sleek dough.
4. Chop the parsley and mix it with oregano.
5. Add rosemary, eggs, and butter.
6. Chop the spinach and add it to the parsley mixture.
7. Chop the Mozzarella cheese and grate the Parmesan cheese.
8. Combine the cheese with the green mixture and stir.
9. Fill the dough with the spinach mixture to form a baguette.
10. Transfer the dish to the strain cooker let it rest for ten minutes.
11. Close the lid and cook the baguette on pressure mode for 30 minutes.
12. Turn its other side and cook it for 15 minutes.
13. When the cheese baguette is cooked remove it from the pressure cooker. Slice it and serve warm.

Nutrition: calories 285, fat 20, fiber 1.5, carbs 5.6, protein 23.6

Lunch Tart

Prep time: 10 minutes |Cooking time: 25 minutes |Servings: 10
Ingredients:
- 9 ounces of sundried tomatoes
- 1 teaspoon of salt
- 7 ounces of soda dough (keto dough)
- 1 egg yolk
- ¼ cup of almond milk
- 2 tablespoons of butter
- 2 white onions
- ½ cup of pork rinds
- 1 teaspoon of nutmeg

COOKING DIRECTIONS:
1. Roll your soda dough using a rolling pin. Put it in the pressure cooker.
2. Place the sundried tomatoes on the rolled dough.
3. Peel the onions and slice them.
4. Add the sliced onion to the tart. Salt it.
5. Add almond milk, butter, nutmeg, and pork rinds.
6. Whisk the egg yolk and pour it over the tart.
7. Close the pressure cooker lid and cook for 25 minutes.

8. When the cooking time ends, release the built-in pressure and remove your lunch tart from the cooker.
9. Serve it in pieces.

Nutrition: calories 218, fat 7.9, fiber 6.4, carbs 21.2, protein 19.4

Warm Lunch Wraps

Prep time: 15 minutes |Cooking time: 10 mins |Servings: 6
Ingredients:
- 4 eggs
- 1 teaspoon of salt
- ½ teaspoon of ground black pepper
- 1 tablespoon of essential olive oil
- 6 keto tortillas
- 4 tablespoons of salsa
- 1 teaspoon of cilantro
- ½ teaspoon of paprika
- 7 ounces of beetroot
- 1 teaspoon of lemon zest
- 1 medium carrot
- 1 red onion
- 1 tablespoon of lemon juice
- 1 cup of lettuce

COOKING DIRECTIONS:
1. Beat the eggs in a mixing bowl and whisk.
2. Add ground black pepper, salt, cilantro, and paprika. Stir.
3. Spray the pressure cooker base with oil and add the egg mixture.
4. Set the cooker's mode to "Sauté" and cook for one minute to form a crepe.
5. Repeat the above procedure until you make 5 crepes. Remove them from the cooker and chill them.
6. Spread the keto tortillas with salsa.
7. Sprinkle them with the freshly squeezed lemon juice and add lettuce.
8. Add the egg crepes.
9. Cut the carrot into strips, chop the beetroot, and slice the onion.
10. Add the vegetables to the tortillas.
11. Add lemon zest to form wraps.
12. Transfer the wraps to the pressure cooker and cook them on manual mode for 3 minutes.
13. Remove the lunch wraps from the cooker and serve warm.

Nutrition: calories 144, fat 8.1, fiber 3, carbs 10.2, protein 8.8

Sausage Pie

Prep time: quarter-hour |Cooking time: 25 minutes |Servings: 8
Ingredients:
- 2 cups of almond flour
- 7 ounces of butter

- 1 teaspoon of salt
- 1 egg
- ¼ cup of almond milk
- 1 pound of sausage
- 1 teaspoon of tomato paste
- 5 ounces of Parmesan cheese
- 1 teaspoon of cilantro
- 1 teaspoon of oregano
- 3 tablespoons of sour cream
- 1 teaspoon of turmeric
- 1 carrot

COOKING DIRECTIONS:
1. Combine butter with almond flour.
2. Add salt, almond milk, and egg. Knead the dough.
3. Chop the sausages and combine them with the tomato paste.
4. Add the cilantro, oregano, and sour cream.
5. Sprinkle the sausage mixture with turmeric.
6. Peel the carrot and slice it.
7. Roll the dough into circular shape using a rolling pin. Put it in the pressure cooker.
8. Add the sausage mixture to the circular dough and flatten it.
9. Add the sliced carrot and milk and close the lid.
10. Cook the mixture for 25 minutes on pressure mode.
11. When the cooking time elapses confirm your sausage pie is cooked using a wooden spoon.
12. Transfer it to a wide flatter and serve.

Nutrition: calories 615, fat 56.4, fiber 3.3, carbs 7.6, protein 23

Spinach Snail

Prep time: quarter-hour |Cooking time: around 30 minutes |Servings: 6
Ingredients:
- 5 sheets of filo pastry
- 1 tablespoon of sesame seeds
- 1 tablespoon of organic olive oil
- 1 teaspoon of butter
- 1 cup of spinach
- A teaspoon of oregano
- ½ teaspoon of nutmeg
- 1 teaspoon of cilantro
- A cup of cheese
- 1 teaspoon of garlic powder
- 1 egg yolk

COOKING DIRECTIONS:
1. Sprinkle the filo pastry sheets with the organic essential olive oil.
2. Chop the spinach and combine it with oregano, nutmeg, cilantro, cheese, and garlic powder. Stir.

3. Place the spinach mixture on the filo pastry sheets and roll them into snail-like shapes.
4. Whisk the egg yolk and pour it over the "snail."
5. Add sesame seeds transfer the mixture to a pressure cooker.
6. Close the lid and set it to pressure mode. Cook the snail spinach in half an hour or until its cooked.
7. Remove the "snail" from the cooker and allow it to cool. Cut into pieces to serve.

Nutrition: calories 80, fat 5.5, fiber 0, carbs 4.37, protein 4

Turkish Rolls

Prep time: ten mins |Cooking time: 25 minutes |Servings: 6
Ingredients:
- 7 ounces of puff pastry
- 1 teaspoon of essential-extra virgin olive oil
- A cup of ground beef
- 1 yellow onion
- A teaspoon of cilantro
- 1 tablespoon of cumin
- 1 egg yolk
- 2 tablespoons of water
- 1 teaspoon of oregano
- ½ teaspoon of turmeric
- ½ teaspoon of ginger
- 1 teaspoon of salt
- ½ tablespoon of freshly squeezed lemon juice

COOKING DIRECTIONS:
1. Peel the onion and dice it.
2. Combine the diced onion with cilantro, oregano, turmeric, ginger, and salt.
3. Mix the ingredient well and add the ground beef. Mix again.
4. Roll the puff pastry using a rolling pin.
5. Subdivide it into medium logs.
6. Add the onion mixture to the puff pastry to create long rolls.
7. Whisk egg yolk with water and add cumin.
8. Spread the pressure cooker with essential organic olive oil and add the Turkey rolls.
9. Brush the logs with the egg mixture and close the lid.
10. Set the cooker to "Pressure" mode and cook for around 25 minutes.
11. Remove your Turkish roll from pressure cooker and allow it to cool before serving.

Nutrition: calories 268, fat 18.2, fiber 1, carbs 17.58, protein 9

Garlic Spaghetti

Prep time: ten mins |Cooking time: 16 minutes |Servings: 7

Ingredients:
- 6 garlic cloves
- 1 tablespoon of garlic powder
- 1 teaspoon of onion powder
- 1 tablespoon of heavy cream
- 3 tablespoons of butter
- 6 ounces of Parmesan cheese
- 2 cups of chicken stock
- 9 ounces of black bean noodles
- ½ cup of fresh parsley
- A teaspoon of white wine
- ½ lemon
- 4 ounces of tomatoes
- 1 cup of ground chicken

COOKING DIRECTIONS:
1. Cook the black beans noodles to al dente following its package instructions.
2. Slice the garlic cloves and combine them with the ground chicken.
3. Add onion powder, garlic powder, cream, white wine, and chicken stock. Stir.
4. Transfer the mixture to the pressure cooker and sauté for 6 minutes or until its ready.
5. Add the black beans noodles.
6. Chop the tomatoes and add them to the pressure cooker contents.
7. Grate the Parmesan cheese.
8. Blend the pressure cooker mixture without damaging the noodles and close its lid.
9. Cook the noodle dish on pressure mode for ten minutes.
10. Transfer your garlic spaghetti to serving plates.
11. Sprinkle it with grated cheese and serve hot.

Nutrition: calories 302, fat 14, fiber 8.5, carbs 15.5, protein 30.9

Salmon Lunch Pie

Prep time: quarter-hour |Cooking time: 35 minutes |Servings: 6

Ingredients:
- 1 pound of salmon fillet (boiled)
- 1 teaspoon of salt
- 7 ounces of butter
- 1 cup of almond flour
- ½ cup of dill
- 1 teaspoon of paprika
- 2 tablespoons of lemon juice
- 1 teaspoon of cilantro
- 5 ounces of dried tomatoes
- ¼ cup of garlic
- 2 sweet peppers
- 1 tablespoon of olive oil

COOKING DIRECTIONS:
1. Shred the boiled salmon fillet and season it with salt and the freshly squeezed lemon juice. Stir.

2. Combine butter with flour, paprika, and cilantro. Knead the dough.
3. Chop the tomatoes, dill, and sweet peppers. Slice the garlic.
4. Mix the ingredients and add them to the shredded salmon.
5. Roll the soft dough using a rolling pin.
6. Spray the strain cooker's base with extra-virgin olive oil and place the rolled dough there.
7. Add the salmon mixture and flatten it.
8. Wrap the dough edges and close the cooker's lid.
9. Cook the pie on pressure mode for 35 minutes.
10. When the salmon pie is ready, allow it to cool.
11. Place it on a flatter and slice. Serve it while warm.

Nutrition: calories 515, fat 44.3, fiber 3.6, carbs 11.7, protein 16.8

Onion Cream Soup

Prep time: quarter-hour |Cooking time: 25 minutes |Servings: 6

Ingredients:
- 1 pound of yellow onions
- 1 cup of cream
- 4 cups of beef stock
- 1 teaspoon of salt
- 1 teaspoon of ground black pepper
- 1 teaspoon of turmeric
- ½ teaspoon of nutmeg
- 1 teaspoon of cilantro
- ½ teaspoon of white pepper
- 1 medium carrot
- 2 ounces of unsalted butter

COOKING DIRECTIONS:
1. Peel the onions and carrot.
2. Dice the onion and grate the carrot.
3. Combine the vegetables in a bowl and add salt, ground black pepper, turmeric, nutmeg, cilantro, and white pepper. Mix the combination.
4. Add the unsalted butter to the pressure cooker and melt.
5. Add the onion mixture and sauté the vegetables while stirring frequently until they turn golden brown.
6. Add beef stock and cream and stir. Set the pressure cooker mode to "Sauté" and close the lid.
7. Cook the soup for quarter-hour.
8. When the cooking time ends, transfer the onion cream soup to a bowl and let it cool.
9. Serve and enjoy.

Nutrition: calories 277, fat 23.8, fiber 2, carbs 11.58, protein 5

Gnocchi

Prep time: 10 mins |Cooking time: quarter-hour |Servings: 4

Ingredients:

- 8 ounces of turnip(flaked)
- ½ cup of coconut flour
- 1 teaspoon of salt
- 4 servings of water
- 1 teaspoon of oregano
- ½ teaspoon of white pepper
- 1 teaspoon of paprika

COOKING DIRECTIONS:

1. Put turnips in the pressure cooker.
2. Add coconut flour, water, salt, oregano, paprika, and white pepper. Stir the portions and close the cooker's lid. Set the cooking mode to manual and cook for 10 minutes. Stir and transfer it to a large bowl.
3. Knead the dough and subdivide it into small balls or gnocchi.
4. Pour 3 cups of water in the cooker and heat.
5. Dip the gnocchi into the water and mix.
6. Close the lid and set the cooker to steam mode.
7. Steam the balls for 7 to 10 minutes or until they get cooked.
8. Remove your gnocchi from the cooker and place it on a flatter.
9. Allow it to rest and serve alongside your favorite sauce.

Nutrition: calories 89, fat 2.7, fiber 7.5, carbs 13.4, protein 3.7

Bacon Pie

Prep time: quarter-hour |Cooking time: a half-hour |Servings: 8

Ingredients:

- 1 pound of rutabaga
- 8 ounces of sliced bacon
- 1 onion
- ½ cup of cream
- 1 tablespoon of organic olive oil
- 1 teaspoon of salt
- A teaspoon of cilantro
- 1 teaspoon of oregano
- ½ teaspoon of red chili pepper
- 5 ounces of Mozzarella cheese

COOKING DIRECTIONS:

1. Slice the bacon and sprinkle it with salt and cilantro. Stir.
2. Peel the rutabaga and slice it.
3. Spray the pressure cooker's base with extra-virgin olive oil.
4. Add half of the sliced bacon in the pressure cooker.
5. Add the sliced rutabaga followed by oregano and red chili pepper.
6. Peel the onion and slice it.
7. Slice the Mozzarella cheese.
8. Add the sliced ingredients to the pressure cooker content to form a pie. Add the cream.
9. Cover the pie with the remaining spices and sliced bacon. Close the lid.
10. Set pressure cooker mode to "Pressure" and cook for thirty minutes.
11. Release pressure and check whether the pie is cooked.
12. Remove your bacon pie and let it chill.
13. Serve it in pieces.

Nutrition: calories 255, fat 17.7, fiber 1.8, carbs 7.6, protein 16.5

Oregano Chicken Wings

Prep time: a quarter-hour |Cooking time: ten mins |Servings: 6

Ingredients:

- 12 chicken wings (boneless)
- 1 tablespoon of oregano
- 1 teaspoon of paprika
- 1 teaspoon of turmeric
- ½ teaspoon of salt
- 2 tablespoons of butter(melted)
- 1 teaspoon of cayenne
- ½ teaspoon of extra-virgin olive oil
- ½ teaspoon of minced garlic

COOKING DIRECTIONS:

1. Mix oregano with paprika, turmeric, salt, melted butter, cayenne, essential olive oil, and minced garlic to make a chicken marinade.
2. Brush each chicken wing with the mixture and leave it for 10 minutes to marinate.
3. Put the wings in the cooker basket and close its crisp lid.
4. Cook the chicken wings for 10 minutes or until they turn light brown.
5. Serve alongside your favorite dish.

Nutrition: calories 361, fat 25.8, fiber 0.9, carbs 11.9, protein 19.7

Halloumi Salad with Beef Tenderloins

Prep time: a quarter-hour |Cooking time: 10 minutes |Servings: 6

Ingredients:

- 7 ounces of halloumi cheese
- 1 tablespoon of orange juice
- 1 teaspoon of sesame oil
- ½ teaspoon of cumin
- ½ cup of arugula
- 1 pound of beef tenderloins
- 1 tablespoon of freshly squeezed lemon juice
- 1 teaspoon of apple cider vinegar treatment
- A teaspoon of salt

- 1 teaspoon of ground white pepper
- A tablespoon of organic essential olive oil
- 1 teaspoon of rosemary
- 1 cup of romaine lettuce

COOKING DIRECTIONS:

1. Tenderize the beef tenderloins and cover them with cumin, freshly squeezed lemon juice, apple cider vinegar, ground white pepper, salt, and rosemary.
2. Marinate the meat for around ten minutes.
3. Transfer the meat to the pressure cooker and sauté for 10 minutes or until its ready.
4. Flip its other side to verify it's well cooked.
5. Chop the beef tenderloins roughly and pour them on a flatter.
6. Tear the lettuce and add it to meat bowl.
7. Slice the halloumi cheese and sprinkle it with sesame oil.
8. Chop the arugula.
9. Add the prepared ingredients to the meat mixture.
10. Sprinkle the salad with orange juice and mix well.
11. Serve it immediately.

Nutrition: calories 289, fat 16.9, fiber 0, carbs 4.53, protein 29

Pho

Prep time: fifteen minutes |Cooking time: 32 minutes |Servings: 9

Ingredients:

- 5 glasses of water
- 4 ounces of scallions
- 3 ounces of shallot
- 1 teaspoon of salt
- 1 teaspoon of paprika
- ½ tablespoon of red chili flakes
- 1 teaspoon of ground white pepper
- ½ cup of fresh basil
- 1 tablespoon of garlic sauce
- 2 medium onions
- ½ lime
- 1 teaspoon of nutmeg
- 2 pounds of chicken breast

COOKING DIRECTIONS:

1. Peel the onions and slice them.
2. Place the sliced onions in the pressure cooker.
3. Chop the shallot and scallions and add them into the pressure cooker.
4. Sprinkle the mixture with white pepper, chili flakes, paprika, salt, and nutmeg.
5. Stir the amalgamation and sauté it for a few seconds.
6. Add water and dip the chicken breast.

7. Close the lid and cook the amalgamation on pressure mode for 30 minutes.
8. When the cooking time elapses, release the remaining pressure and open the cooker's lid.
9. Take off the chicken from the cooker. A colander may be essential in draining excess liquid from your chicken. Shred the chicken using a hand mixer and put it in serving bowls.
10. Sprinkle the dish with the garlic sauce.
11. Squeeze lime juice from your lime and pour it over the chicken. Serve while warm.

Nutrition: calories 139, fat 2.7, fiber 1.2, carbs 5.6, protein 22.2

Crispy Asparagus Pie

Prep time: quarter-hour |Cooking time: half an hour |Servings: 8

Ingredients:

- 10 ounces of butter
- 3 cups of almond flour
- 1 egg
- 1 teaspoon of salt
- 1 pound of asparagus
- 2 tablespoons of olive oil
- ½ cup of pork rind
- 1 teaspoon of paprika
- ½ cup of dill

COOKING DIRECTIONS:

1. Combine the soft butter with almond flour and egg in a mixing bowl.
2. Knead the dough until smooth.
3. Chop the asparagus and dill and mix.
4. Add salt, half of the pork rinds, and paprika to the mixture.
5. Transfer the almond dough to a pressure cooker and flatten.
6. Add the chopped asparagus mixture.
7. Sprinkle the pie with pork rinds and essential olive oil. Close the lid.
8. Cook the pie at pressure mode for half an hour.
9. When the dish is cooked, release the remaining pressure and let the pie rest.
10. Cut it into pieces and serve.

Nutrition: calories 622, fat 58, fiber 6.2, carbs 11.6, protein 7.4

Mushroom Soup

Prep time: 15 minutes |Cooking time: 50 minutes |Servings: 8

Ingredients:

- 1 cup of Enoki mushrooms
- 7 servings of water
- A cup of dill
- 4 tablespoons of salsa
- 1 jalapeno pepper
- ½ cup of cream

- 2 teaspoons of salt
- 1 teaspoon of white pepper
- 1 white onion
- 1 sweet red bell pepper
- A pound of chicken
- 1 teaspoon of soy sauce

COOKING DIRECTIONS:

1. Place Enoki mushrooms in a pressure cooker.
2. Chop the chicken and add it to the mushrooms.
3. Add water and cook the mushrooms at pressure mode for 35 minutes.
4. Meanwhile, chop the dill and jalapeno peppers.
5. Slice the onions and chop the bell pepper.
6. Add vegetables to the bean mixture and close the lid.
7. Set the cooker to pressure mode and cook for 15 minutes.
8. Sprinkle the soup with cream, salsa, white pepper, and soy sauce.
9. Stir the soup and continue cooking for 5 minutes.
10. Remove your mushroom soup from the pressure cooker and allow it to cool.
11. Ladle it on serving bowls and enjoy.

Nutrition: calories 101, fat 2.3, fiber 1.6, carbs 6.7, protein 13.9

Mushroom Cream Soup

Prep time: twenty possibly even minutes |Cooking time: 40 minutes |Servings: 6

Ingredients:

- 1 cup of cream
- 6 servings of water
- ¼ cup of garlic
- 1 teaspoon of salt
- 9 ounces of cremini mushrooms
- 1 teaspoon of butter
- 5 ounces of shallot
- 3 ounces of rutabaga
- 2 ounces of celery
- 1 teaspoon of fresh thyme leaves

COOKING DIRECTIONS:

1. Peel the garlic and slice it.
2. Slice the cremini mushrooms and combine them with the sliced garlic.
3. Toss the combination into the pressure cooker and sprinkle it with butter.
4. Sauté the amalgamation for 7 minutes while stirring frequently.
5. Peel the rutabaga and chop them.
6. Add the chopped rutabaga into the mushroom mixture.
7. Chop celery and shallot.

8. Add the chopped ingredients into the pressure cooker contents.
9. Sprinkle the mixture with salt, cream, and water.
10. Chop the fresh thyme leaves and it to the mixture and stir.
11. Close the lid and set the cooker to pressure mode.
12. Cook for half an hour.
13. When the cooking time ends, unplug the cooker and blend the soup using a hand mixer.
14. When you obtain a creamy texture, transfer your mushroom soup to serving bowls. Enjoy.

Nutrition: calories 75, fat 3, fiber 0.9, carbs 10.4, protein 2.8

Cauliflower Slice

Prep time: fifteen minutes |Cooking time: 25 minutes |Servings: 8

Ingredients:

- 1 pound of cauliflower florets
- 1 tablespoon of salt
- 7 ounces of filo pastry sheets
- 2 tablespoons of butter
- 7 eggs
- 8 ounces of Parmesan cheese
- ½ cup of cottage cheese
- A tablespoon of paprika
- ½ teaspoon of nutmeg
- 1 tablespoon of extra virgin organic olive oil
- ¼ cup of cream

COOKING DIRECTIONS:

1. Wash the cauliflower and chop its florets. Season them with salt.
2. Add the eggs in a mixing bowl and whisk.
3. Add cheese and paprika and stir the mixture.
4. Add nutmeg and cream.
5. Combine the ingredients in a bowl.
6. Spray the filo pastry sheets with extra virgin essential olive oil and put them in the pressure cooker.
7. Add the cauliflower filling and close its lid.
8. Cook the dish on pressure mode for 25 minutes.
9. When your cauliflower slice is cooked, release the remaining pressure and let it rest. Slice and serve.

Nutrition: calories 407, fat 27.5, fiber 2, carbs 21.13, protein 19

Baked Apple Salad

Prep time: quarter-hour |Cooking time: a half-hour |Servings: 8

Ingredients:

- 8 ounces of turkey breast
- A cup of arugula

- ½ cup of lettuce
- 2 tablespoons of orange juice
- 1 teaspoon of sesame oil
- A tablespoon of sesame seeds
- 1 tablespoon of apple cider vinegar treatment
- A teaspoon of butter
- ½ teaspoon of ground black pepper
- 7 ounces of red apples
- ¼ cup of walnuts
- ½ lime
- 2 cucumbers
- 1 tablespoon of mustard
- 1 teaspoon of liquid honey

COOKING DIRECTIONS:
1. Sprinkle the turkey breast with the apple cider vinegar treatment, ground black pepper, and mustard. Blend to mix.
2. Transfer the meat to a pressure cooker.
3. Add butter and cook it on pressure mode for 25 minutes.
4. Remove the turkey breast from the cooker and allow it to chill.
5. Meanwhile, sprinkle the apples with liquid honey and walnuts.
6. Transfer the fruits to the pressure cooker and cook them for 5 minutes on pressure mode.
7. Remove the apples and chill them.
8. Tear the lettuce and arugula and add them to the mixing bowl.
9. Add sesame oil and chop the cucumbers.
10. Add the chopped cucumbers to the mixture.
11. Squeeze the lime juice in the salad.
12. Chop the cooked apples and chicken and add them to the salad mixture.
13. Add orange juice and sesame seeds.
14. Stir the salad well using a wooden spoon. Serve your apple salad immediately.

Nutrition: calories 198, fat 16.1, fiber 1, carbs 6.97, protein 7

Ground Meat-Rice Mixture

Prep time: fifteen minutes |Cooking time: 20 mins |Servings: 4
Ingredients:
- 1 cup of cauliflower rice
- 2 cups of ground beef
- ¼ cup of tomato paste
- 1 tablespoon of ground black pepper
- 3 glasses of water
- 1 tablespoon of extra-virgin organic olive oil
- 1 tablespoon of freshly squeezed lemon juice
- 1 tablespoon of cilantro
- 1 teaspoon of salt
- ¼ cup of soy sauce
- 1 teaspoon of sliced garlic

COOKING DIRECTIONS:
1. Put the ground beef in the pressure cooker.
2. Add the black pepper, cilantro, salt, and sliced garlic.
3. Sprinkle the amalgamation with essential olive oil and stir.
4. Set the load cooker mode to "Sauté" and cook the meat for 6 minutes. Stir.
5. Add cauliflower rice and mix.
6. Add tomato paste, water, and lemon juice. Stir the mix and close the lid.
7. Set the pressure cooker mode to "Slow Cook" and cook for twenty minutes.
8. When your ground meat rice is cooked, sprinkle it with soy sauce and stir.
9. Transfer the dish to serving bowls and enjoy.

Nutrition: calories 194, fat 11.9, fiber 1.9, carbs 7, protein 15.5

FISH AND SEAFOOD RECIPES

Tender Octopus

Prep time: 5 minutes | Cooking time: 15 minutes | Servings: 6

Ingredients:

- 1 teaspoon of salt
- 10 ounces of octopus
- 1 teaspoon of cilantro
- 2 tablespoons of organic olive oil
- A teaspoon of garlic powder
- 1 teaspoon of lime juice
- A cup of water

COOKING DIRECTIONS:

1. Place the octopus in the pressure cooker.
2. Sprinkle it with cilantro, garlic powder, and salt. Mix well.
3. Add water in the pressure cooker and close the lid.
4. Set the cooker's mode to "pressure" and cook for 8 minutes.
5. Remove the spiced octopus from the cooker and place it on a tray.
6. Sprinkle it with essential organic olive oil.
7. Preheat the oven to 360 F and place the tray on the oven.
8. Cook the dish for 7 minutes.
9. When the octopus is cooked, remove it from the oven and season it with lemon juice.
10. Let it rest briefly before serving.

Nutrition: calories 80, fat 5, fiber 0, carbs 1.49, protein 7

Tasty Cuttlefish

Prep time: twenty minutes | Cooking time: 13 minutes | Servings: 6

Ingredients:

- 1 pound of squid
- 1 tablespoon of minced garlic
- A teaspoon of onion powder
- 1 tablespoon of freshly squeezed lemon juice
- A tablespoon of chives
- 1 teaspoon of salt
- 1 teaspoon of white pepper
- 3 tablespoons of fish sauce
- 2 tablespoons of butter
- ¼ Chili pepper

COOKING DIRECTIONS:

1. Slice the squid.
2. Combine the minced garlic with onion powder, chives, salt, and white pepper in a mixing bowl and stir well. Chop the chili pepper and add it to the spice mixture.
3. Combine the sliced squid with the spice mixture and stir.
4. Sprinkle the seafood mixture with fresh lemon juice and fish sauce. Stir.
5. Let the amalgamation rest for 10 minutes.
6. Set pressure cooker mode to "Sauté" and add butter.
7. When the butter melts, add the squid mixture and close the lid.
8. Cook the dish for 13 minutes.
9. When your tasty cuttlefish is cooked, transfer it to a flatter.
10. Serve alongside its fluid.

Nutrition: calories 112, fat 4.9, fiber 0, carbs 3.92, protein 12

Calamari in Tomato Sauce

Prep time: ten mins |Cooking time: 13 minutes | Servings: 4

Ingredients:

- 12 ounces of calamari
- 1 white onion
- 1 teaspoon of cilantro
- 3 garlic cloves
- 1 teaspoon of ground ginger
- ¼ cup of fish stock
- 1 teaspoon of fresh thyme
- ¼ cup of wine
- ¼ cup of water
- 1 tablespoon of organic extra virgin olive oil
- 3 medium tomatoes
- ½ teaspoon of ground white pepper
- 1 teaspoon of lime juice

COOKING DIRECTIONS:

1. Wash the calamari carefully and peel it.
2. Slice it into medium-thick slices.
3. Slice the garlic cloves, dice the onion, and chop the fresh thyme and tomatoes.
4. Set the pressure cooker mode to "Sauté" mode.
5. Put the sliced calamari into pressure cooker and sprinkle it with organic olive oil.
6. Saute the dish for 5 minutes.
7. Add the garlic, onion, thyme, and tomatoes to the calamari mixture.
8. Sprinkle it with water, wine, ground ginger, lime juice, and fish stock. Stir well and close the lid.
9. Set the pressure cooker to "Sauté" mode.
10. Stew the dish for 8 minutes.
11. Remove your sauced calamari from the pressure cooker. Serve it hot.

Nutrition: calories 238, fat 6.1, fiber 2, carbs 16.64, protein 29

Marjoram Salmon

Prep time: ten mins | Cooking time: a quarter-hour | Servings: 6

Ingredients:
- 1 pound of salmon fillet
- A tablespoon of marjoram
- ½ teaspoon of rosemary
- 1 tablespoon of salt
- ½ cup of dill
- 1 cup of water
- A teaspoon of cilantro
- 1 tablespoon of paprika
- A teaspoon of butter
- 1 teaspoon of onion powder

COOKING DIRECTIONS:
1. Combine the marjoram with rosemary and salt in a small bowl.
2. Rub the salmon fillet with the spice mixture.
3. Chop the dill and combine it with onion powder and paprika in a mixing bowl.
4. Add cilantro and stir well.
5. Put the salmon fillet on the steamer rack and place it in the pressure cooker.
6. Set the cooker's mode to Steam and add the dill mixture.
7. Close pressure cooker and cook the fish for fifteen minutes.
8. When the cooking time ends, release the built-in pressure and allow your marjoram salmon to rest.
9. Transfer the dish to serving plates and enjoy.

Nutrition: calories 127, fat 6.2, fiber 1, carbs 1.17, protein 16

Fish Curry

Prep time: 10 minutes | Cooking time: 10 minutes | Servings: 5

Ingredients:
- A tablespoon of curry paste
- 1 teaspoon of curry
- A cup of cream
- 1 pound of salmon fillet
- ¼ cup of garlic oil
- ½ tablespoon of salt
- 1 teaspoon of cilantro
- ¼ cup of fish sauce
- ½ cup of water
- 1 onion
- A teaspoon of red chili flakes
- 1 tablespoon of fresh ginger

COOKING DIRECTIONS:
1. Chop the salmon fillet and put them in the pressure cooker.
2. Combine cream with fish sauce in a mixing bowl.
3. Sprinkle the liquid mixture with curry paste and curry. Blend until smooth.
4. Peel the garlic cloves and onion.
5. Chop the vegetables and add them to the cream mixture.
6. Grate the ginger and add mix it with chili flakes, water, salt, and cilantro. Mix well.
7. Pour the mixture over the chopped salmon for coating.
8. Put the curried fish in the pressure cooker.
9. Close the lid having set it to pressure mode and cook for 10 minutes.
10. When the cooking time ends, release the remaining pressure and open the lid.
11. Transfer your fish curry to serving bowls.

Nutrition: calories 264, fat 16.2, fiber 2, carbs 7.99, protein 22

Seafood Paella

Prep time: ten mins | Cooking time: quarter-hour | Servings: 5

Ingredients:
- 1 cup of cauliflower rice
- 8 ounces of shrimp
- 5 ounces of mussels
- 2 cups of fish stock
- 1 cup of water
- 1 tablespoon of sea salt
- 1 small chili pepper
- 1 teaspoon of curry
- A teaspoon of turmeric
- 1 tablespoon of oregano
- A tablespoon of fish sauce
- 1 teaspoon of paprika
- 3 garlic cloves
- A tablespoon of butter

COOKING DIRECTIONS:
1. Peel the shrimp and combine it with mussels.
2. Place the seafood in the pressure cooker.
3. Add cauliflower rice, salt, curry, turmeric, oregano, and paprika and stir well.
4. Combine the fish stock with fish sauce and butter in a mixing bowl and blend well.
5. Pour the mixture over the shrimp mixture.
6. Peel the garlic and slice it.
7. Chop the chili pepper.
8. Sprinkle the cauliflower rice mixture with sliced garlic and chopped chili pepper. Stir well using a wooden spoon.
9. Close the pressure cooker lid and set its mode to steam. Cook for quarter-hour.
10. When the seafood paella is cooked, remove it from the pressure cooker and put it in a serving bowl.

Nutrition: calories 130, fat 4.7, fiber 1.3, carbs 4.9, protein 16.8

Cod Stew

Prep time: quarter-hour | Cooking time: a half-hour | Servings: 8
Ingredients:
- 1 pound of cod
- 1 large onion
- ¼ cup of garlic cloves
- 3 red peppers
- 1 teaspoon of cilantro
- 1 tablespoon of oregano
- 1 teaspoon of turmeric
- 4 cups of chicken stock
- 1 cup black soybeans (canned)
- 1 teaspoon of sea salt
- ¼cup of fish sauce
- ½ cup of water
- 1 teaspoon of red chili flakes
- A tablespoon of fresh ginger
- ½ cup of parsley
- 1 tablespoon of ground black pepper
- A teaspoon of white pepper

COOKING DIRECTIONS:
1. Chop the cod roughly and put it in a mixing bowl.
2. Peel the onion and garlic cloves and dice them. Add them to the cod.
3. Combine cilantro with turmeric, sea salt, chili flakes, ground black pepper, and white pepper in a separate bowl and mix.
4. Add the spice mixture to the cod.
5. Add the canned black soybeans and ginger.
6. Chop the parsley.
7. Put the cod mixture in the pressure cooker.
8. Add chicken stock, water, and fish sauce.
9. Sprinkle the stew mixture with the chopped parsley.
10. Stir the stew mixture using a wooden spoon and close the lid.
11. Set the load cooker to "Sauté" mode and cook the contents for half-hour.
12. When the cod stew is cooked, leave it to cool before serving.
Nutrition: calories 203, fat 2.2, fiber 5, carbs 27.8, protein 19

Fish Pie

Prep time: quarter-hour | Cooking time: around 30 minutes | Servings: 8
Ingredients:
- 1 tablespoon of curry paste
- A teaspoon of curry
- 1 cup of cream
- A pound of salmon fillet
- ¼ cup of garlic cloves
- ½ tablespoon of salt
- 1 teaspoon of cilantro
- A teaspoon of essential olive oil
- ¼ cup of fish sauce
- 1 onion
- 1 teaspoon of red chili flakes
- 1 tablespoon of fresh ginger
- 10 ounces of keto dough

COOKING DIRECTIONS:
1. Roll the keto dough using a rolling pin.
2. Spray the pressure cooker base with olive oil.
3. Place the rolled dough into pressure.
4. Combine curry paste with curry, cream, salt, cilantro, fish sauce, water, chili flakes, and fresh ginger in a mixing bowl. Stir well.
5. Chop the salmon fillet and put them in a mixing bowl.
6. Add curry paste mixture and mix well.
7. Put the fish mixture in the pie crust.
8. Grate the fresh ginger and sprinkle it over the pie.
9. Peel the onion, slice it, and add it. Close the lid.
10. Set the cooker mode to pressure and cook for half-hour.
11. When your fish pie is cooked, take it off from the cooker and slice. Serve the pie warm.
Nutrition: calories 256, fat 8.5, fiber 5.3, carbs 13, protein 32.8

Mackerel and Zucchini Patties

Prep time: 10 mins | Cooking time: quarter-hour | Servings: 6
Ingredients:
- 10 ounces of mackerel
- 1 medium zucchini
- ½ cup of coconut flour
- 2 eggs
- 1 teaspoon of baking soda
- 1 tablespoon of fresh lemon juice
- 1 teaspoon of oregano
- 1 tablespoon of extra virgin olive oil
- 2 garlic cloves
- 1 teaspoon of red chili flakes

COOKING DIRECTIONS:
1. Mince the mackerel in a mixing bowl.
2. Wash the zucchini and grate it.
3. Add the grated zucchini in the minced fish.
4. Sprinkle the mix with baking soda, squeezed fresh lemon juice, oregano, and chili flakes.
5. Peel the garlic cloves and slice them.
6. Add the garlic to the fish mixture.
7. Whisk the eggs in a separate bowl.
8. Add the whisked eggs to the fish mixture.
9. Sprinkle the amalgamation with coconut flour and knead dough until smooth.
10. Spray the pressure cooker with using extra virgin olive oil.

11.   Set the cooker to "Sauté" mode.
12.   Make medium-sized patties and drop them in the pressure cooker.
13.   Saute the patties for 5 minutes.
14.   Flip their other side and continue sauting for 10 more minutes.
15.   When the cooking time ends, open the pressure cooker lid and take off the cooked patties.
16.   Let your mackerel and zucchini patties to rest. Serve warm.
Nutrition: calories 213, fat 13.7, fiber 3.8, carbs 7.1, protein 15

Spicy Whitebait

Prep time: 10 minutes | Cooking time: ten mins |Servings: 3
Ingredients:
- 1 teaspoon of red chili flakes
- A tablespoon of sour cream
- 4 tablespoons of garlic sauce
- 1 pound of whitebait
- 3 tablespoons of butter
- ½ teaspoon of sage
- A teaspoon of oregano
- 1 teaspoon of essential olive oil
- ½ cup of almond flour
- ¼ cup of milk
- 1 egg
- ½ teaspoon of ground ginger

COOKING DIRECTIONS:
1.   Make fillets from the whitebait.
2.   Combine the chili flakes with sage, oregano, and ground ginger in a bowl and mix.
3.   Rub the whitebait fillets with the spice mixture.
4.   Let the fish rest for 5 minutes.
5.   Meanwhile, beat an egg in a separate bowl and whisk.
6.   Add milk and flour and stir until smooth.
7.   Add the sour cream and stir.
8.   Dip the whitebait fillets in the egg mixture.
9.   Set the cooker to pressure mode.
10.   Add the butter into the pressure cooker and melt.
11.   Add the whitebait fillets and close the cooker.
12.   Cook the dish for 10 minutes.
13.   When the cooking time ends, release the remaining pressure and open the cooker's lid.
14.   Transfer the spicy whitebait into a serving plate.
Nutrition: calories 472, fat 29.8, fiber 3.1, carbs 7.4, protein 43.2

Mackerel Salad

Prep time: 10 minutes | Cooking time: ten mins | Servings: 6

Ingredients:
- 1 cup of lettuce
- 8 ounces of mackerel
- 1 teaspoon of salt
- A teaspoon of paprika
- 1 tablespoon of essential olive oil
- ½ teaspoon of rosemary
- 1 garlic oil
- ½ cup of fish stock
- 1 teaspoon of oregano
- 7 ounces of tomatoes
- 1 large cucumber
- 1 red onion

COOKING DIRECTIONS:
1.   Wash the lettuce and chop it.
2.   Rub the mackerel with salt, paprika, and rosemary. Set the cooker to pressure mode.
3.   Put the spiced mackerel in the cooker.
4.   Add the fish stock and close the lid. Cook the dish for ten minutes.
5.   Peel the garlic cloves and slice it.
6.   Peel the red onion and slice it.
7.   Combine the sliced onion with the chopped lettuce.
8.   Slice the cucumber and chop tomatoes.
9.   Add the vegetables to the lettuce mixture.
10.   When the mackerel is cooked, take it off from the cooker and set it aside.
11.   Chop the fish roughly.
12.   Add the chopped fish to the lettuce mixture.
13.   Sprinkle the salad with organic essential olive oil and stir without damaging the fish. Serve immediately.
Nutrition: calories 123, fat 6.5, fiber 1, carbs 5.29, protein 11

Monkfish Stew

Prep time: ten mins | Cooking time: a half-hour | Servings: 7
Ingredients:
- 1 pound of monkfish fillet
- ½ cup of white wine
- 1 teaspoon of salt
- 1 teaspoon of white pepper
- 1 medium carrot
- 2 white onions
- 1 cup of fish stock
- 3 tablespoons of fish sauce
- A tablespoon of olive oil
- 1 teaspoon of oregano
- ½ teaspoon fresh rosemary
- 1 cup of water
- A teaspoon of sugar
- 1 teaspoon of thyme
- A teaspoon of coriander

COOKING DIRECTIONS:

1.   Chop the monkfish fillet roughly and sprinkle it with salt, white pepper, fish sauce, oregano, fresh oregano, sugar, thyme, and coriander. Stir well.
2.   Let the fish rest for 5 minutes.
3.   Peel the onions and carrot and chop the vegetables. Set the load cooker to "Sauté" mode.
4.   Put the chopped vegetables and monkfish in the pressure cooker.
5.   Sprinkle the combination with white wine, water, and essential extra virgin olive oil.
6.   Mix well and close the cooker's lid.
7.   Cook the dish on pressure mode for half-hour.
8.   When the monkish stew is cooked, open the pressure cooker lid and allow it to rest for ten minutes.
9.   Transfer the stew into a serving bowl and serve.
Nutrition: calories 251, fat 14, fiber 5, carbs 15, protein 17

Cod Chowder

Prep time: ten mins | Cooking time: 35 minutes | Servings: 8
Ingredients:
- 2 tablespoons of fresh marjoram
- 1 teaspoon of salt
- 3 glasses of water
- 1 cup of cream
- 1 onion
- 7 ounces of eggplant
- 1 carrot
- 7 ounces of cod
- 1 teaspoon of ground black pepper
- 1 teaspoon of butter
- 3 tablespoons of chives
- ½ teaspoon of nutmeg
- ½ cup of dill
- 2 ounces of fresh ginger

COOKING DIRECTIONS:
1.   Combine water with cream, butter, and ground black pepper in a bowl and mix well.
2.   Pour the cream mixture into the pressure cooker.
3.   Sprinkle the amalgamation with salt, chives, nutmeg, and fresh ginger.
4.   Peel the onion, eggplants, and carrot.
5.   Grate the carrot and add it to the cooker.
6.   Dice the onion and chop the eggplant.
7.   Set the pressure cooker to "Sauté" mode.
8.   Add cod followed by vegetables into the pressure cooker.
9.   Sprinkle the mixture with fresh marjoram. Chop the dill.

10.   Close the pressure cooker lid and cook the dish for 35 minutes.
11.   When the cooking time ends, release the remaining pressure and open the cooker.
12.   Ladle your cod chowder into serving bowls and sprinkle it with chopped dill.
Nutrition: calories 99, fat 3.1, fiber 3, carbs 11.7, protein 7.7

Fish Tacos

Prep time: ten mins | Cooking time: 10 mins | Servings: 7
Ingredients:
- 7 almond tortilla
- 8 ounces of salmon
- 2 red onions
- 2 red sweet peppers
- 1 tablespoon of mustard
- A tablespoon of mayo sauce
- 1 garlic herb
- 2 tablespoons of essential olive oil
- A teaspoon of sesame seeds
- 1 teaspoon of salt
- ¼ cup of lettuce

COOKING DIRECTIONS:
1.   Combine mustard with mayo sauce in a bowl and stir well.
2.   Sprinkle the salmon with the mustard sauce to coat. Set the pressure cooker to "Steam" mode.
3.   Spread its base with organic extra virgin olive oil.
4.   Add the coated salmon to the cooker and close the lid.
5.   Cook the fish for ten minutes.
6.   Meanwhile, remove seeds from the peppers.
7.   Cut the sweet peppers into strips.
8.   Peel the onion and slice it.
9.   Tear the lettuce.
10.   Peel the garlic and mince its cloves.
11.   Sprinkle the tortilla shell with the minced garlic, salt, sesame seeds, and organic essential olive oil.
12.   Add the bell pepper strips, sliced onions, and lettuce to the tortilla.
13.   When the salmon is cooked, get rid of it from the strain cooker.
14.   Shred the salmon and add it to the tortilla.
15.   Wrap your fish tacos.
Nutrition: calories 160, fat 9.8, fiber 2.5, carbs 8.7, protein 10.6

Sriracha Shrimp

Prep time: 10 minutes | Cooking time: 8 minutes | Servings: 6
Ingredients:
- 1 pound of shrimp
- 3 tablespoons of minced garlic

- 1 tablespoon of sriracha
- A tablespoon of oil
- 1 teaspoon of salt
- 1 teaspoon of ground black pepper
- A teaspoon of ground ginger
- ½ cup of fish stock
- 1 tablespoon of butter

COOKING DIRECTIONS:

1. Peel the shrimp and combine them with sriracha in a mixing bowl.
2. Stir well and add sesame oil, minced garlic, salt, ground black pepper, ground ginger, and fish stock. Stir again. Toss everything well.
3. Put the sriracha shrimp mixture in the pressure cooker having set it to pressure mode.
4. Add butter and close the pressure cooker lid. Cook the dish for 8 minutes.
5. When the sriracha shrimp is cooked, remove it from the cooker and allow it to rest. Serve warm.

Nutrition: calories 125, fat 5.4, fiber 0, carbs 2.33, protein 16

Tuna and Shirataki Noodles Salad

Prep time: ten mins | Cooking time: 12 minutes | Servings: 6

Ingredients:

- 5 ounces of Shirataki noodles
- 1 pound of tuna
- A tablespoon of essential organic olive oil
- 1 teaspoon of ground black pepper
- 3 tablespoons of sour cream
- 1 teaspoon of ground ginger
- 5 tablespoons of fish stock
- 1 tablespoon of soy sauce
- 6 ounces of parmesan cheese
- 1 cup of black olives
- A cup of hot water

COOKING DIRECTIONS:

1. Combine the black pepper with ground ginger in a bowl and mix.
2. Chop the tuna and mix it with the ginger mixture.
3. Cut the cheese into the cubes. Set the pressure cooker to "Steam" mode.
4. Place the chopped tuna in the pressure cooker and cook for 12 minutes.
5. Combine the sliced black olives with cheese cubes, extra virgin olive oil in a mixing bowl.
6. Add soy sauce and fish stock.
7. Sprinkle the amalgamation with sour cream.
8. When the tuna is cooked, release the pressure and open the lid. Chill the chopped tuna.
9. Dip noodles in warm water allow them to sit for quarter-hour.
10. Rinse the noodles and add them to the black olive mixture.
11. Add the chilled chopped tuna and toss the salad gently. Transfer the salad to serving bowls.

Nutrition: calories 301, fat 18.3, fiber 3.4, carbs 3.3, protein 30.2

Tomato Snapper

Prep time: ten mins | Cooking time: fifteen minutes | Servings: 4

Ingredients:

- ½ cup of tomato juice
- 1 large onion
- ½ teaspoon of salt
- 1 tablespoon of basil
- 1 teaspoon of oregano
- 4 garlic cloves
- 1 tablespoon of butter
- ½ cup of chicken stock
- A pound of snapper
- 2 tablespoons of fish sauce

COOKING DIRECTIONS:

1. Remove the snapper's skin, slit it and set it aside.
2. Peel the onion and slice it.
3. Combine salt with basil, oregano, and fish sauce in a mixing bowl and stir.
4. Rub the peeled fish with the spice mixture.
5. Peel the garlic cloves and slice them. Set pressure cooker to "Pressure" mode.
6. Fill the snapper with sliced garlic and onion and put it in the pressure cooker.
7. Add tomato juice and close the lid.
8. Cook the dish on pressure mode for quarter-hour.
9. When the cooking time ends, remove your snapper from the cooker without damaging it.
10. Sprinkle the fish with tomato juice from the cooker and allow it to rest. Serve.

Nutrition: calories 204, fat 5.1, fiber 1.2, carbs 6.5, protein 31.2

Mussel Soup

Prep time: 10 MINUTES | Cooking time: 8 MINUTES | Servings: 6

Ingredients:

- 1 cup of cream
- 3 cups of chicken stock
- 2 tablespoons of essential organic olive oil
- 8 ounces of mussels
- 1 tablespoon of minced garlic
- ½ chili paper
- 1 teaspoon of red chili flakes
- 1 onion
- ½ tablespoon of salt
- ½ cup of parsley

- 7 ounces of shallot
- A tablespoon of lime juice
- 1 teaspoon of black-eyed peas

COOKING DIRECTIONS:

1. Peel the onion and slice it.
2. Chop the shallot and parsley. Set the pressure cooker to "Sauté" mode.
3. Pour the essential olive oil in the pressure cooker.
4. Add the shallot and onion and cook the content for 4 minutes while stirring frequently.
5. Add chicken stock, cream, minced garlic, chili flakes, salt, lime juice, and black-eyed peas into the shallot mixture.
6. Add mussels and sprinkle the amalgamation with chopped parsley. Close the cooker and set it to pressure mode.
7. Cook the dish for 4 minutes.
8. When the cooking time ends, release the built-in pressure and open the cooker's lid.
9. Ladle your mussel soup into serving bowls and enjoy.

Nutrition: calories 231, fat 14.7, fiber 1, carbs 15.63, protein 10

Smoked Salmon Bars

Prep time: quarter-HOUR | Cooking time: 25 MINUTES | Servings: 6

Ingredients:

- 9 ounces of keto dough
- 1 tablespoon of essential olive oil
- 1 teaspoon of butter
- ½ teaspoon of rosemary
- 1 teaspoon of salt
- 9 ounces of smoked salmon
- 6 ounces of mozzarella cheese
- 1 teaspoon of fresh thyme
- A tablespoon of tomato paste
- 1 teaspoon of garlic sauce

COOKING DIRECTIONS:

1. Roll the dough using a rolling pin.
2. Spread the pressure cooker base with butter.
3. Place the rolled dough into the cooker.
4. Sprinkle the dough with extra virgin olive oil and rosemary.
5. Chop the smoked salmon and sprinkle it with salt. Stir to mix.
6. Slice the mozzarella cheese.
7. Sprinkle the keto dough with the garlic sauce and tomato paste.
8. Add the smoked salmon and sliced cheese.
9. Sprinkle the dish with fresh thyme and close the lid.
10. Cook the salmon recipe in saute mode for 25 minutes.

11. When the cooking time ends, open the load cooker and let the dish rest.
12. Cut the dish into squares pieces when serving.

Nutrition: calories 310, fat 11.7, fiber 5.9, carbs 11.1, protein 40.5

Halibut while using Soy Ginger Sauce

Prep time: 10 MINUTES | Cooking time: 9 MINUTES | Servings: 6

Ingredients:

- 1 pound of halibut
- 1 tablespoon of butter
- 3 tablespoons of fish sauce
- 1 teaspoon of rosemary
- A tablespoon of cream
- 1 teaspoon of ground white pepper
- ½ cup of soy sauce
- 2 tablespoons of fresh ginger
- 1 teaspoon of organic olive oil
- A teaspoon of ground ginger

COOKING DIRECTIONS:

1. Cut the halibut into fillets and sprinkle them with rosemary and ground white pepper.
2. Set pressure cooker mode "Sauté" mode and add butter. Allow it to melt.
3. Place the fish in the pressure cooker.
4. Sauté the halibut fillets for two minutes on every side.
5. Combine the fish sauce with cream, soy sauce, fresh ginger, extra virgin olive oil, and ground ginger in a bowl. Sprinkle the halibut fillet with ginger sauce and close the pressure cooker lid.
6. Cook the dish on "Pressure" mode for 5 minutes.
7. When the cooking time ends, open the cooker's lid and remove your halibut fillets carefully without damaging them. Allow your meal to rest before serving.

Nutrition: calories 240, fat 17.5, fiber 1, carbs 7.01, protein 13

Stuffed Snapper with Onions

Prep time: ten MINUTES | Cooking time: twenty or so MINUTES | Servings: 4

Ingredients:

- 1 pound of snapper
- 2 white onions
- ½ cup of dill
- 1 tablespoon of extra virgin olive oil
- 3 garlic cloves
- 1 teaspoon of Erythritol
- ½ tablespoon of sea salt
- A teaspoon of turmeric
- 1 teaspoon of oregano
- ½ teaspoon of cumin

- 1 teaspoon of ground coriander
- 1 teaspoon of dried celery root
- 4 ounces of mushrooms

COOKING DIRECTIONS:

1. Peel the snapper and cut it crosswise.
2. Sprinkle the fish with sea salt.
3. Peel the onions and dice them. Peel the garlic cloves and slice them.
4. Pour the organic olive oil into the pressure cooker and heat it on sauté mode.
5. Add the diced onions and sliced garlic.
6. Stir the mixture and cook it for 4 minutes. Mix well.
7. Remove the onion mixture from the cooker and allow it to chill.
8. Chop the dill and combine it with the onion mixture.
9. Add Erythritol, turmeric, oregano, cumin, ground coriander, and celery root.
10. Dice the mushrooms.
11. Add the mushrooms to the onion mixture.
12. Fill the snapper with the onion mixture and wrap the fish in aluminum foil.
13. Place the wrapped fish on the trivet and hang it in the cooker.
14. Cook the trivet contents on steam mode for twenty minutes.
15. When your stuffed snapper is cooked, open the pressure cooker lid.
16. Take off the fish from the cooker and unwrap it. You can serve it in chops.

Nutrition: calories 230, fat 6.1, fiber 2.7, carbs 12, protein 32.7

Crunchy Cod

Prep time: ten mins | Cooking time: 10 MINUTES | Servings: 5

Ingredients:

- 12 ounces of cod fillet
- 3 eggs
- 1 cup of coconut flour
- A cup of pork rinds
- 1 teaspoon of salt
- 2 tablespoons of extra virgin organic olive oil
- 1 teaspoon of ground white pepper
- A teaspoon of ground ginger
- 1 tablespoon of turmeric
- 2 teaspoons of sesame seeds
- ¼ teaspoon of red chili flakes

COOKING DIRECTIONS:

1. Whisk the eggs in a bowl using a hand mixer.
2. Add the coconut flour and mix it again to attain a smooth texture.

3. Sprinkle the cod fillets with salt, ground ginger, white pepper, chili flakes, and turmeric. Mix.
4. Dip the cod fillets in the egg mixture.
5. Sprinkle the fish with pork rinds and sesame seeds.
6. Pour essential olive oil in the pressure cooker and heat it on sauté mode.
7. Add the cod fillets to the oil and cook them for 5 minutes.
8. When the cod fillets are cooked, remove them from the cooker and drain excess oil using a paper towel.
9. Allow it to rest and serve while warm.

Nutrition: calories 198, fat 12, fiber 1.6, carbs 3.5, protein 19.9

Sweet Mackerel

Prep time: ten MINUTES | COOKING time: 28 MINUTES | Servings: 5

Ingredients:

- 1 teaspoon of Erythritol
- 2 tablespoons of water
- ¼ cup of cream
- 1 pound of mackerel
- 1 teaspoon of ground white pepper
- 3 tablespoons of oregano
- 1 teaspoon of extra-virgin olive oil
- ¼ cup of water
- ¼ teaspoon of cinnamon

COOKING DIRECTIONS:

- Chop the mackerel roughly and sprinkle it with water, Erythritol, ground white pepper, organic olive oil, and cinnamon. Stir well.
- Place the fish mixture in the pressure cooker and add more water. Close the lid.
- Cook the treated mackerel on Sauté mode for 20 minutes without stirring.
- When the cooking time ends, remove your sweet mackerel from the cooker and place it on serving plates. Enjoy!

Nutrition: calories 263, fat 18.1, fiber 1.3, carbs 3.3, protein 22.1

Red Chili Anchovy

Prep time: quarter-hour | Cooking time: 8 minutes | Servings: 3

Ingredients:

- A red Chili pepper
- 10 ounces of anchovies
- 4 tablespoons of butter
- 1 teaspoon of sea salt
- ½ teaspoon of paprika
- 1 teaspoon of red Chili flakes
- A tablespoon of basil
- 1 teaspoon of dried dill
- A teaspoon of rosemary

- 1cup of breadcrumbs

COOKING DIRECTIONS:

1. Remove the Chili pepper seeds and slice it.
2. Combine the Chili flakes with paprika, sea salt, basil, dry dill, and rosemary in a shallow bowl. Stir well. Sprinkle the anchovies with the spices and mix the combination using your hands.
3. Add sliced Chili pepper and let the amalgamation rest for 10 minutes.
4. Set the pressure cooker to sauté mode and spread it with butter. Allow it to melt.
5. Mix the spiced anchovies with the breadcrumbs and pour the mixture into the melted butter.
6. Cook the anchovies for 4 minutes.
7. When the fish is cooked, remove it from the cooker and drain any excess oil using a paper towel. Serve immediately.

Nutrition: calories 356, fat 25, fiber 1, carbs 4.17, protein 28

Parsley Marinated Shrimps

Prep time: 20 MINUTES | Cooking time: 7 minutes | Servings: 3

Ingredients:

- 2 tablespoons of fresh cilantro
- 2 tablespoons of apple cider vinegar
- 1 tablespoon of freshly squeezed lemon juice
- ½ teaspoon of lemon zest
- ½ tablespoon of salt
- ¼ cup of white wine
- 1 teaspoon of brown sugar
- ½ teaspoon of ground ginger
- 1 tablespoon of extra virgin organic olive oil
- ½ tablespoon of minced garlic
- A teaspoon of nutmeg
- 1 cup of water
- 5½ pound of shrimp
- 1 cup of parsley

COOKING DIRECTIONS:

1. Chop the cilantro and parsley.
2. Combine the fresh lemon juice with apple cider vinegar treatment, lemon zest, salt, white wine, and sugar in a bowl.
3. Stir the amalgamation until sugar and salt dissolves.
4. Peel the shrimp and devein and dip them in the freshly squeezed lemon juice mixture.
5. Add the chopped cilantro and parsley and stir well.
6. Add ground ginger, organic olive oil, nutmeg, and water. Mix the shrimp mixture well and allow it to marinate for quarter-hour.
7. Set the cooker to pressure mode and add the marinated shrimp. Cook them for 7 minutes.

8. When the cooking time ends, release the remaining pressure and open the cooker's lid.
9. Serve the shrimp warm or store in a refrigerator (dipped in a marinade.)

Nutrition: calories 143, fat 6, fiber 1, carbs 5.63, protein 16

Fish Pho

PREP TIME: 10 MINUTES|COOKING TIME: 25 MINUTES|SERVINGS: 6

Ingredients:

- 4 ounces of salmon
- 7 ounces of squid
- 5 cup of water
- 1 garlic clove
- ½ cup of fresh dill
- 1 tablespoon of salt
- ¼ cup of soy sauce
- 1 teaspoon of ground black pepper
- ½ tablespoon of coriander
- ¼ teaspoon of thyme
- 1 jalapeño pepper
- 8 ounces of rice noodles
- 5 ounces of bok choy
- 1 teaspoon of red Chili flakes

COOKING DIRECTIONS:

1. Put water, salt, fresh dill, soy sauce, ground black pepper, coriander, thyme, and chili flakes into a pressure cooker.
2. Set the load cooker to sauté mode.
3. Stir the combination, close the cooker's lid, and sauté the contents for quarter-hour.
4. Chop the salmon and squid.
5. Peel the garlic herb and slice it.
6. When the cooking time ends, open the pressure cooker lid and remove all ingredients except their soup.
7. Add chopped salmon, squid, and garlic and stir. Season it with salt.
8. Close the cooker and cook the salmon mixture on pressure mode for ten minutes.
9. Open the pressure cooker lid and ladle the seafood in the serving bowls.

Nutrition: calories 140, fat 4, fiber 1, carbs 14.47, protein 11

Juicy Lobster's Tails

Prep time: ten MINUTES | Cooking time: 7 MINUTES | Servings: 4

Ingredients:

- A pound of lobster tails
- 1 tablespoon of sea salt
- A teaspoon of white pepper
- 1 cup of water
- 2 tablespoons of butter
- 1 teaspoon of garlic powder

COOKING DIRECTIONS:

1. Peel the lobster tails and sprinkle them with sea salt and white pepper.
2. Add the garlic powder and stir the lobster mixture carefully.
3. Pour water into the cooker and place the tails on a trivet.
4. Set the pressure cooker mode to steam.
5. Place the trivet in the cooker and close its lid. Cook the dish for 7 minutes.
6. When your lobster tails are cooked, release the cooker's pressure and open the lid.
7. Transfer the cooked dish to a serving plate and allow it to cool.

Nutrition: calories 143, fat 6.6, fiber 0, carbs 0.98, protein 19

Scallops with Berry Sauce

Prep time: 10 MINUTES | Cooking time: 14 minutes | Servings: 4

Ingredients:

- 10 ounces of sea scallops
- 1 teaspoon of salt
- 6 ounces of blackberries
- 1 tablespoon of butter
- 1 teaspoon of Erythritol
- 1 teaspoon of cilantro
- ½ cup of fish stock
- 1 tablespoon of liquid stevia
- 1 teaspoon of essential organic olive oil

COOKING DIRECTIONS:

1. Slice the scallops roughly and sprinkle them with salt. Stir.
2. Set the pressure cooker to sauté mode.
3. Smear its base with butter and allow it melt.
4. Transfer the sliced scallops in the pressure cooker and cook them for 2 minutes on both sides.
5. Combine the blackberries with Erythritol, cilantro, fish stock, liquid stevia, and extra virgin olive oil in a bowl and stir well.
6. Pour the berry sauce into the cooker and stir gently.
7. Close the cooker's lid and cook the dish on sauté mode for 10 minutes.
8. When your scallops are cooked, remove them from the cooker and spread them with hot berry sauce. Serve.

Nutrition: calories 121, fat 5, fiber 2.3, carbs 6.8, protein 13.2

Fish Pizza

Prep time: 10 MINUTES | Cooking time: 40 MINUTES | Servings: 6

Ingredients:

- 9 ounces of keto dough
- 1 tablespoon of butter
- 8 ounces of shrimp
- 1 teaspoon of basil
- A tablespoon of coriander
- 8 ounces of smoked salmon
- 1 tablespoon of fresh lemon juice
- ¼ teaspoon of ground black pepper
- 1 tablespoon of tomato paste
- 4 ounces of green olives
- 1 teaspoon of sour cream
- A teaspoon of organic essential olive oil
- 8 ounces of parmesan

COOKING DIRECTIONS:

1. Roll the dough using a rolling pin and cut it into medium-sized pizza crust.
2. Pour butter into the pressure cooker and put the rolled dough there.
3. Slice the smoked salmon and place it on your pizza crust.
4. Peel the shrimp and chop them.
5. Sprinkle the chopped shrimp with coriander, basil, lemon juice, and sour cream in a mixing bowl and stir well. Put the chopped shrimp mixture on the keto dough.
6. Slice the olives and add them on the pizza.
7. Sprinkle the dish with tomato paste and ground black pepper.
8. Grate the parmesan cheese and pour it over the pizza.
9. Set the pressure cooker to sauté mode.
10. Close the cooker lid and cook the dish on stew mode for 40 minutes.
11. When the cooking time ends, open the cooker and check whether your pizza is ready using a toothpick. Remove your fish pizza from the cooker and place it in a flatter. Serve it in pieces.

Nutrition: calories 405, fat 16.4, fiber 6.3, carbs 13.1, protein 52.6

Glazed Mackerel with Fresh Ginger

Prep time: ten MINUTES | Cooking time: 10 MINUTES | Servings: 6

Ingredients:

- 1 pound of mackerel
- ½ cup of soy sauce
- ½ cup of fish stock
- 3 tablespoons of Erythritol
- 1 tablespoon of fresh ginger
- A teaspoon of minced garlic
- ½ lime
- 2 tablespoons of sesame oil

COOKING DIRECTIONS:

1. Cut the mackerel into fillets.
2. Sprinkle the mackerel fillets with Erythritol and minced garlic.
3. Set the pressure cooker to sauté mode and spray its base with sesame oil.

4. Put the fillets and sauté it for 3 minutes on each side.
5. Add fish stock, soy sauce, fresh ginger, and squeezed lime juice.
6. Close the pressure cooker lid and cook the dish on pressure mode for 4 minutes.
7. Release the cooker's pressure and open its lid. Transfer your graze mackerel to serving plates and enjoy.

Nutrition: calories 258, fat 18.2, fiber 0.5, carbs 3, protein 20

Cheddar Tilapia

Prep time: quarter-hour | Cooking time: 14 MINUTES | Servings: 5
Ingredients:
- 12 ounces of tilapia
- 5 ounces of Cheddar cheese
- ½ cup of cream
- 1 tablespoon of butter
- A teaspoon of ground ginger
- 1 onion
- 1 teaspoon of ground black pepper

COOKING DIRECTIONS:
1. Cut the tilapia into medium fillets.
2. Combine ginger with ground black pepper in a mixing bowl and stir.
3. Rub the tilapia fillets with the spice mixture and set it aside for 5 minutes.
4. Grate the Cheddar cheese.
5. Peel the onion and slice it. Set the cooker to pressure mode.
6. Add the butter into the cooker and melt it.
7. Add the tilapia fillets and cook them for 2 minutes on each side.
8. Cover the tilapia fillets with sliced onion.
9. Sprinkle the dish with grated cheese and add cream.
10. Close the cooker's lid and cook the dish on sauté mode for 10 minutes.
11. When the cooking time ends, open the pressure cooker lid and remove your cheddar tilapia. Serve hot.

Nutrition: calories 194, fat 10.7, fiber 1, carbs 6.51, protein 18

Mango Snapper

Prep time: 15 MINUTES | Cooking time: 13 MINUTES | Servings: 6
Ingredients:
- 8 ounces of mango
- 1 tablespoon of Erythritol
- A teaspoon of liquid stevia
- 9 ounces of snapper
- 1 red onion
- A teaspoon of ground white pepper
- 1 teaspoon of extra virgin olive oil
- A teaspoon of fresh lemon juice
- 1 tablespoon of butter

COOKING DIRECTIONS:
1. Peel the mango and dice it.
2. Peel the snapper and cut it into pieces.
3. Rub it with ground white pepper and sprinkle it with the freshly squeezed lemon juice.
4. Set the pressure cooker to sauté mode and spray it with extra virgin organic olive oil.
5. Add the chopped mango followed by erytritol, liquid stevia, and butter.
6. Peel the onion and dice it.
7. Add the diced onion into the pressure cooker and stir well. Saute for 5 minutes.
8. Remove the mango mixture from the cooker and leave it to cool.
9. Fill the snapper with the mango mixture and wrap the fish in aluminum foil.
10. Transfer the stuffed snapper into the cooker and close its lid.
11. Cook the dish on pressure mode for 8 minutes.
12. When the cooking time ends, release the remaining pressure and open its lid.
13. Remove the fish from the load cooker and unwrap it. Serve.

Nutrition: calories 110, fat 3.6, fiber 1.1, carbs 7.6, protein 11.7

Salmon Casserole

Prep time: fifteen minutes | Cooking time: half an hour | Servings: 7
Ingredients:
- 14 ounces of boneless salmon
- 4 garlic cloves
- ¼ teaspoon of clove
- 1 teaspoon of salt
- A teaspoon of ground black pepper
- 1 cup of cream cheese
- 1 cup of cauliflower rice
- 3 cups of fish stock
- 1 teaspoon of oregano
- 2 eggs
- ½ cup of white onion
- 1 teaspoon of mussel juice
- A green bell pepper
- 2 tablespoons of butter
- 1 teaspoon of essential olive oil

COOKING DIRECTIONS:
1. Take salmon and chop it into medium-sized cubes.
2. Peel the garlic and slice it.
3. Combine the garlic with ground black pepper, salt, and oregano in a mixing bowl.
4. Combine the spice mixture with the chopped salmon and stir well. Chop the onion.

5. Put the chopped salmon mixture into the cooker and add the chopped onion.
6. Add cauliflower rice and stir.
7. Remove the bell pepper seeds and chop it.
8. Add the bell pepper to the mixture.
9. Add butter and essential organic olive oil in the pressure cooker.
10. Combine the cream cheese with fish stock, and mussel juice in a bowl and stir well.
11. Add 2 eggs and whisk until smooth.
12. Pour the liquid into the cooker and close the lid.
13. Set pressure cooker to sauté mode and cook for half-hour.
14. When your salmon casserole is cooked, transfer it to bowls and allow it to cool. Serve warm.

Nutrition: calories 296, fat 21.8,, fiber 1, carbs 4.8, protein 20.3

Crab Dip

Prep time: quarter-HOUR |Cooking time: 7 MINUTES |Servings: 6
Ingredients:
- A teaspoon of crab boil spices
- 1 pound of crabmeat
- 2 cups of water
- 1 teaspoon of salt
- ½ cup of cream cheese
- 1 tablespoon of minced garlic
- 2 tablespoons of sour cream
- 1 teaspoon of freshly squeezed lemon juice
- ½ teaspoon of lime zest
- 1 teaspoon of onion powder
- A cup of fresh dill
- 1 teaspoon of fish sauce

COOKING DIRECTIONS:
1. Chop the crab meat roughly and place it into pressure.
2. Add the crab boil spices using your hands.
3. Add water and close the lid.
4. Set the cooker to pressure mode and cook the dish for 7 minutes.
5. When the cooking time ends, release the remaining pressure and open the cooker lid.
6. Transfer the cooked crabmeat into a blender.
7. Wash the dill, chop it and add it to the blender contents.
8. Blend the crabmeat mixture until smooth.
9. Add salt, cream cheese, minced garlic, sour cream, freshly squeezed lemon juice, lime zest, onion powder, and fish sauce to the blender mixture.
10. Puree for 2 minutes and pour the crab dip into a serving bowl. Serve.

Nutrition: calories 138, fat 7, fiber 0, carbs 1.96, protein 16

Seafood Casserole

Prep time: quarter-hour | COOKING time: 33 MINUTES | Servings: 10
Ingredients:
- 10 ounces of sea bass
- 1 cup of broccoli rice
- 2 red onion
- 4 cups of chicken stock
- 1 tablespoon of salt
- 1 teaspoon of white pepper
- 3 tablespoons of sour cream
- 1 teaspoon of minced garlic
- A tablespoon of ground ginger
- 1 cup of coconut milk
- 1 cup of coconut flour
- 1 teaspoon of turmeric
- 2 carrots
- 1 tablespoon of butter
- 1 teaspoon of extra-virgin olive oil
- 6 ounces of scallions

COOKING DIRECTIONS:
1. Cut the sea bass into strips.
2. Sprinkle it with salt, white pepper, and ground ginger. Stir.
3. Combine the coconut milk with coconut flour in a bowl and whisk until they smoothen.
4. Peel the carrot, grate it, and chop the scallions.
5. Peel the onions and dice them.
6. Add the onions, carrot, and scallions into the pressure cooker having set it to pressure mode.
7. Add butter and cook for 5 minutes while stirring frequently.
8. Add broccoli rice and sprinkle it with extra virgin essential olive oil.
9. Stir it and cook for 3 minutes.
10. Add sea bass strips, chicken stock, sour cream, turmeric, and milk mixture.
11. Stir the casserole mixture using a wooden spoon.
12. Close the lid and cook for 25 minutes.
13. When the cooking time ends or the seafood casserole is ready, remove it from the cooker and serve.

Nutrition: calories 204, fat 12.3, fiber 7.1, carbs 15.7, protein 9.8

Cod Bowl

Prep time: 10 mins | Cooking time: 12 MINUTES | Servings: 8
Ingredients:
- 1 pitted avocado
- 1 cup of broccoli rice
- 3 cups of fish stock
- 1 teaspoon of salt
- A teaspoon of cilantro

- 10 ounces of cod
- 1 onion
- 3 garlic cloves
- 1 sweet red pepper
- A tablespoon of fish sauce
- 1 teaspoon of nutmeg
- 4 ounces of tomatoes
- A teaspoon of extra-virgin olive oil
- 2 tablespoons of butter
- 8 ounces of mushrooms
- 1 jalapeño pepper
- 1 teaspoon of paprika

COOKING DIRECTIONS:
1. Peel the avocado and chop it.
2. Combine the fish stock with salt, cilantro, fish sauce, nutmeg, essential olive oil, butter, and paprika in a mixing bowl.
3. Stir the amalgamation until the salt dissolves.
4. Peel the onion and chop it.
5. Chop the tomatoes roughly.
6. Place onion and tomatoes into a pressure cooker and add the fish stock mixture.
7. Slice the jalapeño pepper and garlic cloves. Also, chop the cod.
8. Add the chopped cod and sliced vegetables into the pressure cooker and stir well.
9. Add the broccoli rice and close the lid.
10. Set the pressure cooker mode to slow mode and cook for 12 minutes.
11. When your cod bowl is ready, remove it from the cooker and let it chill.
12. Sprinkle it with chopped avocados and serve.

Nutrition: calories 162, fat 9.7, fiber 3.2, carbs 7.6, protein 12.5

Tilapia Bites

Prep time: ten MINUTES | Cooking time: 8 MINUTES | Servings: 8
Ingredients:
- 3 eggs
- ½ cup of half and half
- 1 teaspoon of salt
- A pound of tilapia fillets
- 1 teaspoon of cayenne
- 1 tablespoon of lemon juice
- 3 tablespoons of extra virgin organic olive oil
- 1 teaspoon of coriander
- A teaspoon of cinnamon
- ½ lemon

COOKING DIRECTIONS:
1. Beat the eggs in a bowl.
2. Add salt, cayenne, and half and half, and eggs and stir well.

3. Grate the lemon and squeeze its juice.
4. Chop the tilapia fillets into large cubes.
5. Sprinkle the fish with coriander and cinnamon and stir.
6. Set the pressure cooker to Sauté mode and spray it with essential extra virgin olive oil.
7. Dip the tilapia cubes in the egg mixture.
8. Transfer the fish mixture in the pressure cooker.
9. Sauté it for 4 minutes or until it turns golden brown.
10. Place the cooked tilapia bites on a paper towel to drain excess oil. Serve.

Nutrition: calories 158, fat 9.9, fiber 0, carbs 2.31, protein 15

Fish Balls

Prep time: 10 MINUTES | Cooking time: 4 MINUTES | Servings: 6
Ingredients:
- 1 teaspoon curry
- A teaspoon of ground black pepper
- 1 teaspoon of salt
- 10 ounces of tilapia
- A tablespoon of almond flour
- 1 cup of pork rind
- 1 egg
- 1 teaspoon of oregano
- ½ cup of coconut milk
- 1 cup of organic olive oil

COOKING DIRECTIONS:
1. Grind the tilapia and put it in a mixing bowl.
2. Sprinkle the fish with salt, ground black pepper, almond flour, and oregano.
3. Mix coconut milk with an egg and stir.
4. Make small balls from the tilapia mixture.
5. Dip the fish balls in the pork rind.
6. Set the pressure cooker to sauté mode.
7. Pour the organic olive oil into the cooker and preheat it.
8. Add the fish balls to the cooker and cook for 4 minutes.
9. When the fish balls become golden brown, drain excess oils using a paper towel. Serve immediately.

Nutrition: calories 341, fat 27.1, fiber 1.3, carbs 2.8, protein 24.8

Cod Nuggets

Prep time: 10 MINUTES | Cooking time: 6 MINUTES | Servings: 6
Ingredients:
- 1 cup of pork rind
- 3 eggs
- A cup of coconut cream
- 12 ounces of cod
- 1 teaspoon of kosher salt

- ½ teaspoon of cumin
- ½ cup of coconut flour
- 1 cup of essential extra virgin olive oil
- A teaspoon of nutmeg
- 1 teaspoon of onion powder
- A teaspoon of garlic powder
- 1teaspoon of red pepper cayenne

COOKING DIRECTIONS:

1. Chop the cod roughly and transfer it into a blender. Blend until you get a smooth texture.
2. Transfer the puree into a mixing bowl.
3. Sprinkle it with kosher salt, cumin, nutmeg, onion powder, and garlic powder.
4. Add coconut flour and stir with a wooden spoon.
5. Beat the eggs in a separate bowl and add cayenne pepper and coconut cream. Stir well.
6. Set the cooker to sauté mode and spread it with organic olive oil.
7. Make medium-sized nuggets from the fish mixture and dip them in the egg mixture.
8. Dip the nuggets in the pork rind.
9. Put the nuggets into the pressure cooker and cook them for 6 minutes (each side.)
10. When your cod nugget is cooked, take them off from the cooker and drain excess oils using a paper towel. Serve warm.

Nutrition: calories 397, fat 26.6, fiber 4.5, carbs 8.6, protein 32.5

Garlic Mussels

Prep time: 5 MINUTES | Cooking time: 5 MINUTES | Servings: 5
Ingredients:

- ½ cup of water
- ½ cup of wine
- 1 teaspoon of cilantro
- 13 ounces of mussels
- 1 teaspoon of salt
- A teaspoon of chervil
- 2 ounces of butter
- 4 garlic oil
- ½ cup of fish sauce

COOKING DIRECTIONS:

1. Add white wine to water in a wide bowl.
2. Open the mussel shells and sprinkle them with salt, cilantro, chervil, and fish sauce.
3. Pour the wine mixture in the pressure cooker.
4. Peel the garlic cloves and slice them and set the cooker to pressure mode.
5. Add garlic to the pressure cooker contents.
6. Immediately they start boiling, add the mussels and cook for 1 minute.
7. When your dish is cooked, remove it from the cooker and transfer it to serving bowls.

8. Add the mussel liquid and serve.

Nutrition: calories 157 fat 10.9, fiber 0, carbs 4.53, protein 10

Pineapple Salmon

Prep time: quarter-HOUR | Cooking time: 12 MINUTES | Servings: 6
Ingredients:

- 1 pound of salmon fillet
- ½ cup of fresh parsley
- 1 teaspoon of kosher salt
- 1 teaspoon of sugar
- ½ tablespoon of liquid stevia
- 9 ounces of pineapple
- 2 tablespoons of extra virgin olive oil
- 2 tablespoons of freshly squeezed fresh lemon juice
- 1 teaspoon of lime zest

COOKING DIRECTIONS:

1. Combine kosher salt with sugar, honey, and freshly squeezed lemon juice in a very mixing bowl. Stir until they smoothen.
2. Rub the salmon fillet with the sugar mixture and allow it rest for 10 minutes.
3. Chop the pineapple and combine it with lemon zest in another mixing bowl.
4. Chop parsley and add it to the pineapple mixture. Stir well.
5. Set the pressure cooker to sauté mode and spray it with the essential olive oil.
6. Add the pineapple mixture and sauté it for 5 minutes.
7. Add the marinated salmon and close the lid.
8. Cook the dish on pressure mode for 7 minutes.
9. When your pineapple salmon is cooked, release the cooker's pressure and open its lid.
10. Ladle it to plates and add salmon. Serve while warm.

Nutrition: calories 167, fat 9.5, fiber 0.8, carbs 6.7, protein 15.1

Seafood Gumbo

Prep time: 10 MINUTES |Cooking time: ten MINUTES | Servings: 9
Ingredients:

- ½ cup of organic olive oil
- 1 cup of white onion
- 1 celery of stalk
- 2 cups of beef broth
- 3 ounces of okra
- 1 cup of tomatoes
- ¼ cup of garlic cloves
- 1 pound of crabmeat
- 8 ounces of shrimp
- 1 tablespoon of mussel juice

- 8 ounces of codfish
- 1 teaspoon of salt
- 2 teaspoons of file powder

COOKING DIRECTIONS:
1. Pour the organic olive oil into the pressure cooker and preheat it on pressure mode.
2. Peel the onion and dice it.
3. Chop the celery stalk, tomatoes, and okra.
4. Peel the garlic cloves and slice them. Chop the crab meat.
5. Peel the shrimp and chop them roughly.
6. Chop the codfish.
7. Put the onion, okra, and stalk in the pressure cooker and cook for 3 minutes while stirring frequently.
8. Add sliced garlic, crabmeat, and tomatoes to the seafood and stir.
9. Sprinkle the amalgamation with file powder and mussel juice and stir well.
10. Close the lid and cook the mixture on saute mode for 5 minutes.
11. When your seafood gumbo is cooked, remove it from the cooker and serve.

Nutrition: calories 197, fat 10.5, fiber 1, carbs 8.41, protein 17

Poached Mackerel

Prep time: 10 MINUTES | Cooking time: 10 MINUTES | Servings: 5
Ingredients:
- ½ cup of water
- 1 teaspoon of sesame oil
- A teaspoon of paprika
- 1 teaspoon of salt
- 12 ounces of mackerel
- 1 tablespoon of fish sauce
- 1 teaspoon of cayenne
- ½ cup of cherry tomatoes
- 1 teaspoon of ground nutmeg

COOKING DIRECTIONS:
1. Rub the mackerel with salt, paprika, red pepper cayenne, and ground nutmeg.
2. Sprinkle the fish with the organic extra virgin olive oil and leave it for 5 minutes.
3. Chop the tomatoes and add them to the pressure cooker.
4. Add water and cook the tomatoes on pressure mode for 5 minutes.
5. Add the mackerel, close the lid, and continue cooking for 5 minutes.
6. When the poached mackerel is cooked, release the cooker's pressure and open the lid.
7. Transfer the mackerel to a serving plate and sprinkle it with fish sauce before serving.

Nutrition: calories 151, fat 8.1, fiber 0, carbs 0.89, protein 18

Buttery Shrimps

Prep time: ten mins | Cooking time: 7 minutes | Servings: 6
Ingredients:
- 1 pound of shrimp
- ½ cup of butter
- 1 teaspoon of Erythritol
- A teaspoon of salt
- 1 tablespoon of soy sauce
- 1 garlic oil
- ½ teaspoon of sage
- 1 teaspoon of red chili flakes

COOKING DIRECTIONS:
1. Peel the shrimp and sprinkle it with soy sauce and red Chili flakes.
2. Set the pressure cooker to sauté mode and add butter. Let it melt.
3. Peel the garlic oil and slice it.
4. Add the sliced garlic to the sage and pour both into the load cooker.
5. Stir the amalgamation and sauté for two minutes.
6. Remove garlic and sage from the cooker and add the peeled shrimp. Saute for two minutes.
7. Add salt followed by Erythritol and stir.
8. Close the lid and cook the mixture on pressure mode for 3 minutes.
9. When your buttery shrimps are cooked, transfer them to bowls.
10. Sprinkle them with the cooker's liquid and serve warm.

Nutrition: calories 183, fat 11.5, fiber 0.1, carbs 1.6, protein 17.5

Shrimp Risotto

Prep time: 10 MINUTES | COOKING time: 5 minutes | Servings: 5
Ingredients:
- 1 cup of broccoli rice
- 2 servings of water
- 9 ounces of shrimp
- 1 tablespoon of butter
- 1 teaspoon of olive oil
- A teaspoon of salt
- 1 teaspoon of ground black pepper
- 1 stalk of green onion
- 1 tablespoon of miso paste
- 3 tablespoons of fish stock
- ½ teaspoon of cloves

COOKING DIRECTIONS:
1. Peel the shrimp, sprinkle them with cloves, and stir.
2. Set pressure cooker to sauté mode and add broccoli rice.
3. Add the water, butter, extra-virgin olive oil, salt, and ground black pepper. Stir.

4. Chop the green onion and add it into the broccoli rice mixture.
5. Add fish stock and stir the broccoli rice.
6. Close the lid and cook the dish on saute mode for 3 minutes.
7. Add shrimp and close the lid.
8. Cook the broccoli mixture on pressure mode for two minutes.
9. When shrimp risotto is cooked, take it off from the pressure cooker and leave it to cool.
10. Stir continuously and serve.
Nutrition: calories 106, fat 4.5, fiber 0.9, carbs 3.4, protein 12.8

Almond Milk Cod

Prep time: 20 mins | Cooking time: 13 MINUTES | Servings: 4
Ingredients:
- 3 tablespoons of almond flakes
- ½ cup of almond milk
- 8 ounces of cod
- ¼ cup of fish sauce
- 3 tablespoons of soy sauce
- A tablespoon of lime zest
- 1 teaspoon of minced garlic
- 1 tablespoon of butter

COOKING DIRECTIONS:
- Chop the cod roughly and transfer it to a mixing bowl.
- Add fish sauce and soy sauce and stir.
- Sprinkle the fish with lime zest followed by minced garlic and stir.
- Add almond milk and leave it for 10 minutes to marinate.
- Set the pressure cooker to sauté mode and add butter. Allow it to melt.
- Pour cod into the pressure cooker and close its lid. Cook the mixture on sauté mode for 10 minutes.
- When the cooking time ends, open the pressure cooker lid and add the almond flakes.
- Stir the dish gently and cook for 3 minutes. Remove your almond milk cod from the pressure cooker and serve.
Nutrition: calories 128, fat 6.1, fiber 1, carbs 7.19, protein 11

Catfish with Herbs

Prep time: ten MINUTES | Cooking time: 9 minutes | Servings: 6
Ingredients:
- 1 teaspoon fresh parsley
- 1 teaspoon dill
- 1 tablespoon organic olive oil
- 14 ounces catfish
- ¼ cup fresh thyme
- 3 garlic cloves
- ¼ cup of water
- 2 tablespoons soy sauce
- 1 tablespoon salt

COOKING DIRECTIONS:
1. Wash parsley and thyme and chop them.
2. Combine the greens with dill and salt. Stir.
3. Peel the garlic cloves and slice them. Set the pressure cooker to sauté mode and spray its base with extra virgin olive oil.
4. Put the sliced garlic in the cooker and sauté for 1 minute.
5. Combine the catfish with greens followed by soy sauce and water. Stir well.
6. Transfer the mixture to the strain cooker and sauté for 4 minutes or until the fish turns golden brown.
7. When your catfish is cooked, take it off from the cooker and serve.
Nutrition: calories 103, fat 5.2, fiber 0, carbs 2.42, protein 11

Alaskan Cod Strips

Prep time: ten MINUTES | Cooking time: ten minutes | Servings: 7
Ingredients:
- 2 pounds of Alaskan Cod
- 1 teaspoon of turmeric
- A teaspoon of ground celery
- 1 teaspoon of salt
- A teaspoon of red chili flakes
- 1 teaspoon of ground black pepper
- 1 tablespoon of apple cider vinegar
- 2 tablespoons of extra virgin olive oil
- 1 cup of pork rinds
- 3 eggs
- 1 cup of half and half

COOKING DIRECTIONS:
1. Cut the fish into strips.
2. Sprinkle them with turmeric, ground celery, salt, chili flakes, and ground black pepper and stir.
3. Pour apple cider vinegar treatment over the spiced fish.
4. Whisk the eggs in a separate bowl and add half and half.
5. Dip the fish strips in the egg mixture.
6. Set the pressure cooker to sauté mode and spray it with extra virgin olive oil.
7. Add fish strips and pork rind and sauté each side for 5 minutes.
8. When your Alaskan cod strips are cooked, remove them from the cooker and drain excess oil using paper towel. Serve while hot.
Nutrition: calories 330, fat 17.8, fiber 0.2, carbs 2.1, protein 39.2

Tilapia Pot Pie

Prep time: quarter-HOUR | Cooking time: 35 minutes | Servings: 8
Ingredients:

- 2 oz of puff pastry
- 1 tablespoon of fennel
- 6 ounces of shallot
- 1 white onion
- 13 ounces of tilapia
- A cup of cream
- 1 teaspoon of ground black pepper
- 1 teaspoon of salt
- 6 ounces of parmesan
- 1 tablespoon of coconut flour
- 1 egg
- A teaspoon of olive oil

COOKING DIRECTIONS:
1.   Roll your puff pastry using a rolling pin.
2.   Sprinkle the puff pastry with coconut flour. Set the pressure cooker to saute mode and add extra virgin olive oil.
3.   Put the puff pastry in the oiled cooker.
4.   Chop tilapia into small pieces.
5.   Season the fish with salt and ground black pepper.
6.   Add the chopped fish into the pressure cooker and sprinkle the mixture with fennel.
7.   Peel the white onion, dice it, and add it to the pastry.
8.   Grate parmesan cheese and sprinkle it over the fish pastry.
9.   Close the cooker's lid and cook the dish on sauté mode for 35 minutes.
10.   When your tilapia pot pie is cooked, allow it to cool. Slice it to serve.
Nutrition: calories 207, fat 10.8, fiber 1.1, carbs 11, protein 17.8

Seafood Cauliflower Rice

Prep time: ten mins | Cooking time: 5 minutes | Servings: 5
Ingredients:

- ½ cup of mussel juice
- 2 cups of fish stock
- 1 cup of cauliflower rice
- 1 tablespoon of essential olive oil
- 7 ounces of crabmeat
- A cup of fresh thyme
- 1 tablespoon of fresh rosemary
- A tablespoon of fresh dill
- ½ tablespoon of rice vinegar
- ½ teaspoon of nutmeg
- 1 garlic herb

COOKING DIRECTIONS:
1.   Chop the crab meat roughly and sprinkle it with essential olive oil and fresh thyme.
2.   Sprinkle the seafood with nutmeg and stir.

3.   Set the pressure cooker to sauté mode and transfer the crabmeat there. Sauté it for 3 minutes while stirring frequently.
4.   Peel the garlic cloves.
5.   Remove thyme from the cooker and add garlic, cauliflower rice, fish stock, and mussel juice.
6.   Sprinkle the mixture with rosemary and dill. Stir well and close pressure cooker lid.
7.   Cook the mixture on pressure mode for 5 minutes.
8.   When the cooking time ends, release the cooker's pressure and open its lid.
9.   Sprinkle the cauliflower rice mixture with rice vinegar and stir using a wooden spoon.
10.   Transfer your seafood cauliflower rice into serving bowls and enjoy.
Nutrition: calories 98, fat 4.2, fiber 2.3, carbs 10.1, protein 6

Ginger Scallops

Prep time: fifteen minutes | Cooking time: 5 minutes | Servings: 6
Ingredients:

- 8 ounces of sea scallops
- 3 ounces of fresh ginger
- 1 tablespoon of essential extra virgin olive oil
- A teaspoon of Erythritol
- 1 tablespoon of lemon juice
- A teaspoon of ground ginger
- 3 garlic cloves
- 1 teaspoon of ground black pepper
- 1 teaspoon of salt
- ¼ teaspoon of red chili flakes
- ¼ cup of fish sauce

COOKING DIRECTIONS:
1.   Cut the scallops by half.
2.   Grate the ginger and sprinkle it over the scallops.
3.   Combine sugar with fresh lemon juice, ground ginger, ground black pepper, salt, and chili flakes in a mixing bowl.
4.   Stir the ingredients and cover them with the spice mixture.
5.   Leave the seafood to rest for ten minutes.
6.   Peel the garlic cloves and mince them. Set the pressure cooker to sauté mode.
7.   Pour the organic olive oil into the pressure cooker and add garlic followed by fish sauce.
8.   Stir the mixture and sauté it for 1 minute or before garlic is fragrant.
9.   Add the scallops and sauté for 2 minutes.
10.   When the ginger scallops are cooked, remove them from the pressure cooker.
11.   Let the dish rest briefly and serve.
Nutrition: calories 11, fat 3.5, fiber 1.9, carbs 12.9, protein 8.4

Sesame Seed-crusted Catfish Bites

Prep time: a quarter-hour | Cooking time: 8 minutes | Servings: 7

Ingredients:

- 4 eggs
- 1 cup of cream
- ½ cup of coconut Flour
- 1 teaspoon of salt
- A teaspoon of paprika
- 1 teaspoon of turmeric
- ¼ cup of organic essential olive oil
- 1 teaspoon of cilantro
- ½ teaspoon of oregano
- 1 pound of catfish fillet
- A tablespoon of sesame seeds
- A teaspoon of ground ginger

COOKING DIRECTIONS:

1. Whisk the eggs in a bowl and add cream. Stir.
2. Sprinkle the egg mixture with paprika, salt, turmeric, cilantro, oregano, and ground ginger and stir.
3. Cut the catfish into medium-sized bites.
4. Add the codfish bites to the egg mixture and set it aside.
5. Set the pressure cooker to sauté mode and spread extra virgin olive oil on its base.
6. After the oil heats, sprinkle the codfish with coconut flour and sesame seeds.
7. Put the codfish bites to the pressure cooker and sauté each side for 4 minutes.
8. When your catfish dish is cooked, remove it from the cooker and drain excess oils with a paper towel.

Nutrition: calories 221, fat 17.4, fiber 0.8, carbs 2.6, protein 14

Creamy Tilapia Soup

Prep time: 10 mins | Cooking time: 16 minutes | Servings: 8

Ingredients:

- 1 cup of cream
- 4 servings of water
- 1 pound of tilapia
- 2 teaspoons of organic extra virgin olive oil
- 6 ounces of shallots
- ½ tablespoon of mussel juice
- 1 teaspoon of salt
- A teaspoon of ground black pepper
- 1 onion
- 2 garlic cloves
- ½ teaspoon of cloves
- 4 tablespoons of chives
- 1 teaspoon of cilantro
- 2 carrots

COOKING DIRECTIONS:

1. Chop the tilapia into small pieces.
2. Sprinkle it with salt and ground black pepper.
3. Peel the onion and dice it.
4. Set the pressure cooker to sauté mode and spray its base with the organic olive oil. Add the onion.
5. Sauté the vegetables for 3 minutes while stirring frequently.
6. Peel the carrots and grate them.
7. Add the grated carrot to the pressure cooker.
8. Chop the tilapia and shallots and add them into the cooker.
9. Add the mussel juice, water, and cream. Cook the soup while stirring frequently for 5 minutes.
10. Peel the garlic and mince it and add it to the soup.
11. Close the pressure cooker lid and cook the dish on pressure mode for 8 minutes.
12. When the cooking time ends, release the remaining pressure and open the cooker's lid.
13. Ladle the soup into serving bowls. Add sour cream (if desired) and serve.

Nutrition: calories 106, fat 3.4, fiber 0.8, carbs 7.9, protein 11.7

Spring Tuna Wraps

Prep time: ten mins | Cooking time: 7 minutes | Servings: 6

Ingredients:

- 6 cabbage leaves
- ½ cup cauliflower rice (cooked)
- 9 ounces of tuna
- 1 teaspoon of butter
- A teaspoon of salt
- 1 teaspoon of oregano
- 1 teaspoon of cilantro
- A tablespoon of mayonnaise
- ½ cup of lettuce
- 2 tablespoons of essential extra virgin olive oil

COOKING DIRECTIONS:

1. Chop the tuna and sprinkle it with salt, oregano, and cilantro. Stir.
2. Combine the chopped tuna with cauliflower rice and mix well.
3. Spread the cabbage leaves with mayonnaise, lettuce, and tuna mixture. Make the wraps.
4. Pour the organic olive oil into the pressure cooker and add butter.
5. Set pressure cooker to sauté mode and add tuna wraps. Saute each side of the mixture for 3 minutes.
6. Close the pressure cooker lid and cook on pressure mode for 1 minute.

7. Transfer the cooked dish to your serving bowl and enjoy.
Nutrition: calories 141, fat 9.6, fiber 0.7, carbs 2.2, protein 11.7

Seafood Stew

Prep time: ten mins | Cooking time: 25 MINUTES | Servings: 8
Ingredients:
- A cup of chicken stock
- 3 cups of fish stock
- 1 tablespoon of sour cream
- ¼ cup of cream
- 1 cup of parsley
- A teaspoon of salt
- 1 teaspoon of ground black pepper
- ½ Chili pepper
- 1 jalapeño pepper
- 3 sweet peppers
- 2 onions
- 9 ounces of shrimp
- 9 ounces of salmon
- 1 teaspoon of red Chili flakes
- A carrot

COOKING DIRECTIONS:
1. Combine fish stock with chicken stock and pour them into the pressure cooker.
2. Add sour cream and cream and stir.
3. Chop the parsley and slice Chili peppers.
4. Extract the jalapeno pepper seeds and grind its fresh.
5. Peel the shrimp and chop the salmon and add the ingredients to the pressure cooker.
6. Sprinkle the dish with the grind jalapeño pepper, chopped peppers, parsley, sliced Chili pepper, ground black pepper, and chili flakes.
7. Peel the onions and carrot.
8. Chop the vegetables roughly add them to the pressure cooker contents.
9. Close the pressure cooker lid and cook the dish on stew mode for 25 minutes.
10. When your seafood stew is cooked, remove it from the cooker and serve immediately.
Nutrition: calories 162, fat 5.7, fiber 2, carbs 10.44, protein 18

Mustard Salmon Fillets

Prep time: quarter-hour | Cooking time: 12 minutes | Servings: 8
Ingredients:
- 3 tablespoons of Dijon mustard
- 2 pounds of salmon fillet
- 1 tablespoon of lemon juice
- ½ cup of half and half
- 1 teaspoon of organic olive oil
- A tablespoon of cilantro
- ½ cup of fresh dill
- 1 cup of almond flour
- 3 egg yolks
- 1 teaspoon of tomato paste
- 3 tablespoons of fish sauce

COOKING DIRECTIONS:
1. Combine mustard with freshly squeezed fresh lemon juice, half and half, cilantro, and egg yolks in a mixing bowl. Whisk them until smooth.
2. Add the tomato paste and stir again.
3. Sprinkle the salmon fillets with fish sauce.
4. Chop the dill.
5. Combine the fish fillets with mustard mixture and mix well.
6. Let the salmon marinate for ten minutes and set the cooker to sauté mode .
7. Pour the extra virgin essential olive oil into the pressure cooker.
8. Sprinkle the salmon fillets with almond flour and put them in the pressure cooker.
9. Sauté each side of the mixture for one minute and close the cooker's lid.
10. Saute again for 10 minutes or until the meal is ready.
11. Remove the salmon fillets from the cooker and drain excess oils using paper towels. Serve.
Nutrition: calories 294, fat 18.1, fiber 2.1, carbs 6.3, protein 27.7

Crabmeat

Prep time: fifteen minutes | Cooking time: 10 MINUTES | Servings: 6
Ingredients:
- 1 pound of crabmeat
- A teaspoon of salt
- 1 cup of water
- 1 teaspoon of oregano
- 1 teaspoon of cumin
- ½ tablespoon of fresh lemon juice
- A cup of almond milk

COOKING DIRECTIONS:
1. Combine salt with water and fresh lemon juice in a mixing bowl.
2. Stir the mixture to dissolve the salt.
3. Add oregano and cumin and mix well.
4. Set the pressure cooker to pressure mode and add the mixture followed by crabmeat.
5. Cook the dish for 7 minutes.
6. When the cooking time ends, release the remaining pressure and open the cooker's lid.
7. Drain all the liquid from the cooker leaving crabmeat.
8. Add almond milk and close the pressure cooker lid. Cook for 3 minutes.
9. Transfer your crabmeat to a flatter and enjoy.

Nutrition: calories 105, fat 3.7, fiber 0.8, carbs 12.4, protein 6.2

Salmon with Blackberry Sauce

Prep time: a quarter-hour | Cooking time: 11 minutes | Servings: 6

Ingredients:

- ½ cup of water
- A cup of blackberries
- 1 teaspoon of Erythritol
- 1 teaspoon of cilantro
- A tablespoon of butter
- A teaspoon of rosemary
- ½ tablespoon of salt
- 12 ounces of salmon fillet
- 1 teaspoon of mustard
- ½ teaspoon of ground cumin
- 3 lemon wedges
- 1 chili pepper

COOKING DIRECTIONS:

1.   Wash the blackberries and put them in a blender.
2.   Puree the blackberries until they smoothen and add Erythritol, rosemary, and water. Puree again for 3 minutes.
3.   Rub the salmon fillets with mustard, ground cumin, salt, and cilantro.
4.   Chop the Chili pepper and lemon wedges and add then to the salmon fillets.
5.   Set the pressure cooker to sauté mode add butter. Allow it to melt.
6.   Put the salmon fillets in the melted butter and sauté them fish for 6 minutes (three minutes per side.)
7.   Pour the blackberry sauce into the pressure cooker and close its lid. Cook the dish for 5 minutes.
8.   Remove your cooked salmon fillets from the cooker and serve.

Nutrition: calories 107, fat 5.8, fiber 1.5, carbs 3.6, protein 11.6

Garlic Trout

Prep time: fifteen minutes | Cooking time: 12 minutes | Servings: 5

Ingredients:

- 10 ounces of trout
- 3 tablespoons of minced garlic
- 1 tablespoon of turmeric
- A teaspoon of ground black pepper
- 1 teaspoon of salt
- 2 tablespoons of garlic sauce
- 1 tablespoon of sesame oil
- 2 ounces of fresh ginger
- ¼ cup of soy sauce

COOKING DIRECTIONS:

1.   Cut the trout into medium-sized fillets.
2.   Sprinkle the fillets with turmeric, ground black pepper, salt, and soy sauce.
3.   Let the fish rest for 5 minutes.
4.   Combine the minced garlic and ginger in a mixing bowl and pour them over the trout for coating.
5.   Set the load cooker to "Pressure" mode and spray it with sesame oil.
6.   Add the trout fillets and close the lid. Cook for 12 minutes.
7.   When the cooking time ends, release the residual pressure from the cooker and transfer your garlic trout to a serving plate.

Nutrition: calories 177, fat 9.4, fiber 1, carbs 9.4, protein 14

Stuffed Trout while using the Parsley

Prep time: 10 mins | Cooking time: 13 minutes | Servings: 6

Ingredients:

- 1 red onion
- 1 cup of parsley
- 2 pounds of trout
- 1 teaspoon of white pepper
- ½ lemon
- ½ tablespoon of salt
- 1 teaspoon of fish sauce
- A teaspoon of butter
- 1 tablespoon of organic olive oil
- ½ teaspoon of red chili flakes
- ¼ cup of water
- 1 teaspoon of coriander

COOKING DIRECTIONS:

1.   Peel the onion and slice it.
2.   Wash the parsley and chop it.
3.   Combine the sliced parsley and chopped onion in a mixing bowl.
4.   Sprinkle the combination with fish sauce, chili flakes, and coriander.
5.   Slice the lemon and season the trout with white pepper and salt.
6.   Fill the trout with the parsley mixture.
7.   Combine the essential olive oil with butter in a bowl and pour it over the fish mixture for coating.
8.   Set the cooker to pressure mode and add the coated fish. Cover it with the lemon and close the pressure cooker lid. Cook for 13 minutes.
9.   When the cooking time ends, release the cooker's pressure and open the cooker's lid.
10.   Transfer your stuffed trout to a serving plate and subdivide it into pieces. Serve.

Nutrition: calories 263, fat 13, fiber 1, carbs 3.05, protein 32

SIDE DISHES

Tender Collard Greens

Prep time: ten mins |Cooking time: 20 minutes |Servings: 2

Ingredients:
- 2 cups of collard greens (chopped)
- ½ cup of water
- 3 tablespoons of heavy cream
- 1 teaspoon of salt
- A teaspoon of paprika
- ¼ cup walnuts (chopped)

COOKING DIRECTIONS:
1. Place collard greens in the cooker.
2. Sprinkle the greens with salt and paprika followed by heavy cream and water. Stir.
3. Close the cooker's lid and cook them for 3 minutes on high-pressure mode.
4. Allow pressure to escape naturally for at least 10 minutes.
5. Open the cooker's lid and add walnuts.
6. Stir your tender collard greens and serve.

Nutrition: calories 190, fat 18, fiber 3, carbs 5.3, protein 5.4

Cabbage Hash Brown

Prep time: quarter-hour |Cooking time: 13 minutes |Servings: 6

Ingredients:
- 1-pound of white cabbage (shredded)
- A white onion (diced)
- 1 tablespoon of apple cider vinegar treatment
- A teaspoon of salt
- 1 teaspoon of ground black pepper
- 3 oz of bacon (chopped)
- 1 cup of heavy cream
- ½ cup of water
- ½ teaspoon of tomato paste
- A teaspoon of paprika
- 1 garlic clove (diced)
- 1 oz of pork rinds

COOKING DIRECTIONS:
1. Put the shredded cabbage in a mixing bowl.
2. Sprinkle it with apple cider vinegar, salt, ground black pepper, and paprika.
3. Stir the mixture well and transfer it in a pressure cooker.
4. Add chopped bacon, heavy cream, water, tomato paste, garlic cloves, and pork rinds.
5. Mix it carefully and close the lid.
6. Cook the hash brown on high-pressure mode for 13 minutes.
7. Allow the cooker's pressure to release naturally for ten minutes.

8. Open the lid and mix your cabbage hash brown well. You can serve alongside your favorite sauce.

Nutrition: calories 202, fat 15.2, fiber 2.5, carbs 7.6, protein 10

Wrapped Asparagus

Prep time: ten mins |Cooking time: 7 minutes |Servings: 4

Ingredients:
- 1-pound of asparagus
- 7 oz of bacon (sliced)
- ½ teaspoon of salt
- 1 teaspoon of organic extra virgin olive oil
- ½ teaspoon of cayenne

COOKING DIRECTIONS:
1. Sprinkle the sliced bacon with salt, cayenne, and organic olive oil.
2. Wrap asparagus in the sliced bacon and set them in the cooker basket.
3. Close the planet fryer lid and cook the mixture for 7 minutes.
4. Serve while hot.

Nutrition: calories 302, fat 22.1, fiber 2.4, carbs 5.2, protein 20.9

Cauliflower Rice

Prep time: 10 mins |Cooking time: 5 minutes |Servings: 4

Ingredients:
- 1 ½ cup of cauliflower
- 1 cup of water
- A tablespoon of butter
- ¼ cup of heavy cream
- 1 tablespoon of dried dill
- A teaspoon of salt

COOKING DIRECTIONS:
1. Chop the cauliflower roughly and put it in the mixer.
2. Blend the vegetables to obtain cauliflower rice.
3. Put the "cauliflower rice" in the cooker.
4. Add butter, salt, dried dill, heavy cream, and water.
5. Close and seal the lid.
6. Cook the meal on high-pressure mode for 5 minutes.
7. Use quick pressure release and open the lid. Stir the cauliflower rice and serve hot.

Nutrition: calories 63, fat 5.7, fiber 1.1, carbs 2.6, protein 1.1

Carrot Puree

Prep time: a quarter-hour |Cooking time: 25 minutes |Servings: 6

Ingredients:
- 5 medium carrots
- ½ cup of water
- ½ cup of orange juice
- 1 teaspoon of butter
- ½ teaspoon of cinnamon

COOKING DIRECTIONS:
1. Wash the carrots and peel them.
2. Slice the carrots and place them in a mixing bowl.
3. Sprinkle the vegetables with cinnamon and mix well.
4. Leave the mixture for ten minutes to emit the carrot juice.
5. Transfer the mixture in a pressure cooker and add water followed by orange juice.
6. Close the lid and set the cooker to sauté mode. Cook the mixture for around 25 minutes or until the carrots soften.
7. Allow the carrots to cool and transfer the vegetable dish in a blender.
8. Blend the dish to obtain a smooth texture and add butter. Stir. Serve your carrot puree warm.

Nutrition: calories 36, fat 0.7, fiber 1.4, carbs 7.3, protein 0.6

Shumai

Prep time: twenty or so minutes |Cooking time: 10 mins |Servings: 7

Ingredients:
- 6 ounces of wonton wraps
- 1 cup of ground beef
- 6 ounces of tiger shrimp
- 1 teaspoon of salt
- 2 tablespoons of fish sauce
- A cup of soy sauce
- 1 teaspoon of ground ginger
- A teaspoon of white pepper
- 1 teaspoon of salt
- ½ teaspoon of cilantro
- 3 ounces of green onions
- 1 teaspoon of oregano
- 2 teaspoons of ground white pepper

COOKING DIRECTIONS:
1. Combine the ground beef with salt, cilantro, and oregano in a bowl.
2. Mince the tiger shrimp and combine it with the ground white pepper.
3. Chop the green onion and add it to the shrimp mixture.
4. Add the fish sauce, soy sauce, and ground ginger.
5. Combine the shrimp mixture and the ground beef mixture and mix well.
6. Place the meat mixture on the wonton wraps and wrap the shumai to obtain an open top.

7. Pour water into the pressure cooker.
8. Place shumai in the steamer and transfer it to the pressure cooker.
9. Close the pressure cooker lid and cook the mixture for 5 minutes on steam mode.
10. Allow it to rest for at least 10 minutes and release the built-in steam.
11. Remove your ready shumai from the cooker and serve.

Nutrition: calories 142, fat 3, fiber 1, carbs 19.68, protein 9

Japanese Style Black Bean Pasta

Prep time: ten mins |Cooking time: 8 minutes |Servings: 6

Ingredients:
- 7 oz of black beans pasta
- 1 cup of water
- 1 tablespoon of rice vinegar
- A teaspoon of Erythritol
- 1 teaspoon of sesame seeds
- A teaspoon of red chili flakes
- 1 teaspoon of salt

COOKING DIRECTIONS:
1. Place black beans pasta in the cooker.
2. Add water, salt, and chili flakes and close the lid.
3. Cook the pasta for 8 minutes on high-pressure mode.
4. Quick release the built-in pressure and open the lid.
5. Drain water from the mixture and transfer pasta into a bowl.
6. In a separate bowl, mix rice, vinegar, Erythritol, and sesame seeds. Stir gently.
7. Add the mixture to pasta and shake gently. Transfer the meal to serving bowls.

Nutrition: calories 111, fat 1.4, fiber 7.2, carbs 10.2, protein 14.9

Cabbage Rice

Prep time: quarter-hour |Cooking time: 3 minutes |Servings: 2

Ingredients:
- 8 oz of white cabbage
- ½ cup of water
- ¾ cup of cream
- 1 teaspoon of salt

COOKING DIRECTIONS:
1. Shred the cabbage and add rice to attain a cabbage-rice mixture.
2. Add salt and mix up it.
3. Transfer mixture to the pressure cooker and add water followed by cream. Mix up.
4. Close and seal the lid and cook the cabbage rice on high-pressure mode for 3 minutes.

5. Allow the built-in pressure to release naturally for ten minutes.
6. Open the lid and transfer hot cabbage rice in into the serving plates and enjoy..
Nutrition: calories 86, fat 5.1, fiber 2.8, carbs 9.4, protein 2.2

Mashed Turnips with Chives

Prep time: 10 mins |Cooking time: 6 minutes |Servings: 4
Ingredients:
- 2 cups of turnips (peeled and chopped)
- 2 tablespoons of chives (chopped)
- A tablespoon of butter
- 3 servings of water
- 1 teaspoon of salt
- A teaspoon of garlic powder

COOKING DIRECTIONS:
1. Put turnip in the cooker.
2. Add water and salt.
3. Cook it on high-pressure mode for 6 minutes.
4. Quick-release the cooker's built-in pressure and open the lid. Drain water.
5. Transfer dry turnip to the mixer.
6. Add butter and garlic powder.
7. Blend it to attain a smooth texture.
8. Transfer the turnip mash to serving bowls and sprinkle with chives. Mix up the meal gently.
Nutrition: calories 63, fat 2.9, fiber 2.1, carbs 8.6, protein 1.2

Garlic Cauliflower Florets

Prep time: quarter-hour |Cooking time: 5 minutes |Servings: 6
Ingredients:
- 15 oz of cauliflower florets
- 1 teaspoon of salt
- A tablespoon of garlic powder
- 1 tablespoon of avocado oil
- 1 teaspoon of butter (melted)
- ½ teaspoon of dried oregano

COOKING DIRECTIONS:
1. Mix salt, garlic powder, avocado oil, melted butter, and dried oregano in a bowl.
2. Brush the cauliflower floret with the garlic mixture and leave it for 10 minutes to marinate.
3. Transfer the vegetables into the cooker basket.
4. Sprinkle them with the remaining garlic mixture.
5. Lower the crisp lid and cook the cauliflower for 5 minutes/ until it turns light brown/ tenders.
6. Transfer your cooked cauliflower florets into serving plates and enjoy.
Nutrition: calories 31, fat 1, fiber 2.1, carbs 5, protein 1.7

Spaghetti Squash

Prep time: quarter-hour |Cooking time: ten mins |Servings: 3
Ingredients:
- 10 oz of spaghetti squash
- A tablespoon of butter
- 1 teaspoon of ground black pepper
- 1 cup of water for smoking

COOKING DIRECTIONS:
1. Pour water into the pressure cooker and insert a trivet.
2. Cut the spaghetti squash into halves and detach its seeds.
3. Place the squash on the trivet and seal its lid.
4. Cook the vegetable on high-pressure mode ten minutes.
5. Remove the cooker's pressure instantly and open the lid.
6. Transfer the spaghetti squash to a plate and shred it using a fork.
7. Sprinkle it with ground black pepper and add butter. Stir your spaghetti squash and serve hot.
Nutrition: calories 65, fat 4.4, fiber 0.2, carbs 7, protein 0.7

Turmeric Mushroom Hats

Prep time: quarter-hour |Cooking time: 25 minutes |Servings: 6
Ingredients:
- 2 tablespoons of turmeric
- 1 tablespoon of garlic powder
- A teaspoon of minced garlic
- 1 teaspoon of sea salt
- ½ cup of parsley
- A tablespoon of olive oil
- 1 tablespoon of butter
- 10 ounces of large mushroom caps

COOKING DIRECTIONS:
1. Wash the mushroom caps and detach its stems and gills.
2. Wash the parsley and chop it alongside the mushroom stems.
3. Place the parsley in a blender and pulse to attain a smooth texture.
4. Transfer the blended parsley in a mixing bowl and add butter, minced garlic, sea salt, garlic powder, and turmeric. Stir.
5. Fill the mushroom caps with the parsley mixture.
6. Spray the pressure cooker base with extra virgin olive oil. Transfer your mushroom caps there and close the lid. Cook the mushroom mixture on sear/sauté mode for 25 minutes.
7. When the cooking time ends, open the lid and leave the mushroom caps to chill for 5 minutes.

8.	Remove your mushroom hats from the cooker and serve.

Nutrition: calories 66, fat 4.5, fiber 0.8, carbs 4.3, protein 2

Sautéed Spinach

PREP TIME: TEN MINUTES|COOKING TIME: 13 MINUTES |SERVINGS: 5

Ingredients:

- 3 cups of spinach
- 1 cup of half and half
- A teaspoon of essential organic olive oil
- 1 teaspoon of cilantro
- ½ teaspoon of rosemary
- 1 tablespoon of butter
- A teaspoon of kosher salt
- 1 lemon

COOKING DIRECTIONS:

1.	Wash the spinach and chop it.
2.	Pour organic olive oil into the pressure cooker and heat it on sauté mode.
3.	Transfer the chopped spinach in the pressure cooker.
4.	Sprinkle it with kosher salt, rosemary, and cilantro.
5.	Stir the amalgamation and sauté for 3 minutes. Stir again.
6.	Add butter followed by half and half and close the lid.
7.	Cook the spinach on sauté mode for 10 minutes.
8.	Squeeze the freshly squeezed lemon juice over the spinach and mix well.
9.	Remove your sautéed spinach from the cooker and rest briefly. Transfer it to serving plates.

Nutrition: calories 99, fat 8.9, fiber 0.8, carbs 3.9, protein 2.1

Butternut Squash with Garlic

Prep time: 10 mins |Cooking time: a quarter-hour |Servings: 4

Ingredients:

- 1 pound of butternut squash
- A tablespoon of minced garlic
- 3 tablespoons of butter
- ½ teaspoon of white pepper
- A teaspoon of paprika
- 1 teaspoon of extra virgin olive oil
- A teaspoon of turmeric

COOKING DIRECTIONS:

1.	Wash the butternut squash.
2.	Melt butter and combine it with minced garlic and stir.
3.	Spray the pressure cooker with extra virgin olive oil.
4.	Place the squash in a pressure cooker and sprinkle them with turmeric and paprika.

5.	Top it with garlic butter and close the lid. Cook the spiced butternut on pressure mode for 15 minutes or until they softens.
6.	When the cooking time ends, remove your butternut squash from the cooker and allow it to cool. Serve warm.

Nutrition: calories 145, fat 10, fiber 3, carbs 14.99, protein 2

Celery Root Cubes

Prep time: ten mins |Cooking time: 8 minutes |Servings: 6

Ingredients:

- 12 oz of celery root (peeled)
- 1 teaspoon of salt
- A teaspoon of ground black pepper
- 1 tablespoon of butter
- A teaspoon of essential olive oil
- 1 teaspoon of minced garlic
- 1 tablespoon of fresh parsley(chopped)
- ¾ cup of heavy cream

COOKING DIRECTIONS:

1.	Chop the celery root into medium cubes.
2.	Preheat the Ninja Cooker and add butter followed by organic olive oil. Melt the butter on sauté mode.
3.	Add chopped celery root, ground black pepper, salt, and minced garlic. Stir well and sauté them for 5 minutes. Add chopped parsley and cream and stir well.
4.	Close the lid and cook the celery mixture on high-pressure mode for 3 minutes.
5.	Allow the pressure to exit naturally for around 10 minutes.
6.	Allow your celery root cubes to cool until they reach the room temperature and serve.

Nutrition: calories 101, fat 8.4, fiber 1.1, carbs 6.1, protein 1.3

Broccoli Salad

Prep time: ten mins |Cooking time: ten mins |Servings: 6

Ingredients:

- 1 white onion
- 1 pound of broccoli
- ½ cup of chicken stock
- 1 tablespoon of salt
- A teaspoon of extra virgin essential olive oil
- 1 teaspoon of garlic powder
- 3 tablespoons of raisins
- 2 tablespoons of walnuts (crushed)
- 1 teaspoon of oregano
- A tablespoon of freshly squeezed lemon juice

COOKING DIRECTIONS:

1. Wash the broccoli and separate subdivide into florets.
2. Place the broccoli in a pressure cooker and season it with salt.
3. Close the lid and cook the vegetables on pressure mode for ten minutes.
4. Transfer the broccoli into a serving bowl.
5. Peel the onion and slice it.
6. Add the onion to the broccoli.
7. Sprinkle the combination with garlic powder, oregano, crushed walnuts, raisins, and fresh lemon juice.
8. Add extra virgin olive oil and stir gently before serving.
Nutrition: calories 68, fat 3, fiber 3, carbs 4.09, protein 4

Green Asian-style Zucchini Strips

Prep time: ten mins |Cooking time: 5 minutes |Servings: 6
Ingredients:
- 2 tablespoons of sesame oil
- 3 green zucchini
- A tablespoon of cilantro
- 1 teaspoon of basil
- A tablespoon of kosher salt
- 1 tablespoon of butter
- ½ cup of pork rinds
- ½ cup of coconut milk
- 4 eggs
- 1 tablespoon of cumin

COOKING DIRECTIONS:
1. Wash the zucchini and cut it into strips.
2. Place the zucchini strips in a mixing bowl.
3. Sprinkle them with kosher salt, basil, and cilantro. Stir.
4. Pour the sesame oil into the pressure cooker and heat it on saute mode.
5. Combine eggs with coconut milk and whisk.
6. Dip the zucchini strips in the egg mixture.
7. Coat the vegetables with the pork rind.
8. Place the zucchini strips in the pressure cooker and sauté them for 1 minute on either side.
9. Sprinkle the dish with cumin and serve.
Nutrition: calories 225, fat 18.5, fiber 1.6, carbs 3.8, protein 12.4

Sweet Glazed Onion

Prep time: 5 minutes |Cooking time: 12 minutes |Servings: 6
Ingredients:
- 1 pound of white onions
- 3 tablespoons of butter
- ½ cup of Erythritol
- 1 teaspoon of thyme
- ½ teaspoon of white pepper
- 1 tablespoon of paprika

- ¼ cup of cream

COOKING DIRECTIONS:
1. Peel the onions and slice them.
2. Sprinkle the sliced onions with Erythritol.
3. Add thyme, white pepper, and paprika. Stir.
4. Place the onion mixture in the pressure cooker.
5. Add butter to the cooker and sauté it for 7 minutes while stirring frequently with a wooden spoon.
6. Add cream and blend well.
7. Close the lid and cook the glazed onion at pressure mode for 5 minutes.
8. Remove the cooked onions from the cooker and let it cool before serving.
Nutrition: calories 92, fat 6.6, fiber 2.2, carbs 8.2, protein 1.2

Cream Spinach

Prep time: ten mins |Cooking time: ten mins |Servings: 4
Ingredients:
- 4 cups of spinach (chopped)
- 1 tablespoon of butter
- A cup of cream
- 1 teaspoon of salt
- 4 oz of Cheddar cheese(shredded)
- 1 teaspoon of cayenne
- A teaspoon of paprika
- 1 tablespoon of organic essential olive oil

COOKING DIRECTIONS:
1. Pour cream in the cooker.
2. Add salt, butter, cayenne, and paprika. Preheat them on saute mode.
3. When the mixture starts boiling, add chopped spinach.
4. Stir well and sauté the greens for 5 minutes.
5. After that, sprinkle the spinach with shredded cheese and stir well.
6. Close the lid and sauté the meal for 5 more minutes. Switch off the Ninja Pressure cooker and open its lid. Mix and serve.
Nutrition: calories 218, fat 19.4, fiber 1, carbs 3.9, protein 8.6

Red Beetroot Salad

Prep time: ten mins |Cooking time: 35 minutes |Servings: 7
Ingredients:
- 1 pound of beetroot
- 1 red onion
- 3 tablespoons of sunflower oil
- 1 tablespoon of pumpkin seeds
- 8 ounces of feta cheese
- 1 tablespoon of basil
- ½ cup of fresh parsley
- 4 servings of water

COOKING DIRECTIONS:
1.	Peel the beetroot and drop it in the pressure cooker.
2.	Add water and close the lid.
3.	Cook the beetroot on manual mode for 35 minutes.
4.	Meanwhile, peel the onion and slice it.
5.	Crumble the cheese and chop the parsley.
6.	When the beetroot is cooked, remove it from pressure cooker and set it aside.
7.	Chop it into medium cubes and combine them with the sliced onion.
8.	Add pumpkin seeds and crumbled feta cheese.
9.	Sprinkle the amalgamation with basil and sunflower oil. Stir your beetroot salad well and transfer it to serving plates.
Nutrition: calories 180, fat 13.6, fiber 2, carbs 9.42, protein 6

Creamed Onions Halves
Prep time: 10 minutes |Cooking time: 25 minutes |Servings: 10
Ingredients:
•	A cup of cream
•	1 cup of coconut milk
•	6 big white onions
•	1 teaspoon of ground black pepper
•	½ tablespoon of salt
•	1 tablespoon of paprika
•	½ cup of fresh dill
•	½ cup of basil
•	1 tablespoon of cilantro
•	A teaspoon of mint
•	1 teaspoon of minced garlic
COOKING DIRECTIONS:
1.	Peel the onions and cut them into thick slices.
2.	Place the sliced onion in the pressure cooker.
3.	Combine the coconut milk and cream in a mixing bowl.
4.	Add ground black pepper, salt, and paprika and stir the amalgamation.
5.	Add the cilantro, mint, and minced garlic. Stir.
6.	Pour the cream mixture for the onion slices.
7.	Wash the fresh dill and basil and chop them.
8.	Sprinkle the onions with the chopped seasonings and close the pressure cooker lid.
9.	Set the cooker to sauté mode and cook the onions for 25 minutes or until they soften.
10.	Release the pressure and open the cooker's lid.
11.	Transfer the onions to serving plates and sprinkle them with gravy.

Nutrition: calories 116, fat 7.4, fiber 3.2, carbs 12.5, protein 2.4

Balsamic Onions
Prep time: 10 mins |Cooking time: 17 minutes |Servings: 4
Ingredients:
•	4 medium white onions
•	1 tablespoon of ground black pepper
•	2 tablespoons of freshly squeezed lemon juice
•	1 tablespoon of apple cider vinegar treatment
•	1 teaspoon of Erythritol
•	½ teaspoon of salt
•	½ teaspoon of oregano
•	1 tablespoon of organic essential olive oil
COOKING DIRECTIONS:
1.	Peel the onions and chop them roughly.
2.	Combine the ground black pepper with Erythritol, salt, and oregano in a mixing bowl and stir.
3.	Sprinkle the chopped onions with the spice mixture and mix using your hands.
4.	Add the onions to the cooker and sprinkle the mixture with extra virgin olive oil.
5.	Set the cooker to sauté mode and cook onions for 10 minutes while stirring frequently.
6.	Add apple cider vinegar treatment to the lemon juice. Stir.
7.	Sauté the dish for 7 minutes and open the cooker's lid.
8.	Remove the dish from the pressure cooker and allow it to cool before serving. Enjoy!
Nutrition: calories 81, fat 3.7, fiber 2.9, carbs 11.6, protein 1.5

Keto Tortillas
Prep time: ten minutes |Cooking time: 6 minutes |Servings: 4
Ingredients:
•	1 cup of almond flour
•	½ cup of coconut flour
•	½ teaspoon of salt
•	3 tablespoons of organic extra virgin olive oil
•	½ cup of water
COOKING DIRECTIONS:
1.	In a mixing bowl, add almond flour, coconut flour, salt, and water.
2.	Stir the mixture using a spoon/fork until it becomes homogenous.
3.	Add extra virgin olive oil and knead non-sticky soft dough.
4.	Subdivide it into four and portions (tortillas) and roll each piece using a rolling pin.

5. Preheat the cooker on sauté mode and place one tortilla in the cooker. Cook it for one minute.
6. Repeat step 5 for the three remaining tortillas.
7. Cover the cooked tortillas using a towel to maintain their freshness.
Nutrition: calories 330, fat 27.5, fiber 8, carbs 13, protein 2

Zucchini Noodles

Prep time: ten mins |Cooking time: 10 mins |Servings: 6
Ingredients:
- 2 medium green zucchini
- 1 tablespoon of wine vinegar
- 1 teaspoon of white pepper
- ½ teaspoon of cilantro
- ¼ teaspoon of nutmeg
- 1 cup of chicken stock
- A garlic oil

COOKING DIRECTIONS:
1. Wash the zucchini and use a spiralizer to produce zucchini noodles.
2. Peel the garlic and chop it.
3. Combine the cilantro with chopped garlic oil, nutmeg, and white pepper in a mixing bowl.
4. Sprinkle the zucchini noodles with the spice mixture.
5. Pour the chicken stock in a pressure cooker and sauté it on manual mode until it boils.
6. Add the zucchini noodles to the wine vinegar and stir.
7. Cook the combination on sauté mode for 3 minutes.
8. Remove your zucchini noodles from the cooker and serve.
Nutrition: calories 28, fat 0.7, fiber 1, carbs 3.94, protein 2

Romano Cheese Zucchini Circles

Prep time: ten minutes |Cooking time: a half-hour |Servings: 6
Ingredients:
- 1 pound of yellow zucchini
- 3 tablespoons of minced garlic
- ½ cup of coconut flour
- 3 tablespoons of organic olive oil
- 3 eggs
- ¼ cup of coconut milk
- 7 ounces of Romano cheese
- A teaspoon of salt

COOKING DIRECTIONS:
1. Wash the zucchini and slice them.
2. Combine the minced garlic with salt and mix.

3. Mix the minced garlic mixture and zucchini in a bowl.
4. Add the eggs in the mixing bowl and whisk the amalgamation.
5. Add coconut milk and coconut flour. Stir.
6. Grate the Romano cheese and add to the egg mixture and stir.
7. Pour extra-virgin olive oil in a pressure cooker and preheat it.
8. Dip the sliced zucchini in egg mixture.
9. Transfer the dipped zucchini in the pressure cooker and cook the dish on sauté mode for two minutes.
10. When your Zucchini circles are cooked, remove them from the cooker and drain excess fats with a paper towel. Serve while warm.
Nutrition: calories 301, fat 21.6, fiber 5.1, carbs 12.5, protein 16

Spicy Chinese Green Beans

Prep time: ten mins |Cooking time: quarter-hour |Servings: 8
Ingredients:
- 12 ounces of green beans
- 1 teaspoon of garlic powder
- A teaspoon of onion powder
- 4 garlic cloves
- 2 tablespoons of organic olive oil
- 1 teaspoon of red pepper cayenne
- 1 jalapeno pepper
- 1 teaspoon of butter
- ½ teaspoon of salt
- A cup of water

COOKING DIRECTIONS:
- Wash the green beans and cut them into two.
- Toss the green beans in a mixing bowl.
- Sprinkle the vegetables with the onion powder, chili pepper, and salt and stir.
- Remove the jalapeno pepper seeds and chop it into tiny pieces.
- Add the chopped jalapeno in the green beans mixture.
- Peel the garlic and slice it.
- Combine the sliced garlic with extra virgin olive oil.
- Blend the amalgamation and transfer it to the strain cooker. Add water and stir.
- Put the green beans in the pressure cooker and close its lid.
- Set the pressure cooker mode to sauté and cook the vegetables for 15 minutes.
- When your spicy green beans are ready, remove them from the cooker and drain excess fluids. Serve dry.

Remember, ready green beans should be firm but not crunchy.
Nutrition: calories 49, fat 4.1, fiber 1, carbs 3, protein 1

Parmesan Tomatoes

Prep time: 7 minutes |Cooking time: 7 minutes |Servings: 5
Ingredients:
- 10 ounces of big tomatoes
- 7 ounces of Parmesan cheese
- ½ teaspoon of paprika
- 3 tablespoons of organic olive oil
- 1 tablespoon of basil
- A teaspoon of cilantro
- 1 teaspoon of onion powder

COOKING DIRECTIONS:
1. Wash the tomatoes and cut them into thick slices.
2. Spray the pressure cooker with extra virgin olive oil.
3. Add the tomato slices into the cooker.
4. Combine paprika with basil and cilantro and mix well.
5. Grate the Parmesan cheese and pour it alongside the spice mixture over the tomato slices.
6. Close the pressure cooker lid and cook on sauté mode for 7 minutes.
7. When the cooking time ends, open the pressure cooker lid and allow your parmesan tomatoes to rest.. Transfer it to the serving plates and enjoy.
Nutrition: calories 250, fat 19.3, fiber 1, carbs 7.85, protein 12

Bok Choy with Mustard Sauce

Prep time: ten mins |Cooking time: 12 minutes |Servings: 7
Ingredients:
- 1 pound of bok choy
- 1 cup of water
- ½ cup of soy sauce
- 1 teaspoon of salt
- 1 teaspoon of red chili flakes
- 5 tablespoon of mustard
- 1cup of cream
- A teaspoon of cumin seeds
- 1 teaspoon of ground black pepper
- 1 tablespoon of butter
- ¼ cup of garlic cloves

COOKING DIRECTIONS:
1. Wash the bok choy and chop it into pieces.
2. Combine water with soy sauce, salt, chili flakes, cumin seeds, and ground black pepper in a bowl and mix.
3. Peel the garlic cloves and cut into thin slices.

4. Add butter and sliced garlic into the pressure cooker and sliced garlic.
5. Set the cooker to sauté mode and cook for 1 minute.
6. Add cream, soy sauce mixture, and bok choy and close the lid. Cook the mixture for 10 more minutes.
7. Drain excess fluid from the cooker and sprinkle the bok choy mixture with mustard. Stir.
8. Continue cooking on manual mode for around two minutes and transfer the delicacy to a serving bowl.
Nutrition: calories 83, fat 4.8, fiber 2.1, carbs 7.4, protein 4.2

Cloud Bread

Prep time: quarter-hour |Cooking time: 7 minutes |Servings: 4
Ingredients:
- An egg
- ¾ teaspoon of cream of tartar
- 1 tablespoon of cream cheese
- ¾ teaspoon of onion powder
- ¾ teaspoon of dried cilantro

COOKING DIRECTIONS:
1. Separate the egg white and egg yolk and put them in separate bowls.
2. Whisk the egg white using cream of tartar to achieve a strong peak.
3. Whisk the cream cheese with the egg white until fluffy.
4. Add onion powder and dried cilantro. Stir gently.
5. After this, carefully add egg white and stir it.
6. Scoop the mixture into the Ninja cooker to attain "clouds" and close the crisp lid.
7. Cook the bread for 7 minutes at 360 F or until it becomes light brown. Chill little before serving.
Nutrition: calories 27, fat 0.2, fiber 0, carbs 0.9, protein 1.6

Turmeric Rice

Prep time: 10 mins |Cooking time: 5 minutes |Servings: 2
Ingredients:
- 1 cup of cauliflower
- A tablespoon of turmeric
- ½ teaspoon of onion powder
- ½ teaspoon of garlic powder
- 1 teaspoon of dried dill
- ½ teaspoon of salt
- 1 teaspoon of butter
- 2 pecans (chopped)
- ½ cup of water

COOKING DIRECTIONS:

1. Chop the cauliflower roughly and put it in the blender.
2. Pulse it for 3-4 times or until you get some cauliflower rice.
3. Transfer the vegetables into the cooker and add onion powder, garlic powder, dried dill, and salt.
4. After that, add chopped pecans and water. Stir gently using a spoon and close the cooker's lid.
5. Cook it on high-pressure mode for 5 minutes.
6. Quick release the cooker's pressure and open the lid.
7. Drain excess water using colander.
8. Transfer the cauliflower rice to a big bowl and add turmeric followed by butter. Mix them well and serve while warm.
Nutrition: calories 145, fat 12.3, fiber 3.6, carbs 8.1, protein 3.1

Seasoned Eggs

Prep time: fifteen minutes |Cooking time: 5 minutes |Servings: 7
Ingredients:
- 1 tablespoon of mustard
- ¼ cup of cream
- 1 teaspoon of salt
- 8 eggs
- 1 teaspoon of mayonnaise
- ¼ cup of dill
- 1 teaspoon of ground white pepper
- A teaspoon of minced garlic

COOKING DIRECTIONS:
1. Put raw eggs in the pressure cooker and add water.
2. Cook the eggs on high pressure for 5 minutes.
3. Remove the eggs from pressure cooker and allow them chill.
4. Peel them and cut by half.
5. Remove the egg yolks and mash it.
6. Add mustard, cream, salt, mayonnaise, ground white pepper, and minced garlic on the mashed egg yolks. Chop the dill and pour it over the egg yolk mixture. Mix well until smooth.
7. Transfer the egg yolk mixture to your pastry bag and fill it with the egg whites. Serve immediately.
Nutrition: calories 170, fat 12.8, fiber 0, carbs 2.42, protein 11

Asparagus Mash

Prep time: 6 minutes |Cooking time: 6 minutes |Servings: 1
Ingredients:
- ½ cup of asparagus
- ½ cup of water
- 1 tablespoon of heavy cream

- 1 tablespoon of fresh basil(chopped)
- ½ teaspoon of salt
- ¾ teaspoon of freshly squeezed lemon juice

COOKING DIRECTIONS:
1. Put asparagus in a Ninja cooker.
2. Add water and salt and seal the lid.
3. Cook the vegetables on high-pressure mode for 6 minutes.
4. Quick release the cookers pressure and open its lid.
5. Drain half of the cooker's fluid and add fresh basil into the vegetables.
6. Transfer it into a blender and puree.
7. Add fresh lemon juice and heavy cream to the mixture.
8. Stir the mash and pour it into the serving bowls.
Nutrition: calories 67, fat 5.7, fiber 1.5, carbs 3.2, protein 1.9

Tender Salsa

Prep time: 7 minutes |Cooking time: ten mins |Servings: 5
Ingredients:
- 1 cup of tomatoes
- 1 teaspoon of cumin
- A teaspoon of ground coriander
- 1 tablespoon of cilantro
- ½ cup of fresh parsley
- 1 lime
- A sweet green pepper
- 1 red onion
- A teaspoon of garlic powder
- 1 teaspoon of essential olive oil
- 5 garlic cloves
- 1 bell pepper

COOKING DIRECTIONS:
1. Remove the sweet green pepper's seed and cut it by half.
2. Peel the onion and garlic cloves.
3. Place the vegetables in the pressure cooker and sprinkle them with ½ teaspoon of essential olive oil.
4. Close the cooker's lid and set it to sauté mode. Cook for 10 minutes.
5. Meanwhile, chop the tomatoes and fresh parsley.
6. Peel the lime and squeeze its juice.
7. Combine lime juice with chopped parsley, cilantro, ground coriander, and garlic powder and stir well. Sprinkle the chopped tomatoes with the lime mixture.
8. Remove the vegetables from the pressure cooker.

9. Chop onions and the bell pepper roughly and add them to the tomato mixture. Mix your tender salsa well and serve.

Nutrition: calories 38, fat 1.2, fiber 1, carbs 6.86, protein 1

Sweet Tomato Salsa

Prep time: 10 mins |Cooking time: 8 minutes |Servings: 6
Ingredients:

- 2 cups of tomatoes
- 1 teaspoon of sugar
- ½ cup of fresh cilantro
- 2 white onions
- 1 teaspoon of ground black pepper
- A teaspoon of cayenne pepper
- ½ jalapeno pepper
- 1 teaspoon of extra virgin olive oil
- 1 tablespoon of minced garlic
- ½ cup of green olives
- 1 teaspoon of paprika
- ½ cup of basil
- 1 tablespoon of Erythritol

COOKING DIRECTIONS:
1. Peel the onions and detach jalapeno pepper seeds.
2. Transfer the vegetables to the pressure cooker and sprinkle them with organic olive oil.
3. Close the cooker's lid and cook the components on sauté mode for 8 minutes.
4. Meanwhile, wash the tomatoes and chop them.
5. Place the chopped tomatoes in a bowl.
6. Chop the cilantro. Add the chopped cilantro, ground black pepper, chili pepper, and minced garlic in the chopped tomatoes.
7. Add green olives (chop them or leave them whole as desired.)
8. Chop basil and add it to the salsa mixture.
9. Add paprika and organic olive oil.
10. When the vegetables are cooked, take them off from the cooker and chill.
11. Sprinkle your sweet tomato salsa with Erythritol. Mix well and serve.

Nutrition: calories 41, fat 1.1, fiber 1.9, carbs 7.7, protein 1.2

Pickled Garlic

Prep time: 10 minutes |Cooking time: 9 minutes |Servings: 12
Ingredients:

- 2 cups of garlic
- 1 tablespoon of salt
- A tablespoon of extra virgin olive oil
- 1 teaspoon of fennel seeds
- ½ teaspoon of black peas

- 3 servings of water
- 5 tablespoons of apple cider vinegar
- 1 teaspoon of freshly squeezed lemon juice
- A teaspoon of lemon zest
- 1 tablespoon of stevia
- A teaspoon of red chili flakes

COOKING DIRECTIONS:
1. Place the salt, extra virgin olive oil, fennel seeds, black peas, freshly squeezed fresh lemon juice, lemon zest, stevia, and chili flakes in a pressure cooker.
2. Add water and stir.
3. Preheat the liquid on pressure mode for 5 minutes.
4. Peel the garlic and add it to the preheated liquid.
5. Add apple cider vinegar treatment and stir the mix.
6. Close the lid and cook the garlic on pressure mode for 4 minutes.
7. Open pressure cooker's lid and leave the garlic to rest for around 7 minutes.
8. Transfer your pickled garlic in a glass jar (like a Mason jar) and seal it tightly.
9. Store it in your refrigerator for 24 hrs. before serving.

Nutrition: calories 46, fat 1.3, fiber 0.6, carbs 7.7, protein 1.5

Marinated Spicy Olives

Prep time: ten mins |Cooking time: 17 minutes|Servings: 7
Ingredients:

- 3 cups of olives
- 1 tablespoon of red chili flakes
- A teaspoon of cilantro
- ½ cup of organic olive oil
- 4 tablespoons of apple cider vinegar
- 3 tablespoons of minced garlic
- 1 cup of water
- 3 garlic cloves
- 1-ounce of bay leaf
- ¼ cup of water
- 1 teaspoon of clove
- 4 tablespoons of lime juice

COOKING DIRECTIONS:
1. Combine chili flakes with cilantro, apple cider vinegar treatment, minced garlic, bay leaf, water, and lime juice in a mixing bowl and stir.
2. Peel the garlic cloves and chop them roughly.
3. Add the chopped garlic to the chili flake mixture.
4. Add water to the cooker's mixture.
5. Close its lid and cook the chili flake mixture on pressure mode for 10 minutes.

6. Add organic extra virgin olive oil and olives.
7. Stir the amalgamation and cook for 7 minutes.
8. When the cooking time ends, remove your marinated spicy olives from the cooker and transfer it to a sealed container. Store it for around 2 hours before serving.
Nutrition: calories 186, fat 16.9, fiber 4, carbs 10.57, protein 1

Soft Garnish Dumplings

Prep time: 10 mins |Cooking time: quarter-hour |Servings: 6
Ingredients:
- 1 cup of cottage cheese
- ½ cup of almond flour
- 1 teaspoon of baking soda
- 1 teaspoon of salt
- 2 tablespoons of Erythritol
- 4 tablespoons of coconut milk
- 1 teaspoon of basil
- 3 eggs

COOKING DIRECTIONS:
1. Blend the cottage cheese in a blender.
2. Add eggs and continue blending until it smoothens.
3. Transfer the mix to a bowl and add baking soda followed by almond flour.
4. Sprinkle the mixture with salt, Erythritol, coconut milk, and basil.
5. Knead the dough and mold small logs from it.
6. Set the pressure cooker mode to steam and add the dough logs.
7. Close the cooker's lid and cook for quarter-hour.
8. When the cooking time ends, take off your garnished dumplings from the cooker and serve immediately.
Nutrition: calories 102, fat 6.5, fiber 0.5, carbs 2.6, protein 8.7

Carrot Fries

Prep time: ten minutes |Cooking time: 18 minutes |Servings: 2
Ingredients:
- 2 carrots (peeled)
- 1 teaspoon of salt
- A tablespoon of organic olive oil
- 1 teaspoon of dried parsley

COOKING DIRECTIONS:
1. Cut the carrots into fries. Add dried parsley and season with salt.
2. Mix the contents and transfer them to a Ninja cooker.
3. Close the lid and cook the fries on mid-air crisp mode for 18 minutes (385F.)

4. When the time elapses, open the lid and shake your fries.
5. Cook the carrot fries for more minutes to acquire a crunchy crust. Serve hot.
Nutrition: calories 85, fat 7, fiber 1.5, carbs 6, protein 0.5

Mint Green Peas

PREP TIME: 10 MINUTES |COOKING TIME: 17 MINUTES |SERVINGS: 5
Ingredients:
- 2 cups of green peas
- ½ cup of fresh mint
- 1 tablespoon of dried mint
- A cup of water
- 1 teaspoon of salt
- A tablespoon of butter
- ½ teaspoon of peppercorn
- 1 teaspoon of extra virgin organic olive oil

COOKING DIRECTIONS:
1. Wash mint and chop it.
2. Transfer the chopped mint in the pressure cooker.
3. Add water and close the cooker's lid.
4. Cook the mixture on pressure mode for 7 minutes.
5. Set your mint leaves aside and add green peas, dried mint, salt, peppercorn to the cooker's liquid.
6. Cook them on pressure mode for 10 minutes.
7. Rinse the cooked green peas using colander.
8. Put the peas in a serving bowl and add butter followed by essential organic olive oil.
9. Stir your mint green peas until butter dissolves.
Nutrition: calories 97, fat 4.6, fiber 4, carbs 11.48, protein 3

Veggie Salad with Feta Cheese

Prep time: 10 mins |Cooking time: quarter-hour |Servings: 7
Ingredients:
- 2 medium carrots
- 7 ounces of turnips
- 1 tablespoon of organic olive oil
- 1 red onion
- 4 garlic cloves
- 5 ounces of feta cheese
- 1 teaspoon of butter
- A teaspoon of onion powder
- 1 tablespoon of salt
- A teaspoon of ground black pepper
- 1 red sweet bell pepper

COOKING DIRECTIONS:
1. Wash the carrots and peel them.

2. Peel turnips, onion, and garlic cloves and put them in a pressure cooker.
3. Cook them on steam mode for a quarter-hour or until the vegetables tenders.
4. Chop the vegetables into small pieces and pour them in a mixing bowl.
5. Add butter and stir.
6. Sprinkle the amalgamation with onion powder, salt, ground black pepper.
7. Extract the bell pepper's seeds and chop it.
8. Crumble the feta cheese and add each component into the salad.
9. Mix carefully and serve the salad warm.
Nutrition: calories 107, fat 6.9, fiber 1.6, carbs 8.2, protein 3.8

Eggplant Casserole

Prep time: ten minutes |Cooking time: 20 minutes |Servings: 8
Ingredients:
- 3 eggplants (chopped)
- A white onion (chopped)
- 1 bell pepper (chopped)
- A turnip (chopped)
- 1 teaspoon of salt
- 1 teaspoon of ground black pepper
- A teaspoon of red pepper cayenne
- ½ teaspoon of white pepper
- 1 cup of cream
- 5 oz of Parmesan (grated)

COOKING DIRECTIONS:
1. Mix white onion, bell pepper, and turnip in a bowl.
2. Add salt, ground black pepper, red pepper cayenne, and white pepper.
3. In the cooker, put eggplants, onion mixture, cheese, and cream.
4. Close and seal the lid.
5. Cook the casserole for ten minutes on high-pressure mode.
6. Quick release the cooker's pressure and leave it to cool until it reaches the room temperature.
Nutrition: calories 144, fat 6, fiber 8.1, carbs 17.3, protein 8.5

Turnip Fries

Prep time: quarter-hour |Cooking time: 14 minutes |Servings: 5
Ingredients:
- 1-pound turnips (peeled)
- A tablespoon of avocado oil
- 1 teaspoon of dried oregano
- A teaspoon of onion powder
- ½ teaspoon of salt
- 1 teaspoon of turmeric

COOKING DIRECTIONS:

1. Cut the turnips into fries and sprinkle them with dried oregano, avocado oil, onion powder, and turmeric.
2. Mix the turnip and permit it soak the spices for 5-ten minutes.
3. Put them in a Ninja basket and close the lid.
4. Set the cooker to Air crisp mode (390F) and cook the fries for 14 minutes or until it turns light brown.
5. Transfer it to the serving plates and sprinkle with salt.
Nutrition: calories 34, fat 0.4, fiber 1.9, carbs 7, protein 0.9

Aromatic Radish

PREP TIME: TEN MINUTES|COOKING TIME: 8 MINUTES |SERVINGS: 5
Ingredients:
- 3 cups of radish (trimmed)
- 1 tablespoon of extra virgin essential olive oil
- A tablespoon of butter
- 1 teaspoon of salt
- A teaspoon of dried dill

COOKING DIRECTIONS:
1. Cut the radishes into halves and put them in a mixing bowl.
2. Sprinkle them with organic olive oil, salt, and dried dill. Shake.
3. After this, transfer them to a Ninja cooker and add butter.
4. Close the lid and set the cooker in air crisp mode.
5. Cook the radishes for 8 minutes at 375F. When half of the cooking time passes, stir.
6. Transfer the radishes to serving plates and serve them hot.
Nutrition: calories 56, fat 5.2, fiber 1.1, carbs 2.5, protein 0.5

Turmeric Butternut Squash Strips

Prep time: ten mins |Cooking time: fifteen minutes |Servings: 5
Ingredients:
- 1 pound of butternut squash
- A teaspoon of salt
- ¼ cup of water
- 2 tablespoons of turmeric
- 3 tablespoons of peanut oil

COOKING DIRECTIONS:
1. Wash the butternut squash and peel it.
2. Cut the butternut squash into strips.
3. Sprinkle the cubes with salt, turmeric, and peanut oil. Stir.
4. Place the strips in a pressure cooker having set to sauté mode and cook for ten minutes. Stir.
5. Add water and close the cooker's lid.

6.   Cook the dish on pressure mode for 5 minutes or tenders.

7.   When the cooking time ends, transfer your turmeric strips into serving bowls and enjoy.

Nutrition: calories 124, fat 8.3, fiber 3, carbs 13.13, protein 1

Vegetable Pasta Salad

Prep time: ten mins |Cooking time: 8 minutes |Servings: 10

Ingredients:

- 8 ounces of black bean pasta
- 3 servings of water
- 1 cup of pork rind
- ½ cup of cream cheese
- 3 medium cucumbers
- 1 teaspoon of oregano
- ½ cup of spinach
- 2 tomatoes
- 1 red onion
- A teaspoon of paprika

COOKING DIRECTIONS:

1.   Put the bean pasta in a pressure cooker and add water.

2.   Close the lid and cook it on pressure mode for 8 minutes.

3.   Rinse the pasta with water and put them in a mixing bowl.

4.   Peel the red onion and slice it.

5.   Wash the spinach and chop it.

6.   Chop the tomatoes and cucumbers.

7.   Add the sliced onion, chopped spinach, tomatoes, and cucumbers in a pasta bowl.

8.   Sprinkle the salad with oregano and paprika.

9.   Add cream cheese and blend the mixture to smoothen.

10.   Add pork rind and stir the salad well.

Nutrition: calories 201, fat 9.1, fiber 6, carbs 12.7, protein 19.2

Eggplant Cubes

Prep time: quarter-hour |Cooking time: quarter-hour |Servings: 6

Ingredients:

- 3 eggplants (trimmed)
- 1 tablespoon of salt
- 1 tablespoon of butter
- A teaspoon of minced garlic
- 1 teaspoon of onion powder
- A teaspoon of chili flakes
- 1/3 cup of heavy cream

COOKING DIRECTIONS:

1.   Chop the eggplants roughly and place them on a mixing bowl.

2.   Sprinkle the vegetables with the salt and stir well.

3.   Leave them for 10 minutes.

4.   Drain the liquid squeezed from the vegetables.

5.   Transfer dry eggplants into a pressure cooker.

6.   Add butter, minced garlic, onion powder, chili flakes, and heavy cream. Stir.

7.   Cook the vegetables on saute mode for quarter-hour when stirring.

8.   The eggplants become ready when they tender. Serve hot.

Nutrition: calories 111, fat 4.9, fiber 9.7, carbs 16.8, protein 2.9

Mushroom Puree

Prep time: 10 mins |Cooking time: 20 mins |Servings: 8

Ingredients:

- 12 ounces of cremini mushrooms
- 3 tablespoons of butter
- A teaspoon of organic olive oil
- 1 big white onion
- ¼ cup of cream
- 1 teaspoon of salt
- A teaspoon of ground black pepper
- 1 teaspoon of chicken stock

COOKING DIRECTIONS:

1.   Wash the mushrooms and chop them.

2.   Add the butter in the pressure cooker and melt it on pressure mode.

3.   Add the chopped mushrooms and sprinkle them with salt, ground black pepper, and chicken stock.

4.   Peel the onion and dice it.

5.   Add the diced onion into the mushroom mixture.

6.   Sprinkle it with essential extra virgin olive oil and stir well.

7.   Close the lid and cook the dish at sauté mode for around twenty minutes.

8.   When the cooking time ends, transfer the mushrooms into a mixing bowl.

9.   Puree the mixture using an immersion blender.

10.   Transfer the mushroom puree to a serving bowl. Add cream, mix, and serve.

Nutrition: calories 192, fat 6.8, fiber 5, carbs 34.17, protein 5

Savory Braised Onions

Prep time: 7 minutes |Cooking time: quarter-hour |Servings: 6

Ingredients:

- A cup of liquid stevia
- 1 teaspoon of sea salt

- A pound of white onion
- 4 tablespoons of butter(unsalted)
- 1 teaspoon of ground ginger
- ½ teaspoon of cinnamon

COOKING DIRECTIONS:
1. Combine the liquid stevia with sea salt.
2. Add ground ginger and cinnamon and stir.
3. Peel the onion and slice it.
4. Combine the sliced onion with the stevia mixture and stir.
5. Leave the onions for 5 minutes.
6. Add the butter into the pressure cooker and sauté to melt.
7. Add the onion mixture and stir gently.
8. Close the lid and cook the onions for 15 minutes.
9. When the cooking time ends, open the pressure cooker lid and remove the braised onions. Serve hot.

Nutrition: calories 100, fat 7.8, fiber 1.8, carbs 7.4, protein 1

Sour Cream Pumpkin Cubes

Prep time: ten mins |Cooking time: ten minutes |Servings: 5

Ingredients:
- A pound of pumpkin
- 3 tablespoons of Erythritol
- 1 teaspoon of ground ginger
- ¼ teaspoon of nutmeg
- ½ teaspoon of ground coriander
- ½ cup of water
- ½ cup of sour cream

COOKING DIRECTIONS:
1. Peel the pumpkin and cut it into big cubes.
2. Add Erythritol followed by ginger and mix well.
3. Add nutmeg and ground coriander.
4. Set the pumpkin aside for around 5 minutes to release some juice. Drain it.
5. Transfer the pumpkin cubes into a pressure cooker and add water.
6. Close the lid and cook the dish on pressure mode for ten minutes.
7. When the cooking time ends, release the cooker's lid.
8. Transfer the cooked pumpkin cubes to the serving plate and sprinkle it with sour cream. Enjoy.

Nutrition: calories 82, fat 5.1, fiber 2.7, carbs 8.6, protein 1.8

Sliced Chili Onions

Prep time: quarter-hour |Cooking time: 4 minutes |Servings: 3

Ingredients:
- 2 white onions (sliced)
- 1 tablespoon of chili pepper

- A tablespoon of apple cider vinegar
- 1 tablespoon of organic olive oil
- ½ teaspoon of salt
- 1 teaspoon of butter
- ¾ cup of water

COOKING DIRECTIONS:
1. Slice the onions and place them in a mixing bowl.
2. Add chili pepper, apple cider vinegar treatment, extra virgin essential olive oil, and salt.
3. Add onions and stir. Leave the ingredients for 10 minutes to marinate.
4. After this, pour water into the cooker and add the remaining onions and butter.
5. Close and seal the lid and cook the vegetables on high-pressure mode for 4 minutes.
6. Quick release the built-in pressure and open the lid.
7. Stir your chili onions well using a spoon and transfer the contents to serving plates.
Remember, the cooked vegetables should be tender and not marshy.

Nutrition: calories 84, fat 6.1, fiber 1.8, carbs 7.4, protein 0.9

Bok Choy

Prep time: ten minutes |Cooking time: 8 minutes |Servings: 2

Ingredients:
- 9 oz of bok choy
- 1 tablespoon of essential organic olive oil
- A teaspoon of lemon juice
- 1 teaspoon of ground black pepper

COOKING DIRECTIONS:
1. Wash and trim the bok choy.
2. Cut the vegetables into halves and sprinkle them with lemon juice.
3. Transfer them into a cooker and add extra virgin olive oil followed by the ground black pepper.
4. Mix the vegetables using a wooden spatula and set your cooker to air crisp mode. Close the lid.
5. Cook the vegetables for 8 minutes having stirred them after 4 minutes of cooking.
6. Ladle your dish to serving bowls and enjoy.
7. Your cooked bok choy should have a very tender texture.

Nutrition: calories 77, fat 7.3, fiber 1.3, carbs 2.8, protein 1.9

Artichoke Petals in Creamy Sauce

Prep time: 8 minutes |Cooking time: 8 minutes |Servings: 5

Ingredients:
- A pound of artichoke petals
- 1 cup of heavy cream
- 3 oz of Cheddar cheese (shredded)
- 1 teaspoon of minced garlic

- A teaspoon of garlic powder
- 1 teaspoon of chili flakes
- A teaspoon of almond flour
- 1 tablespoon of butter
- ½ teaspoon of salt

COOKING DIRECTIONS:
1. Mix artichoke petals with minced garlic, garlic powder, and chili flakes in a bowl.
2. Add salt and transfer the amalgamation into a cooker.
3. Add shredded cheese, almond flour, and cream and mix.
4. Close the lid and cook the contents on high pressure mode for 8 minutes.
5. Quick release the pressure and open the lid.
6. Mix in the artichoke petals with sauce and transfer it into serving bowls.

Nutrition: calories 220, fat 17.2, fiber 5, carbs 11.1, protein 7.9

Kabocha Squash

Prep time: 10 mins |Cooking time: a number of hours |Servings: 2
Ingredients:
- 1 ½ cup of Kabocha squash (chopped)
- ½ teaspoon of ground cinnamon
- ½ teaspoon of Erythritol
- A tablespoon of butter
- ½ teaspoon of ground ginger
- ½ cup of water

COOKING DIRECTIONS:
1. Mix Kabocha squash, ground cinnamon, ginger, and Erythritol in a bowl.
2. Add butter and water and close the lid.
3. Cook the vegetable on low-pressure mode until it tenders.
4. Transfer your Kabocha squash into the serving bowl and add some gravy. Enjoy.

Nutrition: calories 84, fat 5.8, fiber 1.4, carbs 7.8, protein 1.1

Soy Sauce Thai Zucchini Strips

Prep time: 10 mins |Cooking time: quarter-hour |Servings: 8
Ingredients:
- 3 medium green zucchini
- 1 teaspoon of ground black pepper
- ½ cup of soy sauce
- 1 tablespoon of sesame seeds
- A teaspoon of salt
- ½ tablespoon of Erythritol
- 1 tablespoon of butter
- A tablespoon of heavy cream
- 1 teaspoon of cilantro
- An egg
- 1 teaspoon of cumin seeds

- ½ cup of almond flour

COOKING DIRECTIONS:
1. Wash the zucchini and strip them.
2. Combine the ground black pepper with sesame seeds, salt, and cilantro in a mixing bowl.
3. Add cumin seeds followed by Erythritol and soy sauce. Blend.
4. Whisk an egg in a mixing bowl and pour it over zucchini strips. Mix them well using your hands.
5. Sprinkle the zucchini strips with almond flour and the ground black pepper mixture.
6. Add butter to the pressure cooker followed by cream.
7. Add the zucchini strips to form its layer.
8. Cook the zucchini on pressure mode for 5 minutes.
9. Add another bunch of zucchini to form a second layer.
10. Repeat this until all your zucchini are cooked.
11. Put the cooked zucchini strips in a pressure cooker.
12. Add the soy sauce mixture and close the lid. Saute the spiced dish for 3 minutes.
13. When the cooking time ends, transfer your sauced-Thai zucchini strips to serving plates.

Nutrition: calories 61, fat 4.2, fiber 1.3, carbs 3.7, protein 2.8

Carrots Wrapped with Bacon

Prep time: ten mins |Cooking time: ten mins |Servings: 8
Ingredients:
- 1 pound of carrots
- 9 ounces of sliced bacon
- 1 teaspoon of salt
- ½ teaspoon of ground black pepper
- A teaspoon of ground white pepper
- 1 teaspoon of paprika
- ¼ cup of chicken stock
- 1 tablespoon of organic essential olive oil
- ¼ teaspoon of marjoram

COOKING DIRECTIONS:
1. Wash the carrots and peel.
2. Sprinkle them with ground black pepper and add salt, ground white pepper, paprika, and marjoram. Stir the amalgamation.
3. Coat the sliced bacon with the spice mixture.
4. Wrap the carrots in the sliced bacon.
5. Pour the essential olive oil in a pressure cooker and add the wrapped carrots.
6. Close the cooker's lid and sauté the carrot for 10 minutes.
7. Add chicken stock and cook the dish on pressure mode for 8 minutes.

8.   When the cooking time ends, release the cooker's pressure and open the lid. Serve your bacon delicacy warm.
Nutrition: calories 141, fat 11.4, fiber 3, carbs 7.91, protein 4

Healthy Turnip-Broccoli Mash

Prep time: quarter-hour |Cooking time: 25 minutes |Servings: 6
Ingredients:
- 8 ounces of turnip
- 5 ounces of broccoli
- 2 cups of chicken stock
- ¼ cup of cream
- 1 tablespoon of salt
- A teaspoon of cilantro
- 2 tablespoons of butter
- 1 teaspoon of thyme

COOKING DIRECTIONS:
1.   Peel the turnip and cut the broccoli into florets.
2.   Chop the turnip and broccoli florets and put them in a pressure cooker.
3.   Add salt, cilantro, and butter. Blend well.
4.   Add chicken stock and close the lid.
5.   Set the pressure cooker to steam mode and cook for 25 minutes.
6.   When the cooking time ends, remove the vegetables from the cooker.
7.   Ensure that it has left at least a half cup of the vegetable liquid.
8.   Place the vegetables in very blender.
9.   Add the vegetable liquid and cream. Puree the combination until smooth.
10.   Add butter and blend them for two minutes.
11.   Serve your potato-broccoli mash warm.
Nutrition: calories 62, fat 4.7, fiber 1.3, carbs 4.6, protein 1.4

Sautéed Pineapple

Prep time: 5 minutes|Cooking time: 10 minutes |Servings: 5
Ingredients:
- 9 ounces of pineapple
- 1 tablespoon of Erythritol
- ¼ cup of freshly squeezed lemon juice
- 3 tablespoons of water
- 1 teaspoon of cinnamon
- A teaspoon of peanut oil
- ½ teaspoon of paprika

COOKING DIRECTIONS:
1.   Peel the pineapple and cut it into cubes.
2.   Pour peanut oil in the pressure cooker and add pineapple cubes.
3.   Set the load cooker to sauté mode and cook the fruits for 3 minutes while stirring frequently.

4.   Add Erythritol, freshly squeezed lemon juice, water, cinnamon, and paprika. Blend the combination gently. Close the lid and sauté the pineapple mixture for 7 minutes.
5.   When the cooking time ends, remove your sautéed pineapple and serve warm.
Nutrition: calories 38, fat 1.1, fiber 1.1, carbs 7.5, protein 0.4

Enoki Mushrooms

Prep time: ten mins |Cooking time: 9 minutes |Servings: 4
Ingredients:
- 1-pound of Enoki mushrooms
- A teaspoon of salt
- 1 teaspoon of sesame seeds
- 1 tablespoon of canola oil
- A tablespoon of apple cider vinegar
- 1 teaspoon of paprika
- 1 tablespoon of butter
- ½ teaspoon of lemon zest
- 1 cup of water (for cooking)

COOKING DIRECTIONS:
1.   Slice the mushrooms roughly and put them in the cooker.
2.   Add water and salt and close the cooker's lid.
3.   Cook the vegetables on high-pressure mode for 9 minutes.
4.   Allow the built-in pressure to release naturally and open the cooker's lid.
5.   Drain excess fluids and transfer the mushrooms into a bowl.
6.   Sprinkle it with sesame seeds, canola oil, apple cider vinegar treatment, paprika, butter, and lemon zest. Mix well and serve.
Nutrition: calories 113, fat 7.2, fiber 3.4, carbs 9.3, protein 3.2

Melted Cabbage Wedges

Prep time: 10 minutes |Cooking time: 25 minutes |Servings: 8
Ingredients:
- 10 ounces of cabbage
- 3 tablespoons of tomato paste
- 1 cup of chicken stock
- A teaspoon of butter
- 1 sweet bell pepper
- ¼ cup of sour cream
- 1 teaspoon of cilantro
- A teaspoon of basil
- 1 medium yellow onion

COOKING DIRECTIONS:
1.   Wash the cabbage and cut it into wedges.
2.   Place the cabbage wedges into the pressure cooker.

3.　　Combine chicken stock with butter, tomato paste, sour cream, cilantro, and basil in a mixing bowl. Blend.

4.　　Peel the onion and detach the bell pepper seeds. Chop the vegetables and add them to the cabbage mixture. Add chicken stock sauce and mix well using a wooden spoon or spatula.

5.　　Close the pressure cooker lid and cook the dish on pressure mode for 25 minutes.

6.　　When the cooking time ends, open the cooker's lid and allow the amalgamation rest. Do not stir it.

7.　　Transfer your melted cabbage wedges into serving plates and enjoy.

Nutrition: calories 45, fat 2.2, fiber 1.6, carbs 6, protein 1.3

Sauteed Celery Stalk

Prep time: ten mins |Cooking time: 3 minutes |Servings: 4

Ingredients:

- 1-pound of celery stalk
- An oz of pork rind
- 1 teaspoon of ground black pepper
- A teaspoon of organic extra virgin olive oil
- 1 teaspoon of salt
- 1 cup of water (for cooking)

COOKING DIRECTIONS:

1.　　Chop the celery stalk roughly and put them in a pressure cooker.

2.　　Add water and close the cooker's lid.

3.　　Cook the celery mixture on high-pressure mode for 3 minutes.

4.　　Allow pressure to release naturally and open the lid.

5.　　Drain water and transfer celery stalk in the bowl.

6.　　Add ground black pepper, essential olive oil, salt, and pork rind and stir.

7.　　Transfer the components to a serving bowl (plates) and enjoy.

Nutrition: calories 70, fat 3.94, fiber 2, carbs 3.7, protein 5.4

VEGETABLE MEALS RECIPES

Zucchini Gratin

Prep time: ten mins | Cooking time: 3 hours | Servings: 6
Ingredients
- 2 zucchini (sliced)
- 1 cup of cream cheese
- 4 oz of Cheddar cheese (shredded)
- A teaspoon of ground black pepper
- 1 teaspoon of salt
- ¼ cup of fresh dill (chopped)
- ¾ cup of walnuts(chopped)
- 1 teaspoon of essential organic olive oil

COOKING DIRECTIONS:
1. Brush the cooker basket with olive oil.
2. Make a layer of sliced zucchini inside.
3. Spread it with cream cheese and walnuts.
4. Add shredded cheese, salt, and dill.
5. Repeat the above procedure until your ingredients are exhausted.
6. Close the lid and cook the gratin on low-pressure mode for 3 hours.
7. Allow your zucchini gratin to cool to room temperature and transfer it to serving bowls.

Nutrition: calories 331, fat 30, fiber 2.1, carbs 6.4, protein 12.6

Steamed Kale

Prep time: ten MINUTES | Cooking time: 6 minutes | Servings: 6
Ingredients
- 1-pound of kale
- A teaspoon of garlic powder
- 1 teaspoon of essential organic olive oil
- ¾ cup of heavy cream
- 1 tablespoon of almonds(chopped)
- A teaspoon of salt
- 1 cup of water (for cooking)

COOKING DIRECTIONS:
1. Chop the kale roughly.
2. Pour water into the pressure cooker and insert trivet.
3. Place the chopped kale on the trivet.
4. Close the cooker's lid and steam the greens for 6 minutes.
5. Meanwhile, mix organic olive oil, cream almonds, and salt.
6. When your steamed kale is cooked, transfer it to the serving bowls and sprinkle it with heavy cream mixture.

Nutrition: calories 103, fat 6.8, fiber 1.3, carbs 8.9, protein 2.9

Herb Carrots

Prep time: ten MINUTES | Cooking time: 20 MINUTES |Servings: 5
Ingredients
- 1 pound of carrots
- 1 teaspoon of salt
- 1 teaspoon of cilantro
- ½ teaspoon of ground ginger
- 1 teaspoon of paprika
- A tablespoon of basil
- ¼ teaspoon of rosemary
- ½ cup of half and half
- 1 teaspoon of minced garlic
- A teaspoon of white pepper

COOKING DIRECTIONS:
1. Peel the carrots and cut them into bite-sized pieces.
2. Combine salt with cilantro, ground ginger, paprika, basil, white pepper, and rosemary in a mixing bowl.
3. Stir the spice mixture and add the carrots.
4. Set the pressure cooker's mode to steam and fix a trivet.
5. Place the carrots on the trivet and cook for 20 minutes.
6. When the cooking time ends, eliminate the dish from the cooker and transfer your herb carrots in a serving plate.
7. Combine the half and half with the minced garlic and mix well.
8. Pour the cream over the carrots and serve.

Nutrition: calories 45, fat 0.5, fiber 3, carbs 9.75, protein 1

Fragrant Jicama

Prep time: ten minutes | Cooking time: 8 MINUTES | Servings: 2
Ingredients
- 7 oz jicama (chopped)
- 1 teaspoon of dried oregano
- ½ teaspoon of dried cilantro
- 1 tablespoon of canola oil
- 1 teaspoon of onion powder
- ½ teaspoon of ground ginger

COOKING DIRECTIONS:
1. Place the chopped jicama in the cooker.
2. Sprinkle it with dried oregano, cilantro, canola oil, onion powder, and ground ginger.
3. Mix the ingredients gently and close the lid.
4. Set the cooker to air crisp mode (375F) and cook the meal for 8 minutes.
5. When your fragrant jicama is tender, transfer it into serving bowls and enjoy.

Nutrition: calories 108, fat 7.2, fiber 5.3, carbs 10.5, protein 1

Zucchini Fries

Prep time: 10 mins | Cooking time: ten minutes | Servings: 6

Ingredients

- 1 zucchini
- A tablespoon of organic olive oil
- 1 teaspoon of ground black pepper

COOKING DIRECTIONS:

1. Trim the zucchini and cut it into fries.
2. Place the vegetables in the cooker and sprinkle with organic olive oil. Stir gently.
3. Close the lid and set your cooker to air crisp mode.
4. Cook the fries for 10 minutes at 370 F.
5. Stir and spread over it ground black pepper.

Nutrition: calories 262, fat 2.4, fiber 0.5, carbs 1.3, protein 0.4

Sweet Sriracha Carrots

Prep time: ten MINUTES | Cooking time: 17 MINUTES | Servings: 7

Ingredients

- 2 tablespoons of sriracha
- 1 cup of water
- A teaspoon of Erythritol
- 2 tablespoons of organic olive oil
- ½ cup of dill
- 1 pound of carrots
- 1 teaspoon of oregano

COOKING DIRECTIONS:

1. Wash the carrots, peel, and slice them.
2. Set the pressure cooker to sauté mode.
3. Pour the organic extra virgin olive oil in the cooker and add the sliced carrots.
4. Sprinkle the vegetables with oregano and dill.
5. Sauté the dish for quarter-hour while stirring frequently.
6. Sprinkle the carrot with Erythritol, water, and sriracha. Mix well.
7. Close the cooker's lid and cook the dish on pressure mode for 2 minutes.
8. When the cooking time ends, release the accumulated pressure and open the lid.
9. Transfer your sweet srirarcha carrots to a serving plate and enjoy.

Nutrition: calories 74, fat 4.2, fiber 2.2, carbs 9.3, protein 1.2

Brussels Sprouts

Prep time: 7 minutes | Cooking time: 4 minutes | Servings: 6

Ingredients

- 13 ounces of Brussels sprouts
- 1 teaspoon of salt
- A teaspoon of cumin
- ½ teaspoon of coriander
- ½ teaspoon of chili powder
- 1 cup of chicken stock
- A teaspoon of thyme
- 1 tablespoon of butter
- A teaspoon of organic olive oil

COOKING DIRECTIONS:

1. Wash the Brussels sprouts and put them in the pressure cooker.
2. Combine salt with cumin, coriander, chili powder, and thyme and mix well.
3. Sprinkle the Brussels sprouts with the spice mixture and stir.
4. Add organic olive oil, butter, and chicken stock.
5. Set the cooker to pressure mode and close its lid. Cook for 4 minutes.
6. When the cooking time ends, release the built-in pressure and open the lid.
7. Transfer your Brussels sprouts to serving bowls.

Nutrition: calories 67, fat 3.5, fiber 3, carbs 7.22, protein 3

Stewed Cabbage

Prep time: 10 minutes | Cooking time: thirty MINUTES | Servings: 7

Ingredients

- 13 ounces of cabbage
- 2 red bell pepper
- ¼ chili pepper
- 1 cup of tomato juice
- A tablespoon of extra virgin organic olive oil
- 1 teaspoon of salt
- 1 teaspoon of paprika
- A teaspoon of basil
- ½ cup of dill (chopped)

COOKING DIRECTIONS:

1. Wash the cabbage and chop it into tiny pieces.
2. Sprinkle the chopped cabbage with salt, paprika, and basil. Mix well using your hands.
3. Transfer the cabbage to a pressure cooker and add tomato juice, organic olive oil, and chopped dill.
4. Chop Chili and red bell peppers and add them to the cooker's contents.
5. Close the pressure cooker's lid and cook the dish on sauté mode for half an hour.
6. When your stewed cabbage is ready transfer it to a bowl and allow them to cool before serving.

Nutrition: calories 46, fat 2.2, fiber 2, carbs 6.62, protein 1

Broccoli Casserole

Prep time: ten MINUTES | Cooking time: 25 MINUTES | Servings: 8
Ingredients

- 10 ounces of broccoli
- 1 cup of cream
- 7 ounces of mushrooms
- 1 onion
- 1 bell pepper
- ½ cup of chicken stock
- 8 ounces of crackers
- A tablespoon of butter
- 1teaspoon of ground black pepper
- 1 tablespoon of salt
- ½ cup of green peas

COOKING DIRECTIONS:
1. Chop the broccoli and slice the mushrooms.
2. Crush the crackers, combine them with ground black pepper, and stir.
3. Chop the bell pepper and onion.
4. Place the broccoli in a pressure cooker and make a layer of the chopped bell pepper and onion.
5. Combine cream with salt and stir. Add green peas.
6. Pour the cream mixture into the pressure cooker.
7. Add chicken stock and butter.
8. Sprinkle the casserole mixture with the crushed crackers.
9. Close the pressure cooker lid and cook the dish on sauté mode for 25 minutes.
10. When the cooking time ends, allow your broccoli casserole to rest briefly before serving.
Nutrition: calories 317, fat 15.4, fiber 5, carbs 41.89, protein 7

Crunchy Broccoli Florets with Egg

Prep time: 10 MINUTES | Cooking time: 6 MINUTES | Servings: 6
Ingredients

- 14 ounces of broccoli
- 1 cup of coconut flour
- 4 eggs
- 1 teaspoon of salt
- 1 teaspoon of ground black pepper
- ¼ cup of essential extra virgin olive oil
- 1 teaspoon of ground cumin

COOKING DIRECTIONS:
1. Wash the broccoli and separate it into florets.
2. Beat the eggs in a mixing bowl and add salt, ground black pepper, and ground cumin.
3. Sprinkle the egg mixture with coconut flour and stir.
4. Dip the broccoli in the egg mixture for coating.

5. Pour olive oil in the pressure cooker and preheat it on saute mode.
6. Transfer the broccoli to the pressure cooker and sauté each side for two minutes.
7. Close the cooker's lid and cook the dish on pressure mode for two minutes.
8. When your broccoli florets are cooked, allow them to unwind before serving.
Nutrition: calories 210, fat 15.9, fiber 2, carbs 8.68, protein 9

Marinated Roasted Mushrooms

Prep time: ten mins | Cooking time: 13 minutes | Servings: 6
Ingredients

- 10 ounces of mushrooms
- 1 onion
- 1 garlic cloves
- 1 ounce of bay leaf
- ¼ teaspoon of black-eyed peas
- 3 tablespoons of apple cider vinegar treatment
- 1 tablespoon of extra virgin olive oil
- A teaspoon of sea salt
- 1 teaspoon of ground black pepper

COOKING DIRECTIONS:
1. Peel the onion and garlic cloves.
2. Slice the vegetables and sprinkle them with the black-eyed peas.
3. Add bay leaf and apple cider vinegar.
4. Chop the mushrooms and put them in the onion mixture.
5. Add sea salt and ground black pepper and mix well. allow the mixture to rest for ten minutes.
6. Set the cooker to sauté mode and pour organic olive oil followed by the mushroom mixture.
7. Close the cooker's lid and sauté the dish for 13 minutes.
8. When the cooking time ends, stir your roasted mushrooms and transfer them to a serving bowl.
Nutrition: calories 189, fat 3.2, fiber 7, carbs 42.64, protein 5

Cauliflower Puree with Scallions

Prep time: fifteen minutes | Cooking time: 7 minutes | Servings: 6
Ingredients

- 1 head of cauliflower
- 4 servings of water
- 1 tablespoon of salt
- 4 tablespoons of butter
- 3 ounces of scallions
- 1 teaspoon of chicken stock
- ¼ teaspoon of sesame seeds
- 1 egg yolk

COOKING DIRECTIONS:

1. Wash the cauliflower and chop it roughly.
2. Place the cauliflower in a pressure cooker and add water. Season your watery mixture with salt.
3. Close the cooker's lid and cook the vegetables on pressure mode for 5 minutes.
4. Release the accumulated pressure and open the cooker's lid.
5. Remove the cauliflower from the cooker and set it aside.
6. Pour your warm cauliflower mixture in the blender.
7. Add butter, chicken stock, and sesame seeds.
8. Blend the amalgamation well.
9. Chop the scallions.
10. Add an egg yolk to the blender mixture and puree them for 30 seconds.
11. Remove the cauliflower puree from the blender and combine it with the chopped scallions. Mix well and serve.

Nutrition: calories 94, fat 8.7, fiber 1, carbs 3.39, protein 2

Vegetable Tart

Prep time: quarter-HOUR | Cooking time: 25 MINUTES | Servings: 9
Ingredients
- 7 ounces of puff pastry
- 1 egg yolk
- 2 red bell peppers
- 5 ounces of tomatoes
- 1 red onion
- 1 eggplant
- 3 ounces of zucchini
- A teaspoon of salt
- 1 teaspoon of essential olive oil
- A teaspoon of ground black pepper
- 1 tablespoon of turmeric
- 7 ounces of goat cheese
- ¼ cup of cream

COOKING DIRECTIONS:
1. Whisk the egg yolk and combine it with the ground black pepper. Stir well.
2. Roll the puff pastry using a rolling pin.
3. Spray the pressure cooker with extra virgin olive oil and add puff pastry.
4. Spread the puff pastry with whisked egg.
5. Chop the tomatoes and dice the onions.
6. Chop the eggplants and zucchini.
7. Combine the vegetables and season them with salt, turmeric, and cream.
8. Mix the vegetables well and transfer them into the pressure cooker.
9. Chop the red sweet peppers and add it to the cooker's content.
10. Grate the goat cheese and sprinkle the tart with cheese.

11. Close the cooker's lid and cook the mixture at pressure mode for 25 minutes.
12. When your vegetable tart is cooked, release the accumulated pressure and open the cooker's lid.
13. Transfer it in a flatter and serve it while sliced.

Nutrition: calories 279, fat 18.8, fiber 3, carbs 18.42, protein 10

Zucchini Pizza

Prep time: 10 minutes | Cooking time: 8 minutes | Servings: 2
Ingredients
- 1 zucchini
- ½ teaspoon of tomato paste
- 5 oz of parmesan (shredded)
- ½ teaspoon of chili flakes
- ¼ teaspoon of dried basil
- 1 teaspoon of extra virgin olive oil

COOKING DIRECTIONS:
1. Cut the zucchini into halves.
2. Pour tomato sauce over the zucchini halves.
3. Fill them with shredded cheese and sprinkle the mixture with chili flakes, dried basil, and essential olive oil. Put the zucchini pizzas in the cooker and close its lid.
4. Cook the pizzas on air crisp mode (375F) for 8 minutes.
5. Place it on a flatter and slice it before serving.

Nutrition: calories 331, fat 21.9, fiber 1.1, carbs 6, protein 28.1

Black Beans in Tomato Sauce

Prep time: ten MINUTES | Cooking time: 19 minutes | Servings: 7
Ingredients
- 8 ounces of black beans
- 1 onion
- 1 cup of tomato paste
- A tablespoon of minced garlic
- 1 teaspoon of ground black pepper
- 4 ounces of celery stalk
- 4 cups of chicken stock
- 1/2 teaspoons of Chili pepper
- ½ teaspoon of turmeric

COOKING DIRECTIONS:
1. Place black beans in the pressure cooker.
2. Peel the onion and chop it.
3. Add the tomato paste, garlic, ground black pepper, chicken stock, Chili pepper, and turmeric in the cooker. Mix well and close the load cooker lid. Cook the dish on pressure mode for quarter-hour.
4. When the cooking time ends, release pressure and open the cooker's lid.
5. Add chopped onion and mix well.

6. Close the pressure cooker lid and cook the dish on sauté mode for 4 minutes.
7. Open the pressure cooker lid and mix well.
8. Transfer the cooked black beans to a serving bowl.
Nutrition: calories 109, fat 2.1, fiber 3, carbs 17.59, protein 6

Roasted Veggie Mix

Prep time: ten MINUTES | Cooking time: half an hour | Servings: 10
Ingredients
- 2 eggplants
- 2 yellow sweet peppers
- 1 tablespoon of salt
- 8 ounces of tomatoes
- 2 turnips
- 1 zucchini
- 1 tablespoon of oregano
- 2 carrots
- 3 tablespoons of sesame oil
- 4 cups of beef broth

COOKING DIRECTIONS:
1. Peel the eggplants and chop them.
2. Sprinkle the eggplants with salt and stir.
3. Remove the seeds from your sweet peppers and chop them.
4. Slice the tomatoes and chop turnips.
5. Chop the zucchini.
6. Peel the carrots and grate.
7. Transfer the prepared vegetables to a pressure cooker.
8. Add oregano, sesame oil, and beef broth.
9. Mix well and close the pressure cooker lid.
10. Cook the veggie mix on steam mode for thirty minutes.
11. When the cooking time ends, transfer the dish to serving bowls.
Nutrition: calories 107, fat 5, fiber 5.6, carbs 13.2, protein 4

Soft Cabbage Petals

Prep time: ten mins | COOKING time: fifteen minutes | Servings: 4
Ingredients
- A pound of cabbage
- 1 tablespoon of chives
- 1 bell pepper (chopped)
- A teaspoon of salt
- 1 teaspoon of white pepper
- ¾ cup of water
- ½ cup of almond milk

COOKING DIRECTIONS:
1. Remove the cabbage petals.
2. Subdivide each petal into 4 pieces and place them in the pressure cooker.

3. Sprinkle the vegetables with chives, chopped bell pepper, salt, white pepper, and almond milk.
4. Add water and stir.
5. Close the cooker's lid and cook the cabbage on steam mode for 15 minutes.
6. When the cooking time elapses, open the lid and stir the petals gently.
7. Transfer your cooked cabbage into serving bowls.
Nutrition: calories 108, fat 7.4, fiber 4.1, carbs 10.9, protein 2.5

Green Beans with Pecans

Prep time: 10 minutes | Cooking time: 10 mins | Servings: 8
Ingredients
- 14 ounces of green beans
- 5 ounces of pecans
- 1 cup of water
- 1 tablespoon of minced garlic
- 4 ounces of raisins
- 1 teaspoon of salt
- A tablespoon of butter
- ¼ teaspoon of curry

COOKING DIRECTIONS:
1. Cut the green beans into halves and sprinkle them with garlic, raisins, salt, and curry. Mix well.
2. Crush the pecans and combine them with the green bean mixture.
3. Add water in the cooker.
4. Place your green beans mixture on a trivet and fit it in the pressure cooker.
5. Close the cooker's lid and cook on steam mode for ten minutes.
6. When the cooking time ends, transfer your cooked green beans to a serving plate.
7. Add butter and mix well before serving.
Nutrition: calories 190, fat 14.5, fiber 3, carbs 16.21, protein 3

Glazed Onion Rings

Prep time: 5 minutes | Cooking time: ten minutes | Servings: 4
Ingredients
- 3 big white onions
- A tablespoon of liquid stevia
- 1 tablespoon of fresh lemon juice
- A teaspoon of lemon zest
- 1 tablespoon of butter
- A teaspoon of ground white pepper
- ¼ cup of soy sauce
- 1 teaspoon of ground ginger

COOKING DIRECTIONS:

1. Combine liquid stevia with freshly squeezed lemon juice, lemon zest, butter, ground white pepper, ground ginger, and soy sauce. Mix well.
2. Peel the onions and slice them into rings.
3. Place the sliced onions in the pressure cooker and add the soy sauce mixture.
4. Close the pressure cooker's lid and cook for 5 minutes on pressure mode.
5. When the cooking time ends, remove your glazed onion rings from the cooker and allow it to cool before serving.

Nutrition: calories 83, fat 3.1, fiber 2.8, carbs 12.6, protein 2.4

Carrot Soufflé

Prep time: 10 MINUTES | Cooking time: 25 minutes | Servings: 7

Ingredients

- 5 big carrots (boiled)
- 1 cup of coconut flour
- A cup of half and half
- ½ cup of cream
- 1 teaspoon of vanilla sugar
- ½ teaspoon of cinnamon
- 1 cup of erythritol
- ½ teaspoon of baking soda
- A tablespoon of apple cider vinegar treatment
- 1 tablespoon of butter
- 1 teaspoon of ground anise

COOKING DIRECTIONS:
1. Mash the carrots using a blender.
2. Combine the carrots with coconut flour, half and half, cream, vanilla sugar, cinnamon, Erythritol, baking soda, apple cider vinegar treatment, butter, and ground anise. Mix until they smoothen.
3. Place the carrot mixture in the pressure cooker and close its lid. Cook them on steam mode for 25 minutes.
4. When the cooking time ends, remove your carrot soufflé from the cooker and allow it rest before serving.

Nutrition: calories 133, fat 6.2, fiber 7.1, carbs 16, protein 3.2

Crunchy Green Beans

Prep time: 10 mins | Cooking time: 4 minutes | Servings: 5

Ingredients

- 15 oz of green beans (chopped)
- 1 tablespoon of extra virgin olive oil
- A teaspoon of salt
- 1 teaspoon of red pepper
- 1 cup of water for smoking

COOKING DIRECTIONS:
1. Pour water into the cooker and add green beans.

2. Close the cooker's lid and cook them on high-pressure mode for 5 minutes.
3. Quick release the cooker's pressure and open its lid.
4. Drain water and transfer the green beans into the ice water to maintain its color.
5. Return the green beans in the cooker and sprinkle them with extra virgin olive oil, salt, and red pepper.
6. Stir gently and close the lid.
7. Set the cooker to air crisp mode and cook the meal for 4 minutes (380F) or until the vegetables are light crispy.

Nutrition: calories 58, fat 3, fiber 3.2, carbs 7.9, protein 1.0

Stuffed Bell Peppers

Prep time: 5 minutes | Cooking time: ten MINUTES | Servings: 9

Ingredients

- 1 cup of cauliflower rice(cooked)
- 10 ounces of green bell pepper
- ½ cup of cheese
- 1 tablespoon of paprika
- ½ teaspoon of salt
- 1 teaspoon of onion powder
- A cup of chicken stock
- ½ cup of sour cream
- 1 teaspoon of organic olive oil
- 1 large onion
- A tablespoon of cilantro

COOKING DIRECTIONS:
1. Remove the sweet peppers' seeds.
2. Combine cauliflower rice with cheese, paprika, salt, onion powder, sour cream, and cilantro. Stir well.
3. Peel the onion and dice it.
4. Set the pressure cooker to sauté mode and spread its base with organic olive oil.
5. Add the diced onion and sauté it for two minutes.
6. Add the cooked onion to the cheese mixture and stir.
7. Fill the sweet peppers with the cheese mixture and place them on a trivet.
8. Fit the trivet in the cooker and close its lid.
9. Cook the trivet content on steam mode for 10 minutes.
10. When the cooking time ends, remove the stuffed peppers from the pressure cooker and leave it to rest.
11. Serve your delicacy warm.

Nutrition: calories 99, fat 4, fiber 2.7, carbs 13.9, protein 4.1

Artichoke Gratin

Prep time: 10 MINUTES | Cooking time: 11 minutes | Servings: 5
Ingredients

- 1 pound of artichoke
- A teaspoon of red Chili flakes
- 1 teaspoon of sea salt
- A teaspoon of oregano
- 1 white onion
- 1 cup of pork rinds
- ¼ cup of wine
- 6 ounces of parmesan cheese
- 2 garlic cloves
- 1 teaspoon of fresh dill

COOKING DIRECTIONS:

1. Chop artichoke and sprinkle it with red Chili flakes followed by sea salt.
2. Add oregano and dill and mix well.
3. Pour wine into the pressure cooker.
4. Add garlic cloves and artichokes.
5. Close the cooker's lid and cook for ten minutes (on pressure mode.)
6. Grate the Parmesan cheese, blend it with pork rinds and mix well.
7. When the artichokes are cooked, strain them and combine with the cheese mixture.
8. Mix well and continue cooking on pressure mode for 1 minute.
9. Release the cooker's pressure and open its lid.
10. Transfer your artichoke gratin into a serving bowl and enjoy.

Nutrition: calories 366 fat 19.5, fiber 5.6, carbs 13.8, protein 35.9

Asparagus Tart

Prep time: ten MINUTES | Cooking time: 25 minutes | Servings: 8
Ingredients

- 7 ounces of keto soda dough
- 10 ounces of asparagus
- 1 cup of walnuts
- 3 tablespoons of butter
- 1 teaspoon of salt
- A teaspoon of ground black pepper
- 1 cup of tomato paste
- 1 onion
- 1 carrot
- An egg yolk

COOKING DIRECTIONS:

1. Roll your dough with a rolling pin.
2. Spread the pressure cooker's base with butter and place the rolled dough.
3. Chop the asparagus and transfer it to your blender.
4. Add walnuts, salt, ground black pepper, tomato paste, and egg yolk.

5. Peel the onion and carrot.
6. Grate the carrot and chop the onion.
7. Add the onion to the blender and puree until smooth.
8. Combine the asparagus mixture with l the carrot and mix well.
9. Spread the dough using the asparagus mixture.
10. Close the cooker's lid and cook the mixture at pressure mode for 25 minutes.
11. When the cooking time ends, release the accumulated pressure and open the cooker's lid.
12. Transfer the tart to a flat plate. Cut into pieces and serve.

Nutrition: calories 191, fat 9.2, fiber 5.4, carbs 11.8, protein 17.5

Spinach Tarts

Prep time: 10 MINUTES | Cooking time: quarter-hour | Servings: 8
Ingredients

- 6 ounces of butter
- 1 cup of coconut flour
- A teaspoon of salt
- ½ teaspoon of Erythritol
- 3 cups of spinach
- ½ cup of sour cream
- 1 teaspoon of ground white pepper
- ½ tablespoon of oregano
- A teaspoon of cayenne pepper

COOKING DIRECTIONS:

1. Chop butter and combine it with coconut flour and salt.
2. Add Erythritol and knead the dough.
3. Roll the dough using a rolling pin and set it in the pressure cooker.
4. Chop the spinach and combine it with sour cream.
5. Sprinkle the mixture with ground black pepper, oregano, and cayenne.
6. Mix well and spread it on your dough.
7. Close the cooker's lid and cook the dough on pressure mode for quarter-hour.
8. When the cooking time ends, allow your spinach tart to rest.
9. Transfer the tart to a serving plate and slice. Serve warm.

Nutrition: calories 248, fat 22.4, fiber 5.5, carbs 9.5, protein 3

Lettuce Warm Wraps

Prep time: ten MINUTES | Cooking time: 20 MINUTES | Servings: 5
Ingredients

- 7 ounces of lettuce
- 1 white onion
- 1 eggplant

- 5 ounces of mushrooms
- 1 tablespoon of organic essential olive oil
- ½ tablespoon of salt
- A teaspoon of butter
- ½ teaspoon of red chili flakes
- ½ teaspoon of red pepper cayenne
- A tablespoon of fresh basil

COOKING DIRECTIONS:
1. Peel the onion and chop it.
2. Chop the eggplant into tiny pieces.
3. Combine the chopped vegetables in a mixing bowl.
4. Chop the mushrooms and add them to the mixture.
5. Sprinkle it with salt, red Chili flakes, and cayenne. Mix well.
6. Add basil and mix again.
7. Add butter and essential olive oil to the pressure cooker.
8. Saute the mixture for 3 minutes or until the butter melts.
9. Add the eggplant mixture and cook for 15 minutes (on pressure mode.)
10. When the vegetable mixture is cooked, remove it from the pressure cooker and leave it to rest.
11. Place the vegetable mixture in the lettuce leaves and wrap. Serve immediately.

Nutrition: calories 157, fat 4.1, fiber 8, carbs 31.02, protein 5

Spicy Asparagus Mash

Prep time: 10 minutes | Cooking time: 10 MINUTES | Servings: 5

Ingredients
- 3 cups of beef broth
- 16 ounces of asparagus
- 1 tablespoon of butter
- A teaspoon of red pepper cayenne
- ½ teaspoon of Chili pepper
- 1 tablespoon of sriracha
- 2 teaspoons of salt
- ½ cup of sour cream
- 1 teaspoon of paprika

COOKING DIRECTIONS:
1. Wash asparagus and chop it roughly.
2. Place the chopped asparagus in the pressure cooker.
3. Add cayenne and beef broth.
4. Season with salt and close the cooker's lid.
5. Cook the dish on pressure mode for 10 minutes.
6. Remove the asparagus from the cooker and strain it.

7. Place it in a mixer and add Chili pepper, butter, sriracha, and sour cream. Blend the amalgamation until smooth.
8. Place your asparagus mash in a serving bowl and enjoy.

Nutrition: calories 72, fat 4.5, fiber 2, carbs 5.14, protein 4

Creamy Vegetable Stew

Prep time: 10 MINUTES | Cooking time: 25 MINUTES | Servings: 10

Ingredients
- 2 eggplants
- 2 yellow sweet peppers
- 1 zucchini
- 1 cup of green beans
- 8 ounces of mushrooms
- 1 tablespoon of salt
- ½ teaspoon of ground black pepper
- 1 cup of chicken stock
- 3 cups of beef broth
- ½ cup of tomato juice
- 1 tablespoon of Erythritol

COOKING DIRECTIONS:
1. Peel the eggplants and chop them.
2. Sprinkle the chopped eggplants with salt and stir the mixture.
3. Remove the seeds from your sweet peppers.
4. Chop the sweet peppers and zucchini.
5. Combine the ingredients in a mixing bowl and add Erythritol. Stir.
6. Place the vegetable mixture in a pressure cooker and sauté for 5 minutes while stirring frequently.
7. Add tomato juice, beef broth, chicken stock, green beans, and mix well.
8. Close the cooker's lid and sauté the mixture for 25 minutes.
9. When your vegetable stew is cooked, transfer it into a bowl and serve.

Nutrition: calories 61, fat 0.9, fiber 5.1, carbs 11.4, protein 4.1

Crunchy Chili Peppers

Prep time: 10 mins | Cooking time: 10 minutes | Servings: 5

Ingredients
- 5 chili peppers
- ½ cup of half and half
- 1 cup of extra virgin organic olive oil
- A cup of coconut flakes
- 1 teaspoon of cilantro
- ¼ cup of coconut flour
- 1 egg
- 1 teaspoon of ground thyme

COOKING DIRECTIONS:

1. Remove the seeds from the Chili peppers and combine them with the coconut flour.
2. Beat an egg in a bowl and pour it over the flour mixture.
3. Add coconut flakes, cilantro, and ground thyme and mix well.
4. Pour the essential olive oil in a pressure cooker and heat.
5. Add the chili peppers to the cooker and roast it on saute mode for 8 minutes per side.
6. When your chili peppers are cooked, remove them from the cooker and allow them to cool.
Nutrition: calories 221, fat 22.6, fiber 1.9, carbs 4.4, protein 2.5

Sauteed Red Cabbage

Prep time: ten minutes | Cooking time: 30 MINUTES | Servings: 4
Ingredients
- 10 oz of red cabbage (shredded)
- ½ cup of water
- 1 oz of raisins (chopped)
- A teaspoon of paprika
- 1 teaspoon of ground coriander
- A teaspoon of ground cinnamon
- ½ teaspoon of apple cider vinegar treatment
- ½ cup of heavy cream

COOKING DIRECTIONS:
1. Place the shredded cabbage in the cooker.
2. Sprinkle it with paprika, ground coriander, ground cinnamon, apple cider vinegar, and raisins.
3. Add heavy cream and mix.
4. Add water and close the lid.
5. Cook the meal on saute mode for half an hour while stirring regularly.
6. When your cabbage gains a soft texture, remove it from the cooker and serve.
Nutrition: calories 94, fat 5.7, fiber 2.5, carbs 10.9, protein 1.5

Oregano Croquettes

Prep time: 10 MINUTES | Cooking time: 6 minutes | Servings: 6
Ingredients
- 1 pound of turnip (boiled)
- 1 cup of fresh oregano
- An egg
- ¼ cup of coconut flour
- 1 teaspoon of onion powder
- A tablespoon of salt
- 4 tablespoons of organic olive oil
- 1 teaspoon of nutmeg
- 1 teaspoon of dill
- Boiled potatoes

COOKING DIRECTIONS:

1. Mash the turnips using a fork or masher.
2. Mince oregano and add it to potatoes.
3. Beat the egg in the mixture and add coconut flour, onion powder, nutmeg, and dill.
4. Knead the dough.
5. Pour extra virgin olive oil in the pressure cooker and preheat it on steam mode.
6. Make medium-sized croquettes from the turnip mixture and put them in the cooker.
7. Cook the croquettes for 6 minutes on either side or until golden brown.
8. Remove your oregano croquettes from the pressure cooker, drain excess oil using a paper towel, and serve.
Nutrition: calories 155, fat 11.6, fiber 6.8, carbs 13.6, protein 3.1

Parmesan Zucchini Balls

Prep time: 10 mins | Cooking time: quarter-hour | Servings: 6
Ingredients
- 7 ounces of parmesan
- 2 zucchini
- 1 teaspoon of salt
- 1 egg
- 1 teaspoon of ground black pepper
- ½ cup of coconut flour
- 3 tablespoons of butter
- ¼ cup of parsley

COOKING DIRECTIONS:
1. Grate zucchini and sprinkle it with salt and ground black pepper. Mix well.
2. Grate the Parmesan cheese.
3. Beat an egg in a separate bowl and whisk.
4. Add the whisked egg to the zucchini mixture followed by cheese.
5. Chop parsley and add it to the zucchini mixture.
6. Add coconut flour and knead dough.
7. Make small balls from the zucchini mixture and place them on a trivet.
8. Transfer the trivet to the cooker and cook the mixture on steam mode for 15 minutes.
9. When your zucchini balls are cooked, remove them from the pressure cooker and serve.
Nutrition: calories 185, fat 13.9, fiber 1.3, carbs 4.5, protein 12.7

Tomato Jam

Prep time: ten MINUTES | Cooking time: twenty roughly minutes | Servings: 5
Ingredients
- 10 ounces of tomatoes
- 1 tablespoon of fresh basil
- ½ teaspoon of cinnamon
- ½ cup of Erythritol
- ½ teaspoon of ground ginger

- 1 tablespoon of nutmeg
- A tablespoon of butter
- 1 teaspoon of anise

COOKING DIRECTIONS:

1. Wash your tomatoes and chop them.
2. Combine basil with cinnamon, Erythritol, ground ginger, nutmeg, and anise. Mix well.
3. Put the chopped tomatoes in the pressure cooker and add the spice mixture.
4. Add butter and mix well.
5. Cook the dish on saute mode for twenty minutes.
6. When the cooking time ends, open the cooker's lid and stir.
7. Transfer your tomato jam to a serving dish and allow it to chill before serving.

Nutrition: calories 39, fat 2.9, fiber 1.1, carbs 3.2, protein 0.7

Jalapeno Crisps

Prep time: ten MINUTES | Cooking time: 5 MINUTES | Servings: 5

Ingredients

- 5 jalapeno peppers (sliced)
- 1/3 cup of coconut flour
- 2 eggs(whisked)
- 1 teaspoon of salt
- A teaspoon of organic essential olive oil

COOKING DIRECTIONS:

1. Whisk eggs and salt in a bowl.
2. Add sliced jalapeno peppers and stir.
3. Dip the jalapeno slices in coconut flour for coating.
4. Transfer the jalapeno slices in the cooker and sprinkle it with essential organic olive oil.
5. Close the lid and cook them on air crisp mode for 5 minutes (380F).
6. Stir them well and continue cooking for around 3 minutes or until jalapeno slices becomes crispy.

Nutrition: calories 71, fat 3.7, fiber 3.8, carbs 6.5, protein 3.5

Sliced Mushrooms with Turmeric

Prep time: ten mins | Cooking time: 7 minutes | Servings: 5

Ingredients

- 1 tablespoon of turmeric
- A pound of cremini mushrooms
- 1 cup of sour cream
- 1 onion
- A tablespoon of paprika
- 3 tablespoons of organic olive oil
- 1 teaspoon of salt
- ½ teaspoon of cayenne

COOKING DIRECTIONS:

1. Peel the onions and dice them.

2. Pour the essential olive oil into a pressure cooker and add onions.
3. Saute them for three minutes while stirring frequently.
4. Chop the mushrooms and combine them with paprika, salt, and red pepper cayenne. Stir.
5. Add the chopped cremini mixture in the pressure cooker and cook for two minutes.
6. Add sour cream and mix well.
7. Add turmeric and stir again.
8. Close the load cooker and continue cooking for 2 minutes.
9. When the assigned time elapses, release the cooker's inbuilt pressure and open its lid.
10. Transfer your sliced mushrooms to a serving bowl and enjoy.

Nutrition: calories 422, fat 14.2, fiber 12, carbs 75.79, protein 11

Veggie Chili

Prep time: fifteen minutes | Cooking time: 25 minutes | Servings: 12

Ingredients

- 5 ounces of rutabaga
- ¼ teaspoon of cayenne pepper
- A teaspoon of salt
- ½ teaspoon of ground black pepper
- 8 ounces of tomatoes
- 1 cup of black beans (cooked)
- 1 carrot
- 2 eggplants
- 1 teaspoon of essential organic olive oil
- A teaspoon of oregano
- 3 cupsof chicken stock

COOKING DIRECTIONS:

1. Peel the rutabagas and dice them.
2. Set the pressure cooker to sauté mode and pour the essential olive oil.
3. Add rutabaga and sauté it for 5 minutes.
4. Meanwhile, chop the tomatoes and eggplants.
5. Combine red pepper cayenne with salt, ground black pepper, and oregano in a mixing bowl.
6. Peel the carrot and grate it.
7. Combine the prepared vegetables and sprinkle them with the spice mixture.
8. Put the spiced vegetables in the cooker and add chicken stock and black beans. Mix well and close the cooker's lid.
9. Cook the mixture on sauté mode for twenty minutes.
10. When the cooking time ends, remove the veggie chilli from the cooker and leave them to cool. Serve warm.

Nutrition: calories 94, fat 1, fiber 6.4, carbs 18, protein 4.9

Vegetarian Shepherd's Pie

Prep time: 15 minutes | Cooking time: 16 minutes | Servings: 7

Ingredients

- 2 white onions
- 1 carrot
- 10 ounces of cauliflower mash
- 3 ounces of celery stalk
- 1 tablespoon of salt
- A teaspoon of paprika
- 1 teaspoon of curry
- 1 tablespoon of tomato paste
- 3 tablespoons of essential olive oil

COOKING DIRECTIONS:

1. Peel the carrot and grate it.
2. Chop the celery stalk and mix the vegetables well.
3. Put the vegetable mixture in the pressure cooker and add paprika, curry, tomato paste, extra virgin olive oil, and salt. Stir.
4. Cook the mixture on pressure mode for 6 minutes while stirring frequently.
5. Spread the vegetable mixture with the cauliflower mash and close the cooker's lid.
6. Cook the dish on pressure mode for 10 minutes.
7. When the cooking time ends, release the built-in pressure and open the cooker's lid.
8. Transfer your shepherd pie to a serving plate. Cut into slices and serve.

Nutrition: calories 107, fat 9.3, fiber 2.3, carbs 6.2, protein 1.6

Fresh Thyme Burgers

Prep time: 10 minutes | Cooking time: quarter-hour | Servings: 8

Ingredients

- A cup of black soybeans (cooked)
- 1 onion
- 1 carrot
- 1 cup of fresh thyme
- A cup of spinach
- ¼ cup of coconut flour
- An egg
- 1 tablespoon of salt
- A teaspoon of ground black pepper
- 1 teaspoon of Dijon mustard
- 3 tablespoons of starch

COOKING DIRECTIONS:

1. Wash thyme and spinach and chop them.
2. Place them in a blender and add lentils.
3. Blend the mixture for 1 minute and transfer the puree to a mixing bowl.
4. Sprinkle it with coconut flour, egg, salt, ground black pepper, Dijon mustard, and starch.
5. Peel the onion and carrot and grate them.

6. Add the vegetables to the thyme mixture and stir.
7. Make medium-sized "burgers" from the mixture.
8. Place the burgers on a trivet and fit it in the pressure cooker.
9. Cook them on steam mode for quarter-hour.
10. When your thyme burgers are cooked, leave them to cool. Transfer them to a wide plate and serve warm.

Nutrition: calories 155, fat 5.8, fiber 5.1, carbs 17.2, protein 10.1

Celery Fries

Prep time: 10 mins | Cooking time: 8 minutes | Servings: 2

Ingredients

- 6 oz of celery root (peeled)
- 1 teaspoon of white pepper
- Cooking spray

COOKING DIRECTIONS:

1. Cut the celery root into fries and sprinkle them with the white pepper.
2. Mix the vegetables and transfer them to the Ninja cooker basket.
3. Spray the fries with cooking spray gently and close the lid.
4. Cook the fries at 385F (on air crisp mode) for 8 minutes.
5. Stir your celery fries after 4 minutes of cooking and serve.

Nutrition: calories 38, fat 0.3, fiber 1.8, carbs 8.5, protein 1.4

Cinnamon Pumpkin Puree

Prep time: 10 MINUTES | Cooking time: 10 mins | Servings: 5

Ingredients

- A pound of sweet pumpkin
- 2 portions of water
- 1 tablespoon of butter
- A teaspoon of Erythritol
- 1 teaspoon of cinnamon
- ½ teaspoon of ground black pepper
- ¼ teaspoon of nutmeg

COOKING DIRECTIONS:

1. Peel the pumpkin and chop it.
2. Put the chopped pumpkin in the pressure cooker.
3. Add water and ground pepper.
4. Close the cooker's lid and cook the mixture on pressure mode for ten minutes.
5. Strain the pumpkin and place it in a mixer.
6. Add Erythritol, butter, cinnamon, and nutmeg. Blend a mixture until smooth.
7. Transfer your pumpkin puree to serving bowls and enjoy.

Nutrition: calories 233, fat 8.7, fiber 2, carbs 38.28, protein 3

Onions Soup

Prep time: ten MINUTES | Cooking time: fifteen MINUTES | Servings: 14

Ingredients

- 5 onions
- 1 cup of cream
- 3 cups of chicken stock
- A tablespoon of salt
- 1 teaspoon of organic extra virgin olive oil
- 2 tablespoons of butter
- ½ tablespoon of ground black pepper

COOKING DIRECTIONS:

1. Peel the onions and grate them.
2. Place the grated onions in the pressure cooker.
3. Add virgin olive oil and sauté the onions for 5 minutes while stirring frequently.
4. Add salt, chicken stock, cream, butter, and ground black pepper.
5. Cook the ingredients on pressure mode for ten minutes.
6. When your onion soup is cooked, ladle it to serving bowls..

Nutrition: calories 47, fat 3.1, fiber 0.9, carbs 4.5, protein 0.8

Carrot Bites

Prep time: ten mins | Cooking time: 5 minutes | Servings: 7

Ingredients

- 5 carrots
- 1 cup of coconut flour
- ½ cup of whey
- 1 teaspoon of baking soda
- A tablespoon of freshly squeezed lemon juice
- 1 teaspoon of salt
- A teaspoon of cilantro
- ½ teaspoon of turmeric
- 1 tablespoon of essential olive oil
- A teaspoon of nutmeg

COOKING DIRECTIONS:

1. Peel the carrots and grate them.
2. Combine the grated carrot with coconut flour, whey, baking soda, freshly squeezed lemon juice, salt, cilantro, turmeric, and nutmeg.
3. Knead the dough and make long logs from it.
4. Set the pressure cooker to sauté mode and pour essential olive oil.
5. Make small pieces from the carrot mixture and put them in the pressure cooker.
6. Sauté the carrot bites for 5 minutes or until they turn golden brown on both sides.

7. Transfer the carrot bites to a flatter and drain excess oil using a paper towel. Leave your bites to cool and serve warm.

Nutrition: calories 115, fat 4.5, fiber 6.9, carbs 15.5, protein 3

Vegetable Risotto

Prep time: 10 MINUTES |Cooking time: 26 minutes | Servings: 5

Ingredients

- 4 ounces of parsnips
- 1 cup of cauliflower rice
- 1 teaspoon of salt
- 3 cups of chicken stock
- 1 tablespoon of turmeric
- ½ cup of green peas
- A teaspoon of paprika
- 2 carrots
- 1 onion
- ½ teaspoon of sour cream

COOKING DIRECTIONS:

1. Chop the parsnip.
2. Peel the onion and carrots.
3. Chop the vegetables into tiny pieces and combine them with parsnip.
4. Sprinkle the vegetable mixture with salt, turmeric, paprika, and sour cream.
5. Place the vegetable mixture in the pressure cooker and cook it on pressure mode for 6 minutes while stirring frequently.
6. Add the cauliflower rice, green peas, and chicken stock and stir using a wooden spoon.
7. Close the pressure cooker's lid and cook the mixture at slow mode for 20 minutes.
8. When the cooking time ends, open the cooker's lid and stir.
9. Transfer your vegetable risotto into serving bowls.

Nutrition: calories 65, fat 0.8, fiber 3.9, carbs 13.3, protein 2.5

Bacon Brussel Sprouts Balls

Prep time: ten mins | Cooking time: ten MINUTES | Servings: 2

Ingredients

- 1 cup of Brussels Sprouts
- 1 teaspoon of extra virgin olive oil
- ½ teaspoon of ground black pepper
- 5 oz of bacon (sliced)

COOKING DIRECTIONS:

1. Mix sliced bacon with essential organic olive oil and ground black pepper.
2. Wrap the Brussels sprout in bacon and transfer it to a Ninja cooker basket.
3. Secure the balls with toothpicks and close the cooker's lid having set it to air crisp mode.

4. Cook the meal for ten minutes while stirring frequently.
5. Transfer your cooked Brussels sprout balls to serving bowls.
Nutrition: calories 424, fat 32.1, fiber 1.8, carbs 5.4, protein 27.8

Asparagus Saute

Prep time: quarter-HOUR | Cooking time: 35 MINUTES | Servings: 4
Ingredients
- 2 cups of asparagus (chopped)
- 2 garlic cloves (diced)
- ½ cup of heavy cream
- ½ cup of water
- 1 teaspoon of butter
- A teaspoon of turmeric
- 1 teaspoon of salt

COOKING DIRECTIONS:
1. Place asparagus in the cooker.
2. Add diced garlic, butter, ground turmeric, salt, and high cream.
3. Mix the amalgamation until it gets an orange color. Add water and stir it gently.
4. Close the lid and set your cooker to saute mode.
5. Saute the asparagus for 35 minutes.
6. When the duration elapses, switch off the cooker and let the asparagus rest for quarter-hour.
Nutrition: calories 78, fat 6.7, fiber 1.6, carbs 3.9, protein 1.9

Ratatouille

Prep time: quarter-hour | Cooking time: 25 minutes | Servings: 9
Ingredients
- 2 green zucchini
- 2 eggplants
- 1 cup of tomatoes
- 3 green bell peppers
- 4 garlic cloves
- 2 red onion
- 1 cup of tomato juice
- A teaspoon of extra virgin olive oil
- 1 cup of chicken stock
- 1 teaspoon of ground black pepper

COOKING DIRECTIONS:
1. Slice the zucchini, eggplants, and tomatoes.
2. Remove seeds from the peppers and slice them.
3. Peel the onions and garlic cloves.
4. Chop the onions and garlic.
5. Combine tomato juice with organic olive oil, chicken stock, and ground black pepper in a mixing bowl.
6. Put the sliced vegetables in the cooker and sprinkle them with onion and garlic.

7. Pour the tomato juice mixture into the pressure cooker and close its lid.
8. Cook the mixture on steam mode for 25 minutes.
9. When the cooking time elapses, remove your ratatouille from the cooker and let it rest. Serve warm.
Nutrition: calories 82, fat 1.4, fiber 6, carbs 16.53, protein 4

Pea Stew

Prep time: 10 MINUTES | Cooking time: 35 minutes | Servings: 6
Ingredients
- 2 cups of green peas
- 1 tablespoon of salt
- 4 cups of chicken stock
- 1 carrot
- 1 tablespoon of extra virgin organic olive oil
- 7 ounces of ground chicken
- A cup of tomato juice
- 1 teaspoon of cilantro

COOKING DIRECTIONS:
1. Peel the carrot and chop it roughly.
2. Put the chopped carrot in the pressure cooker and sprinkle it with essential olive oil.
3. Cook the carrot on pressure mode for 5 minutes.
4. Add the green peas.
5. Sprinkle the mixture with salt, chicken stock, ground chicken, tomato juice, and cilantro.
6. Close the cooker's lid and sauté the mixture for thirty minutes.
7. When your pea stew is cooked, transfer it to a large bowl and allow it to cool. Serve warm.
Nutrition: calories 171, fat 7.4, fiber 3, carbs 13.72, protein 13

Curry Squash Saute

Prep time: ten mins | Cooking time: fifteen minutes | Servings: 6
Ingredients
- 2 cups of Kabocha squash (chopped)
- 1 teaspoon of ground cinnamon
- 1 teaspoon of curry paste
- A teaspoon of curry powder
- ½ teaspoon of dried cilantro
- 1 cup of water
- A tablespoon of pumpkin seeds (chopped)
- 1 tablespoon of butter
- ¾ cup of heavy cream

COOKING DIRECTIONS:
1. Place squash in the cooker and sprinkle it with ground cinnamon, curry powder, and dried cilantro.
2. Add butter, water, and pumpkin seeds.

3. Mix heavy cream with curry paste in a separate bowl.
4. Pour the liquid in the cooker and mix.
5. Close the cooker's lid and sauté for 10 minutes on high pressure mode.
6. Allow the cooker to release pressure for 10 minutes naturally.
7. Open the cooker's lid and transfer your curry squash sauté with its gravy into serving bowls.
Nutrition: calories 97, fat 8.7, fiber 0.8, carbs 4.5, protein 1.2

Leek Soup

Prep time: ten MINUTES | Cooking time: 19 minutes | Servings: 7
Ingredients
- 10 ounces of leek
- 2 garlic cloves
- 5 cups of vegetable stock
- A teaspoon of salt
- 1 yellow onion
- 1 tablespoon of organic olive oil
- ½ cup of sour cream
- 1 teaspoon of oregano
- 4 ounces of noodles
- 1 teaspoon of butter
- A teaspoon of ground white pepper

COOKING DIRECTIONS:
1. Chop the leek.
2. Peel the garlic cloves and slice them.
3. Peel the onion and dice it.
4. Combine onion with garlic. Mix them and put them in a pressure cooker.
5. Add butter and sauté the mixture for 7 minutes.
6. Add chopped leek and pour the vegetable stock.
7. Sprinkle the soup mixture with salt, ground white pepper, oregano, and cream.
8. Close the cooker's lid and sauté for another ten minutes.
9. Open the cooker's lid and add the noodles.
10. Mix the soup well and close the strain cooker's lid.
11. Cook the noodle mixture on pressure mode for 2 minutes.

12. Release the accumulated pressure and open the cooker's lid.
13. Stir your leek soup well and then ladle it to serving bowls.
Nutrition: calories 155, fat 5.9, fiber 1, carbs 19.47, protein 6

Veggie Aromatic Stew

Prep time: fifteen MINUTES | Cooking time: 20 MINUTES | Servings: 7
Ingredients
- 2 carrots
- 1 zucchini
- 8 ounces of broccoli
- 4 ounces of cauliflower
- 4 cups of chicken stock
- ¼ cup of tomato paste
- 1 teaspoon of sugar
- ½ tablespoon of salt
- ½ cup of parsley
- 1 tablespoon of butter
- 2 onions
- 1 teaspoon of oregano

COOKING DIRECTIONS:
1. Wash the broccoli and separate its florets.
2. Chop the zucchini and carrots.
3. Place the vegetables in a pressure cooker.
4. Add chicken stock and tomato paste.
5. Sprinkle the amalgamation with sugar, salt, butter, and oregano. Mix well and close the pressure cooker's lid. Cook the ingredients on sauté mode for ten minutes.
6. Peel the onions and chop them roughly.
7. When the cooking time ends, open pressure cooker lid and add some onions.
8. Chop the parsley and add it to the stew mixture followed by butter. Mix well.
9. Close the cooker's lid and cook your stew on pressure mode for 10 minutes.
10. When your aromatic stew is cooked, release the built-in pressure and open its lid.
11. Mix it well and transfer it to serving bowls.
Nutrition: calories 71, fat 2.3, fiber 3.2, carbs 11.7, protein 3

SNACKS AND APPETIZERS RECIPES

Cheesy Bombs

Prep time: ten mins |Cooking time: ten mins |Servings: 8

Ingredients

- 6 ounces of puff pastry
- 1 teaspoon of salt
- 8 ounces of mozzarella pearls
- 1 egg
- ½ cup of coconut flour
- ¼ cup of coconut milk
- ½ teaspoon of oregano
- 2 tablespoons of butter

COOKING DIRECTIONS:

1. Roll the puff pastry using a rolling pin.
2. Add the egg to a mixing bowl and whisk.
3. Add coconut milk and salt. Stir to dissolve salt.
4. Cut the rolled puff pastry into medium-sized squares.
5. Put the mozzarella pearl at the middle of each square and wrap the dough to form balls.
6. Sprinkle the egg mixture with oregano and mix well.
7. Dip the puff pastry balls in the egg mixture then in the coconut flour.
8. Add butter in the pressure cooker and melt it.
9. Place the puff pastry balls in the pressure cooker and close its lid.
10. Cook the dish on pressure mode for ten minutes.
11. When the cooking time ends, release the cooker's inbuilt pressure and open its lid.
12. Transfer your cheesy bombs to serving plates.

Nutrition: calories 269, fat 19.4, fiber 3, carbs 14.1, protein 8.5

Onion Rings

Prep time: ten mins |Cooking time: 8 minutes |Servings: 7

Ingredients

- 1 cup of coconut flour
- 1 teaspoon of salt
- ½ teaspoon of basil
- 1 teaspoon of oregano
- ½ teaspoon of red pepper cayenne
- 3 eggs
- 5 medium white onions
- 3 tablespoons of sesame oil

COOKING DIRECTIONS:

1. Combine coconut flour with salt, basil, oregano, and red pepper cayenne in a mixing bowl.
2. Stir the coconut flour mixture gently.
3. Whisk eggs in a separate bowl.
4. Peel the onions and cut them in to the thick rings.
5. Separate the onion rings and dip them in the egg mixture.
6. Pour sesame oil in the pressure cooker. Preheat it on pressure mode.
7. Dip the onion rings in the flour mixture.
8. Transfer the onion rings to the pressure cooker.
9. Saute the onions for two minutes on both sides.
10. Place your cooked onion rings on a paper towel to drain excess oils.
11. Season with salt and serve hot.

Nutrition: calories 180, fat 10.1, fiber 7.5, carbs 16.8, protein 5.6

Garlic Tomato Slices

Prep time: ten minutes |Cooking time: 5 minutes | Servings: 5

Ingredients

- 5 tomatoes
- ¼ cup of chives
- 1cup of garlic herb
- ½ teaspoon of salt
- ½ teaspoon of ground black pepper
- 1 tablespoon of extra virgin organic olive oil
- 7 ounces of parmesan cheese

COOKING DIRECTIONS:

1. Wash the tomatoes and cut it into thick slices.
2. Place the sliced tomatoes in the pressure cooker.
3. Chop the chives and grate the parmesan cheese.
4. Peel the garlic cloves and mince them.
5. Combine the grated cheese with minced garlic and stir the amalgamation.
6. Sprinkle the tomato slices with chives, ground black pepper, and salt.
7. Sprinkle the sliced tomatoes with the cheese mixture and close the cooker's lid.
8. Cook the mixture on pressure mode for 5 minutes.
9. When the cooking time ends, remove your tomato slices and serve.

Nutrition: calories 224 fat 14, fiber 1, carbs 12.55, protein 13

Deviled Eggs

Prep time: 10 mins |Cooking time: 5 minutes | Servings: 6

Ingredients

- 6 eggs

- 1 avocado (peeled)
- A tablespoon of cream
- ½ teaspoon of minced garlic
- 1 cup water for smoking

COOKING DIRECTIONS:
1. Put the eggs in the Pressure cooker and add water.
2. Close its lid and cook the eggs on high-pressure mode for 5 minutes.
3. Release the cooker's pressure naturally for 5 minutes.
4. Blend avocado, minced garlic, and cream together.
5. Pour the avocado puree into a bowl.
6. Peel the cooked eggs and cut them into halves.
7. Remove the eggs yolks and add them to the avocado puree. Stir well.
8. Fill the egg whites with the avocado mixture and enjoy.

Nutrition: calories 133, fat 11, fiber 2.2, carbs 3.4, protein 6.2

Herbed Butter

Prep time: ten mins |Cooking time: 5 minutes | Servings: 7
Ingredients
- 1 cup of butter
- A teaspoon of minced garlic
- 1 teaspoon of dried oregano
- A teaspoon of dried cilantro
- 1 tablespoon of dried dill
- 1 teaspoon of salt
- ½ teaspoon of ground black pepper

COOKING DIRECTIONS:
1. Set the cooker to sauté mode and spread it with butter.
2. Add minced garlic, dried oregano, dried cilantro, butter, dried dill, salt, and ground black pepper.
3. Stir the combination and sauté it for 4-5 minutes or until butter melts.
4. Shut down the cooker and stir the butter well.
5. Transfer the butter mixture to the butter mold and freeze it.

Nutrition: calories 235, fat 26.3, fiber 0.2, carbs 0.6, protein 0.4

Broccoli Tots

Prep time: quarter-hour |Cooking time: 8 minutes | Servings: 8
Ingredients
- 1 pound of broccoli
- 3 servings of water
- 1 teaspoon of salt
- An egg

- 1 cup of pork rind
- ½ teaspoon of paprika
- 1 tablespoon of turmeric
- 1 cup of almond flour
- 2 tablespoons of extra virgin essential olive oil

COOKING DIRECTIONS:
1. Wash the broccoli and chop it roughly.
2. Put the broccoli in the pressure cooker and add water.
3. Set pressure cooker to steam mode and cook the broccoli for 20 minutes.
4. Remove it from the cooker and leave it to cool.
5. Transfer the broccoli into your blender.
6. Add egg, salt, paprika, turmeric, and almond flour. Blend the amalgamation until smooth.
7. Add pork rind and blend the broccoli mixture for 1 minute.
8. Pour the olive oil in the pressure cooker.
9. Form medium tots from the broccoli mixture and put them in the pressure cooker.
10. Set it to sauté mode and cook the mixture for 4 minutes on each side.
11. When your broccoli tots are cooked, remove them from the cooker and let them cool a bit before serving.

Nutrition: calories 147, fat 9.9, fiber 1.8, carbs 4.7, protein 11.6

Wrapped Halloumi Cheese

Prep time: ten mins |Cooking time: ten mins |Servings: 8
Ingredients
- 1-pound of halloumi cheese
- 8 oz of bacon (sliced)
- 1 teaspoon of extra virgin olive oil

COOKING DIRECTIONS:
1. Subdivide the cheese into 8 sticks.
2. Wrap each stick in sliced bacon and sprinkle it with organic olive oil.
3. Place the wrapped sticks in the cooker basket and close the air fryer lid.
4. Cook your halloumi cheese for 4 minutes. Serve it warm.

Nutrition: calories 365, fat 29.4, fiber 0, carbs 1.9, protein 22.7

Zucchini Tots

Prep time: quarter-hour |Cooking time: 9 minutes |Servings: 8
Ingredients
- 2 medium zucchinis
- 1 egg
- 1 teaspoon of salt
- ½ teaspoon of baking soda
- 1 teaspoon of freshly squeezed lemon juice

- 1 teaspoon of basil
- A tablespoon of oregano
- 1 cup of oatmeal flour
- 1 tablespoon of organic extra virgin olive oil
- A teaspoon of minced garlic
- 1 tablespoon of butter

COOKING DIRECTIONS:
1. Wash the zucchini and grate it.
2. Beat the egg in a mixing bowl and whisk it.
3. Add baking soda, freshly squeezed lemon juice, basil, oregano, and flour in the egg mixture. Stir it carefully until smooth.
4. Combine the grated zucchini with the egg mixture. Knead the dough until smooth.
5. Combine essential olive oil with minced garlic.
6. Set the pressure cooker to sauté mode.
7. Add butter and transfer the amalgamation to the pressure cooker. Melt the amalgamation.
8. Make the tots from the zucchini dough and dip them in the melted butter mixture.
9. Saute the dish for 3 minutes on each side.
10. When your zucchini tots are cooked, take them off from the cooker and serve.

Nutrition: calories 64, fat 4.4, fiber 0, carbs 4.35, protein 2

Cauliflower Fritters

Prep time: quarter-hour |Cooking time: 13 minutes |Servings: 7
Ingredients
- 1 pound of cauliflower
- A medium white onion
- 1 teaspoon of salt
- ½ teaspoon of ground white pepper
- 1 tablespoon of sour cream
- 1 teaspoon of turmeric
- ½ cup of dill
- 1 teaspoon of thyme
- 3 tablespoons of almond flour
- 1 egg
- 2 tablespoons of butter

COOKING DIRECTIONS:
1. Wash the cauliflower and separate it into florets.
2. Chop the florets and place them in a very blender.
3. Peel the onion and dice it.
4. Add the diced onion to the blender contents and puree.
5. Add salt, ground white pepper, sour cream, turmeric, dill, thyme, and almond flour.
6. Pour in the whisked egg and blend until an easy dough forms.
7. Remove the cauliflower dough from the blender and form medium-sized balls.

8. Flatten the balls a bit and set the pressure cooker to saute mode.
9. Add butter to the cooker and melt it.
10. Add cauliflower fritters in the pressure cooker and sauté them for 6 minutes. Flip them once.
11. Cook the dish on "Sauté" stew mode for 7 minutes.
12. When the cooking time ends, take off your cauliflower fritters and serve immediately.

Nutrition: calories 143, fat 10.6, fiber 3.9, carbs 9.9, protein 5.6

Shallot Pancakes

Prep time: 10 mins |Cooking time: quarter-hour |Servings: 8
Ingredients
- 8 ounces of shallot
- 2 tablespoons of chives
- 1 red onion
- 1 cup of coconut flour
- 2 egg
- ¼ cup of sour cream
- 1 teaspoon of baking soda
- A tablespoon of freshly squeezed lemon juice
- 1 teaspoon of salt
- A teaspoon of cilantro
- ½ teaspoon of basil
- 1 tablespoon of essential olive oil
- 1 bell pepper

COOKING DIRECTIONS:
1. Chop the shallot and chives and mix them in a mixing bowl.
2. Peel the onion, dice it, and add it to the bowl.
3. Whisk the eggs in a separate bowl and add baking soda followed by freshly squeezed fresh lemon juice.
4. Stir the amalgamation and add the cream, salt, cilantro, basil, and coconut flour.
5. Blend the combination well until smooth.
6. Remove the seeds from the bell pepper and chop it into tiny pieces.
7. Add the vegetables to the egg mixture. Stir it until it forms a batter.
8. Set the load cooker to saute mode.
9. Pour the organic essential olive oil in the pressure cooker and preheat it.
10. Ladle the batter and cook the pancakes for two minutes on each side.
11. Store the pancakes under an aluminum foil to keep them warm until all the pancakes are cooked.
12. Serve your shallot pancakes while warm.

Nutrition: calories 138, fat 6, fiber 6.5, carbs 17.6, protein 4.7

Breadsticks

Prep time: 25 minutes |Cooking time: 10 minutes |Servings: 8

Ingredients

- 1 teaspoon of baking powder
- ½ teaspoon of Erythritol
- ½ teaspoon of salt
- 1 cup of water
- 2 cups of almond flour
- 5 ounces of Parmesan
- 1 tablespoon of organic essential olive oil
- A teaspoon of onion powder
- 1 teaspoon of basil

COOKING DIRECTIONS:

1. Combine the baking powder with Erythritol, and water in a mixing bowl. Stir the amalgamation well.
2. Add almond flour, onion powder, salt, and basil. Knead the dough until smooth.
3. Subdivide the dough into 10 pieces creating long logs.
4. Twist the logs in braids.
5. Grate the Parmesan cheese.
6. Place the twisted logs in the pressure cooker.
7. Sprinkle them each with the grated Parmesan cheese and essential organic olive oil. Close the lid and cook the breadsticks on pressure mode for ten minutes.
8. When the cooking time ends, release the cooker's pressure and lave them for 10 minutes to cool.
9. You can serve the breadsticks immediately or store them in a sealed container.

Nutrition: calories 242, fat 18.9, fiber 3, carbs 2.7, protein 11.7

Creamy Shallots with Mushrooms

Prep time: quarter-hour | Cooking time: a half-hour | Servings: 7

Ingredients

- 9 ounces of shallot
- 8 ounces of mushrooms
- ½ cup of chicken stock
- 1 tablespoon of paprika
- ½ tablespoon of salt
- ¼ cup of cream
- 1 teaspoon of coriander
- ½ cup of dill
- ½ cup of parsley
- 1 tablespoon of Erythritol

COOKING DIRECTIONS:

1. Slice the shallot and chop the mushrooms.
2. Combine chicken stock with salt, paprika, cream, coriander, and Erythritol in a mixing bowl. Blend well until they smoothen.
3. Chop the dill and parsley.

4. Pour the cream mixture in the pressure cooker.
5. Set the cooker to "Sauté" mode and add sliced shallot followed by chopped mushrooms. Mix the ingredients using a wooden spoon.
6. Close the lid and sauté the amalgamation for thirty minutes.
7. Chop the parsley and dill.
8. When your creamy shallots are cooked, transfer them to serving plates.
9. Sprinkle the cooked dish with the chopped parsley and dill. Do not stir.

Nutrition: calories 52, fat 1, fiber 1.3, carbs 10.2, protein 3

Carrot Spirals

Prep time: 10 minutes | Cooking time: 13 minutes | Servings: 4

Ingredients

- 1 cup of water
- 4 big carrots
- 1 teaspoon of liquid stevia
- 1 tablespoon of turmeric
- A tablespoon of butter
- ½ teaspoon of ground ginger

COOKING DIRECTIONS:

1. Wash and peel the carrots.
2. Use a spiralizer to make carrot curls or spirals.
3. Put the spirals in a pressure cooker.
4. Combine liquid stevia with water, turmeric, and ground ginger in a mixing bowl. Stir the mixture well.
5. Set the pressure cooker to saute mode and add butter followed by carrots and sauté for 3 minutes. Stir the vegetables frequently.
6. Add the stevia mixture and close the lid.
7. Cook the dish on sauté mode for ten minutes.
8. When the carrot spirals are cooked, remove them from the cooker. Drain the stevia liquid and serve.

Nutrition: calories 62, fat 3.1, fiber 2.2, carbs 8.3, protein 0.8

Zucchini Muffins with Poppy Seeds

Prep time: 15 minutes | Cooking time: quarter-hour | Servings: 6

Ingredients

- 1 cup of coconut flour
- 1 medium zucchini
- 1 teaspoon of baking soda
- 1 tablespoon of fresh lemon juice
- ½ teaspoon of salt
- ½ teaspoon of ground black pepper
- 1 tablespoon of butter
- A cup of coconut milk

- 1 teaspoon of poppy seeds
- 2 tablespoons of flax meal

COOKING DIRECTIONS:

1. Wash the zucchini and chop it roughly.
2. Place the chopped zucchini in the blender and puree.
3. Combine salt with baking soda, freshly squeezed lemon juice, poppy, coconut flour, butter, ground black pepper, and flax meal in a bowl.
4. Add milk and the blended zucchini. Knead somewhat sticky dough.
5. Place the muffins in the muffin's tins and transfer the zucchini muffins in the cooker.
6. Cook the muffins on steam mode for fifteen minutes.
7. When the cooking time ends, verify the dish is cooked using a toothpick.
8. If your zucchini muffins are cooked, take them off from the cooker and serve.

Nutrition: calories 146, fat 8.9, fiber 8.1, carbs 13.5, protein 4

Glazed Walnuts

Prep time: 5 minutes |Cooking time: 4 minutes |Servings: 4

Ingredients

- 1 cup of water
- 6 ounces of walnuts
- 5 tablespoons of Erythritol
- ½ teaspoon of ground ginger
- 3tablespoons of psyllium husk powder

COOKING DIRECTIONS:

1. Combine Erythritol and water in a mixing bowl.
2. Add ground ginger and stir the mixture to dissolve sugar.
3. Transfer the walnuts in the pressure cooker and add sweet liquid.
4. Close the cooker's lid and cook the dish on pressure mode for 4 minutes.
5. Remove your glazed walnuts from the cooker and dip them in a Psyllium husk powder before serving.

Nutrition: calories 286, fat 25.1, fiber 8.2, carbs 10.4, protein 10.3

Gratin Mustard Potatoes

Prep time: 8 minutes | Cooking time: 8 minutes | Servings: 6

Ingredients

- 3 tablespoons of mustard
- 10 ounces of red potatoes
- ½ cup of dill
- 2 tablespoons of butter
- 1 teaspoon of salt
- A tablespoon of minced garlic
- 1 teaspoon of paprika

- 1 teaspoon of cilantro
- A tablespoon of oregano
- 4 tablespoons of water

COOKING DIRECTIONS:

1. Wash the potatoes and chop it into medium cubes while using a knife.
2. Sprinkle the red potato cubes with salt and oregano.
3. Stir the combination and put them in the pressure cooker.
4. Add water and butter and close the cooker's lid. Cook the mixture on pressure mode for 8 minutes.
5. Chop the dill.
6. Combine mustard with minced garlic, paprika, cilantro, and chopped dill. Stir.
7. When the red potato cubes are cooked, take them off the cooker and transfer to a serving bowl.
8. Add butter and sprinkle the your gratin mustard with sauce.

Nutrition: calories 75, fat 4.2, fiber 1, carbs 8.7, protein 1

Glazed Jalapeno Slices

Prep time: 5 minutes | Cooking time: 7 minutes | Servings: 10

Ingredients

- 8 ounces of jalapeno pepper
- ¼ cup of Erythritol
- 5 tablespoons of water
- 2 tablespoons of butter
- A teaspoon of paprika

COOKING DIRECTIONS:

1. Wash the jalapeno pepper and take off its seeds.
2. Slice it into thin circles and combine it with paprika and Erythritol. Blend the mixture.
3. Put butter in the cooker and add water. Set the cooker to saute mode.
4. When the butter begins to melt, add the sliced jalapeno in the cooker.
5. Close the lid and sauté the dish for 7 minutes.
6. When the cooking time ends, remove your jalapeno slices from the cooker and allow it to cool. Serve warm.

Nutrition: calories 28, fat 2.5, fiber 0.7, carbs 7.5, protein 0.4

Cashew Cream

Prep time: 8 minutes | Cooking time: 10 minutes | Servings: 10

Ingredients

- 3 cups of cashew
- 2 cups of chicken stock
- 1 teaspoon of salt
- 1 tablespoon of butter
- 2 tablespoons of ricotta cheese

COOKING DIRECTIONS:
1.   Combine the cashews with chicken stock in a pressure cooker.
2.   Add salt and close the pressure cooker lid.
3.   Cook the cashew mixture on pressure mode for ten minutes.
4.   Remove the cashews from the pressure cooker and drain its water.
5.   Transfer the cashews to your blender and add the ricotta cheese followed by butter. Blend to attain your favorite texture.
6.   Transfer your cashew cream to a serving bowl and serve immediately.
7.   You can also store it in your refrigerator and serve later.
Nutrition: calories 252, fat 20.6, fiber 1.2, carbs 13.8, protein 6.8

Crunchy Chicken Skin

Prep time: ten mins |Cooking time: ten mins | Servings: 7
Ingredients
- A teaspoon of red chili flakes
- 1 teaspoon of ground black pepper
- 1 teaspoon of salt
- 9 ounces of chickens skin
- 2 tablespoons of butter
- 1 teaspoon of organic essential olive oil
- A teaspoon of paprika

COOKING DIRECTIONS:
1.   Combine black pepper with chili flakes and paprika. Stir.
2.   Combine the mixture with chicken skin and let it rest for 5 minutes.
3.   Set the pressure cooker to sauté mode and add butter.
4.   Immediately the butter melts, add the chicken skin and sauté it for 10 minutes while stirring frequently. When the chicken skin gets crunchy, take it off from the pressure cooker and place it on a paper towel to drain excess oils. Serve warm.
Nutrition: calories 134, fat 11.5, fiber 0, carbs 0.98, protein 7

Meatloaf

Prep time: 10 minutes |Cooking time: 40 minutes | Servings: 9
Ingredients
- 2 cups of ground beef
- 1 cup of ground chicken
- 2 eggs
- 1 tablespoon of salt
- 1 teaspoon of ground black pepper
- ½ teaspoon of paprika
- 1 tablespoon of butter
- 1 teaspoon of cilantro

- 1 tablespoon of basil
- ¼ cup of fresh dill
- breadcrumbs

COOKING DIRECTIONS:
1.   Combine chicken with ground beef in a mixing bowl.
2.   Add egg, salt, ground black pepper, paprika, butter, cilantro, and basil.
3.   Chop the dill and add it to the ground meat mixture and stir using your hand.
4.   Place the meat mixture on an aluminum foil and add breadcrumbs before wrapping it.
5.   Place it in a pressure cooker and close its lid. Cook the dish on sauté mode and cook for 40 minutes.
6.   When the cooking time ends, remove your meatloaf from the cooker and allow it to cool.
7.   Unwrap the foil, slice it, and serve.
Nutrition: calories 173, fat 11.5, fiber 0, carbs 0.81, protein 16

Dried Tomatoes

Prep time: 5 minutes |Cooking time: 8 hours | Servings: 8
Ingredients
- 5 medium tomatoes
- 1 tablespoon of basil
- 1 teaspoon of cilantro
- 1 tablespoon of onion powder
- 5 tablespoon of organic olive oil
- 1 teaspoon of paprika

COOKING DIRECTIONS:
1.   Wash the tomatoes and slice them.
2.   Combine cilantro with basil and paprika. Stir well.
3.   Place the sliced tomatoes in the pressure cooker and add the spice mixture.
4.   Add organic olive oil and close the lid.
5.   Cook the dish on slow mode for 8 hours.
6.   When the cooking time ends, the tomatoes should be semi-dry. Remove them from the pressure cooker.
7.   Serve your dried tomatoes warm.
Nutrition: calories 92, fat 8.6, fiber 1, carbs 3.84, protein 1

Stuffed Dates

Prep time: 5 minutes | Cooking time: 7 minutes |Servings: 7
Ingredients
- 6 ounces of Parmesan cheese
- 8 ounces of dates (ripe)
- 1 teaspoon of minced garlic
- 1 tablespoon of sour cream
- 1 teaspoon of butter
- ½ teaspoon of ground white pepper
- 1 teaspoon of oregano

COOKING DIRECTIONS:

1.	Remove the stones from the dates by slitting it lengthwise.
2.	Combine the minced garlic with sour cream, ground white pepper, and oregano. Stir.
3.	Grate the Parmesan cheese, and add it to the minced garlic mixture. Blend the mixture.
4.	Stuff the dates with the cheese mixture and put them in a pressure cooker.
5.	Set the cooker to pressure mode and add butter.
6.	Close the cooker's lid and cook the dates for 7 minutes.
7.	When the cooking time ends, remove your stuffed dates from the cooker and let it cool. Serve warm.
Nutrition: calories 203, fat 7.6, fiber 3, carbs 28.35, protein 8

Veggie Nuggets

Prep time: 10 mins | Cooking time: ten minutes | Servings: 8
Ingredients
- 8 ounces of cauliflower
- 1 big red onion
- 2 carrots
- ½ cup of almond flour
- ¼ cup of pork rinds
- 2 eggs
- 1 teaspoon of salt
- ½ teaspoon of red pepper
- 1 teaspoon of ground white pepper
- A tablespoon of organic olive oil
- 1 teaspoon of dried dill

COOKING DIRECTIONS:
1.	Peel the red onion and carrots.
2.	Chop the vegetables roughly and transfer them to the mixer.
3.	Wash the cauliflower and separate it into florets.
4.	Add the cauliflower florets in a blender and puree.
5.	Add eggs and salt. Blend the amalgamation for 3 minutes.
6.	Remove the vegetable mixture from the blender and put it to a mixing bowl.
7.	Add pork rinds, red pepper, ground white pepper, and dill. Blend the amalgamation until smooth.
8.	Form nuggets from the vegetable mixture and dip them in the almond flour.
9.	Spray the load cooker with organic olive oil and add the vegetable nuggets.
10.	Cook the dish on sauté mode while stirring frequently.
11.	When the nuggets are cooked, remove them from the cooker and serve.

Nutrition: calories 85, fat 5.1, fiber 1.8, carbs 5.9, protein 5

Chicken Nuggets

Prep time: 15 minutes | Cooking time: 20 mins | Servings: 6
Ingredients
- 2 cups of ground chicken
- ½ cup of dill
- 1 egg
- 2 tablespoons of pork rinds
- 1 tablespoon of heavy cream
- ½ cup of almond flour
- 3 tablespoons of butter
- 1 tablespoon of canola oil
- 1 teaspoon of ground black pepper

COOKING DIRECTIONS:
1.	Wash the dill and chop it.
2.	Beat the egg in a mixing bowl and whisk.
3.	Add the chopped dill to the ground chicken. Stir.
4.	Sprinkle the dish with ground black pepper and cream. Blend the nugget mixture again.
5.	Form nuggets from the meat mixture and dip them in the almond flour followed by pork rinds.
6.	Sprinkle the pressure cooker with canola oil and butter.
7.	Set the cooker to pressure mode and add your nuggets after the butter melts.
8.	Close your cooker's lid and cook the dish for around 20 minutes.
9.	When the cooking time ends, check if the nuggets are cooked and transfer them to a flatter.
10.	Drain excess oil using paper towel and serve.

Nutrition: calories 217, fat 15.4, fiber 0.9, carbs 3.1, protein 17.4

Barbecue Chicken Wings

Prep time: quarter-hour | Cooking time: 35 minutes |Servings: 6
Ingredients
- 1 pound of chicken wings
- A teaspoon of ground black pepper
- 1 teaspoon of tomato paste
- 1 tablespoon of minced garlic
- 1 teaspoon of soy sauce
- 3 tablespoons of extra virgin organic olive oil
- 1 teaspoon of red pepper
- 1 teaspoon of cilantro
- 1 tablespoon of tomato sauce

COOKING DIRECTIONS:
1.	Combine the ground black pepper with red pepper and cilantro in a mixing bowl and stir.

2.	Place the chicken wings in a separate bowl and sprinkle it with the ground black pepper mixture.
3.	Add tomato paste, minced garlic, soy sauce, and tomato sauce and coat the chicken using your hands.
4.	Transfer the coated meat to a pressure cooker and close its lid.
5.	Cook the chicken on sauté mode for 35 minutes.
6.	When the cooking time ends, remove your chicken wings from the cooker and serve them hot.
Nutrition: calories 165, fat 9.5, fiber 0, carbs 2.02, protein 17

Shredded Chicken in Lettuce Leaves

Prep time: ten minutes | Cooking time: 30 mins | Servings: 6
Ingredients
- 8 ounces of chicken fillet
- ¼ cup of tomato juice
- 5 tablespoons of sour cream
- 1 teaspoon of ground black pepper
- 8 ounces of lettuce leaves
- 1 teaspoon of salt
- ½ cup of chicken stock
- 1 teaspoon of butter
- 1 teaspoon of turmeric

COOKING DIRECTIONS:
1.	Chop the chicken fillet roughly and sprinkle with sour cream, tomato juice, ground black pepper, turmeric, and salt. Mix the ingredients.
2.	Put the chicken spice mixture in a pressure cooker and add chicken stock.
3.	Close the cooker's lid and cook the dish on sear/Sauté mode for 30 minutes.
4.	When the chicken is cooked, take it off from the cooker and shred it.
5.	Add butter and blend well.
6.	Transfer the shredded chicken to lettuce leaves. Serve your shredded chicken warm.
Nutrition: calories 138, fat 7.4, fiber 2, carbs 12.63, protein 6

Japanese Eggs with Soy Sauce

Prep time: thirty minutes | Cooking time: 20 mins |Servings: 4
Ingredients
- 1 cup Chinese master stock
- 4 eggs
- 1 teaspoon salt

COOKING DIRECTIONS:
1.	Pour the Chinese master stock in the pressure cooker and close its lid.
2.	Cook the liquid on pressure mode for ten minutes.
3.	Remove the Chinese master stock from the cooker and chill it.

4.	Meanwhile, put the eggs in the pressure cooker.
5.	Add water and boil the eggs on pressure mode for ten minutes.
6.	When the eggs are cooked, remove them from the cooker and allow them to cool.
7.	Peel the eggs and dip them in the Chinese master stock.
8.	Leave the eggs in the liquid for around 20 minutes.
9.	Remove the eggs from the liquid and cut it to halves while serving.
Nutrition: calories 134, fat 9.7, fiber 1, carbs 2.01, protein 9

Appetizer Pork Shank

Prep time: 15 minutes |Cooking time: 45 minutes | Servings: 6
Ingredients
- 1 pound pork shank
- ½ cup of parsley
- 4 garlic cloves
- 1 teaspoon of salt
- ½ teaspoon of paprika
- 2 tablespoons of extra virgin olive oil
- 1 teaspoon of cilantro
- 1 tablespoon of celery
- 1 carrot
- 1 cup of water
- 1 red onion
- 1cup of wine
- 2 tablespoons of freshly squeezed lemon juice

COOKING DIRECTIONS:
1.	Chop the parsley and slice the garlic cloves.
2.	Combine the vegetables and add salt, paprika, cilantro, wine, and freshly squeezed lemon juice. Stir the amalgamation.
3.	Combine the pork shank with the marinade and set them aside.
4.	Peel the onion and slice it.
5.	Peel the carrot and grate it.
6.	Combine the sliced onion and grated carrot.
7.	Add celery and blend well.
8.	Add the vegetables to the pork shank mixture and stir using your hands.
9.	Place the meat in the pressure cooker and add water.
10.	Close the cooker's lid and cook it on pressure mode for 45 minutes.
11.	When the cooking time ends, take off your meat from the cooker and let it chill.
12.	Slice your appetizer pork shank and serve.
Nutrition: calories 242, fat 19.8, fiber 1, carbs 5.38, protein 11

Pressure-cooked Peanuts+

Prep time: 5 minutes | Cooking time: 1.5 hour | Servings: 8

Ingredients

- 3 cups of peanuts in shells
- 1 tablespoon of salt
- 4 servings of water
- ½ teaspoon of nutmeg

COOKING DIRECTIONS:

1. Combine water with nutmeg, and salt.
2. Stir the mixture well to dissolve salt.
3. Transfer your nutmeg fluid into the pressure cooker.
4. Add peanuts and close the lid.
5. Cook the dish on pressure mode for 90 minutes.
6. When the cooking time ends, remove your cooked peanuts from the cooker and let it cool before serving.

Nutrition: calories 562, fat 36.8, fiber 6, carbs 38.57, protein 28

Spinach Dip

Prep time: ten mins |Cooking time: a quarter-hour |Servings: 8

Ingredients

- 1 cup of spinach
- ½ cup of cream cheese
- ½ cup of cream
- 6 ounces of Romano cheese
- 1 teaspoon of salt
- A teaspoon of paprika
- 1 bell pepper
- 1 white medium onion
- 5 tablespoon of walnuts
- 1 teaspoon of ground ginger
- ½ cup of fresh dill

COOKING DIRECTIONS:

1. Wash the spinach and dill. Chop them.
2. Place the greens in the pressure cooker.
3. Add cream and cream cheese.
4. Grate the Romano cheese and sprinkle the green mixture with grated cheese.
5. Add salt, paprika, walnuts, and ground ginger.
6. Remove the seeds from the bell pepper and peel the onion.
7. Chop the vegetables into pieces and add them to the cooker mixture.
8. Mix your spinach dip using a spoon.
9. Close the lid and cook the dish on steam mode for 15 minutes.
10. When the cooking time ends, remove your spinach dip from the cooker and stir.
11. Transfer it to serving bowls and enjoy.

Nutrition: calories 196, fat 15.9, fiber 1, carbs 4.62, protein 10

Stuffed Jalapeno Peppers

Prep time: ten minutes | Cooking time: 8 minutes |Servings: 8

Ingredients

- 7 ounces of Parmesan cheese
- 8 ounces of jalapeno pepper
- 1 teaspoon of cilantro
- ½ teaspoon of olive oil
- 1 tablespoon of chives

COOKING DIRECTIONS:

1. Wash the jalapeno peppers and cut them crosswise.
2. Combine cilantro with extra virgin olive oil and chives in a bowl. Stir.
3. Slice the Parmesan cheese thinly.
4. Put the sliced cheese in the jalapeno pepper halves.
5. Sprinkle the vegetables with the spice mixture.
6. Transfer the stuffed jalapeno peppers to the pressure cooker and close its lid. Cook the dish on pressure mode for 8 minutes.
7. Release the accumulated pressure from the cooker and open its lid.
8. Remove the stuffed jalapeno peppers the cooker and let it rest.
9. Transfer your dish to the serving plates and enjoy.

Nutrition: calories 103, fat 1.6, fiber 1, carbs 11.79, protein 10

Oregano Mushrooms

Prep time: fifteen minutes |Cooking time: thirty minutes | Servings: 6

Ingredients

- 10 ounces of mushrooms
- 1 tablespoon of oregano
- 1 teaspoon of basil
- ¼ cup of fresh parsley
- 1 teaspoon of ground black pepper
- 1 teaspoon of cilantro
- ½ cup of sour cream
- 1 medium onion
- 1 teaspoon of salt
- 2 tablespoons of butter

COOKING DIRECTIONS:

1. Wash the mushrooms and slice them.
2. Chop the fresh parsley and blend it with oregano
3. Peel the onion and dice it.
4. Combine all of the prepared ingredients in a mixing bowl.
5. Sprinkle the amalgamation with basil, ground black pepper, cilantro, sour cream, and butter. Stir.

6. Set the pressure cooker to sauté mode and add the mushroom mixture.

7. Close the lid and sauté the dish for 30 minutes.

8. Remove the oregano mushrooms from the cooker and let it rest.

9. Serve your oregano mushrooms with crusty bread slices.

Nutrition: calories 97, fat 8.1, fiber 1.4, carbs 5, protein 2.5

Cottage Cheese Prunes

Prep time: 10 minutes |Cooking time: 3 minutes | Servings: 6

Ingredients

- 12 ounces of prunes (pitted)
- 1 cup of cheese
- 2 tablespoons of raisins
- 1 teaspoon of essential olive oil
- 2 ounces of cheddar cheese
- 1 teaspoon of sugar

COOKING DIRECTIONS:

1. Cut the prunes crosswise.

2. Combine cheese and sugar in a bowl.

3. Grate cheddar cheese and add it to the cheese mixture. Mash the combination well using a fork.

4. Mince the raisins and add them to the chesses mixture.

5. Fill the prune halves with the cottage cheese mixture.

6. Spray the pressure cooker base with olive oil.

7. Transfer the prune halves in the pressure cooker and close its lid.

8. Cook the dish on pressure mode for 3 minutes or until the cheese melts.

9. Release the cooker's pressure and open its lid. Chill the dish briefly before serving.

Nutrition: calories 117, fat 2.6, fiber 2, carbs 20.67, protein 4

Lamb Cutlets

Prep time: ten mins | Cooking time: a quarter-hour | Servings: 6

Ingredients

- 10 ounces of lamb cutlets
- 1 onion
- ½ cup of garlic herb
- 1 teaspoon of salt
- A teaspoon of ground black pepper
- 1 tablespoon of heavy cream
- 1 teaspoon of extra virgin olive oil
- 1 tablespoon of cilantro
- ½ tablespoon of paprika
- An egg

COOKING DIRECTIONS:

1. Chop the lamb into tiny pieces and place them in the mixing bowl.

2. Sprinkle the chopped lamb with salt, ground black pepper, cilantro, paprika, and egg.

3. Peel the onion and add it to your lamb mixture.

4. Make medium-sized patties from the meat mixture.

5. Set the pressure cooker to saute mode and spray pressure it with essential organic olive oil.

6. Add the lamb patties into the cooker and sauté them for 10 minutes from each side.

7. Close the lid and cook your dish on pressure mode for 15 minutes.

8 When the cooking time ends, remove your lamb cutlets from the load cooker and let them cool a bit before serving.

Nutrition: calories 177, fat 10.9, fiber 1, carbs 5.47, protein 14

Garlic Tofu Bites

Prep time: ten mins | Cooking time: 8 minutes | Servings: 6

Ingredients

- 10 ounces of tofu
- 2 tablespoons of minced garlic
- 1 teaspoon of paprika
- ½ teaspoon of oregano
- 1 tablespoon of olive oil
- 1 teaspoon of dried dill

COOKING DIRECTIONS:

1. Combine the minced garlic with paprika, oregano, and dill. Stir well.

2. Cut the tofu into medium squares and rub them with minced garlic mixture.

3. Set the pressure cooker to saute mode and spray it with essential extra virgin olive oil.

4. Place the tofu squares in the pressure cooker and sauté them for 4 minutes.

5. Remove your garlic tofu bites from the cooker and serve immediately.

Nutrition: calories 154, fat 11.9, fiber 2, carbs 6.25, protein 8

Sweet Pork Ribs

Prep time: thirty minutes | Cooking time: 40 minutes | Servings: 6

Ingredients

- 1 tablespoon of Erythritol
- 1 tablespoon of liquid stevia
- 2 tablespoons of freshly squeezed lemon juice
- A pound of pork ribs
- 1 tablespoon of lime zest
- 1 teaspoon of salt
- 3 tablespoons of extra virgin olive oil
- ½ tablespoon of oregano

- ½ tablespoon of fresh thyme
- 1 tablespoon of red pepper

COOKING DIRECTIONS:

1. Combine Erythritol with fresh lemon juice, lime zest, salt, oregano, and red pepper and stir.
2. Separate the pork ribs into individual ribs and sprinkle them with the spice mixture.
3. Chop the fresh thyme and add it to the pork ribs mixture.
4. Let the pork ribs sit for about twenty or so minutes to absorb the flavors.
5. Set the cooker to pressure mode and spread its base with essential olive oil.
6. Add the marinated pork ribs and close its lid. Cook the dish on meat mode for 40 minutes.
7. Open the pressure cooker's lid and remove your sweet pork rinds.
8. Transfer the dish to the serving plate and sprinkle it with liquid stevia before serving.

Nutrition: calories 276, fat 20.5, fiber 0.7, carbs 4.7, protein 20.4

Pasta Cake

Prep time: fifteen minutes | Cooking time: 25 minutes | Servings: 8

Ingredients

- 8 ounces of black bean pasta (cooked)
- 4 eggs
- 1 cup of almond flour
- 1 onion
- 1 carrot
- 2 tablespoons of butter
- 1 teaspoon of ground black pepper
- 1 teaspoon of salt
- 1 cup of parsley
- 1 cup of cream
- 1 tomato

COOKING DIRECTIONS:

1. Beat the eggs in a mixing bowl and whisk.
2. Peel the onion and carrot. Grate the vegetables.
3. Sprinkle the grated vegetables with ground black pepper, salt, and cream and stir the amalgamation.
4. Chop the tomato and parsley.
5. Combine the cooked black bean pasta with the chopped parsley and tomato.
6. Add almond flour to the egg mixture.
7. Add the butter to the grated vegetable mixture. Knead the dough until smooth.
8. Pour the dough in the pressure cooker and flatten it using your hands or a spatula.
9. Pour the cream and close the cooker's lid.
10. Cook the dish on steam mode for 25 minutes.

11. When the cooking time ends, remove your solid pasta cake from the cooker. Cut it into slices and serve.

Nutrition: calories 1873, fat 8.4, fiber 7.1, carbs 12.9, protein 16.5

Tuna Balls

Prep time: ten mins | Cooking time: a quarter-HOUR | Servings: 6

Ingredients

- 9 ounces of tuna fillet
- 1 tablespoon of minced garlic
- 1 teaspoon of coriander
- A teaspoon of basil
- 1 teaspoon of butter
- 1 teaspoon of salt
- ½ tablespoon of turmeric
- 2 tablespoons of starch
- 2 tablespoons of organic olive oil
- 1 cup of pork rinds
- An egg
- 2 tablespoons of chives

COOKING DIRECTIONS:

1. Chop the tuna fillet and transfer to a blender.
2. Add minced garlic, coriander, basil, salt, turmeric, starch, and chives.
3. Add an egg and blend it.
4. Remove the tuna mixture from the blender and transfer it to a mixing bowl. Stir it carefully.
5. Make small balls from the fish mixture and dip them in the pork rinds.
6. Spread the cooker's base with butter and let it melt.
7. Put the tuna balls in the cooker and close the lid.
8. Cook the dish on sauté mode for quarter-hour.
9. When the cooking time ends, verify whether your tuna is ready.
10. Remove them from the cooker and let them chill. You can either serve immediately or store them in the refrigerator for later servings.

Nutrition: calories 228, fat 21, fiber 0.2, carbs 4.3, protein 13

Chicken Balls in Melted Butter

Prep time: quarter-hour | Cooking time: 25 minutes | Servings: 8

Ingredients

- 3 cups of ground chicken
- 4 tablespoons of butter
- ½ cup of dill
- 1 teaspoon of salt
- A teaspoon of paprika
- 1 teaspoon of ground black pepper

- 1 tablespoon of garlic powder
- A teaspoon of extra virgin olive oil
- An egg
- ½ cup of pork rinds

COOKING DIRECTIONS:
1. Chop the dill and put them in a mixing bowl.
2. Add salt, paprika, ground black pepper, garlic powder, and ground chicken. Stir using a wooden spoon.
3. Add egg and blend well using your hands.
4. Make medium-sized balls from your ground chicken mixture.
5. Flatten them and put a pat of butter and the middle of each ball.
6. Wrap the ground chicken with butter to make the chicken balls.
7. Dip the chicken balls in the pork rinds.
8. Pour the organic olive oil into the pressure cooker and add the chicken balls.
9. Close the lid and cook the balls on sauté mode on for 25 minutes.
10. When the cooking time ends, open the cooker's lid and transfer the chicken balls to serving plates.

Nutrition: calories 226, fat 14.1, fiber 0.7, carbs 2.8, protein 22.4

Colorful Veggie Skewers

Prep time: ten mins | Cooking time: 10 mins | Servings: 6
Ingredients
- 5 ounces of corn
- 1 sweet bell pepper
- 1 big carrot
- 1 cup of cherry tomatoes
- 1 teaspoon of salt
- 1 teaspoon of basil
- ½ teaspoon of ground black pepper
- 1 teaspoon of sesame oil
- 1 tablespoon of cumin seeds

COOKING DIRECTIONS:
1. Wash each vegetable thoroughly.
2. Remove the seeds from your bell pepper and cut it into medium squares.
3. Peel the carrot and slice it.
4. Transfer the bell pepper squares, sliced carrot, corn, and cherry tomatoes to a mixing bowl.
5. Sprinkle the mixture with salt, ground black pepper, cumin seeds, and sesame oil. Blend it well using your hands.
6. Add the vegetables on wooden skewers.
7. Set the strain cooker to steam mode and place the vegetable skewers in the pressure cooker.
8. Close the lid and steam the dish for 10 minutes.
9. When the cooking time ends, remove them from the cooker and let them cool.

10. Set the pressure cooker to "sauté" mode and sauté your vegetable skewers briefly before serving.

Nutrition: calories 110, fat 2.2, fiber 3, carbs 21.21, protein 3

Cod Fritters

Prep time: quarter-hour | Cooking time: 52 minutes| Servings: 6
Ingredients
- 1 pound of cod fillet
- 1 onion
- 4 garlic cloves
- 1 teaspoon of ground ginger
- 1 teaspoon of ground black pepper
- 1 teaspoon of salt
- ½ tablespoon of cilantro
- ½ cup of parsley
- An egg
- ¼ cup of almond flour
- 1 teaspoon of starch
- 1 teaspoon of coriander

COOKING DIRECTIONS:
1. Chop the cod fillet roughly and transfer it to a blender. Blend the fish fillet to obtain a puree.
2. Pour the fish puree into a big bowl and sprinkle it with ginger, ground black pepper, salt, cilantro, egg, almond flour, starch, and coriander. Blend the amalgamation well using a spoon.
3. Chop the parsley and slice the garlic cloves.
4. Peel the onion and grate it.
5. Add the grated onion, sliced garlic, and chopped parsley to the fish mixture. Stir.
6. Set the cooker to steam mode.
7. Make medium-sized fritters from the cod mixture and put them in the pressure cooker.
8. Close the cooker's lid and cook the fritters for 25 minutes.
9. When the cooking time ends, open the cooker and let the dish rest briefly.
10. Remove your cod fritters from the load cooker and serve the dish immediately. You can also store them either in a sealed container or a refrigerator for later servings.

Nutrition: calories 92, fat 2.1, fiber 0.9, carbs 3.4, protein 15.2

Pakora

Prep time: 5 minutes | Cooking time: 5 minutes | Servings: 4
Ingredients
- 2 cups of almond flour
- 1 tablespoon of fresh ginger
- ½ medium onion
- 3 ounces of habanero
- 1 teaspoon of baking soda

- 1 tablespoon of fresh lemon juice
- 3 tablespoons of organic olive oil
- ½ cup of water
- 1 teaspoon of thyme

COOKING DIRECTIONS:
1. Combine almond flour with fresh ginger, baking soda, water, freshly squeezed lemon juice, and thyme. Stir.
2. Chop the habanero and onion and add the constituents to a mixing bowl. Knead the dough.
3. Set the pressure cooker to sauté mode and spread it with extra virgin olive oil.
4. Take the ladle and add the pakora mixture to the cooker.
5. Sauté the pakora for 4 minutes and drain their excess oils using a paper towel. Allow it to cool before serving.

Nutrition: calories 190, fat 17.7, carbs 7.4, protein 3.7

Kebabs

Prep time: 20 minutes | Cooking time: 25 minutes | Servings: 5

Ingredients
- 1 pound of boneless chicken
- 3 tomatoes
- 1 teaspoon of paprika
- 2 tablespoons of apple cider vinegar
- 3 tablespoons of essential extra virgin olive oil
- 1 red bell pepper
- 1 teaspoon of oregano
- ¼ teaspoon of cayenne

COOKING DIRECTIONS:
1. Chop the boneless chicken meat into cubes.
2. Chop the tomatoes and combine them with paprika, apple cider vinegar, oregano, cayenne, and essential olive oil in a mixing bowl. Stir well.
3. Combine the chopped chicken with the spice mixture in a mixing bowl.
4. Mix the ingredients using your hands and allow the meat mixture rest for 10 minutes.
5. Remove the seeds from the bell pepper and dice it into large chunks.
6. Thread the boneless chicken meat, chopped tomatoes, and bell pepper on the wooden skewers.
7. Transfer the kebabs to a pressure cooker and close its lid.
8. Steam the snack for 25 minutes.
9. When your kebabs are ready, remove them from the cooker to cool before serving.

Nutrition: calories 334, fat 21.3, fiber 3, carbs 25.8, protein 11

Rumaki

Prep time: quarter-hour | Cooking time: quarter-hour | Servings: 6

Ingredients
- 1 pound of chicken livers
- 4 tablespoons of teriyaki sauce
- ½ cup of soy sauce
- 1 tablespoon of minced garlic
- 8 ounces of bacon slices
- 1 teaspoon of salt
- ½ teaspoon of ground black pepper
- 3 tablespoons of organic essential olive oil

COOKING DIRECTIONS:
1. Combine the teriyaki sauce with soy sauce, minced garlic, and ground black pepper in a mixing bowl and whisk well.
2. Put the chicken livers in the teriyaki sauce mixture, stir, and let them rest for ten minutes.
3. Sprinkle the bacon with salt and stir.
4. Remove the chicken liver from the teriyaki sauce mixture.
5. Wrap it in sliced bacon and fasten with toothpicks.
6. Pour the olive oil into the pressure cooker.
7. Transfer the wrapped contents to the cooker and sprinkle it with 3 tablespoons while of teriyaki sauce.
8. Set your cooker to pressure mode and close its lid. Cook the dish for around 14 minutes.
9. When the cooking time ends, open the cooker's lid and remove your rumaki. Transfer it to a serving plate and leave it to rest. Serve warm.

Nutrition: calories 405, fat 31.7, fiber 2, carbs 15.32, protein 17

Cocktail Meatballs

Prep time: fifteen minutes | Cooking time: 25 minutes | Servings: 7

Ingredients
- 2 cups of ground beef
- 1 tablespoon of minced garlic
- 4 ounces of Keto bread
- 1 tablespoon of Erythritol
- 3 tablespoons of tomato paste
- 1 tablespoon of water
- 1 tablespoon of essential olive oil
- An egg
- ¼ cup of cream
- 1 teaspoon of baking powder
- 1 tablespoon of freshly squeezed lemon juice
- 1 teaspoon of salt

COOKING DIRECTIONS:
1. Combine ground beef with minced garlic and salt in a mixing bowl.
2. Beat an egg in a separate mixing bowl and whisk it.
3. Add the Keto bread and cream and stir until smooth.

4.   Add the cream mixture to the ground beef mixture and stir well.
5.   Make small cocktail meatballs through from the ground beef mixture.
6.   Set the pressure cooker to sauté mode and sprinkle it with organic olive.
7.   Add the cocktail meatballs and sauté them for ten minutes.
8.   Combine water with tomato paste, Erythritol, baking powder, and lemon juice in a bowl. Whisk well.
9.   Add the tomato mixture to the cooker and close its lid. Cook them for around 15 minutes.
10.   When the cooking time ends, remove your cocktail meatballs from the cooker and sprinkle it with its gravy while serving.
Nutrition: calories 143, fat 8.2, fiber 1.6, carbs 8.7, protein 11.3

Sweet Pecans
Prep time: ten minutes | Cooking time: ten mins | Servings: 10
Ingredients
- An egg
- ½ cup of Erythritol
- 3 tablespoons of stevia powder
- 1 teaspoon of butter
- 1 cup of pecans
- 1 teaspoon of cinnamon
- ½ teaspoon of ground black pepper

COOKING DIRECTIONS:
1.   Beat the egg in a mixing bowl.
2.   Add cinnamon, Erythritol, and ground black pepper. Stir the mixture.
3.   Add pecans and stir well. Let the pecans soak in the egg liquid.
4.   Set the cooker to pressure mode and add pecans followed by 3 tablespoons of the egg mixture.
5.   Close the cooker's lid and cook the dish on for ten minutes.
6.   When the cooking time ends, release the cooker's pressure and open its lid.
7.   Transfer your sweet pecans to a serving bowl and sprinkle stevia powder. Serve immediately or refrigerate for later use.
Nutrition: calories 13, fat 1, fiber 0.2, carbs 9.9, protein 0.6

Stuffed Cheese-Garlic Bread
Prep time: 10 minutes | Cooking time: ten minutes | Servings: 6
Ingredients
- ½ cup of parsley
- 8 ounces of Keto bread
- 7 ounces of Cheddar cheese
- 1 tablespoon of butter
- 4 ounces of ham

- 1 teaspoon of paprika
- ½ teaspoon of turmeric
- 2 tablespoons of minced garlic
- 1 tablespoon of organic olive oil

COOKING DIRECTIONS:
1.   Take Keto bread and subdivide it into tiny cuts.
2.   Shred the cheese and chop the ham and mix them in a bowl.
3.   Add minced garlic and stir well.
4.   Sprinkle the cheese mixture with paprika, turmeric, and organic olive oil.
5.   Fill Keto bread with the cheese mixture.
6.   Set the cooker to pressure mode and place some butter at the middle of each slice.
7.   Transfer buttered slices into the cooker and close its lid.
8.   Cook the dish for 10 minutes or until cheese melts.
9.   Remove the cooked bread from the cooker and leave it to cool. Serve your cheesed bread in slices.
Nutrition: calories 269, fat 17.6, fiber 3.3, carbs 12, protein 17.1

French Fries
Prep time: ten minutes | Cooking time: 20 mins | Servings: 6
Ingredients
- A teaspoon of baking soda
- 1 pound of Jicama
- 1 tablespoon of salt
- 1 teaspoon of ground black pepper
- 2 tablespoons of essential organic olive oil

COOKING DIRECTIONS:
1.   Cut jicama into thick pieces and sprinkle them with black pepper and salt in a bowl. Toss them well to coat.. Put the trivet in the pressure cooker and place sliced jicama on it.
2.   Set the cooker to steam mode and close its lid.
3.   Cook the dish for 10 minutes and release the cooker's pressure before opening it.
4.   Remove jicama from the trivet and sprinkle it with organic essential olive oil.
5.   Sprinkle the baking soda and stir gently.
6.   Preheat the oven to 365 F and cook the dish for 10 minutes or until it becomes crunchy.
7.   Remove the dish from the load cooker and allow it rest briefly. Serve the fries immediately.
Nutrition: calories 70, fat 4.8, fiber 3.8, carbs 6.9, protein 0.6

Cheesy Bruschetta
Prep time: 10 minutes | Cooking time: 7 minutes | Servings: 7
Ingredients

- 7 slices of Keto bread
- 6 ounces of Cheddar cheese
- 1 teaspoon of minced garlic
- 1 teaspoon of salt
- ½ teaspoon of dried dill
- 1 tablespoon of sour cream
- 1 teaspoon of butter
- 1 bell pepper

COOKING DIRECTIONS:

1. Combine the minced garlic with salt, dried dill, sour cream, and butter in a bowl. Stir to obtain a smooth texture. Rub the bread slices with the minced garlic mixture.
2. Slice Cheddar cheese and remove seeds from the bell pepper.
3. Slice the bell pepper and spread them alongside cheddar cheese around the bread.
4. Set the cooker to pressure mode and transfer the bruschetta into it. Close the cooker's lid.
5. Cook the dish for 7 minutes or until cheese melts.
6. Remove your cheesy bruschetta from the cooker and allow it rest briefly. Serve warm.

Nutrition: calories 184, fat 11.1, fiber 2.6, carbs 10.3, protein 12.1

Pepperoni Mini Pizzas

Prep time: twenty or so minutes | Cooking time: 25 minutes | Servings: 8

Ingredients

- 1 cup of whey
- 1 tablespoon of brown sugar
- ½ teaspoon of salt
- 2 cups of almond flour
- 1 tablespoon of butter
- ½ cup of parsley
- 6 ounces of mozzarella cheese
- 5 ounces of pepperoni
- 1 teaspoon of ground white pepper
- 1 tablespoon of tomato paste
- 2 tomatoes

COOKING DIRECTIONS:

1. Combine almond flour with whey, salt, and ground white pepper. Knead the dough until smooth.
2. Combine tomato paste with butter in a bowl and stir well.
3. Chop the parsley and slice the pepperoni.
4. Slice the tomatoes and grate the mozzarella cheese.
5. Make a long-log shape from your dough and subdivide it into six pieces.
6. Make small pizza rounds from the dough.
7. Spread the pizza crusts with the tomato paste.
8. Add the sliced tomatoes and chopped parsley.
9. Sprinkle the pizzas with the grated cheese.
10. Set the cooker to pressure mode and place the mini pizzas into it.
11. Close the lid and cook the dish for 25 minutes.
12. When the cooking time ends, remove your pepperoni mini pizzas from the cooker and allow them to cool.
13. Cut the pizzas into halves and serve immediately.

Nutrition: calories 221, fat 16.6, fiber 1.4, carbs 6.9, protein 12.3

DESSERT RECIPES

Pineapple Whisked Cake

Prep time: 15 MINUTES |Cooking time: a half-HOUR | Servings: 10

Ingredients

- 9 ounces of pineapple(canned)
- 4 eggs
- 1 cup of almond flour
- 1 cup of sour cream
- 1 teaspoon of baking soda
- 1 tablespoon of freshly squeezed lemon juice
- 1 teaspoon of cinnamon
- ½ cup of erythritol
- 2 tablespoons of butter

COOKING DIRECTIONS:

1. Beat the eggs in a bowl and whisk.
2. Add sour cream and whisk the amalgamation for 1 minute.
3. Add baking soda followed by freshly squeezed lemon juice and stir.
4. Add Erythritol, cinnamon, butter, and almond flour.
5. Mix the ingredients using a hand mixer for 5 minutes.
6. Chop the canned pineapples and add them to dough.
7. Mix the pineapple dough using a spoon.
8. Pour the dough into the pressure cooker and close its lid.
9. Cook the dish on manual mode for thirty minutes.
10. When the cooking time open the cooker and check whether the cake is cooked.
11. Remove your pineapple cake from the cooker and leave it to chill. Serve it in slices.

Nutrition: calories 176, fat 14.2, fiber 1.7, carbs 16.7, protein 5.5

Strawberry Cheesecake

Prep time: ten MINUTES |Cooking time: 24 minutes | Servings: 6

Ingredients

- A cup of strawberries
- 1 cup of cream
- 2 eggs
- ½ cup of Erythritol
- 7 ounces of almond arrowroot crackers
- 5 tablespoons of butter
- 1 teaspoon of vanilla sugar
- ¼ teaspoon of nutmeg
- 3 tablespoons of low-fat caramel

COOKING DIRECTIONS:

1. Crush the crackers well and combine them with butter. Stir.
2. Beat the eggs in a mixing bowl and add sugar, vanilla Erythritol, nutmeg, and cream. Whisk this mixture well. Wash the strawberries and slice them.
3. Put the cracker mixture in the pressure cooker and flatten it to form crust.
4. Pour the cream mixture on the crust and flatten it using a spoon.
5. Dip the sliced strawberries in the cream mixture and close the cooker's lid.
6. Cook the mixture on pressure mode for 24 minutes.
7. When the cooking time ends, remove your strawberry cheesecake from the load cooker and put it in a refrigerator.
8. Sprinkle the cheesecake with caramel. Cut into slices and serve.

Nutrition: calories 148, fat 13.4, fiber 0.5, carbs 21.2, protein 2.4

Keto Donuts

Prep time: 15 MINUTES |Cooking time: 6 minutes | Servings: 8

Ingredients

- 1 cup of coconut milk
- 3 eggs (beaten)
- 1 teaspoon of vanilla flavoring
- 1cup of coconut flour
- ½ cup of almond flour
- 1 teaspoon of baking powder
- ½ cup of Erythritol
- 1 tablespoon of ground cinnamon
- 1 teaspoon of organic essential olive oil

COOKING DIRECTIONS:

1. Mix coconut milk, beaten eggs, vanilla flavoring, coconut flour, and almond flour in a bowl.
2. Add baking powder and organic essential olive oil. Knead the non-sticky dough.
3. Roll the dough to obtain 8 donuts.
4. Place the donuts in the air fryer basket of Ninja Foodie and close its lid.
5. Cook the donuts at 355F for 3 minutes.
6. Combine Erythritol with ground cinnamon and dip each donut in the cinnamon mixture for coating. Enjoy.

Nutrition: calories 204, fat 14.2, fiber 7.9, carbs 26.4, protein 6.3

Chocolate Lava Ramekins

Prep time: 10 MINUTES |Cooking time: 10 minutes | Servings: 4

Ingredients

- ½ cup of Erythritol
- 3 whole eggs
- 1 cup of coconut flour

- 1-ounce of chocolate
- 4 egg yolks
- 1 teaspoon of vanilla sugar
- 8 ounces of butter
- 1 teaspoon of instant coffee

COOKING DIRECTIONS:

1. Beat the eggs in a mixing bowl and whisk it.
2. Add the Erythritol and mix the ingredients using a hand mixer.
3. Melt the chocolate and butter.
4. Add the melted chocolate to the egg mixture.
5. Add the coconut flour, instant coffee, and vanilla sugar to the mixture and stir until it smoothen.
6. Pour the chocolate mixture into the ramekins and place them on a trivet.
7. Transfer the trivet in the pressure cooker and close its lid. Set it to bake/roast mode and cook the contents for 10 minutes.
8. When the cooking time ends, open the pressure cooker and remove the trivet.
9. Let the ramekins cool for a few minutes and serve.

Nutrition: calories 644, fat 57.6, fiber 12.1, carbs 23.3, protein 11.6

Applesauce

Prep time: ten MINUTES |Cooking time: 16 MINUTES |Servings: 5

Ingredients

- ½ pound of apples
- 2 cup of water
- 1 teaspoon of cinnamon
- 1 teaspoon of Erythritol

COOKING DIRECTIONS:

1. Wash the apples and peel them.
2. Chop the apples and place them in a pressure cooker.
3. Add water and mix well.
4. Close the cooker's lid and cook the apples on pressure mode for 16 minutes.
5. Release the cooker's pressure and open its lid.
6. Transfer the cooked apples to a blender and puree.
7. Add cinnamon and Erythritol. Blend until they smoothen.
8. Chill your applesauce in the refrigerator before serving.

Nutrition: calories 13, fat 0.1, fiber 0.8, carbs 3.5, protein 0.1

Chocolate Topping

Prep time: 5 minutes | Cooking time: 2 minutes | Servings: 4

Ingredients

- 1 tablespoon of hot chocolate mix
- 4 tablespoons of butter
- 1 oz of chocolate brown
- 1 tablespoon of Erythritol

COOKING DIRECTIONS:

1. Place butter, hot chocolate mix, and chocolate bars in the Ninja Pressure cooker.
2. Add Erythritol and stir gently.
3. Close the lid and cook the mixture on high-pressure mode for two minutes.
4. Quick release the pressure and open the cooker's lid. Stir.
5. Transfer your chocolate topping into a glass jar and store it in a refrigerator for 72 hours.

Nutrition: calories 143, fat 13.8, fiber 0.6, carbs 8, protein 0.9

Cinnamon Apple Cake

Prep time: ten MINUTES |Cooking time: 18 MINUTES |Servings: 10

Ingredients

- 1 teaspoon of cinnamon
- ½ cup of Erythritol
- 1 cup of coconut flour
- An egg
- 1 apple
- 1 cup of sour cream
- A tablespoon of vanilla sugar
- 1 teaspoon of ground ginger
- 5 ounces of butter
- 1 tablespoon of orange juice
- 12 teaspoons of lemon zest

COOKING DIRECTIONS:

1. Beat the egg in a bowl and whisk for a minute.
2. Add the coconut flour, sour cream, vanilla sugar, orange juice, and lemon zest. Mix until smooth.
3. Remove the seeds from the apple and dice it.
4. Sprinkle the chopped apple with Erythritol, cinnamon, and ground ginger. Mix well.
5. Melt the butter and add it on the dough and stir well.
6. Add the apple dough in the pressure cooker and close its lid. Cook the dough on pressure mode for 18 minutes.
7. When the cooking time ends, open the pressure cooker lid and allow your apple cake to rest.
8. Remove the dessert from the pressure cooker and place it on a serving plate. Slice to serve.

Nutrition: calories 225, fat 18, fiber 5.6, carbs 23.9, protein 3.2

Blueberry Muffins

Prep time: quarter-hour | Cooking time: 10 MINUTES |Servings: 6

Ingredients

- 1 cup of frozen blueberries
- 1 ½ cup of coconut flour
- 1 teaspoon of baking powder

- 1 tablespoon of apple cider vinegar treatment
- 1 tablespoon of coconut
- ½ cup of almond milk
- 2 eggs
- 1 teaspoon of vanilla flavor
- 1 teaspoon of extra virgin olive oil

COOKING DIRECTIONS:

1. Place the coconut flour, baking soda, apple cider vinegar, coconut, almond milk, eggs, and vanilla flavoring in a blender. Blend the mix well.
2. Add the frozen blueberries and blend the mixture for thirty seconds.
3. Take the muffin molds and fill each halfway with batter.
4. Place the muffins molds on a trivet and fix it in the pressure cooker.
5. Close the cooker's lid and cook the molds on pressure mode for 10 minutes.
6. When you blueberry muffins are ready, remove them from the cooker and leave them to cool. Serve while warm.

Nutrition: calories 214, fat 10.4, fiber 13.1, carbs 25.4, protein 6.5

Pumpkin Cake

Prep time: quarter-HOUR | Cooking time: 25 MINUTES |Servings: 10

Ingredients

- 3 cups of canned pumpkin
- 1 teaspoon of cinnamon
- 3 cups of coconut flour
- 2 eggs
- 1 tablespoon of baking powder
- 1 tablespoon of apple cider vinegar
- 1/3 cup of Erythritol
- 1 teaspoon of vanilla flavoring
- 1 teaspoon of essential organic olive oil
- ½ cup of walnuts
- 1 teaspoon of salt

COOKING DIRECTIONS:

1. Mash the canned pumpkin well.
2. Combine the coconut flour with baking powder, apple cider vinegar, Erythritol, vanilla extract, and salt. Stir well.
3. Beat the eggs in a separate bowl.
4. Add the eggs to the coconut flour mixture and stir.
5. Crush the walnuts.
6. Combine the mashed pumpkin with the flour mixture and knead smooth dough.
7. Add crushed walnuts and knead the dough for 1 minute.
8. Spray the pressure cooker with organic olive oil and add the pumpkin dough. Flatten it to acquire a cake shape.

9. Close the cooker's lid and cook the dessert on pressure mode for 25 minutes.
10. Check if your pumpkin cake is cooked using a toothpick and remove it from the cooker. Let it rest, slice, and serve.

Nutrition: calories 228, fat 8.9, fiber 17.1, carbs 31.6, protein 8.2

Strawberry Pie

Prep time: fifteen MINUTES |Cooking time: quarter-hour | Servings: 4

Ingredients

- 1 cup of almond flour
- 1/3 cup of butter (softened)
- 1 tablespoon of swerve
- 1 teaspoon of baking powder
- ¼ cup of almond milk
- ¼ cup of strawberries (sliced)

COOKING DIRECTIONS:

1. Make batter by mixing almond flour, with softened butter, swerve, baking powder, and almond milk.
2. Pour the amalgamation in the Ninja Foodie.
3. Place the sliced strawberries on the batter and press it to create a berry layer.
4. Close the cooker's lid and set it to high-pressure mode. Cook the pie for quarter-hour.
5. Allow the pressure to release naturally for 5 minutes.
6. Chill your strawberry pie well and serve.

Nutrition: calories 214, fat 22.5, fiber 1.3, carbs 7.4, protein 2.1

Lemon Flan

Prep time: a quarter-HOUR | COOKING time: 20 minutes | Servings: 4

Ingredients

- ¼ cup of Erythritol
- 3 tablespoons of water
- ½ cup of coconut cream
- ½ cup of cream
- 2 eggs
- ½ teaspoon of salt
- 1 tablespoon of freshly squeezed lemon juice
- 1 teaspoon of lemon zest
- 1 teaspoon of vanilla flavor

COOKING DIRECTIONS:

1. Combine Erythritol with water and pour it into the pressure cooker. Heat it on pressure mode and mix continuously until a smooth caramel forms.
2. Pour the caramel in the ramekins having set the cooker's mode to sauté.
3. Pour the cream in the pressure cooker and cook it for 30 seconds.
4. Beat the eggs in a mixing bowl and add them to the cream while stirring constantly.

5.   Add salt, lemon zest, vanilla flavoring, and coconut cream.

6.   Add the freshly squeezed lemon juice and mix well. Cook for 1 minute while stirring constantly.

7.   Pour the cream mixture into the ramekins and place it on a trivet.

8.   Fit the trivet in the cooker and cook the contents at pressure mode for 8 minutes.

9.   Remove the ramekins from the pressure cooker and put them in the refrigerator for couple of hours before serving.

Nutrition: calories 181, fat 16.82, fiber 0.5, carbs 3.27, protein 5.12

Vanilla Ice Cream

Prep time: ten MINUTES |Cooking time: 5 MINUTES |Servings: 4
Ingredients
- 1 cup of heavy cream
- 4 egg yolks
- 3 teaspoons of Erythritol
- 1 tablespoon of vanilla flavor

COOKING DIRECTIONS:

1.   Whisk Erythritol and egg yolks together.

2.   Pour heavy cream into the Ninja Foodie.

3.   Add the egg yolk mixture and vanilla flavoring.

4.   Cook the liquid on high-pressure mode for 5 minutes.

5.   Fast release the built-in pressure and open the cooker's lid. Stir the mixture using a hand mixer until it thickens.

6.   Place it in the goodies maker to frozen it.

Nutrition: calories 365, fat 15.6, fiber 0, carbs 5.6, protein 3.3

Hot Vanilla Shake

Prep time: ten MINUTES |Cooking time: 3 minutes | Servings: 3
Ingredients
- 1 cup of almond milk
- 2 tablespoons of swerve
- 1 teaspoon of vanilla flavor
- 1 tablespoon of almond flour
- 2 tablespoons of butter
- 1 tablespoon of walnuts (chopped)

COOKING DIRECTIONS:

1.   Pour almond milk in the Ninja Foodie.

2.   Add swerve and vanilla flavorings.

3.   Add butter and close the lid.

4.   Cook the liquid on high-pressure mode for 3 minutes.

5.   Allow the pressure to release naturally for 10 minutes.

6.   Add almond flour and stir the butter mixture until it smoothens.

7.   Add walnuts and stir gently.

8.   Pour the cooked cake into the serving glasses and serve warm.

Nutrition: calories 286, fat 29.4, fiber 2.2, carbs 8.7, protein 3

Chocolate Muffins

Prep time: ten MINUTES |Cooking time: 10 minutes | Servings: 7
Ingredients
- 3 tablespoons of cocoa
- ½ cup of Erythritol
- 2 eggs
- 1 teaspoon of baking soda
- 1 tablespoon of freshly squeezed lemon juice
- 1 cup of coconut flour
- 1 cup of plain yogurt
- ½ teaspoon of salt
- 1 teaspoon of essential olive oil

COOKING DIRECTIONS:

1.   Beat the eggs in a mixing bowl.

2.   Add cocoa and mix well.

3.   Combine the baking soda with the fresh lemon juice and add it to the egg mixture.

4.   Add Erythritol and yogurt and mix again.

5.   Add the salt and coconut flour. Mix well using a hand mixer until a smooth batter forms.

6.   Spray the muffin with extra virgin essential olive oil.

7.   Pour the batter into the muffin until they are halfway full.

8.   Place the muffins forms in the pressure cooker having set it to pressure mode. Close the lid.

9.   Cook the muffins for 10 minutes.

10.   When the muffins are cooked, remove them from the cooker and let them rest.

Nutrition: calories 123, fat 4.4, fiber 7.6, carbs 29, protein 6.3

Sweet Pudding

Prep time: 10 mins | Cooking time: 21 minutes | Servings: 5
Ingredients
- 1 cup of heavy cream
- ½ cup of half and half
- 2 tablespoons of starch
- 4 egg yolk
- 2 tablespoons of Erythritol
- 1 teaspoon of ground cardamom
- 1 teaspoon of vanilla extract

COOKING DIRECTIONS:

1.   Whisk the heavy cream and combine it with the half and half and starch. Stir the mixture.

2.   Add egg yolks and blend using a hand mixer.

3.   Add Erythritol, ground cardamom, and vanilla flavor. Mix well.

4.   Place the cream mixture in the glass form.

5. Put the trivet in the pressure cooker and add the glass form with uncooked pudding.
6. Close the cooker's lid and cook the mixture on pressure mode for 21 minutes.
7. Remove your sweet pudding from the cooker and store it in the refrigerator for some hours before serving.
Nutrition: calories 175, fat 15.3, fiber 0.1, carbs 11, protein 3.4

Chocolate Bacon

Prep time: ten MINUTES |Cooking time: 4 minutes | Servings: 6
Ingredients
- 6 bacon slices
- 2 oz chocolates, melted

COOKING DIRECTIONS:
1. Place the bacon slices in the cooker basket and close its lid.
2. Set the Air fryer mode and cook the bacon for 4 minutes.
3. Flip its other side and cook for 2 minutes.
4. Dip the cooked bacon in the melted chocolate and allow it to cool to acquire a solid texture.
Nutrition: calories 156, fat 11.3, fiber 0.5, carbs 4.1, protein 8

Lemon Curd

Prep time: ten MINUTES |Cooking time: 13 MINUTES |Servings: 5
Ingredients
- 4 tablespoons of butter
- ½ cup of Erythritol
- 3 egg yolks
- 3 tablespoons of lemon zest
- 1 cup of freshly squeezed lemon juice
- 1 teaspoon of vanilla flavoring

COOKING DIRECTIONS:
1. Place butter in the blender and add Erythritol. Blend the combination for two minutes.
2. Add the egg yolks and lemon zest. Blend the mixture for 3 minutes.
3. Add the fresh lemon juice and vanilla flavoring. Blend for 30 seconds.
4. Pour water into the pressure cooker and fit a trivet.
5. Pour the curd mixture into glass jars and transfer them in the pressure cooker.
6. Close the cooker's lid and cook the lemon curd on pressure mode for 13 minutes.
7. When the lemon curd is cooked, release the accumulated pressure and remove the glass jars containing the curd from the cooker.
8. To attain a better taste, store it in the refrigerator for 8 hours.

Nutrition: calories 130, fat 12.3, fiber 0.4, carbs 2.3, protein 2.2

Lime Pie

Prep time: half an hour | Cooking time: thirty minutes | Servings: 12
Ingredients
- 1 teaspoon of baking powder
- A cup of whey
- 1 teaspoon of salt
- 1 cup of Erythritol
- A lime
- 1 teaspoon of cinnamon
- A tablespoon of butter
- 1 teaspoon of cardamom
- 2 cups of coconut flour

COOKING DIRECTIONS:
1. Combine the baking powder with whey and Erythritol in a mixing bowl. Stir well.
2. Add coconut flour, cardamom, butter, cinnamon, and salt. Mix well and knead the dough.
3. Place the dough on a towel and leave it in warm area for 10 minutes. Slice the limes.
4. Make a lime layer in the pressure cooker.
5. Pour the dough in the pressure cooker and flatten it.
6. Close the cooker's lid and cook it on pressure mode for twenty minutes.
7. When your lime pie is cooked, open the cooker's lid and allow it to chill.
8. Place it on a flat plate and serve in slices.
Nutrition: calories 96, fat 3, fiber 8.3, carbs 31.5, protein 2.9

Blondies

Prep time: 15 MINUTES |Cooking time: 10 MINUTES |Servings: 6
Ingredients
- 1 teaspoon of baking powder
- 1 teaspoon of fresh lemon juice
- 4 tablespoons of butter (softened)
- 1 cup of almond flour
- ¼ cup of flax meal
- 3 tablespoons of Erythritol
- 1 teaspoon of vanilla flavor
- 2 tablespoons of coconut flakes

COOKING DIRECTIONS:
1. Put all the ingredients in a large mixing bowl.
2. Knead non-sticky dough from the ingredients.
3. Place the dough in the Ninja Foodie and cut it into small bars.
4. Close the cooker's lid and cook the dough on high-pressure mode for 10 minutes.
5. Allow the pressure to release naturally for around 10 minutes.

6. Chill your blondies well and transfer it to a serving plate.

Nutrition: calories 123, fat 12.3, fiber 2, carbs 3.1, protein 2.2

Savory Baked Apples

Prep time: ten MINUTES |Cooking time: 15 MINUTES |Servings: 5

Ingredients
- 5 red apples
- 1 tablespoon of stevia (powdered)
- ½ cup of almonds
- 1 teaspoon of cinnamon
- 1 cup of water

COOKING DIRECTIONS:
1. Wash the apples and cut their tops off.
2. Remove its seeds and flesh to create apple cups. Crush the almonds.
3. Sprinkle the apples with cinnamon and stevia.
4. Fill the cups with the almond mixture and cover them using apple tops.
5. Pour water in the pressure cooker.
6. Add the stuffed apples and close the pressure cooker's lid.
7. Cook the apples at saute mode for quarter-hour.
8. When the cooking time ends, transfer your savory baked apple to a serving plate.

Nutrition: calories 172, fat 5.2, fiber 6.8, carbs 33.2, protein 2.6

Pumpkin Pudding

Prep time: ten MINUTES |Cooking time: 35 MINUTES |Servings: 7

Ingredients
- 1 pound of pumpkin
- 1 tablespoon of pumpkin pie spice
- 3 tablespoons of cream
- 1 teaspoon of vanilla flavor
- 4 servings of water
- 1 teaspoon of butter

COOKING DIRECTIONS:
1. Peel the pumpkin and chop it.
2. Place the pumpkin in the pressure cooker and add water.
3. Close the cooker's lid and cook it on pressure mode for 20 minutes.
4. Strain the pumpkin and mash it using a fork.
5. Sprinkle the pumpkin with the pumpkin pie spices, vanilla flavoring, butter, and cream. Mix well until smooth. Pour the pumpkin mixture into a large ramekin, wrap it in aluminum foil, and place it on a trivet.
6. Pour water into the pressure cooker and fit your trivet.

7. Close the cooker's lid and cook the mixture on sauté mode for fifteen minutes.
8. Remove your pumpkin pudding from the cooker and allow it rest. Unwrap the foil and serve.

Nutrition: calories 26, fat 1, fiber 0.8, carbs 4, protein 0.6

Grated Pie

Prep time: 25 minutes | Cooking time: 25 minutes | Servings: 7

Ingredients
- 1 cup of strawberries (mashed)
- 7 ounces of butter
- 1 teaspoon of salt
- A cup of almond flour
- 1 teaspoon of vanilla flavor
- A tablespoon of lemon zest
- 1 tablespoon of turmeric
- 1 teaspoon of nutmeg
- ½ teaspoon of ground ginger

COOKING DIRECTIONS:
1. Grate butter in a mixing bowl.
2. Sprinkle it with salt, vanilla flavoring, lemon zest, turmeric, nutmeg, and ground ginger.
3. Pour the almond flour to a bowl and knead dough using your hands.
4. Place the dough in the freezer for quarter-hour.
5. Remove the dough from the freezer to acquire a hard texture.
6. Grate a portion of the dough and place it in the pressure cooker.
7. Sprinkle the grated dough with strawberries.
8. Flatten it to form a layer.
9. Grate the other portion over the strawberries.
10. Close the cooker's lid and cook the dough on pressure mode for 25 minutes.
11. When the cooking time ends, place your grated pie on a flatter and let it rest. Cut into slices and serve.

Nutrition: calories 309, fat 31.3, fiber 2.5, carbs 6.2, protein 3.9

Condensed Cream

Prep time: 10 MINUTES |Cooking time: 40 minutes | Servings: 7

Ingredients
- 3 cups of cream
- 5 egg yolks
- 1 cup of Erythritol
- 1 teaspoon of vanilla flavoring

COOKING DIRECTIONS:
1. Whisk the yolks in a mixing bowl.
2. Combine cream with Erythritol in a pressure cooker.

3. Set it top sauté mode and add the vanilla flavoring. Cook for ten minutes while stirring frequently.
4. Mix the components and add the egg yolks slowly and stir well.
5. Close the load cooker and cook the mixture on pressure mode for around 30 minutes.
6. When the cooking time ends, transfer your condensed cream into the pressure cooker and refrigerate immediately.
Nutrition: calories 106, fat 8.9, fiber 0, carbs 3.7, protein 2.8

Crème Brule

Prep time: 10 MINUTES |Cooking time: 20 mins | Servings: 6
Ingredients
- 5 tablespoons of Erythritol
- 2 cups of cream
- ½ teaspoon salt
- 10 egg yolks

COOKING DIRECTIONS:
1. Put the egg yolks in a mixing bowl and mix it using a hand mixer.
2. Add salt to the egg mixture.
3. When the combination becomes fluffy, add cream. Mix well for a minute.
4. Sprinkle the glass ramekins with Erythritol and pour the cream mixture on them.
5. Pour some water in the pressure cooker and hang the trivet.
6. Fit the trivet in the strain cooker and close its lid.
7. Cook the contents on steam mode for 20 minutes.
8. When your cream Brule is cooked, allow it to cool a bit. Serve warm.
Nutrition: calories 141, fat 12, fiber 0, carbs 3.5, protein 5.1

Macaroons

Prep time: 10 MINUTES |Cooking time: 3 minutes | Servings: 5
Ingredients
- 3 egg whites
- 2 tablespoons of Erythritol
- 1 teaspoon of vanilla protein powder
- ½ cup of almond flour
- ½ cup of coconut shred
- 1 teaspoon of baking powder

COOKING DIRECTIONS:
1. Whisk the egg whites in a mixing bowl.
2. Add Erythritol, vanilla protein powder, almond flour, coconut shred, and baking powder. Stir the amalgamation well.
3. Make medium-sized balls from the mixer and press them gently.

4. Place the pressed balls (macaroons) in a Ninja Foodie basket.
5. Close the cooker's lid and cook the balls on Air fryer mode (at 360F) for 3 minutes or until it turns light brown. Chill your macaroons before serving.
Nutrition: calories 118, fat 9.4, fiber 2, carbs 9.3, protein 5.5

Coconut Bars

Prep time: 10 minutes | Cooking time: 6 MINUTES |Servings: 8
Ingredients
- 1 cup of coconut shred
- 1/3 cup of coconut flour
- 2 eggs(whisked)
- 3 tablespoons of swerve
- 1 teaspoon of vanilla flavoring
- ¼ cup of pecans (chopped)
- 2 tablespoons of butter

COOKING DIRECTIONS:
1. Mix coconut shred, coconut flour, whisked eggs, swerve, vanilla flavoring, and chopped pecans.
2. Add butter and stir the mass until they become homogenous.
3. Line the Ninja Foodie internally with baking paper and place the coconut mixture onto it.
4. Flatten it to acquire a smooth layer.
5. Close the lid and cook the coconut mixture on high-Pressure mode for 6 minutes.
6. Quick release the cooker's pressure and open its lid.
7. Transfer your coconut bars to a flatter and serve it in slices.
Nutrition: calories 182, fat 15.5, fiber 4.4, carbs 13.6, protein 3.4

Avocado Mousse

Prep time: 10 minutes | Cooking time: 25 minutes | Servings: 4
Ingredients
- ½ cup of almond milk
- 2 egg yolks
- 2 tablespoons of swerve
- 2 avocados (peeled)
- 1 teaspoon of coconut flakes
- 1 teaspoon of vanilla flavoring

COOKING DIRECTIONS:
1. Pour almond milk into the Ninja Foodie.
2. Whisk the egg yolks with swerve and vanilla flavoring.
3. Transfer the amalgamation to the Ninja Foodie and close its lid.
4. Cook the mixture on pressure mode for 3 minutes.
5. Blend the avocado to acquire a soft and smooth mixture.

6. Chill the cooked almond milk mixture and add blended avocado followed by the almond milk mixture. Stir well.
7. Transfer your avocado mousse into serving bowls and sprinkle it with coconut flakes.
Nutrition: calories 308, fat 29.2, fiber 7.4, carbs 11.8, protein 4

Ricotta Pie

Prep time: ten MINUTES |Cooking time: 20 mins | Servings: 8
Ingredients
- 14 ounces of ricotta cheese
- 4 eggs
- 1/3 cup of Erythritol
- 1 cup of coconut flour
- A teaspoon of salt
- 1 tablespoon of butter
- 1 teaspoon of nutmeg
- 1 tablespoon of vanilla flavoring
- ¼ teaspoon of sage

COOKING DIRECTIONS:
1. Whisk the eggs in a mixing bowl and add ricotta.
2. Stir the mixture and sprinkle it with salt, nutmeg, Erythritol, vanilla extract, and butter. Mix well and add coconut flour.
3. Mix the batter until smooth.
4. Pour the batter into the pressure cooker and flatten it using a spatula.
5. Close the cooker's lid and cook the mixture on pressure mode for 25 minutes.
6. When the cooking time ends, release the inbuilt pressure and allow the pie to rest for around 10 minutes. Transfer your ricotta pie to a serving plate. Slice and serve.
Nutrition: calories 126, fat 7.9, fiber 0.7, carbs 12.1, protein 8.7

"Apple" Crumble

Prep time: ten MINUTES |Cooking time: 25 MINUTES |Servings: 6
Ingredients
- A cup of Erythritol
- 1 cup of almond flour
- 8 ounces of butter
- 1 teaspoon of cinnamon
- A tablespoon of nutmeg
- 1 zucchini (chopped)
- 1 tablespoon of vanilla flavoring
- ½ cup of whipped cream

COOKING DIRECTIONS:
1. Place zucchini in the pressure cooker. Set the cooker to sauté mode.
2. Sprinkle the zucchini with Erythritol and nutmeg. Mix well and sauté the mixture for 10 minutes. Slice the butter.

3. Combine cinnamon with vanilla flavoring and almond flour.
4. Add butter and mix well using your hands.
5. Rub the dough with your fingers until a crumbly mixture is formed.
6. Sprinkle the sautéed zucchini with the crumble dough and close the pressure cooker's lid.
7. Cook the dough mixture on pressure for quarter-hour.
8. Release the pressure and allow the dish to rest.
9. Transfer your apple crumble to a serving plate and add whipped cream.
Nutrition: calories 423, fat 43.5, fiber 2.7, carbs 6.1, protein 4.9

Blackberry Compote

Prep time: 8 minutes | Cooking time: 5 minutes | Servings: 5
Ingredients
- 1 ½ cup of blackberries
- 3 tablespoons of Erythritol
- 1 teaspoon of vanilla flavoring
- ¼ cup of water

COOKING DIRECTIONS:
1. Mash the blackberries gently and put them in the Ninja Foodie.
2. Add Erythritol, vanilla flavoring, and water. Stir the berries using a wooden spatula.
3. Close the cooker's lid and seal it.
4. Cook compote on high pressure mode for 5 minutes.
5. Allow pressure to exit from the cooker naturally and let your blackberry compote chill.
Nutrition: calories 21, fat 0.2, fiber 2.3, carbs 11.5, protein 0.6

Sponge Cake

Prep time: quarter-HOUR | Cooking time: 30minutes | Servings: 8
Ingredients
- 6 eggs
- 2 cups of coconut flour
- 1 cup of whipped cream
- ½ cup of Erythritol
- 1 tablespoon of vanilla flavoring

COOKING DIRECTIONS:
1. Separate the egg yolks and egg whites.
2. Combine the egg yolks with Erythritol and stir to attain a fluffy texture using a hand mixer.
3. Whisk the egg whites until you acquire firm peaks.
4. Pour coconut flour and the vanilla flavoring in the egg yolk mixture and stir well.
5. Add the egg whites and fold them using a spatula.

6. Add the sponge cake batter to the pressure cooker.
7. Level the batter using a spatula and close the lid.
8. Cook the cake on pressure mode for thirty minutes.
9. When the dish is cooked, remove your sponge cake from the cooker and set it aside.
10. Cut it crossways to acquire two halves and spread each portion with the whipped cream.
11. Cover it using the second section of the cake and serve.

Nutrition: calories 111, fat 8.4, fiber 1.3, carbs 2.9, protein 5

Zucchini Crisp

Prep time: ten minutes | COOKING time: 20 mins | Servings: 6

Ingredients

- 1 pound of zucchini
- 2 cups of almond flour
- 1/3 cup of Erythritol
- 1 tablespoon of cinnamon
- 1 teaspoon of vanilla flavoring
- 1 teaspoon of baking soda
- 7 ounces of butter
- A cup of water
- ½ cup of flax meal
- 11 tablespoons of freshly squeezed lemon juice

COOKING DIRECTIONS:

1. Chop the zucchini and place them in a pressure cooker.
2. Combine Erythritol with cinnamon, water, and almond flour.
3. Sprinkle the chopped zucchini with Erythritol mixture.
4. Pour some water in the zucchini mixture.
5. Combine the vanilla flavor with the remainder flour, flax meal, baking soda, freshly squeezed lemon juice, and butter in a mixing bowl.
6. Combine until a crumble forms from the mixture.
7. Sprinkle the apple mixture with the crumbles and close the pressure cooker lid.
8. Cook the mixture on pressure mode for twenty minutes.
9. When the cooking time ends, allow your zucchini crisp to rest before serving.

Nutrition: calories 514, fat 49.2, fiber 8.2, carbs 25.5, protein 11.5

Cottage Cheese Prune Soufflé

Prep time: ten MINUTES |Cooking time: 10 mins | Servings: 6

Ingredients

- 6 ounces of prunes
- 1 cup of cheese
- ½ cup of sour cream
- 5 whole eggs
- 1 teaspoon of ground ginger
- 3 egg yolks

COOKING DIRECTIONS:

1. Beat full eggs in a bowl and add the egg yolks.
2. Add cheese and sour cream and mix for 3 minutes.
3. Add ground ginger and mix well.
4. Chop the prunes and add them to the cheese mixture.
5. Put the cheese mixture in ramekins and place them on a trivet.
6. Pour water in the pressure cooker and fit the trivet.
7. Close the cooker's lid and cook the contents on pressure mode for ten minutes. When your prune soufflé is cooked allow it to cool before serving.

Nutrition: calories 208, fat 10.9, fiber 2.1, carbs 21.2, protein 9.3

Walnuts Bars

Prep time: ten MINUTES |Cooking time: quarter-HOUR | Servings: 8

Ingredients

- 1 cup of walnuts
- A cup cream
- 1 tablespoon of starch
- ½ cup of Erythritol
- 5 tablespoons of butter
- 1 cup of almond flour
- 1 teaspoon of baking soda
- 1 teaspoon of fresh lemon juice
- An egg
- ¼ teaspoon of salt
- 1 teaspoon of turmeric

COOKING DIRECTIONS:

1. Put butter, baking soda, freshly squeezed lemon juice, egg, and flour in a blender. Blend the amalgamation until smooth.
2. Place the dough in a silicone form and flatten it using a spatula.
3. Put the dough in the pressure cooker and close its lid. Set its cooking mode to pressure.
4. Combine starch with cream, Erythritol and turmeric. Mix well using a hand.
5. Crush the walnuts and add it to the batter and stir well.
6. When the cooking time ends, release the built-in pressure and allow the crust to chill.
7. Spread it with the cream mixture and return it to the pressure cooker.
8. Cook the walnut bars for 5 minutes and allow them to rest.

Nutrition: calories 265, fat 24.2, fiber 2.6, carbs 6.4, protein 7.6

Pineapple Pie

Prep time: ten mins | Cooking time: 20 MINUTES |Servings: 8

Ingredients

- 9 ounces of fresh pineapple
- 1 tablespoon of apple cider vinegar treatment
- 4 tablespoons of liquid stevia
- 8 tablespoons of butter
- 1 cup of coconut flour
- ½ cup of ground flax meal
- 1 teaspoon of extra virgin olive oil
- ¼ teaspoon of ground ginger

COOKING DIRECTIONS:

1. Slice the pineapple.
2. Combine coconut flour with ground flax meal, butter, Erythritol, ground ginger, and baking soda in a mixing bowl.
3. Sprinkle the amalgamation with apple cider vinegar and knead smooth dough.
4. Transfer the dough to the freezer for ten minutes.
5. Remove the frozen dough and grate it.
6. Sprinkle the pressure cooker with essential extra virgin olive oil.
7. Add half of the grated dough.
8. Make a layer of sliced pineapple and sprinkle it with the remaining portion of grated dough.
9. Close the cooker's lid and cook on sauté mode for 10 minutes.
10. Flip the pie and sauté it for ten minutes. Let your pineapple pie rest before slicing and serving.

Nutrition: calories 218, fat 16.2, fiber 8.5, carbs 16.8, protein 3.8

Sweet Carrot Slow Cook

Prep time: ten minutes | Cooking time: 20 minutes | Servings: 7

Ingredients

- 3 cups of coconut milk
- 2 carrots
- 1 tablespoon of Erythritol
- 1 teaspoon of ground ginger
- ¼ teaspoon of salt

COOKING DIRECTIONS:

1. Peel the carrots and dice them.
2. Transfer them into the pressure cooker and add coconut milk, ground ginger, and salt. Stir well and close cooker's lid.
3. Cook the mixture on slow mode for quarter-hour.
4. Open the cooker's lid and add Erythritol.

5. Stir well and continue cooking on pressure mode for 5 minutes.
6. When the cooking time ends, chill your Slow Cook in the refrigerator before serving.

Nutrition: calories 245, fat 24.5, fiber 2.7, carbs 7.6, protein 2.5

Sweet Poppy Bun

Prep time: quarter-HOUR | Cooking time: half an hour | Servings: 8

Ingredients

- ¼ cup of poppy seeds
- 1 tablespoon of baking powder
- 1 cup of almond milk
- 1 teaspoon of salt
- 1 cup of Erythritol
- 1 teaspoon of vanilla flavor
- An egg
- 2 cups of coconut flour
- 1 teaspoon of organic olive oil

COOKING DIRECTIONS:

1. Combine baking powder with salt and Erythritol in a mixing bowl and stir well.
2. Add the almond milk followed by a cup of coconut flour. Mix until smooth.
3. Whisk the egg and add it to the vanilla flavoring.
4. Add the egg mixture to the baking powder mixture and stir.
5. Add the other cup of flour and knead smooth dough.
6. Combine poppy seeds with Erythritol in another mixing bowl and stir.
7. Subdivide your dough into three parts.
8. Spray the pressure cooker with extra virgin olive oil.
9. Dip each portion partially in the poppy seed mixture.
10. Close the cooker's lid and cook the buns on pressure mode for half an hour.
11. Release the accumulated pressure and open the cooker's lid.
12. Transfer your poppy buns to a serving plate and let it rest. Cut them into pieces and serve.

Nutrition: calories 228, fat 13.2, fiber 13.1, carbs 23.6, protein 6.1

Caramel Bites

Prep time: ten minutes | Cooking time: 9 minutes | Servings: 10

Ingredients

- 7 ounces of puff pastry
- 1 tablespoon of butter
- 1 teaspoon of cinnamon
- 1 egg yolk
- 1 teaspoon of extra virgin olive oil
- 4 tablespoons of low-carb caramel drops

COOKING DIRECTIONS:

1. Roll the puff pastry using a rolling pin.
2. Make circles from your dough using a cutter.
3. Whisk the egg yolk and sprinkle it over the dough circles.
4. Put butter and caramel at the center of each puff pastry circle to acquire small puffs.
5. Spray the pressure cooker with organic extra virgin olive oil.
6. Add the puff pastry bites to the cooker and cook at sauté mode for 6 minutes or until each side turns light brown.
7. Place the caramel bites on a paper towel and drain excess oil. Serve warm.

Nutrition: calories 173, fat 12.4, fiber 1.2, carbs 16, protein 2.1

Puff Pastry Cups

Prep time: quarter-HOUR | Cooking time: 25 MINUTES | Servings: 8

Ingredients

- 10 ounces of puff pastry
- 3 tablespoons of pumpkin puree
- 1 teaspoon of butter
- A tablespoon of almond flour
- 1 tablespoon of Erythritol
- 1 teaspoon of cinnamon
- A cup of water
- 1 teaspoon of extra virgin essential olive oil

COOKING DIRECTIONS:

1. Roll your puff pastry and make grade circles from it.
2. Sprinkle the ramekins base with extra virgin olive oil and place puff pastry squares on them. The puff pastry squares should be larger than ramekins to wrap the dough.
3. Combine the pumpkin puree with almond flour, Erythritol, and cinnamon in a bowl and stir well.
4. Fill the ramekins with the pumpkin puree mixture and wrap the puff pastry gently.
5. Pour water in the pressure cooker and place the ramekins on a trivet.
6. Fit the trivet in the cooker and cook the content on steam mode for 25 minutes.
7. When your puff pastry cups are cooked, remove them from the cooker and transfer them to a flatter. Serve warm.

Nutrition: calories 212, fat 15, fiber 0.9, carbs 16.9, protein 2.9

Cream Cheese Mousse

Prep time: fifteen MINUTES | Cooking time: 4 MINUTES | Servings: 6

Ingredients

- 2 cups of cream cheese
- 1 oz of chocolate
- 1 teaspoon of vanilla flavor
- ½ cup of cream
- ½ cup of Erythritol
- 1 teaspoon of hot chocolate mix

COOKING DIRECTIONS:

1. Combine the chocolate, vanilla flavoring, sugar, powered cocoa, and cream in a bowl. Mix well using a hand mixer.
2. Set the pressure cooker to sauté mode and place the cream mixture in the pressure cooker. Saute it for 4 minutes.
3. Leave the mixture for some time and add the cream cheese. Whisk the amalgamation until smooth.
4. Transfer your cheese mousse to the freezer and chill for ten minutes before serving.

Nutrition: calories 311, fat 29.5, fiber 0.3, carbs 5.7, protein 6.4

Carrot Cake

Prep time: 10 MINUTES | Cooking time: 35 minutes | Servings: 8

Ingredients

- 1 cup of almond flour
- 1 teaspoon of baking soda
- 1 teaspoon of freshly squeezed lemon juice
- A carrot
- 1 teaspoon of apple juice
- ½ cup of yogurt
- ½ cup of coconut milk
- 1 teaspoon of pumpkin pie spices
- 2 eggs
- 4 tablespoons of Erythritol

COOKING DIRECTIONS:

1. Peel the carrot and grate it.
2. Combine the eggs with the grated carrot and whisk.
3. Add yogurt and milk.
4. Sprinkle the mixture with apple juice, fresh lemon juice, baking soda, pumpkin pie spices, semolina, and flour. Knead the dough until smooth. Pour the carrot batter into the pressure cooker.
5. Pour water into the pressure cooker and place a trivet inside.
6. Set the cooker to pressure mode, place the mixture on the trivet, and close the cooker's lid.
7. Cook the dough for 35 minutes.
8. When your carrot cake is cooked, take it off the cooker and let it cool. Cut into slices and serve.

Nutrition: calories 159, fat 11.9, fiber 2.1, carbs 9.4, protein 5.7

Strawberry Jam

PREP TIME: TEN MINUTES | COOKING TIME: TWENTY ROUGHLY MINUTES | SERVINGS: 7

Ingredients

- ½ cup of Erythritol

- 2 cups of strawberries
- 1 teaspoon of lemon zest
- ½ teaspoon of ground cardamom

COOKING DIRECTIONS:

1. Chop the strawberries and sprinkle them with Erythritol. Set the pressure cooker to sauté mode.
2. Stir the mixture and transfer it to the pressure cooker.
3. Sauté the amalgamation for 5 minutes while stirring frequently using a wooden spoon.
4. Sprinkle the strawberry mixture with ground cardamom and lemon zest.
5. Stir well and sauté the amalgamation for quarter-hour or until it reduces by half.
6. Remove your strawberry jam from the cooker and store it in the refrigerator for some time before using it.

Nutrition: calories 14, fat 0.1, fiber 0.9, carbs 14.8, protein 0.3

Sweet Yogurt

Prep time: 25 MINUTES |Cooking time: 9 hours quarter-hour | Servings: 7

Ingredients

- 5 cups of almond milk
- 3 tablespoons of yogurt starter
- 1 cup of strawberries (chopped)
- ½ cup of blueberries

COOKING DIRECTIONS:

1. Pour almond milk in the pressure cooker and close its lid.
2. Set it to slow mode and cook the milk for 15 minutes while stirring frequently.
3. Open the cooker's lid and allow it to sit for fifteen minutes.
4. Add the yogurt starter and stir well using a wooden spoon.
5. Close cooker's lid and cook for 9 hours.
6. Remove your sweet yogurt from the pressure cooker and store it for some hours in the refrigerator.
7. Transfer the yogurt to serving bowls and sprinkle it with strawberries.

Nutrition: calories 407, fat 41, fiber 4.4, carbs 12.6, protein 4.2

Brownie Cups

Prep time: ten MINUTES |Cooking time: 4 minutes | Servings: 2

Ingredients

- 1 oz of chocolate bars(melted)
- 2 eggs (whisked)
- 4 tablespoons of butter
- 2 tablespoons of almond flour
- 1 teaspoon of vanilla flavoring
- 5 drops of liquid stevia

COOKING DIRECTIONS:

1. Mix melted chocolate, whisked eggs, butter, almond flour, and vanilla extract in a bowl.
2. Add liquid stevia and mix the amalgamation until smooth.
3. Pour the brownie mixture in the brownie cups and insert a trivet in the Ninja Foodie.
4. Pour a cup of water and place the cups on a trivet.
5. Cook the brownie cups for 4 minutes on Pressure mode.
6. Release the accumulated pressure and let the dessert chill before serving.

Nutrition: calories 388, fat 35.1, fiber 1.2, carbs 10.6, protein 8.4

Cream Mousse with Strawberries

Prep time: quarter-hour | Cooking time: 7 MINUTES |Servings: 10

Ingredients

- 1 cup of cream cheese
- 1 cup of whipped cream
- 3 egg yolks
- ½ cup of Erythritol
- 1 tablespoon of hot chocolate mix
- A tablespoon of butter

COOKING DIRECTIONS:

1. Whisk the egg yolks with Erythritol and combine the amalgamation with the cream cheese.
2. Set the pressure cooker to sauté mode and add the cream mixture.
3. Cook for 7 minutes while stirring frequently.
4. Transfer the cream cheese mixture to a mixing bowl and add the whipped cream followed by powered cocoa. Add butter and mix the contents using a hand blender.
5. Transfer your cream mousse to serving bowls.

Nutrition: calories 144, fat 14.4, fiber 0.2, carbs 13.5, protein 2.9

Butter Cake

Prep time: 20 MINUTES |Cooking time: 25 MINUTES |Servings: 8

Ingredients

- 2 egg whites
- 10 tablespoons of butter
- 2 cups of almond flour
- ½ cup of almond milk
- ½ cup of Erythritol
- 1 teaspoon of vanilla flavoring
- 1 teaspoon of baking soda
- 1 tablespoon of freshly squeezed lemon juice
- ½ teaspoon of ground cardamom

COOKING DIRECTIONS:

1.   Melt the butter and combine it with almond milk, almond flour, Erythritol, vanilla flavoring, baking soda, fresh lemon juice, and ground cardamom.
2.   Knead smooth dough and place it on a trivet
3.   Pour water into the cooker and insert the trivet.
4.   Close the cooker's lid and cook it on pressure mode for 25 minutes.
5.   Open the pressure cooker's lid and confirm whether it's ready using a toothpick.
6.   Transfer your butter cake to a plate and let it rest.
7.   Whisk the egg whites to acquire peaks form.
8.   Sprinkle the butter cake with icing and allow it to cool before serving.
Nutrition: calories 71, fat 5.8, fiber 1, carbs 17.8, protein 2.4

Zucchini Tacos

Prep time: quarter-HOUR | Cooking time: 5 MINUTES |Servings: 7
Ingredients
*   2 zucchini
*   2 tablespoons of liquid stevia
*   1 teaspoon of cinnamon
*   ½ teaspoon of ginger
*   6 ounces of almond flour tortillas (keto tortilla)

COOKING DIRECTIONS:
1.   Peel the zucchini and chop them.
2.   Sprinkle the chopped zucchini with cinnamon and ginger.
3.   Mix well and leave the zucchini for 5 minutes to squeeze some juice.
4.   Place zucchini in the cooker and cook them on pressure mode for 4 minutes.
5.   Sprinkle the tortillas with liquid stevia.
6.   Remove the cooked zucchini from the pressure cooker and let them rest.
7.   Place the zucchini mixture in the tortillas, wrap them and serve.
Nutrition: calories 140, fat 7.1, fiber 4.3, carbs 9.2, protein 11.1

Lemon Loaf

Prep time: ten MINUTES |Cooking time: 30 minutes | Servings: 8
Ingredients
*   1 cup of fresh lemon juice
*   3 tablespoons of lemon zest
*   3 cups of almond flour
*   ½ cup of cream
*   An egg
*   1 teaspoon of baking soda
*   ½ teaspoon of baking powder
*   2 tablespoons of Erythritol

*   1 teaspoon of turmeric
COOKING DIRECTIONS:
1.   Combine almond flour with baking powder, baking soda, turmeric, and Erythritol in a mixing bowl.
2.   Stir and add the freshly squeezed lemon juice followed by cream.
3.   Add egg and lemon zest.
4.   Knead smooth dough in form of a loaf.
5.   Pour water into the pressure cooker and put the trivet.
6.   Transfer the loaf-form placed on a trivet in the pressure cooker. Close its lid.
7.   Cook the dough on pressure mode for half-hour.
8.   Open the cooker's lid and remove your lemon meatloaf. Let it cool, slice it and serve.
Nutrition: calories 88, fat 6.9, fiber 1.5, carbs 7.9, protein 3.4

Sweet Spaghetti Casserole

Prep time: 10 MINUTES |Cooking time: twenty minutes | SERVINGS: 7
Ingredients
*   8 ounces of black bean pasta (cooked)
*   1 cup of cottage cheese
*   6 eggs
*   ¼ cup of cream
*   A tablespoon of essential organic olive oil
*   1 teaspoon of salt
*   1/3 cup of Erythritol
*   1 teaspoon of vanilla flavor
*   1 teaspoon of nutmeg

COOKING DIRECTIONS:
1.   Combine cheese with cream, eggs, and Erythritol in a blender. Blend them to a puree.
2.   Transfer the cheese mixture to a mixing bowl and add the cooked pasta, nutmeg, and vanilla flavoring. Mix well.
3.   Pour the organic olive oil on the cooker's base and add the cheese mixture.
4.   Close the cooker's lid and cook it on slow mode for around 20 minutes.
5.   When your spaghetti casserole is cooked, open the cooker's lid and allow it to cool.
6.   Cut it into pieces and serve.
Nutrition: calories 2, 13 fat 8.1, fiber 7, carbs 23.2, protein 23.7

Vanilla Cake

Prep time: ten MINUTES |Cooking time: 45 minutes | Servings: 12
Ingredients
*   5 eggs
*   1 teaspoon of vanilla flavor
*   ½ cup of almond flour
*   ½ cup of Erythritol

- 3 cups of almond milk
- 6 ounces of butter

COOKING DIRECTIONS:

1. Melt the butter and combine with the vanilla flavor, Erythritol, almond milk, almond flour, and eggs. Whisk the ingredients.
2. Pour a half cup of water into the pressure cooker.
3. Pour the butter mixture in a glass form.
4. Fit the trivet in the pressure cooker and put glass form there.
5. Cook the mixture on pressure mode for 45 minutes.
6. When the cooking time ends, open the pressure cooker's lid and allow the compound to cool.
7. Place your vanilla cake on a flatter and serve it in pieces.

Nutrition: calories 273, fat 28.2, fiber 1.5, carbs 13.8, protein 4.1

APPENDIX : RECIPES INDEX

Spring Tuna Wraps 107
Sriracha Shrimp 94
Steamed Chicken Cutlets 58
Steamed Kale 127
Stewed Cabbage 128
Strawberry Cheesecake 156
Strawberry Jam 166
Strawberry Pie 158
Stuffed Bell Peppers 132
Stuffed Buns with Egg 40
Stuffed Cheese-Garlic Bread 154
Stuffed Chicken Breast 53
Stuffed Chicken Caprese 78
Stuffed Dates 146
Stuffed Jalapeno Peppers 149
Stuffed Lettuce 29
Stuffed Meatloaf 29
Stuffed Meatloaf 77
Stuffed Snapper with Onions 96
Stuffed Tomatoes with Ground Chicken 71
Stuffed Trout while using the Parsley 109
Suffed Peppers with Eggs 41
Sweet Beef Ribs 18
Sweet Carrot Slow Cook 165
Sweet Chicken Breast 55
Sweet Egg Toasts 44
Sweet Glazed Onion 114
Sweet Mackerel 97
Sweet Pecans 154
Sweet Poppy Bun 165
Sweet Pork Ribs 150
Sweet Pudding 159
Sweet Spaghetti Casserole 168
Sweet Sriracha Carrots 128
Sweet Tomato Salsa 119
Sweet Yogurt 167

T

Tasty Cuttlefish 90
Tender Collard Greens 110
Tender Octopus 90
Tender Salsa 118
Tender Schnitzel 77
Teriyaki Chicken 55
Thai Chicken Fillet 56
Tilapia Bites 102
Tilapia Pot Pie 105
Tomato Chicken Stew 52

Tomato Cups 43
Tomato Ground Chicken Bowl 67
Tomato Jam 135
Tomato Snapper 95
Tortilla Ham Wraps 44
Tuna and Shirataki Noodles Salad 95
Tuna Balls 151
Tuna Salad 82
Turkish Rolls 84
Turmeric Butternut Squash Strips 121
Turmeric Meatballs 20
Turmeric Mushroom Hats 112
Turmeric Rice 117
Turnip Fries 121

V

Vanilla Cake 168
Vanilla Ice Cream 159
Vegetable Pasta Salad 122
Vegetable Risotto 138
Vegetable Tart 130
Vegetarian Shepherd's Pie 137
Veggie Aromatic Stew 140
Veggie Chili 136
Veggie Frittata 41
Veggie Nuggets 147
Veggie Salad with Feta Cheese 120
Vietnam-style Pork Ribs 24

W

Walnuts Bars 164
Warm Chicken Salad 68
Warm Chicken Salad 74
Warm Lunch Wraps 83
Wrapped Asparagus 110
Wrapped Halloumi Cheese 142

Z

Zucchini Crisp 164
Zucchini Egg Cups 35
Zucchini Fries 128
Zucchini Gratin 127
Zucchini Muffins with Poppy Seeds 144
Zucchini Noodles 116
Zucchini Pasta with Chicken 50
Zucchini Pizza 130
Zucchini Quiche 39
Zucchini Scramble 50
Zucchini Tacos 168
Zucchini Tots 142

Printed in the USA
CPSIA information can be obtained
at www.ICGtesting.com
LVHW082014181023
761450LV00016B/1603